Knowing

Knowing How

*Essays on Knowledge,
Mind, and Action*

Edited by
JOHN BENGSON
MARC A. MOFFETT

OXFORD
UNIVERSITY PRESS

OXFORD
UNIVERSITY PRESS

Oxford University Press is a department of the University of Oxford.
It furthers the University's objective of excellence in research, scholarship,
and education by publishing worldwide.

Oxford   New York
Auckland   Cape Town   Dar es Salaam   Hong Kong   Karachi
Kuala Lumpur   Madrid   Melbourne   Mexico City   Nairobi
New Delhi   Shanghai   Taipei   Toronto

With offices in
Argentina   Austria   Brazil   Chile   Czech Republic   France   Greece
Guatemala   Hungary   Italy   Japan   Poland   Portugal   Singapore
South Korea   Switzerland   Thailand   Turkey   Ukraine   Vietnam

Oxford is a registered trade mark of Oxford University Press
in the UK and certain other countries.

Published in the United States of America by
Oxford University Press
198 Madison Avenue, New York, NY 10016

© Oxford University Press 2011

First issued as an Oxford University Press paperback, 2014.

All rights reserved. No part of this publication may be reproduced, stored in a
retrieval system, or transmitted, in any form or by any means, without the prior
permission in writing of Oxford University Press, or as expressly permitted by law,
by license, or under terms agreed with the appropriate reproduction rights organization.
Inquiries concerning reproduction outside the scope of the above should be sent to the Rights
Department, Oxford University Press, at the address above.

You must not circulate this work in any other form
and you must impose this same condition on any acquirer.

Library of Congress Cataloging-in-Publication Data
Knowing how : essays on knowledge, mind, and action/edited by John Bengson and Marc A. Moffett.
p.   cm.
Includes bibliographical references (p.   ).
ISBN 978-0-19-538936-4 (hardcover : alk. paper); 978-0-19-020022-0 (paperback : alk. paper)
1. Knowledge, Theory of.   2. Act (Philosophy)   I. Bengson, John.   II. Moffett, Marc A.
BD161.K5634 2011
121—dc22   2011003179

Contents

Preface — vii
Acknowledgments — xi
Contributors — xiii

The State of Play

1. Two Conceptions of Mind and Action: Knowing How and the Philosophical Theory of Intelligence—JOHN BENGSON AND MARC A. MOFFETT — 3

PART ONE: *Ryle's Legacy*

2. Rylean Arguments: Ancient and Modern—PAUL F. SNOWDON — 59
3. Ryle's *Knowing-How*, and Knowing How to Act—JENNIFER HORNSBY — 80

PART TWO: *Philosophical Considerations*

4. Practical Expertise—JULIA ANNAS — 101
5. Knowing How without Knowing That—YURI CATH — 113
6. Knowledge-How: A Unified Account—BERIT BROGAARD — 136
7. Nonpropositional Intellectualism—JOHN BENGSON AND MARC A. MOFFETT — 161
8. Ideology and the Third Realm (Or, a Short Essay on Knowing How to Philosophize)—ALVA NOË — 196

PART THREE: *Linguistic Perspectives*

9. How to Resolve *How To*—JONATHAN GINZBURG — 215
10. Knowing How and Knowing Answers—DAVID BRAUN — 244
11. Knowledge Ascription by Grammatical Construction—LAURA A. MICHAELIS — 261

PART FOUR: *Implications and Applications*

12. Knowing How and Epistemic Injustice—KATHERINE HAWLEY — 283
13. Knowing What It Is Like—MICHAEL TYE — 300
14. Linguistic Knowledge—MICHAEL DEVITT — 314
15. Inference, Deduction, Logic—IAN RUMFITT — 334

References — 361
Index — 387

Preface

OUR LIVES ARE filled with endeavors and projects, ranging from the mundane to the meaningful, which engage us in myriad activities that we almost invariably know how to do. Such knowledge is not idle but seems to plays a crucial role in enabling the corresponding activity. In the absence of this "know-how"—knowledge how to tie our shoes, ride a bicycle, make coffee, change a light bulb, tell the time, write an e-mail, encourage a friend, use the elevator, calculate a sum, and so on—it is difficult to imagine how we could intelligently navigate, or even reasonably aspire to so navigate, the complex situations in which we often find ourselves. Whether we act (and interact) skillfully or awkwardly, cunningly or stupidly, wisely or foolishly, we do not in any case do so blindly.

Knowledge how to do things is a pervasive and central element of everyday life. Yet it raises many difficult questions that must be considered by anyone who aspires to understand human cognition and agency. What is the connection between knowing how to do things and knowing that something is the case? Is knowledge how to act simply a type of ability or disposition to behavior? Is there an irreducibly practical form of knowledge? How are we to conceive the relation between theory and practice, and between thinking and doing? What is the role of the intellect in intelligent action?

The present book collects fifteen original essays that address these and many other questions about knowledge, mind, and action. The primary aim of this collection is to gather together state-of-the-art work that directly engages the conceptual, empirical, and linguistic issues surrounding knowledge how. Recently, there has been a surge of interest in the nature of knowing how and a corresponding surge of literature—chiefly in the form of articles scattered across sundry journals and general anthologies. The time has come for a single venue in which philosophers and linguists can assess (or reassess) various positions that have emerged (or are emerging), develop new positions that have not yet been formulated, and pursue implications and applications of these positions for other debates in philosophy and cognate disciplines. This book is meant to offer just such a venue.

A second major goal, not unrelated to the first, is to bring out the broader philosophical significance of knowing how. Knowing how has played an important role in recent work in ethics, philosophy of action, epistemology, philosophy of language, philosophy of mind, and cognitive science. This breadth is reflected in this book's chapters, which forge links between diverse areas and sources, historical as well as contemporary, and cover a wide range of topics dealing with tacit and procedural knowledge, the psychology of skill, expertise, intelligence and intelligent action, the nature of ability, the syntax and semantics of embedded questions, the mind-body problem, phenomenal character, epistemic injustice, moral knowledge, the epistemology of logic, linguistic competence, the connection between knowledge and understanding, and the relation between theory and practice. We hope that these chapters contribute to a growing awareness that philosophical discussion of knowledge how is intimately connected to a host of other debates converging on the nature of the mind and its relation to action.

The book begins with a state-of-play chapter that highlights some of these connections within the context of a survey and critical examination of the main issues, arguments, and views—intellectualist as well as anti-intellectualist—in the philosophical debate surrounding knowledge how. Marking significant developments from the seminal work of Gilbert Ryle to the present day, this opening chapter attempts to systematize various strands in recent discussion of knowledge, mind, and action and, in so doing, situate the study of knowledge how in a larger theoretical setting.

The book is thereafter divided into four parts.

Part I, "Ryle's Legacy," includes two chapters investigating Ryle's treatment of knowledge how to act and its potential implications for contemporary debate. In "Rylean Arguments: Ancient and Modern," Paul F. Snowdon critically evaluates the Rylean paradigm, scrutinizing Ryle's handling of intellectualism and his use of various examples, as well as challenging more recent defense of the idea that knowing how and knowing that are strongly contrastable. In "Ryle's *Knowing-How,* and Knowing How to Act," Jennifer Hornsby argues for the merit of several of Ryle's core contentions—in particular, that acting on propositional knowledge requires a sort of knowledge that could not itself be propositional—and defends them against contemporary attack. Despite their apparently conflicting assessments of Ryle's positive views, Snowdon and Hornsby agree that careful attention to Ryle's discussion enables an improved perspective on recent work regarding the relation between knowing and doing.

The five chapters of Part II, "Philosophical Considerations," focus on various aspects of the contemporary debate between intellectualism and anti-intellectualism. In "Practical Expertise," Julia Annas identifies a notion of practical expertise, intimately related to but perhaps not simply identical to knowledge how, whose difference from mere routine and essential connection to reason-giving she subsequently details (with an eye to both ancient philosophy and more recent work by positive psychologist Mihalyi Csikszentmihalyi). In "Knowing How without Knowing That," Yuri Cath takes up the reductive thesis that knowledge how is a form of knowledge that, arguing that it is vulnerable to three distinct types of counterexample; at the same time, this does not yet support a broadly Rylean or anti-intellectualist view, Cath suggests, because the counterexamples can be avoided by linking knowledge how to propositional attitudes other than knowledge that. In "Knowledge How: A Unified Account," Berit Brogaard defends the reductive thesis and discusses the relations between knowledge how and both justification and ability, the latter of which she eventually treats disjunctively. In "Nonpropositional Intellectualism," John Bengson and Marc A. Moffett reject the reductive thesis, arguing that knowledge how is a type of objectual knowledge or understanding that is grounded in, but not reducible to, propositional attitudes. In "Ideology and the Third Realm (Or, a Short Essay on Knowing How to Philosophize)," Alva Noë combines reflection on an intellectualist view of the relation between theory and practice with reflection on styles of argumentation employed in recent discussion of knowledge how, contending that simple appeals to experimental and linguistic data fail to appreciate the "third realm" character of philosophical analysis—which, Noë maintains, like practical knowledge itself, lies between the domain of the provable or the rule governed and the domain of mere taste or feeling.

Part III, "Linguistic Perspectives," includes three essays on the syntax and semantics of knowledge how constructions and their bearing on the debate between intellectualism and anti-intellectualism. In "How to Resolve *How To*," Jonathan Ginzburg argues in a nonreductive spirit that there are epistemically oriented attitude terms, including 'know', that select for both facts and abilities; he subsequently presents a semantics that distinguishes 'that'-clauses from (interrogative) "resolutive" complements, including 'how to' clauses. In "Knowing How and Knowing Answers," David Braun defends an austere version of the reductive view, according to which knowledge how to φ is knowledge of a proposition that answers the question of how to φ; he maintains that insofar as judgments about whether a given proposition answers such a question vary from context to context, this austere view can accommodate natural language data concerning knowledge how ascriptions. In "Knowledge Ascription by Grammatical Construction," Laura A. Michaelis draws on the resources of Construction Grammar in arguing that infinitival complements ('to'-clauses) denote a relation between a person and a procedure, and *wh*-complements (including 'how'-clauses) denote a relation between a person and a "means" variable in a presupposed open proposition, specifically, the ability to identify that variable.

Part IV, "Implications and Applications," brings together four essays discussing the relevance of philosophical work on knowing how for ethics, philosophy of mind and cognitive science, philosophy of language, and the philosophy of logic. In "Knowing How and Epistemic Injustice," Katherine Hawley considers whether and how a distinctively epistemic type of injustice might arise in the case of knowledge how and explores some of the potential social, political, and ethical dimensions of such injustice. In "Knowing What It Is Like," Michael Tye proposes that recent work on knowledge how and, more generally, knowledge-*wh* might shed light on the nature of *knowing what it is like to have an experience*, as opposed to *knowing the phenomenal character of an experience*: both require objectual knowledge, but only the former involves knowledge that. In "Linguistic Knowledge," Michael Devitt argues that philosophical arguments in favor of the view that knowledge of language is reducible to a type of knowledge-that are less compelling than the empirical findings regarding the psychology of skill and procedural knowledge, which he maintains speak against it. In "Inference, Deduction, Logic," Ian Rumfitt seeks to identify fatal flaws in Ryle's influential account of the nature of logic and of its applicability; he then sketches an alternative approach to the topic that attempts to elucidate the way in which knowing how and knowing that interact as thinkers exercise the capacity for deductive argument.

Acknowledgments

WE ARE ESPECIALLY grateful to our contributors, not only for the outstanding original articles produced for this book but also for their patience and commitment throughout the process. We would like to thank Peter Ohlin and the rest of the staff at Oxford University Press for their support in bringing this book to publication. Special thanks to Ray Buchanan, Ulrika Carlsson, David Chalmers, Michael Devitt, Franz-Peter Griesmaier, Jeffrey Lockwood, Aidan McGlynn, Edward Sherline, David Sosa, and Jason Stanley for their help and advice at various stages of the project and to Jennifer Wright for inspiring us to the topic. We are grateful to two anonymous referees for insightful suggestions regarding both form and content and to Sara Qualin for helping to prepare the manuscript.

Individually, John Bengson would like to thank the philosophy departments at the University of Texas at Austin, University of St. Andrews, Yale University, Australian National University, and the University of Wisconsin at Madison for providing intellectual homes during the tenure of this project and Anat Schechtman for her support and encouragement. Marc Moffett would like to thank the philosophy department at the University of Wyoming for teaching relief and additional financial support.

Contributors

JULIA ANNAS is Regents Professor of Philosophy at University of Arizona. She specializes in almost every facet of ancient Greek philosophy, including ethics, psychology, and epistemology. She is a fellow of the American Academy of Arts and Sciences and author of *Hellenistic Philosophy of Mind*, *The Morality of Happiness*, *Platonic Ethics, Old and New*, and *Intelligent Virtue*.

JOHN BENGSON is an Assistant Professor of Philosophy at the University of Wisconsin, Madison. Previously, he was a research fellow in the Centre for Consciousness at the Australian National University. His current research centers on issues in epistemology, philosophy of mind, and philosophy of action.

DAVID BRAUN is Professor of Philosophy at the University at Buffalo and the Patrick and Edna J. Romanell Chair in Philosophy. An expert in philosophy of language, he has written on nonreferring terms, indexicals and demonstratives, attitude ascriptions, and questions and answers.

BERIT BROGAARD is Associate Professor of Philosophy at the University of Missouri at St. Louis. She has written on diverse topics in epistemology, philosophy of language, metaphysics, and other areas; her current research is located at the intersection of philosophy of mind and psychology.

YURI CATH is a postdoctoral research fellow in the Arché Philosophical Research Centre at the University of St. Andrews. His main research interests are philosophy of mind and epistemology, especially knowledge how and philosophical methodology.

MICHAEL DEVITT is Distinguished Professor of Philosophy in The Graduate Center at The City University of New York (CUNY). He specializes in philosophy of language and metaphysics and is author of *Designation*, *Truth and Realism*, *Coming to Our Senses*, *Ignorance of Language*, and *Putting Metaphysics First*.

JONATHAN GINZBURG is Professor of Linguistics at the UFR D'Études Anglophones at Université Paris Diderot (Paris 7). His main research interests are in formal semantics and theory of communication, including modeling dialogue interaction and the grammar of clausal constructions. He is coauthor of *Interrogative Investigations: The Form, Meaning, and Use of English Interrogatives* and author of *The Interactive Stance: Meaning for Conversation*.

KATHERINE HAWLEY is Professor of Philosophy at the University of St. Andrews. She specializes in metaphysics, epistemology, and philosophy of science and is author of *How Things Persist*.

JENNIFER HORNSBY is Professor of Philosophy at Birkbeck College at the University of London. Her main research interests are in the philosophies of action, mind, and language. She is author of *Actions* and *Simple Mindedness: A Defence of Naïve Naturalism in the Philosophy of Mind*.

LAURA A. MICHAELIS is Associate Professor of Linguistics at the University of Colorado at Boulder. Her research is focused on linguistic creativity and, more specifically, on tense and aspect in the developing syntactic model Construction Grammar. She is author of *Aspectual Grammar and Past-Time Reference*.

MARC A. MOFFETT is Associate Professor of Philosophy at the University of Texas, El Paso. His research is focused on issues in epistemology, philosophy of language, philosophy of mind, and metaphysics, including knowledge, understanding, disagreement, the mind-body problem, and intensional content.

ALVA NOË is Professor of Philosophy at the University of California at Berkely. His work focuses on the theory of perception and consciousness and, more generally, philosophy of mind, cognitive science, and phenomenology. He is author of *Perception in Action* and *Out of Our Heads: Why You Are Not Your Brain and Other Lessons from the Biology of Consciousness*.

IAN RUMFITT is Professor of Philosophy at Birkbeck College at the University of London. He works mainly in philosophy of language and logic and in the history of analytic philosophy (Frege), with forays into metaphysics and the philosophy of mathematics.

PAUL F. SNOWDON is Grote Professor of Mind and Logic at University College London. His research interests include philosophy of mind, epistemology, metaphysics, and history of philosophy, focusing on personal identity, perception, and the mind-body problem.

MICHAEL TYE is Professor of Philosophy at the University of Texas at Austin. He is a leading figure in philosophy of mind and cognitive science and author of *Ten Problems of Consciousness*; *Consciousness, Color, and Content*; *Consciousness and Persons*; and *Consciousness Revisited: Materialism without Phenomenal Concepts*. He is coauthor of *Seven Puzzles of Thought (and How to Solve Them): An Originalist Theory of Concepts*.

The State of Play

I

Two Conceptions of Mind and Action

KNOWING HOW AND THE PHILOSOPHICAL THEORY OF INTELLIGENCE

John Bengson and Marc A. Moffett

> Perhaps it is a pity that the Theory of Knowledge and the Theory of Conduct have fallen into separate compartments. (It certainly was not so in Socrates' time, as his interest in the relation between *eidos* and *technê* bears witness.) If we studied them together, perhaps we might have a better understanding of both.
> H. H. PRICE, *Thinking and Representation*

SINCE GILBERT RYLE'S attack on what he unsympathetically labeled the "intellectualist legend," it has been widely accepted that knowledge how to do things is fundamentally distinct from knowledge that something is the case.[1] In recent years, however, this orthodox anti-intellectualist position has come under increasing pressure. At issue in the debate is not simply knowledge how, but altogether different conceptions of the mind and its relation to action.

The present book contains fifteen essays (including this one) that engage various issues in this broader debate, probing the intersection of knowledge, mind, and action. Some of our actions manifest states or qualities of mind, such as intelligence and skill. But what are these states and qualities, and how are they manifested in action? In this chapter, we examine the state of play in the current debate on knowledge how and begin to articulate and evaluate general intellectualist and anti-intellectualist answers to such questions. Inter alia, we attempt to situate

---

1. It has been suggested that a fundamental distinction between knowledge how to act (hereafter, simply 'knowledge how') and knowledge that something is the case (hereafter, simply 'knowledge that') is also found, prior to Ryle, in the work of Dewey (1922), Heidegger (1926), and Piaget (1937) and even earlier in such thinkers as Plato and Aristotle. We will not pursue this suggestion here.

recent discussion of knowledge how in a much larger debate about the nature of intelligence and intelligent action.[2]

Our primary aim is to explore the opposing intellectualist and anti-intellectualist views originating in Ryle's discussion (§1), investigating some of the issues and questions that motivate and sustain the conflict between them (§§2–3). Another aim is to indicate how, and to what extent, an adequate account of knowledge how is not a peripheral philosophical goal. The reason is not simply that such an account may hold the key to integrating the theory of knowledge and the theory of conduct, perhaps leading to a better understanding of both (as Price observed). The current theoretical milieu is one which makes the debate about knowledge how more pressing than at any time since Ryle. Many of the most influential thinkers working in such disparate areas as epistemology, philosophy of action, ethics, philosophy of language, linguistics, theory of education, cognitive ethology, psychology, philosophy of mind, phenomenology, and cognitive science seem to have found the notion of knowledge how central to their theoretical projects (§4). As we shall see, this is not accidental: knowledge how may serve as a hinge on which our general understanding of mind and action turns.

1. Ryle and the Philosophical Theory of Intelligence

Contemporary debates over the nature of knowledge how owe much to Ryle's treatment in his 1945 lecture "Knowing How and Knowing That" and the second chapter of his 1949 monograph *The Concept of Mind*. The aim of this section is to introduce some of the main contours of the dialectic between two very different philosophical perspectives suggested by Ryle's discussion, in which intellectualist and anti-intellectualist views of knowledge how emerge as specific instances of far more general theses about intelligence and intelligent action broadly understood. The plan is to highlight several interrelated questions that seem to have fueled Ryle's own general anti-intellectualism but have been largely neglected or backgrounded in recent discussion of knowledge how.

---

2. Notably, Stanley and Williamson (2001, 444) gesture at this larger debate when, at the close of their recent defense of intellectualism in the specific case of knowledge how, they write: "Neglect of this fact [that knowledge how is a species of knowledge that] impoverishes our understanding of human action, by obscuring the way in which it is informed by intelligence." In his critical response, Noë (2005, 278) likewise gestures at the idea that intellectualism and anti-intellectualism are not simply views about knowledge how, but conflicting accounts of "our mental nature." We believe that these suggestive remarks invite further exploration; hence the present chapter.

1.1 Intellectualism

In chapter 2 of *The Concept of Mind*, Ryle sets out

> to show that there are many activities which directly display qualities of mind, yet are neither themselves intellectual operations nor yet effects of intellectual operations. (1949, 26)

The "many activities" to which Ryle is referring are basically those activities we *know how* to do. However, as he makes clear, Ryle's initial starting point is not knowing how in particular, but rather what he refers to as states (acts, processes, etc.) of "intellect and character" more generally. Such states of agents are designated by "intelligence-epithets" such as 'intelligent,' 'clever,' 'sensible,' 'skillful,' 'canny,' 'wise,' 'prudent,' 'careful,' 'rational,' 'stupid,' 'silly,' and 'idiotic' (see, e.g., 1949, 25, 27, 46, and 280; 1945, 1, 3, 5, and 10); correlatively, "qualities of intellect and character" (1949, 7, 61, and esp. 126 and 135), which are properties of actions, are designated by the corresponding adjectival and adverbial intelligence-epithets such as 'intelligently,' 'cleverly,' and the like.[3]

Interestingly, at various points Ryle uses 'intelligence' in a broad sense that includes all members of this group, including stupidity and idiocy.[4] Hereafter, we reserve 'intelligence' (lowercase 'i') for intelligence in the narrow sense, namely, that which is intelligent but *not* stupid, idiotic, and so forth; we will use 'Intelligence' (capital 'I') as an umbrella term covering all states of intellect

---

3. Although Ryle is not always clear about this distinction, intelligence-epithets can, with equal felicity, designate states of agents (as when we say that an individual is clever) or properties/qualities of actions performed by those agents (as when we say that an individual acted cleverly). The latter may be possessed by action types (e.g., *choosing to eat healthy foods* is sensible), as well as particular actions by particular individuals; we focus on the latter. The relation between the relevant states of agents and qualities of actions is detailed in note 5. The relation between intelligence-epithets and various other evaluative epithets (e.g., 'correctly', 'validly') is discussed in note 28.

4. Thus Ryle (1945, 1) speaks of "the several concepts of intelligence," by which is meant "the more determinate" members of the family of "mental-conduct concepts" expressed by terms such as those listed in the text (1949, 25). This family is a proper subset of mental phenomena (cf. sensations and emotions; see, e.g., 1949, 135 and 204). It does not, prior to theorizing, include propositional or factual attitudes and abilities or dispositions; rather, as we shall see, such attitudes and abilities or dispositions serve as candidate *grounds* or *bases*—intellectual and non-intellectual grounds or bases (analysans, explanans, explicans, etc.), respectively—for the indicated states and qualities. Snowdon (chapter 2) articulates several worries about Ryle's efforts to theorize about this family, a few of which intersect with the present treatment.

and character, including intelligence (in the narrow sense), stupidity, and idiocy.[5]

Such terminology enables us to respect the complex relations between various states of Intelligence. Particular states of Intelligence obviously come apart, and not simply because some have a positive valence (e.g., intelligence) whereas others have a negative valence (e.g., stupidity): for instance, one might play chess intelligently but not cleverly or one might know how to prune trees (Ryle's example) but not yet be skilled at pruning trees (i.e., prune trees skillfully). Of course, it does not follow that the various states of Intelligence are completely dissimilar. Indeed, a philosophical theory of Intelligence—Ryle's concern—aspires to provide an account, not of this or that particular state of intellect and character, but of what all of them have in common, that is, of Intelligence generally.

Intelligence-epithets often modify overt behaviors, such as pruning trees. But Ryle is keenly aware that Intelligent actions, such as pruning trees skillfully, are not distinguishable from non-Intelligent actions in virtue of any *overt* features of the performance; rather, we must "look beyond the performance itself" (1949, 45; cf. 25, 32–33, and 40–41). On what basis, then, are we to draw the distinction between the Intelligent and the non-Intelligent? Call this *the delineation question*, which can be formulated generally, as follows:

The Delineation Question
What makes the difference between behaviors that do, and overtly indistinguishable behaviors that do not, display states of Intelligence?

It is here that an intellectualist conception of mind and action, which privileges the intellect ("intellectual operations") by "defin[ing I]ntelligence in terms of the apprehension of truths" (1949, 27), arises. More generally, Ryle tells us, intellectualism holds:

(1) that Intelligence [involves] those specific internal acts which are called acts of thinking, namely, the operations of considering propositions; (2) that practical activities merit their titles 'intelligent,' 'clever,' and the rest only because they are accompanied by some such internal acts of

---

5. It is natural to think that ordinary thought and language vindicate Ryle's use of a broad sense of 'intelligent.' Correlatively, a broad sense of 'stupid' that designates a lack of all states of intellect and character—the absence of Intelligence—seems to be operative in an assertion such as "It's just a stupid machine; it can't think." As we shall use the term, δ is Intelligent if and only if δ is or exercises or displays a state of Intelligence. A particular behavior or action φ (e.g., pruning trees) by a particular individual x displays a state of Intelligence (e.g., the action displays skill) if and only if x exercises a state of Intelligence in φ-ing (e.g., x exercises skill in pruning trees); in such a case, φ is an exercise of a state of Intelligence (e.g., φ is an exercise of skill), and φ has a quality of Intelligence (e.g., φ is skillful or done skillfully).

considering propositions (and particularly "regulative" propositions). (Ryle 1945, 1; cf. 1949, 26ff. and 137)

Internal, nonovert mental states of grasping propositions thus are said to make the difference between the Intelligent and the non-Intelligent.

As suggested by this quotation from Ryle, intellectualism can be understood as the conjunction of two theses, the first of which concerns the aforementioned states of Intelligence and the second of which concerns the relation between these states and action (the exercise of Intelligence):

[I$_{MIND}$] A state σ is a state of Intelligence if and only if σ is or involves[6] a certain type of internal state of engaging propositional content.

[I$_{ACTION}$] An individual x exercises a state of Intelligence in performing an action φ (i.e., x φ-s Intelligently) if and only if x φ-s and x has some state σ such that (i) σ is or involves a certain type of internal state of engaging propositional content and (ii) σ is appropriately causally (or otherwise explanatorily[7]) related to the production of φ.

Where the broad category picked out by the expression 'internal state of engaging propositional content' includes such intellectual phenomena as having a propositional attitude (a way of "latching onto" propositional content) and reasoning (a way of "manipulating" propositional content), as well as other conceptual attitudes.[8] We will often focus on propositional attitudes.

---

6. We state the theses here and below as specifying what the phenomenon designated by the left-hand side *is or involves*. The relevant relation of *being or involving* is distinct from mere equivalence, which cannot sustain the claim of asymmetric determination, dependence, or priority that seems to be essential to the views in question (for discussion of such a stronger, asymmetric relation, see, e.g., Kim 1974, 1994; Fine 1995; Correia 2005, chs. 3–4; and Schaffer 2009a). Specifically, the theses should be interpreted as saying that the phenomenon designated by the left-hand side *is at least partially grounded in*—and in this sense 'is or involves'—the phenomenon designated by the right-hand side (i.e., the former holds at least partly in virtue of the latter). They may but need not specify, say, identities or analyses, for reasons of the sort discussed in note 11.

7. Some intellectualists may wish to understand the relation in terms of, say, noncausal rationalizing explanation or functional (or teleological) explanation. We will leave this qualification implicit in what follows.

8. While Ryle sometimes focuses on acts of thinking and theorizing, and on knowledge, grasp, or apprehension of truths or facts, as well as acts of considering, it is clear that the relevant category—*intellectual operations*—includes most, if not all, nonaffective, nonsensory states that go by the name of propositional attitudes or factual attitudes (see Vendler 1967) in contemporary philosophical parlance (e.g., acknowledging that p, recognizing that p, judging that p, accepting that p, believing that p, perceiving that p, knowing that p, and so forth). The

These intellectualist theses need not be motivated solely by their status as responses to the delineation question. It is difficult to deny that at least some Intelligent actions are preceded by internal states of engaging propositional content. To take a simple example, many of us still recite "Righty, tighty; lefty, loosey" before unscrewing a bolt. In such a case, we are explicitly considering the regulative proposition on which we subsequently act. To the extent that the Intelligence of the action is not a brute and inexplicable fact but is somehow linked to the presence of such prior considering, such considering (regardless of whether it is conscious or explicit)[9] can be said in general to be what confers Intelligence on subsequent action. Such considering—and states relevantly like it—can in turn be said to have the profile *Producer of Intelligence*. Consequently, intellectualism, which posits just this profile, may be regarded as enjoying prima facie motivation: to wit, Intelligent actions are just those actions that are preceded by internal states of engaging propositional content (e.g., considering a regulative proposition).

Although [I_{MIND}] and [I_{ACTION}] are quite general, they have a variety of specific applications. One important application concerns knowledge how to act, a state of Intelligence to which Ryle devotes much attention (see, e.g., 1945, 7ff. and 1949, 28ff.). Intellectualism entails, by [I_{MIND}], that knowledge how is a matter of possessing some relevant propositional attitude (or combination of propositional attitudes) and, by [I_{ACTION}], that actions which display knowledge how are always produced by a causal process somehow involving the relevant propositional attitude (or combination of propositional attitudes).[10] More precisely:

[$I_{KNOW-HOW}$] A state σ of an individual x is a state of knowing how to φ if and only if σ is or involves x's having some relevant propositional attitude(s) regarding φ-ing.[11]

---

relevant states are "internal" in at least the sense that they are not overt; however, intellectualism is wholly compatible with anti-individualism (Burge 1979) and various other externalist theses.

9. Ryle acknowledges that intellectual operations may be "implicit" (1945, 7) and that their exercise may be "very swift and go quite unmarked by the agent" (1949, 29). Cf. Fodor (1968) and Dennett (1982) on some varieties of implicit (tacit, etc.) representation.

10. 'Relevant' signifies a restriction to a specific type of propositional attitude(s). Such a restriction would be required to avoid rendering each and every state of Intelligence equivalent to knowledge how. All the same, the restriction is not obligatory; the significance of this option is discussed in note 27.

11. Ryle allows that proponents of intellectualism might "reduce" knowledge how to knowledge-that (or a "set" or "sandwich" of "knowings-that"; 1945, 10 and 15), but it is also open to them to find some other propositional attitude (recall note 8) and to treat "know-that...as the

[I$_{KH-ACTION}$] x exercises knowledge how to φ in performing an action φ if and only if x φ-s and x has some state σ such that (i) σ is or involves some relevant propositional attitude(s) regarding φ-ing and (ii) σ is appropriately causally related to the production of x's φ-ing.

Analogous theses apply to other phenomena answering to mental-conduct concepts, including those expressed by terms such as 'intelligence' and 'skill.' Intellectualism entails that the grounds of knowledge how, intelligence, and skill are propositional, and exercises thereof are propositionally guided, through and through.[12]

1.2 Four Arguments against Intellectualism

Ryle is no friend to intellectualism. He takes it to be the "prevailing doctrine" (1945, 1, 2, and 3) and one of the "main supports" for the pernicious "paramechanical myth" of "occult Forces" or internal mental causes (1949, 27; cf.

---

ideal model of all [I]ntelligence" (1945, 5 emphasis added). Nor must the proponent of intellectualism view the relation between knowledge how and intellectual states as strict identity or reduction; a nonreductive approach may be allowed. For example, Ryle—who seems to have used the term 'reduce' broadly to include, e.g., identification as well as grounding—suggests that his opponent may treat knowledge how as "derived from" (1949, 31) propositional attitudes. To summarize: the core contention of intellectualism seems to be that knowledge how and other states of Intelligence are at least partially grounded in intellectual states such as propositional attitudes (see also §2.1). While it might be suggested that this characterization of intellectualism is too broad, it bears emphasizing that, as we shall see, Ryle's basic objections in his 1945 lecture and *The Concept of Mind* apply equally to intellectualism so characterized, and he undoubtedly would have rejected this broad intellectualism as vociferously as a narrower, more reductionistic intellectualism.

12. As indicated in note 10, different states of Intelligence (intelligence, skill, cleverness, stupidity, idiocy, etc.) could be said to require different types of attitude or combination thereof (e.g., believing, accepting, contemplating, choosing, seeming, intending, neglecting, knowing) or different types of proposition or combination thereof (e.g., that step B follows step A, that this is a way of φ-ing, that φ-ing is best done by ψ-ing, that it is rationally required to φ when C). Although determining which attitude(s) or proposition(s) are required for different states of Intelligence may require empirical investigation, it is plausible to think, as Ryle does, that whether any such attitudes or propositions are required *at all* for a given state to be properly understood as an instance of Intelligence (rather than not) is a philosophical question. (Compare the a posteriori functionalist thesis that, roughly, mental states are functional states, although which mental state is which functional state is a partly empirical question.)

A note on skill: It is important to recognize that intellectualists distinguish sharply between skills and abilities or dispositions. Skill is a state of Intelligence, whereas mere ability or disposition is not (recall note 4); consequently, according to intellectualism, skills but not abilities or dispositions must be at least partially grounded in propositional attitudes. This approach might be motivated by the idea that all skills (but not all abilities or dispositions) require at least some Intelligence, which in turn involves knowledge that partly underwrites the skilled agent's power to act as she does, namely, skillfully. We return to the issue of skill later.

18–24).[13] He maintains that it entails a severely mistaken view of education as the mere imparting of truths (1945, 15–16) and, more generally, serves to misrepresent "daily experience" and the "quite familiar" facts of "ordinary life" (e.g., 1949, 32; 1945, 6; 1949, 28). Although Ryle suggests that he "relies on variations of one argument" to make his case against intellectualism (1945, 2), his critical discussion actually mentions several distinct types of argument, centering on four. Each of these four types of argument can be seen as focused on an ordinary question that Ryle takes intellectualism to be unable to answer satisfactorily. We consider each in turn, beginning with Ryle's (1940, 38; 1945; 1949, ch. 2) much discussed regress argument.

Let α be some action that is an exercise of a state of Intelligence (e.g., an exercise of knowledge how). By $[I_{ACTION}]$ (or $[I_{KH\text{-}ACTION}]$), α requires a distinct internal state α^* of engaging propositional content that is causally related to the production of (in short, 'produces') α. But, according to Ryle, a state of engaging propositional content is itself something that can be exercised either Intelligently or not, and, Ryle implies, if it is not (e.g., if one does not consider a proposition Intelligently), then its product, α, cannot be Intelligent (or an exercise of knowledge how)—which *ex hypothesi* it is. So the exercise of α^* must be an exercise of a state of Intelligence (or the exercise of α^* must exercise knowledge how): that is, α^* must be Intelligently exercised.[14] But then, by $[I_{ACTION}]$ (or $[I_{KH\text{-}ACTION}]$), it follows that the Intelligent exercise of α^* also requires a distinct internal state α^{**} of engaging propositional content that produces α^*. Since the same reasoning applies to α^{**} (whose Intelligent exercise will require α^{***}, and so on ad infinitum), a regress ensues.

Of course, this is simply one way to implement or interpret the core idea behind Ryle's regress argument. That core idea appears to be that intellectualists fail to provide a satisfactory, non-regress-inducing answer to the question of what it is for intellectual states themselves to be exercises of states of Intelligence. Ryle summarizes:

---

13. While Ryle's stated target is usually Plato or Descartes, whose doctrines of a tripartite soul and a mind-body dualism (respectively) Ryle vehemently opposed, it is worth noting that an intellectualist perspective was also espoused, albeit in perhaps less blatant forms, by several of Ryle's more immediate influences, including the Oxonian Cook Wilson (see, e.g., 1926, §12), the Phenomenologist Edmund Husserl (see, e.g., 1901/1913), and Gottlob Frege (see, e.g., 1918/1956, 310).

14. Ryle (1949, 31; cf. 10): "According to the [intellectualist] legend, whenever an agent does anything intelligently, his act is preceded and steered by another internal act of considering a regulative proposition appropriate to his practical problem. But what makes him consider the one maxim which is appropriate rather than any of the thousands which are not? Why does the hero not find himself calling to mind a cooking-recipe, or a rule of Formal Logic? Perhaps he does, but then his intellectual process is silly and not sensible." See also Ryle (1940, 39). We return to these issues in §§2.2–4, where we discuss how intellectualists might attempt to resist the idea that an act must itself *exercise* Intelligence in order to *produce* an Intelligent action.

> They postulate an internal shadow-performance to be the real carrier of the [I]ntelligence ordinarily ascribed to the overt act, and think that in this way they explain what makes the overt act a manifestation of [I]ntelligence. They have described the overt act as the effect of a mental happening, though *they stop short... before raising the next question—what makes the postulated mental happenings manifestations of [I]ntelligence and not mental deficiency.* (1949, 50 emphasis added)

Let us call this *the mental appraisal question*, which can be formulated generally as follows:

The Mental Appraisal Question
What makes a given mental act an exercise of a state of Intelligence, rather than not?

It should be clear from [I$_{ACTION}$] that, according to intellectualism, an individual's act is an exercise of a state of Intelligence only when the individual has a distinct mental state of engaging some propositional content that produces the act. But when we ask about the exercise of that distinct mental state itself, inquiring about the state of Intelligence thereby exercised—specifically, when what is being appraised is a *mental* act consisting of the exercise of an internal state of engaging propositional content (e.g., considering a proposition, reasoning, and so forth)—Ryle's regress appears to follow in the manner sketched above. But if that is so, then a distinct state of Intelligently engaging a propositional content cannot make a given mental act an exercise of a state of Intelligence, rather than not. What does? Absent a satisfactory, non-regress-inducing intellectualist answer to this question, opponents of the "intellectualist legend" may well regard themselves as supported in their opposition.

While the regress argument is perhaps Ryle's most famous challenge to intellectualism, it may not be the most influential. This brings us to Ryle's second main argument. It is widely thought that intellectualism is counterintuitive, for it violates an intuitive distinction between the theoretical and the practical. Specifically, according to Ryle, it does

> not [do] justice to the distinction which is quite familiar to all of us between knowing that something is the case and knowing how to do things.... [Intellectualists] concentrate on the discovery of truths or facts, and they either ignore the discovery of ways and methods of doing things or else they try to reduce it to the discovery of facts. They assume

that [I]ntelligence equates with the contemplation of propositions and is exhausted in this contemplation. (1945, 4)

It should be clear that what Ryle here dubs 'knowing that' represents truth or fact-oriented states consisting in the "contemplation of propositions" (what we have called 'internal states of engaging propositional content') more generally, while 'knowing how' represents action-oriented states regarding "ways and methods of doing things" more generally. Of course, the indicated contrast is most salient when we focus, as Ryle often does, on the case of knowledge that something is the case versus knowledge how to do things, for it is here that we find what intuitively looks to be a clear distinction between merely truth or fact-oriented theoretical knowledge versus action-oriented practical knowledge.[15] This raises a question, which we will call *the practical/theoretical question*, of how to account for this intuitive distinction:

The Practical/Theoretical Question
How are we to understand the distinction between practical knowledge (action-oriented states) and mere theoretical knowledge (merely truth or fact-oriented states)?

Absent a satisfactory account of the intuitive distinction between practical knowledge and mere truth or fact-oriented knowledge, intellectualism may be accused of failing to do justice to the complex character of mind and action.

We will return to Ryle's regress and this intuitive distinction later. Before moving on, let us briefly consider two of Ryle's less famous—but, arguably, equally significant—arguments against intellectualism. The first of these is broadly epistemological. Because it understands Intelligence in terms of internal (nonpublic) states of engaging propositional content, it seems that intellectualism entails that no amount of external (public) observation could ever enable one to determine whether an intelligence-epithet is applicable in individual cases. Given that all we have to go on in daily life is just such observation, this threatens the very *rationality*, in daily life, of the ordinary practice of ascribing states and qualities of Intelligence:

---

15. This type of practical knowledge is not to be confused with what Anscombe (1957, §32) labeled 'practical knowledge,' by which she meant knowledge of what one is doing intentionally (for example, that I am writing this note); see §4.3 for possible connections. Propositional attitudes may be understood as truth or fact-oriented insofar as their propositional contents are bearers of truth and falsity; in this way, propositional attitudes may be true or false. Abilities and dispositions, by contrast, cannot be true or false. A state is *merely* truth or fact-oriented when it may be true or false and it is not action-oriented.

> According to this theory, external observers could never know how the overt behavior of others is correlated with their mental powers and processes and so *they could never know or even plausibly conjecture* whether their applications of mental-conduct concepts to these other people were correct or incorrect.... [O]ur characterizations of persons and their performances as intelligent...or as stupid...could never have been made....
> (1949, 21 emphasis added; cf. 1949, 54 and 60)[16]

To resist this argument, the intellectualist must answer what we will call *the rational ascription question*:

The Rational Ascription Question
What is the basis for the rationality of our ordinary practice of ascribing states and qualities of Intelligence?

Absent a viable answer to this question, intellectualism may be charged with upholding an impoverished view of (our view of) our mental lives.

Let us now turn to Ryle's fourth main argument against intellectualism. The central contention is simple but powerful:

> However many strata of knowledge-that are postulated, the same crux always recurs that a fool might have all that knowledge without knowing how to perform.... (1945, 8)

Perhaps Ryle's most effective application of this idea occurs in this passage about chess:

> We can imagine a clever player generously imparting to his stupid opponent so many rules, tactical maxims, "wrinkles," etc., that he could think of no more to tell him; his opponent might accept and memorise all of them, and be able and ready to recite them correctly on demand. Yet he might still play chess [without Intelligence].[17] (1945, 5)

---

16. Some commentators have interpreted passages like this one in a way that commits Ryle to an implausible verificationism (cf. Soames 2003, 97–98; Stanley forthcoming-b, 3n.1). Such an interpretation threatens to miss or obscure the genuine question that this and similar passages pose to intellectualism.

17. Ryle's worry is anticipated by Locke in *The Conduct of the Understanding*: "Nobody is made anything by hearing of rules or laying them up in his memory..., and you may as well hope to make a good painter or musician extempore, by a lecture and instruction in the arts of music

This raises the delineation question anew. If it is possible, as Ryle suggests, that two such individuals grasp all of the same propositions but only one of them possesses Intelligence (e.g., has knowledge how), then Intelligence does not supervene on propositional attitudes (i.e., the facts about propositional attitudes do not fix the facts about Intelligence). But if that is so, then internal states of engaging propositional content cannot make the difference between behaviors that do, and overtly indistinguishable behaviors that do not, display states of Intelligence. What does? Absent a viable answer to this delineation question, intellectualism may be charged with presenting a wholly inadequate conception of mind and action.[18]

1.3 Anti-Intellectualism

Ryle's project is not only to challenge the intellectualist legend but also to piece together an alternative conception of mind and its relation to action centered on the idea that "[I]ntelligence-predicates are definable in terms of knowing-how" (1945, 15; 1949, 27–28), where knowing how is held to be equivalent to a particular type of power, that is, a feature of agents typically expressed by a modal auxiliary such as 'can,' 'could,' or 'would': for instance, an ability or disposition.[19]

According to Ryle (1949, 40–47), knowing how to φ is not merely a regularity of behavior or a habit, but rather a disposition to φ that is (i) trained (i.e., the product of practice, not drill), (ii) trainable (i.e., liable to modification and improvement),[20] and (iii) multitrack (i.e., it may be exercised in diverse ways, including actions other than φ).[21] More generally:

---

and painting, as a coherent thinker or strict reasoner by a set of rules showing him wherein right reasoning consists" (1706/1891, 19).

18. It is important to distinguish Ryle's "fool argument" from his regress argument. While the latter challenges the right-to-left direction of the intellectualist theses stated above, the former challenges the left-to-right direction. Cf. Fantl (2008, 454–455) and Snowdon (chapter 2).

19. To be sure, it might be true in some sense of 'can' that x can φ even though it is not true that x is able or disposed to φ. Following current practice, we focus on abilities or dispositions, but it is important to emphasize that an account of knowledge how and Intelligence that appealed to such a sense of 'can' may still qualify as a form of anti-intellectualism. (The anti-intellectualist theses stated below and the discussion that follows should be read in this light.)

20. The capacity to learn or to modify and improve one's behavior is often held to be one, if not the primary, mark of intelligence. See, e.g., Nowell-Smith (1960) and Bennett (1964, 34ff.).

21. It is sometimes suggested that Ryle did not hold that knowledge how to perform some action φ is equivalent to a type of disposition to φ on the grounds that Ryle (1949, 44) maintained that knowledge how is equivalent to a type of disposition "the exercises of which are indefinitely heterogenous" and his examples (1949, 47) of such exercises invoke mental actions

[AI$_{\text{KNOW-HOW}}$] A state σ of an individual x is a state of knowing how to φ if and only if σ is or involves x's having a certain type of ability or disposition (e.g., a trained, trainable, multitrack disposition) to φ, rather than propositional attitudes.

[AI$_{\text{KH-ACTION}}$] x exercises knowledge how to φ in performing an action φ if and only if x φ-s and x has some state σ such that (i) σ is a certain type of ability or disposition (e.g., a trained, trainable, multitrack disposition) to φ, rather than propositional attitudes, and (ii) x's φ-ing is the actualization of σ.

These theses are instances of a more general conception of mind and action. This conception, which we will call *anti-intellectualism* (hence 'AI'), can be understood as the combination of the following two theses about states of Intelligence, and exercises thereof:

[AI$_{\text{MIND}}$] A state σ is a state of Intelligence if and only if σ is or involves a certain type of ability or disposition (e.g., a trained, trainable, multitrack disposition) to perform some action (or set of actions), rather than propositional attitudes.

[AI$_{\text{ACTION}}$] An individual x exercises a state of Intelligence in performing an action φ if and only if x φ-s and x has some state σ such that (i) σ is a certain type of ability or disposition (e.g., a trained, trainable, multitrack disposition) to perform some action (or set of actions), rather than propositional attitudes, and (ii) x's φ-ing is the actualization of σ.

As should be clear, anti-intellectualism entails that the phenomena answering to mental-conduct concepts, including those expressed by adjectives such as 'intelligent' and 'skillful', are grounded in powers—abilities or dispositions to behavior—rather than attitudes.[22]

Anti-intellectualism denies that internal states of engaging propositional content play any role in accounting for Intelligent action. Recitation of "Righty,

---

such as "deeds imagined" (see, e.g., Weatherson 2007, 436). However, it does not follow from the fact that a disposition D can be *exercised* in diverse ways, including physical and mental actions other than φ, that D is not correctly characterized as a disposition to φ.

22. It would be illuminating to have a complete theory of abilities or dispositions (Ryle himself seems to have endorsed a conditional analysis; see Maier (2010) for helpful discussion of theories of ability). But no such theory is needed to understand and assess these anti-intellectualist theses—no more than a complete theory of propositional attitudes is needed to understand and assess intellectualism.

tighty; lefty, loosey"—understood as a state of considering a regulative proposition—before unscrewing a bolt is deemed irrelevant to the Intelligence of the action (or perhaps denied altogether). Propositional attitudes are replaced with abilities or dispositions. As a result, anti-intellectualism seems to introduce the following answers to the mental appraisal, practical/theoretical, delineation, and rational ascription questions:

1. *Mental appraisal.* What makes a given mental act itself an exercise of a state of Intelligence, rather than not? The answer, according to anti-intellectualism, is that it is a direct exercise of knowledge how, that is, an actualization of a particular type of ability or disposition (for Ryle, a trained, trainable, multitrack disposition to act). Such an actualization, unlike an internal mental act of engaging propositional content (e.g., considering a proposition), is not itself an action that is intelligently or stupidly performed.[23] Since nothing more than the actualization of such an ability or disposition is held to make a given mental act an exercise of a state of Intelligence, regress is averted.

2. *Practical/theoretical.* How are we to make sense of the distinction between action-oriented practical knowledge and mere truth or fact-oriented knowledge? The answer, according to anti-intellectualism, is that practical knowledge regarding some activity φ—such as knowledge *how* to φ—is a particular type of ability or disposition to φ, whereas mere truth or fact-oriented knowledge regarding φ—such as knowledge *that* φ is such and such—is *not* an ability or disposition to φ.[24] To the extent that an ability or disposition to φ is plainly an action-oriented state that does not simply collapse our grasp of "ways and methods of doing things" to the mere "contemplation of propositions," such a view successfully accommodates the intuitive distinction between the theoretical and the practical.

---

23. While it may be possible for an ability or disposition to be exercised Intelligently in some cases, as when Gandhi *sensibly* exercises his disposition to fight systemic injustice by, say, opting to practice various forms of nonviolent resistance rather than guerrilla warfare, the anti-intellectualist may hold that certain abilities or dispositions are non-Intelligently exercised. See §2.2 for related discussion.

24. Ryle (1949, ch. 9) seems to suggest that the latter is a particular type of ability or disposition to say that φ-ing is such and such (out loud or in one's head), to imagine that φ-ing is such and such, and so forth. But such a dispositional account of mere truth or fact-oriented knowledge is wholly optional and is not an essential feature of anti-intellectualism. For relevant discussion, see note 25, which contemplates an extreme anti-intellectualist position that might embrace such an account; it may also (but need not) deny the practical/theoretical distinction.

3. *Delineation.* What makes the difference between behaviors that do, and overtly indistinguishable behaviors that do not, display states of Intelligence? The answer, according to Ryle's anti-intellectualism, is that the former behaviors but not the latter are exercises of knowing how, a particular type of ability or disposition, whose detection requires one to "look beyond the performances themselves," but not (as intellectualism seems to imply) to "pry into some hidden counterpart performance enacted on the secret stage of the agent's inner life" (1949, 45).

4. *Rational ascription.* What is the basis for the rationality of our ordinary practice of ascribing states and qualities of Intelligence? The answer, according to Ryle's anti-intellectualism, is simple:

To find that most people have minds…is simply to find that they are able and prone to do certain sorts of things, and we do this by witnessing the sorts of things they do. Indeed we…discover what specific qualities of intellect and character people have. (1949, 61; cf. 169)

To the extent that observers can determine the presence or absence of the relevant ability or disposition in virtue of witnessing actual performances (in diverse circumstances, on multiple occasions, etc.), the rationality of our ordinary practice of ascribing states and qualities of Intelligence is thus sustained.

2. *Intellectualism after Ryle*

Stripped to its essentials, Ryle's critical project in *The Concept of Mind* is a philosophical gambit to undercut a traditional view of mind and action by making explicit certain of its commitments and arguing that they have very troubling consequences. Any such project faces the danger of specifying too many details of the target view, for such specification tends to introduce the possibility that the target will evade the criticism proffered by simply tweaking—or, if you prefer, fine-tuning—some of those details, all the while retaining its core contention. Such tweaking is one of the topics of this section. In recent years, it has become clear that intellectualism has available a variety of resources that go unmarked in Ryle's discussion. It has also emerged that an adequate account of knowledge how is not a frivolous philosophical aim. After gesturing at the importance of knowledge how to broader debate about mind and action, we survey some of these resources and explore how they might facilitate intellectualist answers to the delineation, practical/theoretical, mental appraisal, and rational ascription questions. (In the next section, we turn to anti-intellectualism to discuss some of the resources to which anti-intellectualists might appeal when attempting to respond to recent intellectualist attacks.)

2.1 Intellectualism, Anti-Intellectualism, and the Importance of Knowing How

'Intellectualism' and 'anti-intellectualism' are, of course, terms of art that can be used in different ways in different contexts, including the various chapters in this book. (The best policy is to refer to the individual chapters to understand how the author is using the terms.) However, we believe that one of Ryle's most important contributions was to uncover a general, theoretically significant fault line in the theory of knowledge, mind, and action, to which these terms helpfully—and quite naturally—apply. The core contention of the intellectualist side of this line is that states of Intelligence and exercises thereof are at least partially grounded in propositional attitudes. The core contention of the anti-intellectualist side, by contrast, is that states of Intelligence and exercises thereof are grounded in powers (abilities or dispositions to behavior), not in propositional attitudes. That is, with respect to Ryle's fault line, some version of $[I_{MIND}]$ and $[I_{ACTION}]$ seems to be essential to any general intellectualist view, while some version of $[AI_{MIND}]$ and $[AI_{ACTION}]$ seems to be essential to any general anti-intellectualist view.[25]

Now, it is worth observing that if anti-intellectualism is simply the denial of the intellectualist thesis that states of Intelligence are at least partially grounded in propositional attitudes, then it is, strictly speaking, consistent with an approach that does not invoke powers. Be that as it may, what remains distinctive of anti-intellectualism is that it does not invoke propositional attitudes; intellectualism, by contrast, does invoke such attitudes. Notice that intellectualists may consistently allow that some states of Intelligence, such as skill, require a corresponding power; they may also allow that mere powers have various roles to play in a

---

25. Attention to Ryle's fault line also allows us to make sense of an extreme anti-intellectualist position, according to which knowing that depends on knowing how, a position that goes beyond $[AI_{MIND}]$ and $[AI_{ACTION}]$. (One version of this position is endorsed by Hartland-Swann (1956, 114; cf. 1958), who holds that "*all* cases of knowing *that* can ultimately be reduced to cases of knowing *how*." See also Brandom 1994, Haugeland 1998, and Hetherington 2006. Cf. Roland 1958, Ducasse 1964, and Beck 1968.) Generalizing somewhat, such a view asserts the following triad: $[AI_{MIND}]$, $[AI_{ACTION}]$, *and* the thesis that propositional attitudes and exercises thereof are at least partially grounded in knowing how and other states of Intelligence—and thus, in turn, corresponding abilities or dispositions. It is an interesting question how (or whether) nonextreme anti-intellectualism (which embraces $[AI_{MIND}]$) can successfully avoid collapsing into extreme anti-intellectualism. There is also room to contemplate an extreme intellectualist position according to which all mental or agentive powers are at least partially grounded in propositional attitudes. We lack the space to explore these positions here.

comprehensive theory of mind and action (as well as explanation of particular actions on particular occasions). What remains distinctive of the intellectualist side of the aforementioned fault line is the thesis that all states of Intelligence, including skill, are at least partially grounded in propositional attitudes, regardless of whether a power is somehow required.[26]

At any rate, given the generality of these views, one might wonder why the specific case of knowledge how merits special consideration. In short: why care about knowledge how? Here is one type of answer (several others will emerge at various points later). Suppose for a moment that knowledge how is *not* grounded in propositional attitudes. Two conclusions would immediately follow. First, intellectualists could not regard knowledge how as a state of Intelligence; however, to the extent that knowledge how is a paradigm example of such a state, this specific case would not be any mere exception to $[I_{MIND}]$ but would undercut its basic motivation. Second, knowledge how would constitute an attractive basis for a general understanding of Intelligent action as *not* grounded in propositional attitudes, just as Ryle maintained, thereby undercutting $[I_{ACTION}]$. For these reasons, the intellectualist about mind and action cannot easily abandon the idea that knowledge how is grounded in attitudes. Likewise for the anti-intellectualist, who (for parallel reasons) cannot easily abandon the idea that knowledge how is grounded in abilities or dispositions, rather than attitudes. Knowledge how is, in this sense, a hinge on which our general understanding of mind and action—in particular, a satisfactory theory of Intelligence and its manifestation in action—turns.[27]

---

26. It might be denied that knowing how, skill, and the various other phenomena that we have been calling states of Intelligence are to be given a uniform intellectualist (or anti-intellectualist) account: from this perspective, some of the phenomena are intellectual; others are not. We lack the space to give this perspective the attention it deserves. Prima facie, however, it faces at least two difficulties. First, it not only abandons but also wholly disallows a general theory of Intelligence; yet, insofar as the theory of Intelligence and Intelligent action is still in its infancy, such an extreme verdict may be viewed as premature. Second, and perhaps more importantly, it seems implausible to deny that knowing how, skill, and other states of Intelligence have something important in common; what is needed is an account of this commonality, which just is the project discussed in the text.

27. Further motivation for treating knowledge how as a focal point centers on the practical/theoretical and delineation questions. Regarding the former, knowledge how is a paradigm of an action-oriented state; understanding such knowledge arguably provides a key to an explanation of the distinction between the theoretical and the practical. Regarding the latter, at a superficial level both the intellectualist and the anti-intellectualist could agree about the proper solution to the delineation question: knowledge how makes the difference between behaviors that do, and overtly indistinguishable behaviors that do not, display states of Intelligence. Of course, this veneer of agreement simply highlights substantial disagreement about how to unpack this solution: to wit, intellectualists and anti-intellectualists are deeply at odds about what knowledge how is. This indicates how understanding knowledge how may play a pivotal

This goes some distance toward making sense of recent (post-Ryle) emphasis on the specific case of knowledge how. It also invites us to use knowledge how as a model or test case when considering how the intellectualist might respond to the challenges posed by the questions highlighted in §1.2: the mental appraisal, delineation, practical/theoretical, and rational ascription questions. Let us discuss each in turn.

2.2 The Mental Appraisal Question

Recall that the mental appraisal question asks about a given mental act: what makes it an exercise of a state of Intelligence, when it is? Notice that the question does not presuppose that *every* mental act, or even every mental act in which one engages propositional content, is an exercise of a state of Intelligence—that is, it does not presuppose that all such actions are done or performed Intelligently. Nor should it. While some mental acts, such as *reasoning sensibly*, may be exercises of Intelligence, other mental acts, such as *contemplating* or *entertaining*, need not be. Contemplating or entertaining (i.e., merely thinking about) the proposition that, say, the number of stars in the universe is odd is a clear case of considering a proposition and thus an exercise of a state of engaging propositional content, but it is not obvious what one could mean by saying that it is done or performed Intelligently: "Gilbert contemplated that proposition stupidly" sounds like a category mistake.

Here it is important to bear in mind the difference between an item *being* a state of Intelligence and an item *being an exercise of* a state of Intelligence (i.e., being something that is done or performed Intelligently). A given state of engaging propositional content may qualify, by [I_{MIND}], as *Intelligent*. But it need not thereby qualify as an *exercise of* Intelligence (i.e., something done or performed Intelligently); to earn that status, it must satisfy [I_{ACTION}], and it is open to the intellectualist to deny, in a given case, that it does.[28] That there is room for such denial is independently motivated by the stars example, which can be usefully

---

role in a substantive account of the difference between the Intelligent and the non-Intelligent. The worry that the dispute between intellectualists and anti-intellectualists is not substantive is discussed and rejected in §4.6.

28. It is crucial not to conflate two different types of evaluation: (1) whether an act was done *correctly* or *validly* (e.g., reasoning according to modus ponens) and (2) whether it was done *Intelligently* (e.g., reasoning sensibly). That is, we must distinguish between evaluative epithets in general and what Ryle calls the "intelligence-epithets" in particular (and not simply because an act might be done correctly but not Intelligently, as several of Ryle's own examples—involving those who act successfully but *not* Intelligently—bring out). As emphasized in §1 and §2.1, intellectualism and anti-intellectualism are theses about the latter only.

contrasted with the case of reasoning sensibly. On the one hand, reasoning sensibly is a state of Intelligence that itself exercises a state of Intelligence (it is reasoning done Intelligently, as implied by the applicability of the intelligence-epithet 'sensibly'); consequently, the intellectualist will hold that reasoning sensibly satisfies both [I$_{\text{MIND}}$] and [I$_{\text{ACTION}}$]. On the other hand, merely contemplating or entertaining the proposition that the number of stars is odd is a state of Intelligence that does *not* itself exercise a state of Intelligence (as implied by the inapplicability of the intelligence-epithet 'stupidly' in the sample sentence at the end of the previous paragraph); consequently, although it may satisfy [I$_{\text{MIND}}$], the intellectualist need not hold that it satisfies [I$_{\text{ACTION}}$].

The intellectualist may exploit these points to deflect Ryle's regress. Intellectualism leads to regress only when clauses (i) and (ii) in [I$_{\text{ACTION}}$] are conjoined with an additional, regress-inducing principle to the effect that the relevant internal states of engaging propositional content are *always exercises of Intelligence* (i.e., Intelligently done or performed)—and, therefore, must themselves satisfy [I$_{\text{ACTION}}$].[29] To be explicit, regress ensues when intellectualism is elaborated as follows:

[I$_{\text{ACTION}}$+] An individual x exercises a state of Intelligence in performing an action φ (i.e., x φ-s Intelligently) if and only if x φ-s and x has some state σ such that (i) σ is or involves an internal state of engaging propositional content, (ii) σ is appropriately causally related to the production of φ, *and* (+) σ is Intelligently exercised rather than not (i.e., σ itself exercises a state of Intelligence).

But intellectualism need not be so elaborated. The condition expressed in (+) is not compulsory, and it should be rejected by intellectualists seeking to avoid regress. But how?

Intellectualists might look to the idea that sometimes one simply *acts on* one's intellectual state—where, just as in the case of contemplating the stars proposition, the relevant state is not itself something that is Intelligently exercised. This is, in effect, Carl Ginet's contention in the following passage:[30]

---

29. Cf. Snowdon (2003, §4).

30. Cf. Stanley and Williamson (2001, §1), who suggest that the key to Ryle's regress—both understanding it and solving it—is attention to the distinction between intentional action and nonintentional action. As discussed here and in §1.2, we believe that Ryle's regress centers on the issue of Intelligence and Intelligent action. The class of actions that are Intelligent might not be coextensive with the class of actions that are intentional: for instance, it is plausible to think that when Gilbert contemplates the stars proposition, he does so intentionally, though he does not do so Intelligently. As we shall see, what is needed to answer Ryle's regress is an account of a certain type of non-Intelligently exercised intellectual state.

I exercise (or manifest) my knowledge *that* one can get the door open by turning the knob and pushing it (as well as my knowledge *that* there is a door there) by performing that operation quite automatically as I leave the room; and I may do this, of course, without formulating (in my mind or out loud) that proposition or any other relevant proposition. (1975, 7 emphasis in original)

Perhaps in some cases a state of engaging propositional content (in Ginet's example, propositional knowledge that one can get the door open by turning the knob and pushing it, together with propositional knowledge that there is a door there) can be appropriately causally related to the production of ('produce') an Intelligent action, although it is not itself an exercise of Intelligence. The intellectual state—a propositional attitude—is such that it is simply exercised, and its being exercised leads directly (non-Intelligently) to an Intelligent action.

(Some may find it infelicitous or misleading to say that propositional attitudes could ever be "exercised" in action. However, the central idea is that attitudes may be *brought to bear on action* (i.e., we *act on* such attitudes), and their being brought to bear on action (acted on) need not itself be an action that is intelligently or stupidly performed. Whether such bringing to bear on action (acting on) is felicitously described as "exercising" is perhaps terminological; indeed, if need be, our usage here may be regarded as technical. On our usage, exercising an attitude is not itself a propositional attitude (i.e., an internal state of engaging propositional content); rather, it is an act of bringing a propositional attitude to bear on action (acting on an attitude), where the subsequent action may be physical or mental. Such exercising is absent from the stars example, which in this respect differs from Ginet's example and the righty-tighty example (from §1.1). While the stars example involves a propositional attitude that is not Intelligently exercised, Ginet's example and the righty-tighty example may involve propositional attitudes that are non-Intelligently exercised: that is, in the stars example, the attitude is *not* exercised (brought to bear on action) at all—one simply has it; in the other two examples, the attitudes *are* exercised (brought to bear on action) but not Intelligently so. What all of these examples have in common is that they involve propositional attitudes that are not exercised Intelligently. Hence, they differ from the case of reasoning sensibly, which involves an attitude that *is* exercised Intelligently (viz., sensibly).)

A satisfactory development of this response to Ryle's regress requires an account of the indicated non-Intelligently exercised propositional attitudes— attitudes that (i) *are* states of Intelligence and (ii) *produce* actions that are exercises of states of Intelligence but (iii) are not themselves *exercises* of states of

Intelligence. What are these attitudes? And how can they produce actions without themselves being exercised Intelligently?

Let us take a moment to reflect on the issue of the non-Intelligent exercise of attitudes that are themselves Intelligent. (Possible characterizations of the relevant attitudes themselves will be discussed in the next section.) There are at least two different approaches that the intellectualist might take to this phenomenon. According to a *personalist* view, the relevant attitudes are exercised through a non-Intelligent act that is performed by the person, for example, the act of *applying* or *utilizing* one's attitude. Thus, the relevant attitudes are not *Intelligently exercised*; rather, they are simply *applied* or *utilized*, and their being applied or utilized produces an Intelligent action.[31] According to a *subpersonalist* view, the relevant attitudes are exercised through a non-Intelligent act that occurs at the subpersonal level (i.e., an act that is *not* performed by the person), for example, the act of *deploying* or *triggering* an attitude (cf. Fodor 1968, 629 and 632–633; Stanley forthcoming-b, 15–17). Thus, one does not *Intelligently exercise* the relevant attitudes; rather, they are simply deployed or triggered, and their being deployed or triggered produces an Intelligent action. Naturally, a *hybrid* view will hold that the relevant attitudes are in some cases non-Intelligently exercised through an act that is performed by the person and in other cases through an act that occurs at the subpersonal level. (The hybrid view may be rendered attractive by the thought that the righty-tighty case seems to involve a *person* applying her knowledge of a regulative principle, whereas in Ginet's example, propositional knowledge regarding the door arguably could be simply triggered or deployed *subpersonally*.) To the extent that these views are able to explain how the relevant attitudes can be non-Intelligently exercised, such views would play a crucial role in helping to elaborate intellectualism in a way that averts regress.[32]

In a moment, after considering (in §2.3) several intellectualist answers to the practical/theoretical question, we will be able to articulate (in §2.4) how

---

31. Such applying or utilizing might be understood in terms of what O'Shaughnessy (1980, ch. 10) refers to as 'sub-intentional actions,' such as agentively but absent-mindedly strumming one's fingers, perhaps in the way suggested by Steward (2009, 308): "they are…our doings, even though they are not the products of our intentions" nor the results of "any antecedent thinkings, wishings, plannings, or the like." In general, a personalist view requires denial of Ryle's (1945, 4) assertion that "whatever 'applying' may be, it is a proper exercise of [I]ntelligence," if this is meant to imply that *each and every* act of applying (or utilizing) is an exercise of Intelligence. For relevant discussion, see Parry (1980, 389–390), who suggests that Ryle's view that applying is a proper exercise of Intelligence implies that anti-intellectualism is itself guilty of regress.

32. Ryle would presumably object to the subpersonalist and hybrid views, which seem to violate the tenet that the locus of Intelligence is always the person or agent. Cf. Nagel (1969) and, e.g., Korsgaard (1999).

intellectualism might attempt to use these ideas to dispel Ryle's regress. But first, it is worth pausing to notice that the personalist and subpersonalist views described here embody an intellectualist approach to the exercise of Intelligence that is, at a certain level of abstraction, of a piece with Ryle's own anti-intellectualist answer to the mental appraisal question, outlined in §1.3. The central difference is that whereas anti-intellectualism invokes *abilities* or *dispositions* such that their exercise is not itself an action that is Intelligently performed,[33] intellectualism invokes *attitudes* such that their exercise is not itself an action that is Intelligently performed. In both cases, one encounters a phenomenon—a type of power (ability, disposition) or a type of state (attitude)—that is non-Intelligently actualized or exercised, and its being so actualized or exercised leads directly to Intelligent action.

2.3 The Practical/Theoretical Question

Of course, this last clause serves to reinforce the point, noted a moment ago, that a complete intellectualist answer to Ryle's regress requires a characterization of the relevant attitude. What is needed is an intellectual state that, in addition to being capable of non-Intelligent exercise, fits the profile *Producer of Intelligence*: a type of propositional attitude that *produces Intelligent action when (non-Intelligently) exercised*. Of course, filling this lacuna is tantamount to identifying a propositional attitude that is practical or action-oriented rather than merely theoretical. In this way, a response to Ryle's regress looks to be inseparable from an answer to the practical/theoretical question—which, from the perspective of intellectualism, can be addressed only by an attitude that is in some sense truth or fact-oriented (insofar as it is an internal state of engaging propositional content), but not *merely* so. What could such an attitude be?

Now, at one level of description, intellectualism might simply offer a broadly functional characterization of the relevant attitude:[34] for example, it is a type of state whose nature or role is to produce Intelligent action under certain conditions, namely, when exercised. Of course, for this to be a satisfactory *intellectualist* response to the practical knowledge question, we must have reason to think that

---

33. Recall note 23.

34. Cf. Craig (1990, 153), who suggests that the central idea behind the intellectualist approach is, roughly, that "the change from 'that' to 'how' marks the fact that we are dealing with [an] information[al state] of the type which characteristically enables a certain kind of action." It is sometimes suggested that acknowledging a distinction between action-oriented states and mere truth or fact-oriented states suffices to establish that knowledge how—or, more generally, Intelligence—is not an intellectual matter, thus vindicating anti-intellectualism. We hope that the present discussion makes clear why this is mistaken.

this state is or involves a propositional attitude (or combination of propositional attitudes). We must also be told how the relevant state could satisfy this functional characterization without simply collapsing into an anti-intellectualist disposition to behavior. Addressing these issues looks to be among the most pressing tasks facing intellectualism.

Here, briefly, are three approaches that might be seen as taking steps in this direction. First, building on a suggestion by Jason Stanley and Timothy Williamson (2001), one might hold that practical knowledge involves contemplating or entertaining a proposition under a "practical mode of presentation," as opposed to a nonpractical—for instance, merely theoretical—mode of presentation.[35] Second, following John Bengson and Marc Moffett (2007; chapter 7), the intellectualist might hold that practical knowledge involves understanding a way of acting, where such understanding—which essentially requires reasonable mastery of certain concepts—is a state that is poised to guide successful, intentional action. A third version of intellectualism might exploit (Ryle's colleague) Herbert Haberly Price's (1946, 36) notion of *familiarity with a universal*, holding that practical knowledge involves familiarity with a "practical" universal, for example, an action-type.[36] (We will return to Price's discussion of familiarity with a universal in §2.5.)

Of course, these approaches do not entail that there is an exclusive or fundamental distinction between knowledge that something is the case and knowledge how to do things. Nevertheless, to the extent that one or another of the indicated notions—a practical mode of presentation, understanding a way of acting, familiarity with a practical universal, or some combination thereof—allows us to identify a type of attitude that, while practical, can be fully characterized without implicitly or explicitly collapsing into an anti-intellectualist ability or disposition to behavior, the result would be an intellectualist-friendly account of the intuitive distinction between practical knowledge (action-oriented states) and mere theoretical knowledge (merely truth or fact-oriented states).

---

35. Cf. Williamson (1999, 44): "one's grasp of the propositional content may be distinctively practical ('φ now!'; 'φ like this!')." For critical discussion of the notion of a practical mode of presentation, see Koethe (2002), Schiffer (2002), Rosefeldt (2004), Fantl (2008, 460ff.), and Williams (2008, §5).

36. Cf. Carr (1981a, 60–61), who focuses on knowledge of rules of a practice or "relations between prescriptions," and Gibbons (2001, 590), who suggests that "knowing how is something like having a non-accidentally effective action plan." In a similar vein, Annas (2001, §§4–6) emphasizes the importance of understanding the subject matter of an area of expertise, which she relates to the Platonic notion of grasping a Form—with which Price's notion of familiarity with a universal likewise bears affinities.

2.4 Intellectualism and Ryle's Regress, Continued

We are now in a position to see how intellectualism might seek to avoid regress.

As indicated in §2.1, knowledge how may serve as our test case. Suppose (for purposes of illustration) that the intellectualist holds, in conformity with [I$_{KH\text{-}MIND}$] (and [I$_{MIND}$]), that x knows how to φ if and only if x possesses intellectual state α*, where α* is appropriately practical—that is, α* is action-oriented; for example (recalling the options canvassed in §2.3), it involves contemplation of a proposition regarding φ-ing under a practical mode of presentation, understanding a way of φ-ing, or familiarity with the action-type φ. Now, let α be an action, such as pruning trees, that an individual might know how to perform. Then [I$_{KH\text{-}ACTION}$] (and [I$_{ACTION}$]) will be true just in case the following holds: x exercises knowledge how to α in performing α if and only if x performs α and (i) x has α* and (ii) α* is appropriately causally related to the production of (again, 'produces') α. As we saw in §2.2, a subpersonalist version of intellectualism will hold that α* is deployed or triggered *but not Intelligently so*; hence, α* *is* knowledge how (i.e., knowledge how to α), but the deployment or triggering of α* does not *exercise* knowledge how, nor any other state of Intelligence. Analogously for a personalist version of intellectualism, according to which α* is applied or utilized. Let 'α**' signify the act of deploying, triggering, applying, or utilizing α*. Since α** does not exercise any state of Intelligence, [I$_{KH\text{-}ACTION}$] does not apply to it; consequently, in neither case—subpersonalist nor personalist—does the intellectualist encounter a need to postulate any further intellectual state (α***) that produces α**. On both views, α** (the act of deploying, triggering, applying, or utilizing α*) is not itself something that is Intelligently done or performed (i.e., it does not exercise a state of Intelligence), and α* is appropriately practical: it is a type of intellectual state such that if its deployment, triggering, application, or utilization produces α, then α exercises knowledge how to α. In this way, by combining an appropriate characterization of the relevant intellectual state with a personalist or subpersonalist view of its non-Intelligent exercise, regress is averted.

The same story might be told mutatis mutandis for other states of Intelligence, such as intelligence and skill, and its overall success will depend on the success of its central characters, discussed in §§2.2–3.

2.5 The Delineation Question

Insofar as an intellectual state that fits the profile *Producer of Intelligence* plays a crucial role in a general intellectualist account of the difference between the Intelligent and the non-Intelligent, an intellectualist answer to the mental appraisal and practical/theoretical questions must be developed in tandem with an answer to the delineation question. What makes the difference between behaviors that do, and overtly indistinguishable behaviors that do not, display states of Intelligence? As we saw in §1.3, an answer to this question must display an appropriate sensitivity to Ryle's fool argument, which contends that two individuals might have all of the same propositional attitudes with respect to some activity φ (e.g., chess), yet one possesses while the other lacks Intelligence and knowledge how with respect to φ. There are several ways that the intellectualist might try to respond to the fool argument and answer the delineation question.[37] We shall consider three.

First, the intellectualist might draw inspiration from Stanley and Williamson's (2001) appeal to a practical mode of presentation in the case of knowledge how (mentioned in §2.3). On this approach, one individual possesses while the other individual lacks knowledge how to φ because only one of them entertains the relevant proposition regarding φ under a practical mode of presentation. Other states of Intelligence could be treated analogously, perhaps as summoning their own distinctive modes of presentation.

Second, the intellectualist might utilize Bengson and Moffett's (2007; chapter 7) appeal to understanding (also mentioned in §2.3). The importance of understanding was perhaps first stressed by Descartes, who wrote in *Discourse on Method* that a careful study of mindless automata as compared with those beings with minds, such as ourselves,

> would reveal that [the automata] were not acting through *understanding* [*connaissance*] but only from the disposition of their organs.[38] (1637/1984, 140 emphasis added)

On the version of the understanding-based approach suggested by Bengson and Moffett, one individual possesses while the other individual lacks knowledge how to φ because only one of them understands a way of φ-ing, where such understanding essentially requires reasonable mastery of concepts in a (possibly implicit) conception of that way. Other states of Intelligence could be held to require reasonable conceptual mastery in much the same way.

---

37. One option that we do not elaborate consists in denying (or rephrasing) Ryle's fool intuition, holding that there would in fact be some propositional attitude that one individual possesses but the other lacks. Of course, the intellectualist would need to provide fairly compelling reasons for such denial; she would also owe an explanation of the original intuition, assuming it persists.

38. See Erion (2001) for discussion of Cartesian "tests" for intelligence and their connection to the famous Turing Test.

Third, the intellectualist might make use of Price's discussion of the role of familiarity with a universal in intelligent action:

> Sometimes...familiarity with a universal enables...an actual real-life instance. If you are up in an aeroplane and ask the pilot what a *stall* is, he may answer by pulling back the control stick and actually doing one. His familiarity with that universal has enabled him to produce an actual instance of it.... This indeed is one of the most striking ways in which familiarity with a universal can show itself. It also illustrates the very intimate connexion which there is between cognition and action.... Our familiarity with the universal, a cognitive state, overflows of itself into an activity which is practical. This is just what we call an intelligent action.[39] (1946, 36)

This idea could be applied to other states of Intelligence as well. On such an approach, one individual possesses while the other individual lacks Intelligence because only one of them is familiar with the relevant universal. (For example, in the case of knowledge how to φ, the relevant universal might be the action-type φ.)

These three types of response to the fool argument open up three types of answer to the delineation question. Specifically, what makes the difference between the Intelligent and non-Intelligent may be said to be a combination of propositional attitudes plus (i) the mode of presentation under which the propositional contents of the relevant attitudes are entertained, (ii) understanding (hence reasonable conceptual mastery), or (iii) familiarity with a relevant universal. These intellectualist answers to the delineation question can be usefully compared to Ryle's own anti-intellectualist answer, outlined in §1.3. Whereas anti-intellectualism invokes *a special type of ability* or *disposition* when accounting for the distinction between the Intelligent and the non-Intelligent, intellectualism invokes *a special type of attitude* when accounting for this distinction. Insofar as this special type of attitude just is a state that fits the profile *Producer of Intelligence*, the result would be a uniform answer to the mental appraisal, practical/theoretical, and delineation questions.

---

39. Price seems to use 'cognition' and 'cognitive' in a traditional sense that opposes the cognitive to the sensory; we will follow this usage here and below. As this passage illustrates, Price's discussion of the relation between cognition and action is extremely rich and suggestive; we lack the space to do it justice here. Price goes on to consider several other ways of manifesting one's familiarity with a universal: for example, in addition to doing (showing, demonstrating) it, one might imagine it, draw it, describe it, or recognize it when it is manifested by others.

2.6 The Rational Practice Question

While the mental appraisal, practical/theoretical, and delineation questions force the intellectualist to theorize about the metaphysics of propositional attitudes, viz., specifying what could make it the case that certain non-Intelligently exercised attitudes have the profile *Producer of Intelligence* and serve to make the difference between the Intelligent and the non-Intelligent, answering the rational ascription question is, by contrast, a largely epistemological project. There are two main epistemological strategies the intellectualist might pursue when seeking to provide a rational basis for our ordinary practice of ascribing states and qualities of Intelligence. We begin with a strategy that focuses on observation and then turn to a strategy that focuses on inference.[40]

The observation strategy has two steps: the first step is to accept the requirement, evidently endorsed by Ryle, that the indicated practice can be rational only if states and qualities of Intelligence are somehow objects of public observation; the second step is to develop a (perhaps nontraditional) account of such observation—of *how* such things are observed (perceived), if intellectualism is true. For example, the observation intellectualist might accept a "rich" view of the objects of perception, allowing that we perceive states and qualities of Intelligence in much the same way that some have said we perceive semantic properties (Peacocke 1992, 89–90) or natural kind properties (Siegel 2006), namely, through perceptual engagement whose scope is improved or increased (albeit still in some sense noninferentially) by other features of our epistemic situation (e.g., our conceptual capacities or background knowledge). Or the observation intellectualist might pursue John McDowell's (1982/1998, 387) suggestion that facts regarding internal states of mind can be perceived indirectly (yet still in some sense noninferentially) via the direct perception—"disclosure to experience"—of certain publicly observable features, for example, their expression or manifestation:

> The idea of a fact being disclosed to experience is in itself purely negative: a rejection of the thesis that what is accessible to experience falls short of the fact in the sense...of being consistent with there being no such fact.... [One] application of the idea...seems appropriate in at least some cases of knowledge that someone else is in an "inner" state, on the basis of experience of what he says and does. Here we might think of what is directly available to experience in some such terms as 'his giving expression to his being in that "inner" state': this is something that, while not

---

40. There is, of course, room for a hybrid approach that allows both observation and inference.

itself actually being the "inner" state of affairs in question, nevertheless does not fall short of it in the sense I explained.

These are just two examples—rich and indirect—of how, in broad outline, the intellectualist might try to carry out step two in the observation strategy.

The inference strategy also has two steps: the first step is to reject the requirement that our ordinary practice of ascribing states and qualities of Intelligence can be rational only if such states and qualities are somehow objects of public observation; the second step is to develop an alternative account of the rational basis of this practice in terms of the rational character of ordinary inferences regarding such states and qualities. For example, the inference intellectualist might hold that we rationally infer states and qualities of Intelligence in much the same way that some have said we rationally infer, say, electrons, namely, through a cogent abductive inference based on perception of publicly observable phenomena. Another option is to revisit the plausibility of much-debated appeals to analogical inference, whose viability Ryle consistently challenged. Or to cite just one more example, the inference intellectualist might pursue the possibility of a valid deductive inference based on perception of publicly observable phenomena, together with (possibly tacit or implicit) beliefs whose contents somehow invoke principles of rational or folk psychology. And so on for various other inferentialist responses to skepticism about other minds.

The observation and inference strategies introduce answers to the rational ascription question that are quite similar to Ryle's own anti-intellectualist answer, outlined in §1.3. In both cases, we detect items that are not wholly overt. Whereas anti-intellectualism allows that we detect *abilities* or *dispositions* in virtue of witnessing actual performances (in diverse circumstances, on multiple occasions, etc.), intellectualism allows that we detect *attitudes* in virtue of witnessing such performances. Either way, we manage to "look beyond the performance itself" to a power (ability, disposition) or intellectual state (attitude) of the individual that is distinct from any particular overt behavior.

The foregoing suggests how intellectualists might answer questions about the appraisal of mental acts, the intuitive distinction between the theoretical and the practical, the delineation of Intelligent action, and the rational basis for ascriptions of states and qualities of Intelligence. Obviously, much depends on the details, which remain to be spelled out (several of this book's chapters can be regarded as contributing to this project). But we hope that this discussion indicates the subtlety and richness of the surrounding issues, as well as some of the resources available to those wishing to elaborate and defend intellectualism.[41]

---

41. These and other resources may be used to develop responses to objections to particular versions of intellectualism (of which there are many; see, in particular, Cath chapter 5), which we

3. Anti-Intellectualism after Ryle

Anti-intellectualists likewise possess a variety of resources that may be used to elaborate and defend their position against recent (post-Ryle) attacks. This section explores some of the issues surrounding four such attacks, each of which can be understood as suggesting that anti-intellectualism is unable to satisfactorily answer certain questions about mind and action. We first identify these questions and sketch how they are, or might be, answered by intellectualists; then we briefly discuss how they might also be answered by anti-intellectualists. While the discussion is concerned with states of Intelligence in general, for the sorts of reasons discussed in §2.1, we often focus on knowledge how, treating it as a model or test case.

3.1 Four Arguments against Anti-Intellectualism

One of the main arguments against anti-intellectualism is that knowledge how—and hence Intelligence—can, and sometimes does, come apart from abilities and dispositions. On one hand, coaches, instructors, and other authorities have been said in some cases to know how to do things—and hence to possess Intelligence with respect to certain activities—that they are not themselves able or disposed to do. For example, Jeffrey King provides the example of a ski instructor who teaches his students how to do complex jumps that he himself is unable or indisposed to perform (see Stanley and Williamson 2001, 416), and Paul Snowdon (2003, 8) describes a situation in which a master chef loses his arms and, in turn, the ability or disposition to cook but nevertheless retains culinary know-how. On the other hand, the lucky and the ignorant have been said in some cases to be able or disposed to do things that they do not themselves know how to do—and, moreover, to exercise such an ability or disposition in actions that wholly lack Intelligence. For example, David Carr (1979, 407) offers the case of a modern dancer who unwittingly performs a semaphore version of Gray's "Elegy," and Katherine Hawley (2003, 27) presents a scenario involving an uninformed hiker who mistakes falling snow for water and subsequently escapes an avalanche by making swimming motions.

---

do not consider here. Additional resources include, for example, allowing variation among the relevant propositional attitudes; allowing variation among the relevant propositional contents of the attitudes; recruiting a notion of nonconceptual content; emphasizing the role of demonstrative concepts (cf. McDowell's (1994, 1996, 2007, and elsewhere) notion of "situation-specific conceptual articulation"); providing a pragmatic, contextual, or epistemic explanation of anti-intellectualism's focus on abilities or dispositions; questioning alleged or assumed equivalences between knowing how and various other phenomena (e.g., so-called procedural knowledge, discussed in §§4.5–6); and so forth. Some of these options are developed in the chapters of this book.

Although such examples have typically focused on the specific case of knowing how, each may be modified to probe other states of Intelligence as well. To illustrate, it seems clear that Carr's dancer and Hawley's hiker, who are able to perform their respective activities while lacking the relevant knowledge how, also lack the relevant intelligence and skill: the dancer does not *intelligently* perform a semaphore version of Gray's "Elegy," and the hiker is not *skilled* at escaping avalanches (though she may be skilled at making swimming motions). Likewise for other intelligence-epithets: the hiker no more escapes the avalanche *idiotically* than she does *sensibly* or *cleverly* (though she does, of course, escape *luckily*). If this is correct, then these examples demonstrate the possibility of ability without intelligence, skill, sensibleness, and cleverness.

It is less straightforward to uncover a gap in the other direction; indeed, many theorists deny that such states of Intelligence can be present in the absence of corresponding ability. Yet, might an individual be a clever (sensible, intelligent, skilled) teacher, but because she develops a debilitating condition be no longer able to teach? Or consider Snowdon's master chef, who has lost his arms: might he still retain his culinary skills? Perhaps not, given that he is now unable to cook. But one might imagine an observer remarking on how tragic it is that the master chef will no longer be able to cook; her interlocutor responds that, fortunately, the master chef's virtuosity will not be wasted, for the master intends to impart his culinary skills by mentoring students who show promise of achieving expertise comparable to his own.

It is possible to view discussion of these cases (and many others like them) as contributing little more than putative counterexamples to anti-intellectualism: if states of Intelligence can come apart from abilities and dispositions, as these cases might be taken to suggest, then the former cannot be grounded in the latter. An alternative—and, perhaps, theoretically more fruitful—perspective consists in seeing them also as challenges to the anti-intellectualist's answer to the delineation question, outlined in §1.3. Such cases seem to suggest that it is possible that two individuals have all of the same abilities or dispositions to behavior, but only one of them has knowledge how. But if this is so, then knowledge how does not supervene on abilities or dispositions (i.e., the facts about abilities and dispositions do not fix the facts about knowledge-how), in which case abilities or dispositions cannot make the difference between behaviors that do, and overtly indistinguishable behaviors that do not, display states of Intelligence. What does?

Recalling the discussion in §§2.2–5, the intellectualist may point to a combination of propositional attitudes plus (i) mode of presentation, (ii) conceptual understanding, or (iii) familiarity with a relevant universal. Individuals who know how to φ while lacking the ability or disposition to φ still possess such intellectual states, whereas individuals who have the ability or disposition to φ

but do not know how to φ lack such intellectual states. It remains to be seen whether the anti-intellectualist can likewise explain the cases in question. Absent such an explanation, which is to say absent a satisfactory answer to the delineation question, opponents of anti-intellectualism may continue to view their opposition as well grounded.

A second type of argument against anti-intellectualism focuses on the role of knowledge how—and hence Intelligence—in phenomena such as practicing complex intentional actions. Coming to possess a disposition or ability to perform a certain action in some cases requires practicing that action; in this vein, Aristotle famously suggested in the *Nichomachean Ethics*,

> For the things we have to learn before we can do them, we learn by doing them, e.g. men become builders by building and lyreplayers by playing the lyre. (350 B.C.E./1908, 1103a32)

Even if Aristotle's remark does not apply across the board, it is difficult to deny that, at least in some cases of complex intentional action (e.g., cooking a soufflé, dancing the tango, shaving, dunking a basketball, surfing, tying a complicated knot, making putts), we practice with the purpose of eventually acquiring a novel disposition or ability. In such cases, however, it seems that we must already know how to do what we are not yet disposed or able to do. (Or, at least, it must be possible to do them sillily or stupidly, and thus Intelligently, prior to acquiring the ability or disposition sought. But let us focus on the role of knowledge how in particular.) Given these actions' complexity, if we did not already know how to perform them, it is not clear how we would go about practicing them.[42] This raises what we will call *the complex practice question*:

> *The Complex Practice Question*
> How are we to explain the possibility of practicing complex intentional actions that we are not yet able or disposed to perform?

If knowledge how to φ involves a (possibly tacit or implicit) attitude whose propositional content represents a way of φ-ing, as intellectualism allows, then

---

[42]. Cf. Bengson and Moffett (2007, 34). We at least do not recommend practicing shaving prior to knowing how to shave! Snowdon (2003, 20) observes that knowledge how to φ may precede practicing φ-ing: "we very often [come] to know how to do something without any practice. Just a glance in the room where I am was enough for me to realise how to reach the chair I am sitting in. I certainly did not need to practice reaching it." This observation may also pose a challenge to Ryle's emphasis on training, discussed in §1.3.

even prior to being able or disposed to φ, one may already have in one's cognitive possession, as it were, a way of φ-ing. Conscious awareness, attention, and concentration may then be applied to individual movements in attempting or endeavoring to act in this way, for example, by coordinating particular parts of the body or executing a series of steps; such a conscious process, though perhaps unnecessary once one has mastered φ-ing (at which point φ-ing may become "automatic"), constitutes practicing φ-ing. Fred Dretske begins to describe this process in "Where Is the Mind When the Body Performs?":

> We begin the learning process aware of the fingers, the arms, the legs—their position and movements. Precisely timed sequences have to be coordinated and the only way to coordinate them is by awareness of the individual movements. In learning to shoot a lay-up, for example, one has to concentrate on elevating from the left foot as one shoots with the right hand. In learning to swim, one has to concentrate on, think about, be aware of, one's breathing in order to time inhalations with the brief interval during which the nose and mouth are out of the water. (1998)

In this way, knowledge how might be said to enable complex practice: coordination of individual movements through (as Dretske describes) awareness of, concentration on, and thinking about particular parts of the body and their role in the execution of the action. Because anti-intellectualism understands states of Intelligence in terms of abilities or dispositions, it entails that knowledge how to φ cannot precede a disposition or ability to φ. Prima facie, this is problematic. To the extent that practicing complex intentional actions requires knowledge how to do what we are seeking to be (and thus are not yet) disposed or able to do, as suggested above, this threatens the very *possibility* of such practice. Absent a viable answer to the complex practice question that somehow manages to dissolve this threat, anti-intellectualism may be charged with offering an untenable view of the relation between mind and action.

A third argument against anti-intellectualism highlights an intuitive distinction between practical knowledge and various other practical phenomena, such as knacks, which do not involve the same type of rational, epistemic achievement. Here, for example, is Julia Annas:

> Either "knowing how" involves "knowing that" or it does not. If it does not, then what we think of as practical knowledge is being construed as a kind of inarticulate practical knack, an ability to manipulate the world which is not at a sufficiently rational level to be judged epistemically. (2001, 248)

It should be clear that Annas is here using 'knowing how' to represent states of practical knowledge more generally, including skill and expertise, and 'knowing that' to represent truth or fact-oriented states more generally (once again, what we have called 'engaging propositional content'). Her idea is that the cognitive character of genuine skill or expertise cannot be accommodated by an approach that focuses solely on successful performance, which can also be found in knack and various potentially non-Intelligent behaviors, such as reflexes and instinctual responses. To appreciate an individual as possessing practical knowledge ('knowing how') and not merely as a "muddler or dabbler" (Annas 2001, 244) who has a non-Intelligent knack, we must, Annas suggests, look beyond the individual's powers ("an ability to manipulate the world") to something that could make sense of her rational, epistemic achievement: namely, her truth or fact-oriented states ('knowing that'), as the intellectualist recommends.[43] The challenge that this suggestion poses to anti-intellectualism has its source in what we will call *the knowledge/knack question*:

The Knowledge/Knack Question
How are we to understand the distinction between states of practical knowledge (in particular, knowing how, skill, and expertise) and mere knacks?

This question is related to but distinct from the delineation question. While the delineation question asks about the difference between *behaviors* that do, and those that do not, display states of Intelligence, the knowledge/knack question asks about the *states* that are held to underlie and explain that difference. The knowledge/knack question can thus be regarded as seeking an explanation of the very *Intelligence* of those states.[44] What is wanted is an understanding of how or why states of practical knowledge embody such Intelligence, which is not present in all

---

43. Cf. Setiya (2008, 405ff.) and Bengson and Moffett (chapter 7); see also Bennett (1964) on the differences between genuine intelligence and "fake" and "frozen" intelligence. Annas (2001, 244; cf. chapter 4) connects the distinction between practical knowledge and mindless or absentminded knack to the issue of learning and practice: "A skill is intellectually complex and requires thought to acquire; it is not just something which can be picked up casually from experience. Hence, it is contrasted with a "knack"..., which you can pick up just by copying other people without thinking much about it." Cf. Dewey (1922, 173 and 178), who contrasts intelligence and intelligent action with impulse and "treadmill activity" and records the worry that "practical work done by habit and instinct in securing prompt and exact adjustment to the environment is not knowledge, except by courtesy."

44. The explanandum here is captured by the striking images of Solomon Andrée's crashed balloon, the *Eagle*, which manage to depict the genuine Intelligence of practical knowledge through an important style of breakdown, yet against the backdrop of an even more significant type of achievement.

action-oriented states. Viewed another way, an adequate theory must distinguish not only between Intelligent and non-Intelligent behaviors but also between, for example, Intelligent-powers and mere knack-powers (e.g., the muddler's mere capacity to act successfully). Intellectualists propose to account for this distinction—and, in turn, address the knowledge/knack question—by citing propositional attitudes (together with, e.g., mode of presentation, conceptual understanding, or familiarity with a relevant universal, as discussed above), which are held to be the source of Intelligence. Anti-intellectualists must provide an alternative account of the source of Intelligence. Absent such an account, which is to say absent a satisfactory answer to the knowledge/knack question, anti-intellectualism may be accused of offering a seriously incomplete account of mind and action.

A fourth type of argument against anti-intellectualism has focused on the syntax and semantics of ascriptions of states of Intelligence, in particular, knowledge how. Stanley explains the rationale behind concern with such linguistic issues as follows:

> Suppose one produces an analysis of knowing how to do something. Surely, it would be a worry with such an analysis if there is no correct compositional semantics of English according to which ascriptions of knowing how to do something express that analysis. If there were no plausible compositional semantics for English ascriptions of knowing how that assigned to them one's favored analysis, then that would show that one's analysis could not possibly be what English speakers mean when they use such ascriptions. (forthcoming-a)

This introduces what we will call *the linguistics question*:

The Linguistics Question
What is the correct semantics (intensional or extensional) for ascriptions of knowledge how and other states of Intelligence?

It is widely held that contemporary theories of the semantics of embedded questions, supported by corresponding syntactic analysis, indicate that a sentence such as 'Gilbert knows how to prune trees' ascribes to the subject (here, Gilbert) propositional knowledge of the answer to a question (here, how to prune trees), no less than does 'Gilbert knows where to prune trees' or 'Gilbert knows when to prune trees.'[45] Thus

---

45. Cf. Brown (1970), Vendler (1972, ch. 5), Ware (1973, 156), Hintikka (1975, 1992), White (1982, ch. 2), Stanley and Williamson (2001), Braun (2006; chapter 10), Schaffer (2007,

it is said that intellectualism is able to accurately specify what English speakers mean when they use such knowledge-*wh* constructions (knowledge how, where, when, who, etc.). This applies pressure to anti-intellectualism. In the absence of a plausible semantics according to which ascriptions of knowing how actually ascribe to the subject an ability or disposition to perform the relevant behavior, anti-intellectualism may be accused of changing the subject: away from our nontechnical, "familiar and everyday" notion (with which Ryle himself was originally concerned; see, e.g., 1949, 7–9 and 62) toward something else altogether.

3.2 The Delineation Question

Let us consider how the anti-intellectualist might respond to the challenges posed by the questions highlighted in the previous section, beginning with the delineation question. What makes the difference between behaviors that do, and overtly indistinguishable behaviors that do not, display states of Intelligence? We have seen that those cases in which knowing how and abilities or dispositions appear to come apart cast doubt on the anti-intellectualist's proposal that the Intelligent and the non-Intelligent can be distinguished in terms of abilities or dispositions.[46] To dispel these doubts, the anti-intellectualist might resolve to tweak—adjust or fine-tune—some of the details of her position, while nevertheless retaining its core contention, namely, that knowledge how and other states of Intelligence are grounded in a type of power.[47] This involves viewing the putative counterexamples in the way recommended by Daniel Bonevac, Josh Dever, and David Sosa:

2009b), Brogaard (2009; chapter 6), and Stanley (2011). See, in particular, Groenendijk and Stokhof (1982, 1984, 1997) and Karttunen (1977).

46. It is important to ensure that the cases do not merely show that knowledge how *one* φ-s (or knowledge how φ-ing *is done*, knowledge how *it is that* φ is performed, or knowledge of *what it takes* to φ) comes apart from abilities or dispositions—to the extent, of course, that the former differs from knowledge how *to* φ (cf. Hornsby 1980, 84; Noë 2005, 284 n. 4; Hetherington 2006, 71 n. 2 and §11; and Bengson and Moffett 2007, §1 and chapter 7, §2). Some theorists have claimed that 'knows how to' is ambiguous, for example, between *knows how one* and *is able to* (cf. Mackie 1974; Hintikka 1975; Carr 1979, 1981; Katzoff 1984; Rumfitt 2003; Rosefeldt 2004; Hetherington 2006; and Lihoreau 2008). Such ambiguity claims, which are both popular and controversial, constitute substantive linguistic theses that are open to standard linguistic tests for ambiguity (such as those described in Zwicky and Sadock 1975; for a critical application of some of these tests, see Bengson, Moffett, and Wright 2009, 393ff.).

47. An alternative approach that we will not elaborate involves denying (or rephrasing) the relevant anti-anti-intellectualist intuitions, holding that knowing how and powers do not in fact come apart in the relevant cases. Of course, the anti-intellectualist would need to provide fairly compelling reasons for such denial; she would also owe an explanation of the original intuitions, assuming they persist.

> Counterexamples refute proposals, more or less, one at a time.... While they can refute specific instances of a style of theory, counterexamples are not in themselves to the style as a whole. Instead, they are tools for refinement, allowing a better choice of specific instance of that style to be endorsed. (forthcoming, §1)

Thus Hawley (2003, 22) has suggested a refinement to the anti-intellectualist style of theory that focuses on a particular counterfactual, namely, if x knows how to φ under certain circumstances, then if x tried to φ in those circumstances, then x would successfully φ (where the circumstances may specify relevant manifestation or enabling conditions; cf. Millikan 2000, ch. 4 and Noë 2005; for critical discussion, see Bengson and Moffett, chapter 7). A slightly more exotic refinement would consist in a nonstandard analysis of a certain type of power, for example, one associated with a conditional possessing distinctive features, for example, one that resists familiar constraints such as centering (and thus differs from the material conditional, the C. I. Lewis strict conditional, and the Lewis/Stalnaker variably strict counterfactual conditional).[48]

Counterfactuals and exotic conditionals may not exhaust the anti-intellectualist's options. For example, she might instead investigate the prospects of a "weak" power (perhaps associated with a "weak" noncounterfactual, nonexotic conditional) that *together with some additional nonpropositional state or states* fully grounds knowledge how. The task would then be to specify the indicated extra state or states. Although it is not clear at this point how such a specification might proceed, the option to pursue it, like the option to pursue an exotic conditional, remains.

3.3 The Knowledge/Knack Question

Insofar as a power that accounts for the difference between the Intelligent and the non-Intelligent must allow for the possibility of practical knowledge, as opposed

---

48. To illustrate, albeit schematically, let C be such a conditional. Suppose it is true that in all of the cases in which the subject knows how to φ while lacking an ability or disposition to φ, an instance of C is still true, and that in all of those cases in which the subject does not know how to φ while possessing an ability or disposition to φ, an instance of C is false; indeed, suppose it were shown that x knows how to φ if and only if C; then, to the extent that C is associated with a type of power (e.g., it can be shown to be typically expressed by a modal auxiliary such as 'can', 'could', or 'would'), rather than propositional attitudes, C would enable an anti-intellectualist explanation of the relevant cases and an answer to the delineation question. One of the most pressing questions facing anti-intellectualism is whether any conditional satisfies this description. For relevant discussion of conditionals, see Bonevac, Dever, and Sosa (2006).

to a mere knack, an anti-intellectualist answer to the delineation question must be developed in tandem with an answer to the knowledge/knack question. How are we to understand the distinction between practical knowledge and a mere knack without appealing to "theoretical" (truth or fact-oriented) cognition? The anti-intellectualist might respond that practical knowledge—knowing how, skill, and expertise—is a type of power that involves distinctively *practical* cognition. This perspective seems to be suggested by Martin Heidegger in *Being and Time* (which Ryle himself reviewed rather favorably)[49]:

> 'Practical' behaviour is not 'atheoretical' in the sense of "sightlessness." The way it differs from theoretical behaviour does not lie simply in the fact that in theoretical behaviour one observes, while in practical behaviour one *acts*, and that action must employ theoretical cognition if it is not to remain blind; for... action has *its own* kind of sight. Theoretical behaviour is just looking, without circumspection. (1926/1962, 99)

The idea is that practical knowledge possesses a proprietary cognitive character (i.e., a cognitive character that is not reducible to the rational, epistemic achievement of truth or fact-oriented states), and it is this proprietary cognitive character that distinguishes it from mere knacks. Of course, a satisfactory development of this style of response to the knowledge/knack question requires an account of the indicated proprietary cognitive character—a type of rational, epistemic achievement that is distinctively practical but at the same time is not merely a matter of successful performance. What is this character, and what makes it a genuinely rational, epistemic achievement?

Anti-intellectualists have several options, besides invoking a primitive (i.e., brute and inexplicable) notion of practical, power-based cognition when attempting to answer this question. First, they may look to Heidegger's notion of circumspection [*Umsicht*] (and the related notions of readiness-to-hand [*Zuhandenheit*] and understanding [*Verstehen*]), which designates "a kind of concern which manipulates things and puts them to use" and in this sense "has its own kind of 'knowledge'" (Heidegger 1926/1962, 95; see also esp. §31).[50]

---

49. See Ryle (1929, 370): "I have nothing but admiration for his [Heidegger's] special undertaking and for such of his achievements in it as I can follow, namely the phenomenological analysis of the root workings of the human soul."

50. Interestingly, the early Ryle (1929, 25) seems to have thought that Heidegger did not succeed in eschewing intellectual states, writing that Heidegger's "attempt to derive our knowledge of 'things' from our practical attitudes towards tools breaks down; for to use a tool involves knowledge of what it is, what can be done with it, and what wants doing." It has been suggested

Second, anti-intellectualists might seek to elaborate Ryle's notion of training (mentioned in §1.3), which was originally intended to help to distinguish practical knowledge from mere habit. Third, they might draw inspiration from Maurice Merleau-Ponty's (1945/1962, 142ff.) emphasis on a kind of "motor grasping or a motor significance," which he himself regarded as implying that "it is the body which 'understands'" (cf. Dreyfus 1967, 1992, ch. 7, and 2002; Kelly 2002; Carman 2008, 111ff.). Kevin O'Regan and Alva Noë's (2001, §3) notion of "knowledge of sensorimotor contingencies," which is said to be related to what Ryle (1949, 230) described as "acquired expectation-propensities" and has affinities with Merleau-Ponty's "motor grasping," as well as James Gibson's (1977) theory of "affordances" (see also Gregory 1970), may be viewed as a fourth option or a sympathetic elaboration of Ryle's or Merleau-Ponty's basic approach.

Of course, it is not enough simply to introduce a notion and claim that it has a proprietary cognitive character; what is needed is a full, noncircular characterization of a phenomenon that does not implicitly or explicitly appeal to any intellectual states but still plausibly underwrites a type of rational, epistemic achievement beyond the kind of regular, successful performance attainable by mere muddlers and dabblers (in short, a theoretically interesting proprietary cognitive character, statable as such without scare quotes).[51] To the extent that one or another of the indicated notions—circumspection, training, motor grasping, knowledge of sensorimotor contingencies, or some combination thereof—can be so characterized, which is of course a non-trivial task, the result may well be an anti-intellectualist-friendly account of the intuitive distinction between practical knowledge and mere knacks.

3.4 The Complex Practice Question

Such an account may perhaps inform an anti-intellectualist treatment of the phenomenon of practicing complex intentional actions that we are not yet able or disposed to perform. As we saw, it seems natural to think that practicing such actions requires knowledge how to do what we are seeking to be, and thus are not yet, able or disposed to do. Still, anti-intellectualists might deny this, maintaining that such knowledge how is not in fact required. Instead, they might invoke a minimal power to φ (e.g., a mere capacity to φ); such a power, in combination with auxiliary information (e.g., lessons or instructions) regarding what it takes

---

to us that Heidegger was in fact a proponent of (a nonstandard version of) intellectualism, rather than anti-intellectualism. There is much to be said on behalf of this suggestion.

51. Here we encounter with urgency Mumford's (1998, 25) counsel, issued in a slightly different context, that "if...appeal[ing to powers] is to bring benefits, it is essential that it be backed up with a credible account of what [the relevant powers or] dispositions are supposed to be."

to φ, could then be said to enable one to practice φ-ing (given the requisite concentration, awareness, etc.). Perhaps ironically, the anti-intellectualist's explication of the practitioner's grasp of the indicated information might exploit the very propositional attitude(s) to which intellectualists appeal when analyzing or grounding knowledge how, for example, knowledge that *w* is a way to φ—or of some other maxim, imperative, or regulative proposition about what to do in order to φ.[52] The difference between the intellectualist and anti-intellectualist is, of course, that the latter will deny that knowing how itself is or involves any such attitude(s); it simply plays a role in practicing complex intentional actions.[53]

This approach to the complex practice question treats knowledge how as a substantive power, in contrast with the indicated (practice-enabling) minimal power. Such an answer requires an account of the difference between these two types of power that is consistent with anti-intellectualism's answers to the delineation and knowledge/knack questions. It also requires dialectical subtlety. For the appeal to propositional attitudes in anti-intellectualism's explanation of complex practice interacts in potentially hazardous ways with the contention (discussed above) that propositional attitudes are unable to sustain the action-oriented character of knowledge how. Arguably, if the relevant propositional attitudes are action-oriented enough to allow such practice, then they are action-oriented enough to qualify as practical (i.e., they are not *merely* theoretical); conversely, if the relevant propositional attitudes are *not* action-oriented enough to qualify as practical (i.e., if they are merely theoretical), then they are *not* action-oriented enough to allow such practice. In these ways, engaging the complex practice question demands sensitivity to the broader debate between intellectualist and anti-intellectualist views of mind and action.

---

52. Ryle (1945, 12): "What is the use of such formulæ if the acknowledgement of them is not a condition of knowing how to act...? The answer is simple. They are useful pedagogically, namely, in lessons to those who are still learning how to act. They belong to manuals for novices [and] are banisters for toddlers...."

53. One way to develop this approach involves distinguishing knowledge how *to* φ from knowledge how one φ-s (or knowledge how φ-ing *is done*, knowledge how *it is that* φ is performed, or knowledge of *what it takes* to φ; recall note 46) and subsequently holding that only the latter is or involves the indicated propositional attitude. Practicing a complex intentional action could then be said to require, not prior knowledge how *to* φ, but rather prior knowledge how *one* φ-s (or knowledge how φ-ing *is done*, or knowledge of *what it takes* to φ, etc.). An entirely different strategy, which we will not evaluate here, allows that practicing a complex intentional action φ may require prior knowledge how to act; however, on this alternative, it is denied that this must be knowledge how to φ. Rather, one knows how to do various other things, and one also knows that doing these other things in such and such order is a way (or what it takes) to φ; together, this enables one to practice φ-ing. Cf. Hornsby (1980, 83) and Brewer (1999, 243–244).

3.5 The Linguistic Question

While the delineation, knowledge/knack, and complex practice questions force the anti-intellectualist to theorize about the metaphysics of powers, specifying what could make it the case that certain powers are rational, epistemic achievements and serve to make the difference between the Intelligent and the non-Intelligent, answering the linguistics question is, by contrast, a broadly semantic project. Setting aside Intelligence-attributions that do not attribute knowledge how, which might be thought to pose no special problem for anti-intellectualism, an anti-intellectualist response to the linguistics question in the prima facie problematic case of knowledge how (recall §3.1) may come in two stages: first, deny that the semantics of knowledge-*wh* constructions, in general, and its relevance to the case of knowledge-how, in particular, are as cut-and-dried as proponents of intellectualism sometimes suggest; second, provide an alternative, anti-intellectualist-friendly semantics that can take the place of the standard, propositional semantics. Let us consider each stage in turn.

As we have seen, intellectualists such as Stanley and Williamson (2001) have claimed that (i) knowledge-how attributions should be treated as embedded questions, on a par with closely related constructions (knowledge where, when, who, etc.), and (ii) the best semantics for embedded questions is propositional in nature. Both claims may be disputed. For example, regarding (i), there is reason to think that a uniform semantic treatment of closely related constructions is not always warranted. To illustrate, consider the following examples offered by Laura Michaelis (chapter 11):

1. x learned to φ.
2. x tried to φ.
3. x knew to φ.
4. x understood to φ.

Despite the overt grammatical similarities, only (3) and (4) can be appropriately paraphrased in terms of normative propositional content (roughly, x knew/understood *that x ought to φ*). In a similar way, anti-intellectualists can maintain that 'how-to'-complements are interpreted differently from other *wh*-complements. This approach might be motivated by the observation that many people seem to be comfortable with an ability-based paraphrase of knowledge-how constructions, whereas an ability-based paraphrase of other knowledge-*wh* constructions is far less natural.

As for (ii), although it may well be that the standard semantics for embedded questions is propositional in nature, this semantics is not without difficulties of its own. For instance, specifying questions by means of sets of propositional answers, as in the standard approach, is potentially problematic. Thus Michaelis (chapter 11) argues that, *pace* the standard view, there is no acceptable existentially quantified proposition that captures the intuitive semantic meaning of sentences such as (5), as suggested by the failure of (6) and (7) to serve as adequate paraphrases:

5. x asked how to φ.
6. $(\exists w)(x$ asked if w is a way to $\varphi)$.
   [In English: There is a way of acting such that x asked if that way of acting is a way to φ.]
7. x asked if $(\exists w)(w$ is a way to $\varphi)$.
   [In English: x asked if there is a way of acting that is a way to φ.]

In a similar vein, Jonathan Ginzburg (1995a; chapter 9; cf. Ginzburg 1995b, 1996, and Ginzburg and Sag 2000) argues that what counts as an acceptable answer to a given *wh*-question seems to be context sensitive in ways that are difficult to square with the standard semantics of embedded questions. The point, of course, is not that such arguments obviously demonstrate once and for all that the standard view is irrelevant or false. Rather, the lesson is simply that the empirical adequacy of the standard view and its applicability to the case of knowing how are far from settled (see also Rumfitt 2003; Collins 2007b, n. 9; Roberts 2009; Stout 2010; Bengson and Moffett chapter 7; Devitt forthcoming-a).

At this point, intellectualists may wish to take refuge in the thought that all of the major historical treatments of embedded questions have been propositional, and that this indicates that *any* plausible semantics for knowledge-how attributions will be propositional. However, a variety of nonpropositional approaches have found their way into the literature in recent years. These approaches center on, not propositional attitudes per se, but rather *de se* attitudes (Roberts 2009), objectual attitudes toward ways of acting (Bengson and Moffett chapter 7), and objectual attitudes toward the free variable in a presupposed open sentence (Michaelis chapter 11).[54] Here we arrive at stage two: providing an anti-intellectualist semantics. To be sure, these approaches may not by themselves deliver complete or exclusive anti-intellectualist semantics; after all, they are consistent with the thesis that the indicated nonpropositional attitudes are eventually grounded in propositional attitudes. Nevertheless, they do locate semantics *compatible* with

---

54. This last proposal might be developed within the context of Discourse Representation Theory (Kamp 1981) as involving an attitude toward a discourse referent assumed to be in the common ground. Another option may be Fine's (1985) theory of arbitrary objects.

anti-intellectualism: in this sense, they yield anti-intellectualist-*friendly* semantics (in turn, whether the indicated nonpropositional attitudes are grounded in propositional attitudes emerges as a philosophical, nonlinguistic debate). Indeed, each approach takes aim in its own way at the propositionalist heterodoxy on which intellectualist answers to the linguistics question have tended to rely and, thereby, opens up space within which anti-intellectualism can maneuver.

There appear to be two further, radical options available to anti-intellectualism. The first radical option consists in resisting the demand for fealty to ordinary usage of 'knowledge how' and to embark instead on a form of philosophical *explication*—wherein, roughly, the ordinary notion of knowledge how is replaced with a stipulatively defined notion that is held to preserve the theoretically interesting features of the original notion while shedding its alleged imperfections (cf. Carnap 1947/1956, §2).[55] The second radical option is to accept the standard semantic view of embedded questions, in general, and knowledge how attributions, in particular, as irreducibly propositional but argue that this is consistent with a version of anti-intellectualism according to which the truth-conditions for such attributions are ultimately grounded in corresponding abilities or dispositions to behavior.[56]

The foregoing suggests how intellectualists and anti-intellectualists might answer questions about the delineation of Intelligent action, learning and practicing, the intuitive distinction between practical knowledge and practical knacks, and the semantics of ascriptions of knowledge how and other states of Intelligence. Given the importance of the details, as well as the potentially far-reaching and interdisciplinary character of the surrounding issues, further investigation is, of course, required (several of the chapters in this book contribute to this venture).

4. *Implications and Applications*

The debate between intellectualism and anti-intellectualism intersects with core issues in disparate philosophical areas, including epistemology, ethics, and philos-

---

55. Presumably, anti-intellectualists must seek a characterization of these alleged imperfections that does not indirectly vindicate intellectualism.

56. This second radical option is roughly the converse of the one taken by Bengson and Moffett (chapter 7), who can be regarded as endorsing a type of radical intellectualism. It is worth emphasizing that this second radical option will not be open to Ryleans or neo-Ryleans aiming to *reductively analyze* or *eliminate* internal mental states (e.g., propositional attitudes). Nevertheless, it is surely a strategy that many philosophers sympathetic to Ryle's project will find tempting (cf. White 1982). Note that would-be intellectualists must be careful not to indirectly (and perhaps unwittingly) vindicate the second radical version of anti-intellectualism.

ophies of action, language, mind, and cognitive science. Focusing on the specific cases of knowing how and skill, this section discusses—or, perhaps more accurately, raises questions about—a few such intersections and gestures at numerous others. (Several are pursued with greater focus and detail in this book's chapters.) The aim is not so much to adjudicate disputes in these areas, but rather to draw attention to the scope and significance of the philosophical theory of Intelligence.

4.1 Epistemology

Knowing how and skill have been explicitly invoked in a variety of epistemological contexts, beyond debate concerning whether there is a type of knowledge that is fundamentally distinct from knowledge that. Some examples include discussion of skepticism (see, e.g., Gellner 1951, 29–30; Unger 1975, 145–146 and 281–283; Hetherington 2008), the a priori (see, e.g., Toulmin 1949, 176; Gellner 1951, 30ff.; Hetherington 2009), inferential warrant and logical knowledge (see, e.g., Ryle 1945, 6ff.; Powers 1978; Kalderon 2001; Besson 2010; Rumfitt chapter 15), episodic memory and mnemonic justification (see, e.g., Soteriou 2008, 480–484), self-knowledge (see, e.g., Yalowitz 2000), testimony (see, e.g., Hawley forthcoming; cf. Craig 1990, ch. 17), the value of knowledge (see, e.g., Riggs 2002), the problem of the criterion (see, e.g., Hetherington forthcoming), and epistemic injustice (see, e.g., Hawley chapter 12).

Another epistemological application occurs in the increasingly popular field of virtue epistemology, whose emphasis on "epistemic skills" or "competences" and "intellectual virtues" brings it into direct contact with the debate between intellectualism and anti-intellectualism. To illustrate, in *A Virtue Epistemology*, Ernest Sosa defines propositional knowledge in terms of apt belief, and apt belief in terms of competent, true belief (2007, ch. 2).[57] The relevant competence is not wholly un-Intelligent but is a state of intellect and character, for example, knowledge how or skill (Sosa 2003, 101). Presumably, this is as it should be, if it is true that propositional knowledge—at least when it is "reflective," in Sosa's terminology—cannot be the product of a mere knack (or combination of knacks). The connection to the debate between intellectualism and anti-intellectualism should be plain. Yet, it remains an open question whether a fully developed virtue epistemology is compatible with intellectualism or in fact entails the type of

---

57. Cf. Sosa (2009, esp. 12–14). In a similar vein, Markie (2006, 130) defends an account of "epistemically appropriate perceptual belief" as the exercise of knowledge how, specifically, "the exercise of knowledge of how to identify objects and their features perceptually." Cf. Reynolds (1991), Zagzebski (1996), Hyman (1999), Bloomfield (2000), Pollard (2003), Battaly (2008), Greco (2009), and Lepock (forthcoming). In their discussions of knowing how and skill (competence, etc.), many of these theorists indicate a commitment to anti-intellectualism.

anti-intellectualism to which Sosa seems to commit when he explicitly characterizes the relevant competence as

> a disposition...that would in appropriately normal conditions ensure (or make highly likely) the success of any relevant performance issued by it.[58] (2007, 29)

Now, if intellectualism is true, then such a disposition is un-Intelligent—in which case it seems unable to do the sort of theoretical work required by virtue epistemology. If anti-intellectualism is true, then such a disposition may do the relevant theoretical work; what is then needed to secure the viability of such virtue epistemology is, among other things, an account (perhaps of the sort described in §3.3) that meets the challenge, hitherto unremarked, to plausibly distinguish such a disposition from an un-Intelligent knack.

4.2 Ethics

The debate between intellectualism and anti-intellectualism may interact in analogous ways with philosophical work in virtue ethics. Allegedly following such thinkers as Aristotle and Thomas Aquinas, it is widely believed or assumed by contemporary virtue ethicists that moral virtues are dispositions (or some other type of power). In a recent survey article, Rosalind Hursthouse summarizes:

> A virtue such as honesty or generosity is...a character trait—*that is*, a [multitrack] disposition which is well entrenched in its possessor. (2009, §2 emphasis added)

To the extent that moral virtues are or involve states of Intelligence (i.e., they are not wholly un-Intelligent),[59] virtue ethics so understood appears to be committed to a form of anti-intellectualism. As indicated by the challenges discussed in §3, such a commitment is not trivial. At any rate, such commitment may be premature. Arguably, there is room to explore an intellectualist approach to moral

---

58. However, Sosa elsewhere suggests that knowing how is "a rather special sort of propositional knowledge" (2003, 101). Notice that if propositional knowledge in general is held to require knowing how or skill, as in Sosa's virtue epistemology, and knowing how or skill in turn requires at least some propositional attitudes, as Sosa here suggests, then regress threatens.

59. Some but not all virtue ethicists characterize virtue as a skill (see, e.g., Annas 1995, 2011; cf. Zagzebski 1996, II.2.4). However, to our knowledge, none denies that the relevant virtues are Intelligent.

virtues, according to which it is mistaken to think that the core of virtue (and character) can be discerned through a narrow focus on traits and their kin. Rather, on this intellectualist approach, moral virtues are at least partially grounded in intellectual states—which may be said, in turn, to be regularly exercised in appropriate actions. For example, the honest or generous person must have certain propositional attitudes, to which exercises of her honesty or generosity must—in order to qualify as being genuinely honest or generous—be causally related.[60] Ryle (1940; 1945, 13–14; cf. 1949, 110ff.) himself contemplated, and predictably rejected, a moral view of this sort, but in light of the intellectualist resources discussed in §2, such a view may be regarded as now meriting reevaluation.

This is not the only place where intellectualist and anti-intellectualist views make an appearance in core debates in moral theory broadly construed. Questions concerning the role of propositional attitudes (internal acts of engaging regulative propositions, rules, maxims, or principles) in ethical deliberation, practical reasoning, rationality, and moral judgment have animated much contemporary work in metaethics, ethics, and moral psychology (see, e.g., Dewey 1922; Ryle 1940; Smart 1950; Gould 1955; Cross 1959; Bennett 1964; Geach 1966; Kenny 1966; Kupperman 1970, 140ff.; Hintikka 1974b; Mackie 1974; Carr 1981a; Dreyfus and Dreyfus 1982, 1991; Gauthier 1994, e.g. 701–702; Churchland 1996, 143ff. and 2000; Blackburn 1996; Clark 1996, 2000; McDowell 1996; Sayre-McCord 1996; Carr and Steutal 1999; Varela 1999; Audi 2001, ch. 8; Dancy 2004, 142ff.; van Willegenburg 2004; Bartsch and Wright 2005; Railton 2006, 2009; Andreou and Thalos 2007; Wiggins 2009). Participants in the corresponding debates frequently juxtapose propositional attitudes with knowing how or skill, as it is widely believed or assumed that the latter are nonpropositional. One wonders what might happen if this anti-intellectualist supposition is lifted (or at least suspended).

To see what we have in mind, consider first that a similar anti-intellectualist supposition pervades moral epistemology, where the nature and status of moral knowledge remains controversial. In a neglected passage, Ryle himself proposed that

> moral knowledge, if the strained phrase is to be used at all, is knowing how to behave in certain sorts of situations in which the problems are neither merely theoretical nor merely technical. (1949, 316)

---

60. The possibility that virtues are partially grounded in intellectual states might suggest a hitherto unexplored connection between virtue ethics and deontology. Intellectualists might also question the popular idea that moral virtues require corresponding abilities or dispositions to act virtuously. Similarly for practical wisdom: see, e.g., Whitcomb (2011), who argues that wisdom does not require a reliable disposition to act wisely. If intellectualism is true, this conclusion is compatible with Ryan's (1996, 1999) suggestion that wisdom is or involves a type of knowledge how.

Given Ryle's anti-intellectualism, this implies the view that moral knowledge is grounded in abilities or dispositions, rather than propositional attitudes. Annas (1995, 2001, 2011; chapter 4) has argued that this view can and should be resisted: although she defends the thesis that (a significant portion of) our moral knowledge is knowledge how or skill, she maintains that such knowledge or skill cannot be understood without reference to propositional attitudes (see, e.g., 2001, 248). Regardless of whether Annas is correct to recommend intellectualism, surely she is right to implicitly separate the following two types of question:

[Q1] Does moral knowledge (virtues, ethical deliberation, practical reasoning, rationality and rational agency, etc.) involve knowing how or skill (Intelligence)?
[Q2] If so, is such knowing how or skill (Intelligence) grounded in abilities or dispositions, rather than propositional attitudes?

While [Q1] is, of course, a type of question belonging to moral theory, the project of answering [Q2], by contrast, is ultimately a matter of engaging the philosophical theory of Intelligence.

4.3 Philosophy of Action

Contemporary work in philosophy of action has fruitfully investigated the metaphysics and the epistemology of intention and intentional action. There is room here to explore intellectualist and anti-intellectualist views about these and kindred phenomena (e.g., volitions, voluntary action, free action, plans, endeavoring).[61] Are intentions to act grounded in propositional attitudes or, rather, abilities or dispositions to behavior? Are intentional actions produced by the former or, rather, actualizations of the latter? Is knowledge of what one is doing when one acts intentionally—what we might call 'Anscombian practical knowledge' (see Anscombe 1957)—a matter of having propositional attitudes or, rather, some type of power?

Given the connections between intentional action and Intelligent action, it is reasonable to expect discussion of these questions to somehow implicate

---

61. See, for example, Ryle's (1949, 64ff.; cf. 1945, 3) discussion of intellectualist theories of volition and voluntary action, which persist still today. For example, Velleman (2000, 195ff.) has recommended what looks to be an intellectualist view of intentional action as behavior preceded by "accepting a proposition in such a way as to make it true," where such acceptance is a type of propositional attitude that he labels 'directive cognition.' Cf. Bratman's (1987) work on plans, Chisholm's (1976, 57ff.; 1988) treatment of undertaking or endeavoring, and Thompson's (2008, 93ff.) remarks on "the intellectual aspect" of action, which he deems "all-important."

knowledge how and other states of Intelligence. For instance, Jennifer Hornsby (chapter 3) suggests that an adequate account of agency must acknowledge that the application of knowledge in processes of acting requires a type of general knowledge—specifically, knowledge how to act—that because of its generality, cannot be exhausted by knowledge of particular propositions applied. And Kieran Setiya (2008, 404) has recently argued that, insofar as it is a general principle (which he endorses) that "If A is doing φ intentionally, A knows how to φ, or else he is doing it by doing other things that he knows how to do," we are compelled to admit that "Knowledge how belongs at the core of any intentional action." Setiya proceeds to argue that knowledge how also belongs at the core of "dynamic epistemology" and Anscombian practical knowledge:

> Knowing how to φ is the state or condition that, with knowledge of ability [viz., knowledge that if I intend to φ, I will be doing so in fact], provides the epistemic warrant for decision. Together, they justify the transition in which one forms the intention and belief that one is doing φ or that one is going to do it.... Knowledge how thus plays a role in dynamic epistemology, in our entitlement to form and revise beliefs. This happens continuously in the performance of intentional action...[s]o my knowing how to [act] is constantly implicated in knowledge of what I am doing. (Setiya 2008, 407; cf. Paul 2009 and Setiya 2009)

This attempt to integrate the metaphysics and epistemology of intentional action seems to exploit the simultaneously practical and cognitive—or, recalling Heidegger, the circumspective—character of knowing how, which is not an epistemically inert, arational knack (recall §3), but is rather a paradigm example of Intelligence and source of Intelligent action (recall §§1–2). At the same time, as we have seen, these aspects of knowing how remain to be fully characterized and adequately explained. It is fair to say that further investigation will be needed to determine which of intellectualism or anti-intellectualism is best positioned to offer the requisite illumination vis-à-vis intention and intentional action.[62]

---

62. Knowing how and skill have both played prominent roles in several other debates in the philosophy of action, including criticism of the so-called causal theory of action (see, e.g., Ruben 2003, 131ff.; Clarke 2010) and more general issues surrounding the metaphysics and epistemology of agency (see, e.g., Hornsby 1980, ch. 6; Archer 2000; Stanley and Williamson 2001, 442ff.; Gibbons 2001; Kelly 2002; Bengson and Moffett 2007, §4; Leist 2007; Lekan 2007; Stanley forthcoming-b). Theorists may also explore intellectualist versus anti-intellectualist accounts of the difference between *akratic* action (weakness of will) and, for example, compulsion or addiction; capacities-based accounts are explored in Holton (1999, 2004), G. Jones (2003), Smith (2003), and Cohen and Handfield (2011).

4.4 Philosophy of Language and Linguistics

Such investigation may also enable a lucid assessment of appeals to knowing how and skill (or "mastery") in the philosophy of language and linguistics. For example, Robert Brandom (1994, 131) has advanced the inferentialist-cum-pragmatist view that "there is nothing more to conceptual content than its broadly inferential articulation," which is grounded in "a kind of know-how" (87ff.), which in turn "is a matter of practical ability" (23). An anti-intellectualist perspective similarly pervades appeals to knowing how and skill in discussion of nonsense and ineffability (see, e.g., Wittgenstein 1953/1968; Moore 1997; cf. Williamson 1999), Dummettian realism and antirealism (see, e.g., Dummett 1982 and 2006),[63] imperatives (see, e.g., Ryle 1940; Hare 1972, 3), and rule-following (see, e.g., Ryle 1940, 1945, 1949; Wittgenstein 1953/1968; Kripke 1982; Boghossian 1989; Wright 1989; Brandom 1994, 20ff. and 65ff.; Haugeland 1998, ch. 13; Martin and Heil 1998; Tanney 2000; Kalderon 2001). In each of these cases, one wonders—as in §4.2 (recall the distinction between [Q1] and [Q2])—if an anti-intellectualist perspective of the relevant phenomena is compulsory. Viewed another way, it seems reasonable to ask in each case whether the explanandum is an instance of Intelligence: if not, then the appeal to knowing how must be deemed either misleading or superfluous, but if so, then we can begin to consider the further question of whether such Intelligence is best understood in intellectualist or anti-intellectualist terms.

Recent debates over the nature and status of linguistic knowledge appear to be premised on the reasonable assumption that such knowledge is or involves a form of Intelligence (see, in particular, Bennett 1964, §5). Noam Chomsky has argued that the knowledge of language that ordinary speakers possess—in other words, their knowledge how to speak their language—is factual knowledge and cannot be understood in anti-intellectualist terms.[64] In an obvious allusion to Ryle, Chomsky writes:

> Evidently, possession of this knowledge [of language] cannot be identified with ability to speak and understand or with a system of dispositions... or

---

63. Loux (2003, 642 emphasis added) suggests that Dummett's case for antirealism is linked to the idea that "to understand a statement is to *know how* to use it properly; and to know that is to have the *ability* to recognize when the assertion of that statement would be correct."

64. Chomsky (1988, 62–63 emphasis added; cf. 1975, 1980a, 1992): "We may think of the language faculty as a complex and intricate network of some sort associated with a switch box consisting of an array of switches.... When these switches are set, the child has command of a particular language and *knows the facts* of that language: *that* a particular expression has a particular meaning, and so on."

habits. We cannot exorcise the "ghost in the machine" by reducing [such] knowledge to ability, behavior, and dispositions. (1988, 10–11)

Chomsky's opponents ably disagree, of course, and thus the nature and status of knowledge of language remains highly controversial (see, e.g., Wittgenstein 1953/1968; Ware 1973, §§4–5; Putnam 1988, 32 and 1996; Dummett 1991, 93ff. and 1993, ch. 3; Devitt 1981, 1984/1997, 2006b, and chapter 14; Schiffer 2003; Hornsby 2005; Stanley 2005; Longworth 2008).

4.5 Philosophy of Mind, Phenomenology, Cognitive Science, Ethology, and Psychology

In *The Concept of Mind*, Ryle himself approached the issue of knowing how and skill through the philosophy of mind (specifically, the mind-body problem), treating them as centerpieces in his attack on a Cartesian dualism of mental and physical that espouses "the dogma of the ghost in the machine."[65] Although most philosophers today deem Ryle's attack unsuccessful,[66] it is difficult to deny that it was—and remains—influential, and not simply because its quips and gibes presented anti-Cartesians with a sizable rhetorical advantage.

Such polemical contests aside, knowing how and skill have featured prominently in a variety of other well-known controversies in recent (post-Ryle) philosophy of mind, phenomenology, and cognitive science. These include debates over the nature and possibility of machine or artificial intelligence (see, e.g., MacIntyre 1960; Nowell-Smith 1960; Dreyfus 1967, 1992, 2002; Winograd 1975; Searle 1980; Block 1981; Dreyfus and Dreyfus 1982; Brooks 1991; Haugeland 1998), representationalist theories of mind and knowledge (see, e.g., Dreyfus and Dreyfus 1982; Dreyfus 1992, 2002; Clark and Toribio 1994; Haugeland 1998; Kelly 2002; Clarke 2010, §4; Cummins and Roth forthcoming; Stanley forthcoming-a), Frank Jackson's (1982) Mary argument against physicalism (see, e.g., Nemirow 1980, 1990; Lewis 1983, 1988; Mellor 1993; Raymont 1999; Alter 2001; Stanley and Williamson 2001; Tye 2004; Cath 2009; Glick forthcoming), issues concerning nonconceptual content and concept possession (see, e.g., Noë 2005 and chapter 8; Bengson and Moffett 2007 and chapter 7; Toribio 2007; Kumar 2011; Devitt forthcoming-a; Glick forthcoming), the proper understanding of knowledge of phenomenal character and "what it is like" (see Tye, chapter 13),

---

65. This connection is revisited by Snowdon (2003, 16) and Hornsby (chapter 3); see also Churchland (1996).

66. Though Rylean approaches have recently seen defense by Mesler (2004) and Stout (2006).

and the relation between perception and action (see, e.g., Varela, Thompson, and Rosch 1991; Grush 1998; Mandik 1999; O'Regan and Noë 2001; Noë 2004; Schellenberg 2007; Reitveld 2008; Bengson in progress).

It is also common to find knowing how and skill invoked by philosophers, cognitive scientists, ethologists, and psychologists in discussion of the status of animal cognition (see, e.g., MacIntyre 1960, 1999 ch. 3; Nowell-Smith 1960; Bennett 1964; Noë 2005; Wallis 2008; Adams 2009; Bengson, Moffett, and Wright 2009; Devitt forthcoming-a), embodied and situated cognition (see, e.g., Paillard 1960, 1991; Varela et al. 1991; Haugeland 1998; Kelly 2002; Gallagher 2005, ch. 10), automaticity and flow (see, e.g., Annas chapter 4), tacit representation (see, e.g., Fodor 1968; Dennett 1982; Cummins 1986; Haugeland 1998, ch. 8; Ramsey 2007, ch. 5; cf. Polanyi 1958, 1966), and so-called procedural knowledge or memory (see, e.g., Winograd 1975; Bechtel and Abrahamsen 1991, 106; Pollock and Cruz 1999, 127ff.; Bzdak 2008; Adams 2009; Young 2009; Devitt forthcoming-a; Glick forthcoming).[67] Such discussions must be approached cautiously, however, as calibration with respect to both topic and terminology awaits confirmation.

To illustrate, consider the apparently prima facie exclusive distinction between procedural knowledge and declarative knowledge. While this distinction is often seductively glossed using the language of 'knowing how' and 'knowing that,' it may be hazardous to simply assume that such a gloss is meant to implicate a genuine equivalence—that whatever the notion of declarative knowledge designates is equivalent to knowledge that (or a subset of propositional attitudes) and that whatever the notion of procedural knowledge designates is equivalent to knowledge how. In this vein, cognitive scientists Neil Stillings, Steven Weisler, Christopher Chase, Mark Feinstein, Jay Garfield, and Edwina Rissland warn:

---

67. This list does not purport to be exhaustive. For example, knowing how and skill are also discussed in empirical literature on child development, language acquisition, implicit learning, motor learning and "double disassociation," expert systems, and the popular theory of multiple intelligences, among other areas. See Kaufman, Kaufman, and Plucker (forthcoming) for a review of contemporary psychological theories of intelligence.

There are still further areas where the debate between intellectualism and anti-intellectualism may have implications: for example, philosophy of education (see, e.g., Ryle 1945, 15–16; Beck 1968; Carr 1981b, 1984; Schön 1983; Cunliffe 2005; Winch 2009), aesthetics and the theories of art and creativity (see, e.g., Carr 1984, 1987, 1999; Gaut 2009), the study of religion (see, e.g., Ryle 1949, 23; Griffiths 2003, 39ff.; Moore 2003), discussion of the status of *Dasein* and the question of Being (arising from Heidegger 1926/1962), and non-Western thought and comparative philosophy (see, e.g., Raphals 1992; Ivanhoe 1993; Lai 2007; Stalnaker 2010).

Traditional [Ryle-inspired] epistemology distinguishes between *knowing how* and *knowing that*.... [T]his distinction is not the same as the one psychologists draw between procedural and declarative knowledge.... Much of our knowledge-that is probably encoded declaratively, since much of it is mobilized in controlled processes. Similarly, the kinds of automated, production-style skills we have are typically demonstrated in situations where 'know-how' is the most apt characterization of the knowledge in question.... However, these distinctions do not coincide exactly.[68] (1995, 369)

Similar warnings may be applied elsewhere, for example, to the notions of automaticity and tacit representation. To borrow a metaphor due to Wilfred Sellars (1962), it is fair to say that our understanding of both the manifest image and the scientific image would benefit from further investigation of the connections, if any, between the everyday notions of knowing how and skill, which are paradigm instances of states of Intelligence, and the technical or semitechnical notions of procedural knowledge, automaticity, and tacit representation (for example) figuring prominently in contemporary cognitive science, ethology, and psychology.[69]

---

68. Devitt (forthcoming-a, §3) characterizes the distinction thus: "declarative knowledge is explicit, accessible to consciousness, and conceptual, [whereas] procedural knowledge is implicit, inaccessible to consciousness, and subconceptual." This characterization nicely highlights one difficulty that arises from assuming the equivalence thesis: it is not obvious that knowledge that and knowledge how possess the indicated features (for example, even Ryle allowed that knowledge that may be implicit; recall note 9). A second difficulty is that a variety of non-Intelligent entities such as calculators, visual systems, and dishwashers represent rules or procedures—the standard characterization of procedural knowledge—whereas they do not possess knowledge how. This is related to a third difficulty: given that such entities possess procedural knowledge, it is far from clear that so-called procedural knowledge is in fact a form of knowledge (cf. Ramsey 2007, 169–173). A fourth difficulty is that the representation of rules or procedures is not obviously nonpropositional; consequently, it may not be of any use to anti-intellectualists wishing to defend Ryle's claim that there is an exclusive (or fundamental) distinction between knowledge how and knowledge that. Fifth, there is reason to think that Ryle himself would have been very unhappy with internal mental representations of rules or procedures (cf. Dennett 1982, 214 and Tanney 2009), regardless of what label such representations are given.

69. In this connection, consider MacIntyre's (1960, 90) interesting remarks on nonstandard uses of Intelligence-epithets: "Provided the psychologist is clear and consistent in his usage, is it not open to him to use 'intelligence' as he likes? This...ignores the point of the psychologist's enterprise. For the psychologist claims to be able to provide us with predictive techniques for assessing intelligence in our sense of the word, or at least in a sense akin to our sense. It is open to the psychologist to invent any technical terms that he can find a need for; there is no *a priori* reason for giving fewer rights to 'G' than to 'meson' or to 'chromosome.' But like 'meson' and 'chromosome' in the end 'G' has to be made intelligible in terms which start from the nontechnical." Cf. Thompson (2008, 10).

4.6 The Substantive Character of Ryle's Fault Line

To some, these observations will serve to uncover the possibility that the "theoretically interesting" states designated by the aforementioned technical or semitechnical notions (e.g., so-called 'procedural knowledge') lie elsewhere than knowing how and skill. Might this possibility render the philosophical debate between intellectualism and anti-intellectualism nonsubstantive, or merely terminological, and therefore uninteresting? No.

To see this, consider the following scenario. It may turn out that what is needed for a given theory (e.g., an account of what Jackson's Mary learns upon leaving her black-and-white room, or a so-called enactive theory of vision)[70] to succeed may just be the existence of at least one "anti-intellectual" state; that is, what matters is simply that there is *some state or other* that is grounded in powers, rather than propositional attitudes, and that plays the relevant theoretical role. An anti-intellectualist who endorses the indicated theory might then allow that everyday knowing how or skill is not such a state, but add—perhaps in a deflationary tone of voice—that this merely implies that theorizing about everyday knowledge how or skill is ultimately less important than studying the relevant type of power. One problem with this addition (and the accompanying tone) is that while it would be a triviality that *the state in question* is grounded in powers rather than propositional attitudes, it would remain a substantive question whether *states* of *Intelligence and Intelligent action* are grounded in powers rather than propositional attitudes. Viewed another way, the problem is that it would still be a substantive question whether the "anti-intellectual" state in question was in fact an instance of Intelligence and a Producer of Intelligence: a state of intellect and character, like knowing how and skill. Perhaps it is not. Nor, perhaps, are all of the states designated by the technical or semitechnical notions discussed at the end of the previous subsection (§4.5). This is a possibility that cannot be ruled out by mere stipulation. Nor, arguably, is it settled by the relevant empirical science alone. After all, while such states might play a crucial theoretical role in extant explanations of *behavior* (perhaps even agentive behavior), they might not play such a role in a philosophically adequate explanation of *Intelligent action*. On the other hand, they might. The substantive character of these issues should make clear why an appreciation of and sensitivity to distinctions, or potential distinctions, like those sketched at the end of the previous subsection, does not induce trivialization.

These considerations can be used to highlight the broader significance of the philosophical theory of Intelligence, as described in §1.1 and §2.1. Insofar as the

---

70. See the citations in §4.5.

indicated theoretical role requires a state that is an instance of Intelligence and a Producer of Intelligence, the approach taken by our imaginary anti-intellectualist will not be available, for intellectualism entails that *all* of the candidate states— all instances of Intelligence and Producers of Intelligence, and thus *all the states that could play the requisite theoretical role*—are grounded in propositional attitudes. So the proposed shift simply cannot be made. The same point applies mutatis mutandis to intellectualists who attempt an analogous shift in the other direction. In general, any such shift emerges as untenable once we attend to the fault line uncovered by Ryle's discussion and consequently make plain the "bigger picture". To the extent that this fault line implies a division between intellectualist and anti-intellectualist conceptions of mind and action of the sort described in §2.1, sustained attention to the aforementioned arguments and issues centering on knowing how, skill, and other states of Intelligence promises to bear substantial—and substantive—theoretical fruit.[71]

---

71. Thanks to Bruin Christensen, Sue Deuber, Stephen Hetherington, Jeff Lockwood, Leon Leontyev, John Maier, Matthieu Marion, Aidan McGlynn, Elliot Paul, Raul Saucedo, Susanna Schellenberg, and Jennifer Wright for helpful comments and discussion.

PART I
Ryle's Legacy

2

Rylean Arguments: Ancient and Modern

Paul F. Snowdon

RYLE CAN BE credited with opening the debate about the nature of knowing how and also with thinking out and presenting a conception of knowing how that became the accepted conception among philosophers for about fifty years. That is, surely, a very significant achievement. It is clear, too, that many philosophers still regard it as more or less correct. I want to devote this chapter to considering some of Ryle's arguments and views and also to considering a recent attempt by Wiggins to defend Ryle's picture. My own view, in contrast, is that the Rylean 'paradigm' is some distance from the truth, and I shall argue for that evaluation of it.[1] I want to begin by listing some fairly obvious things about knowing how.

1. Some Obvious Things

Here are some things about knowing how that seem to me pretty clear. The first four are, I think, evidence, not conclusive but strong, that the Rylean paradigm is questionable. The fifth gives some aid and comfort to Ryle.

> 1. There is an argument by equivalence to show that knowing how is knowing that, which has been proposed by a number of people. Thus, (i) if S knows how to F, then S knows a way to F, and (ii) if S knows a way to F, then S knows that so and so-ing is a way to F. So knowing how is revealed as knowing that by two very simple equivalences. But there are other arguments by equivalence. Thus, (iii) if S knows how to F, then S knows what to do to F, and

---

1. I tried to support such an evaluation in Snowdon (2003). The present chapter aims to add more weight to that evaluation, but I have tried not to repeat the earlier treatment. It needs stressing that it is impossible here to consider everything that Ryle says or that his supporters say.

(iv) if S knows what to do to do F, then S knows that so and so-ing is what to do to F. Again, these simple equivalences seems to reveal knowing how as a form of knowing that. What, though, do such arguments by purported equivalence achieve? The answer is, I believe, that committed Ryleans will reject them by denying the second suggested equivalence in each argument. There is, of course, no forcing people to accept these equivalences, and, indeed, it should be conceded that they *may* not be equivalent. It is not, however, outrageous to hold that these *are* equivalences, so as arguments, it seems to me, they have some weight.

2. The spread and take-up of know-how seems exactly the same as the spread of knowledge that. Thus, S buys a new computer and wants to learn how to switch it on. S reads the instructions and learns from them that the way to switch it on is to do so and so. There is, surely, no manifest contrast in such obvious cases between knowing how and knowing that.

3. We should also remember that we talk of people realizing how to do something, of its dawning on them how to do it, of them working out how to do it, of them telling someone how to do it, and also of them showing someone how to do it. In these completely normal ways of speaking, it seems we are treating the possession of knowledge how as a form of information possession. Further, we can ask someone, do you have any idea how to F? The focus of such a question is on the subject's cognitive appreciation of an issue. It is like asking, what do you think is the way to do this? In the light of these obvious aspects of our language, it surely seems quite wrong to think that the default view about knowing how should be that it is a *quite different sort of thing* from knowing that.

4. As a rough-and-ready contrast, we can distinguish two points of view when we consider the question whether another person S knows how to do F. One is where our point of view is whether S is going to be in a position to do F. We have no interest in gaining from S the relevant know how. Either we already have it—we know how to ride a bicycle, and our interest is whether S can join us—or we do not want to know how but want someone who does know how; for example, we want someone who knows how to repair our complex but currently malfunctioning boiler, something we are sure we shall never know how to do. But very often our interest is in finding someone who can impart to us the relevant know-how. Does S know how to open the safe we are trying to open? If so, he can impart his knowledge to us. Now, when our interest is, as it very often is, of the latter sort, it is completely natural to think of a particular bit of knowing how as a piece of information (a datum) that someone can convey to us. There is no appeal in thinking of such knowing how as strongly distinct from information as to

what is the case, information that can be imparted. These points indicate, I wish to suggest, that Ryle's emphasis on the contrast between knowing how and knowing that is not in any way obviously right. I stress that I do not think that these remarks are strong evidence that *all* knowing how is knowing that. They do not indicate that. I take them, rather, to indicate that it is not the case that all (or the standard central cases of) know how is definitely not know that.

The four (according to me) obvious things that I have so far listed I interpret as indicating that there are reasons not to treat the Rylean view as the default view (in the way, I suspect, that philosophers still do). But there is another obvious thing that I wish to add to the list that makes the picture more complex.

> 5. Although no one has ever satisfactorily formulated what the condition is exactly, it seems obvious that a condition on knowing that P is that the knower accepts that P, and so there is a formulation of the claim that P that would, other things being equal, elicit assent from the knower. This is part of the point, though not the whole point but rather the relatively uncontroversial part of the point, of talking of knowledge as a standing in the space of reasons.[2] I shall call this the AP-component (short for assent-to-P component) in knowing that P. Now what seems plainly possible is that human agents when faced with the task of achieving goal G might have the capacity to choose the appropriate means (call them M) without there being any claim P that they would assent to that says that M is (a) means to achieve G. Putting these claims together, they amount to showing that complex behavioral capacities are, in principle, independent of factual knowledge. Now, that possibility is precisely what Ryle is relying on, and I am suggesting it cannot be ruled out. We can then say that the status that Ryle seems to have been tempted to ascribe to knowing how is a status that represents a conceptual possibility.

I turn now to a consideration of (some of) the points that Ryle makes.

2. Ryle's Discussion: Some Themes

Ryle presented his views in two places. The second, and more famous, was in *The Concept of Mind*, but the first was his article "Knowing How and Knowing That"

---

2. I myself am unconvinced that the rest of what is conveyed by Sellars's famous slogan (famously endorsed, of course, by McDowell) is similarly correct.

in the *Proceedings of the Aristotelian Society*. These were highly effective in presenting a conception of the nature of knowing how. Now, as I have suggested in §1, the Rylean paradigm should not strike us as a good one, and the question that we should really be asking is just how far from the truth is it? In a further defense of this outlook, I want to begin by investigating Ryle's presentation of his paradigm in his early article.[3]

(A) Intellectualism

Ryle's paper begins with a three-and-a-half-page preamble, which reads like a long abstract or summary. What stands out is that in the preamble Ryle *never* mentions know how. According to the preamble, Ryle's topic is "the logical behaviour of the several concepts of intelligence, as these occur when we characterise either practical or theoretical activities as clever, wise, prudent, skilful, etc." (Ryle 1945, 1). Ryle sets out the 'prevailing doctrine,' which he subsequently calls 'intellectualism' and which says that practical activities merit the application of "intelligence concepts" in virtue of being accompanied by "internal acts of considering propositions" (and particularly "regulative propositions"). Now, there are a number of aspects of Ryle's discussion of intellectualism that are unclear.

   1. We have no clear idea as to what range of concepts it is supposed to apply to. What exactly is an "intelligence concept"? Ryle does not say or give any hint as to the boundaries of this range of concepts. One might be tempted to suggest that an 'intelligence' concept is one the application of which has implications about the intelligence of the subject. But Ryle's list includes 'wittily' and 'scrupulously,' and it is surely not part of our understanding of these notions that their application indicates intelligence (or lack of intelligence). The scope of intellectualism is, then, more or less impossible to determine.
   2. It is clear from his discussion that he does include what we might call 'negative' intelligence concepts, such as stupid, unwise, and imprudent. But Ryle gives no indication what sort of account of these the 'intellectualist' is committed to giving. Presumably, the intellectualist will adopt an account with the same structure for the negative cases, but it then becomes clear that as sketched by Ryle, a central element in intellectualism is completely missing. We have no idea what makes an internal

---

3. I reread Ryle's early article as a result of engaging with the paper by Wiggins (2009) that I shall discuss later. I am very grateful to Wiggins for causing me to reread it.

accompaniment a ground for the application of a positive intelligence concept and what makes it a ground for a negative application. (And of course, we similarly have no idea what differentiates between the different positive and the different negative concepts according to the theory either.) Possibly Ryle's idea is that the intellectualist approach to the negative concepts is that their application is grounded in the absence of the internal accompaniments.[4] Well, we simply do not know.

3. There is another puzzling thing about intellectualism. All those who have played chess know full well, perhaps from their own case or, if they are lucky, from observing others, that it is possible to make a bad or poor move after considerable thought about what to do. It is simply obvious that a move does not count as clever, intelligent, or even sensible simply in virtue of being preceded by and being the result of considerable thinking.[5] But on the face of it, that obvious falsehood is what intellectualism is committed to. So either intellectualism is obviously false, or Ryle's formulation of it quite fails to convey what it is actually saying about the relation between an action's being preceded and caused by 'theorizing' and its being, say, an intelligent action.

4. There is a further question to be asked about the doctrine of intellectualism. What sort of theory is it? It would be perfectly possible to treat intellectualism as what one might call a psychological theory. Read this way, it is not claiming to analyze the concept of, say, acting intelligently, but it is postulating a psychological process that brings it about that there is intelligent action. Now, it is clear that Ryle himself treats intellectualism as a conceptual thesis. This is clear from, among other things, the way he describes the sort of mistake it is on his conception: he calls it a type mistake, which seems to be his term (in 1945) for what he later called a category mistake, that is, a serious conceptual misconception. Ryle is obviously at liberty to define his own target as he wishes, but it is quite another matter, if he has in mind a point of view accepted by actual thinkers, that they were really aiming at conceptual analysis, rather than psychological explanation. Ryle gives us no help in this matter since his treatment of the position is virtually *ahistorical*. His understanding

---

4. Or perhaps on Ryle's conception, intellectualism would say that an act falls under the negative intelligence concepts if *eithe*r it is not accompanied by inner thought *or* is accompanied by the wrong sort. We do not know what the theory says, nor do we know what might be meant by the 'wrong' sort.

5. The frequent pointlessness of thought by chess players is beautifully and humorously shown in chapter 1 of Alexander Kotov's classic book, *Think Like a Grandmaster*. It represents an unanswerable refutation of intellectualism (on its most obvious understanding).

of it is not anchored in, or answerable to, a correct reading of any actual figures that he names. So although it is clear what Ryle takes the general status of intellectualism to be, namely, a conceptual thesis, we have no reason to accept that as the best characterisation of the debate.

This observation can be linked to a more general one about Ryle. Ryle's approach to the myth of the ghost in the machine is that it represents a conceptual confusion—a category mistake. It is refuted by displaying the correct conceptual account. To maintain this view, Ryle has to regard the doctrine under attack as a conceptual claim. Any target of his philosophical criticism in the philosophy of mind must, it seems, be a conceptual thesis, and his understanding of intellectualism fits that. It is hard not to feel, though, that this conception is a mistake. The ontological theories that Ryle opposes are better viewed as bad theories, intelligible in themselves, (perhaps) not well supported and not consonant with other assumptions that we make, and so to be rejected. Ryle's approach to intellectualism is, therefore, of a piece with his approach to the philosophy of mind in general, an approach that has not, in my view, proved fruitful. It represents a distortion of what the fundamental debates in the philosophy of mind are about.

5. This links with a further lacuna in Ryle's presentation of intellectualism. We have no sense of why anyone should accept it. Now, I would have thought that the root of its appeal is the simple idea that intelligent performance requires *thought*. If this is the root of its appeal, it confers on intellectualism more the character of a *psychological thesis* than a piece of conceptual analysis. I suggest, then, that Ryle's reading of intellectualism does not fit what should strike us as its main ground.

6. When Ryle sketches 'intellectualism,' he stresses that the 'thinking' that it postulates involves considering "particularly 'regulative' propositions." If applied to his case of chess, that would mean, presumably, that according to intellectualism, the thinker contemplates and recites such propositions as, say, "Do not move your queen in the first four moves." Why, though, does Ryle characterize the postulated thinking in this way? As far as I can see, there is no reason for him to do so. Presumably, what should guide the characterization is a careful survey of the kind of thinking intelligent players do engage in when they play chess. Now, I am not such a player but have been in the company of such players, and it is quite obvious that they do not repeat to themselves such 'regulative' principles. What they consider is what moves are available, what responses to those moves are available, and so on, and, further, what the resulting positions mean or amount to. So another aspect of Ryle's characterization is quite unwarranted. As one might put it, why did not Ryle

simply locate intellectualism as the idea that intelligent action is action resulting from a process of thought about action? Why build in the characterization of the thinking in the way that he does?

7. Growing out of this question is a related observation. In the way he seems to be thinking, Ryle views intellectualism in two different ways. The first is that intellectualism essentially postulates as the ground of intelligent action a certain process—a process of (inner) thinking. The second conception is that intellectualism essentially grounds intelligent action as emanating from factual knowledge. It is, surely, obvious that in fact these are not the same idea, but Ryle at times seems to think that they are. Consider the following passage right at the start of the main section:

They assume that intelligence equates with the contemplation of propositions and is exhausted in this contemplation.... I hope to show that a number of cruces and paradoxes remain insoluble if knowing-that is taken as the ideal model of all operations of intelligence. (Ryle 1945, 4–5)

The last sentence is fixing on *knowing that* as the crucial ingredient, whereas the first sentence is clearly fixing on a *process* of "contemplating propositions." It should be clear that there is a shift in emphasis here, between making a process central and making knowledge that central. But it should also be clear that this is a confusion; since knowing that something is the case is a state (or standing condition), it simply cannot be regarded as a model of an operation. Once again, this is very hard to follow.

Ryle's intellectualism is a monster, not so much monstrous in what it says, but monstrous as a target for philosophical discussion. There are two final aspects of it, or of Ryle's discussion of it, that I want to highlight briefly.

8. It seems fair to me to say that Ryle's dominant conception of intellectualism is the process account, where the process grounding intelligence is inner thinking, which gives rise to the action. It is hard not to feel, though, that Ryle has an odd conception of the 'thinking' in question. He describes it as "the operation of considering propositions," and he stresses the involvement of "regulative propositions" (Ryle 1945, 1). This is surely a very etiolated conception of thinking. Thinking is not well characterized as simply contemplating a proposition—rather as one might contemplate a remembered face or remembered tune. The thinking that intellectualism postulates should be thought of as a purposive inner activity engaged in with a certain goal—to determine

what to do, which is to say, to determine an answer to a practical question. It is a real problem how the process of thinking achieves this resolution, but it is surely wrong to build the characterization of intellectualism around an impoverished understanding of thinking.

9. What ultimately is the account of 'intelligence' concepts that Ryle offers? Toward the end of his paper, Ryle puts his own conception this way.

> When a person knows how to do things of a certain sort, we call him 'acute', 'shrewd' 'scrupulous'...'a good general' or a 'good examiner'. In doing so we are describing a part of his character, or crediting him with a certain dispositional excellence. Correspondingly when we describe some particular action as clever, witty or wise, we are imputing to the agent the appropriate dispositional excellence.... His dispositional excellences are actualised in those performances.... It is second nature in him to behave thus.... (Ryle 1945, 14)

This is hardly satisfactory. Clearly, knowing how to do something is not a character trait. I know how to start the computer I am working on, but not the computer you are working on. What sort of character does that make me? Ryle has yoked together two completely different things—know-how and character. Further, in thinking of standing conditions such as cleverness, Ryle is evidently thinking of them as dispositions to action; thus, the clever person is the person who is disposed to perform clever actions. But that need not be so. A witty person, say, might never utter the witticisms that occur to him; the clever chess player might not play chess but merely observe and think about it. Finally, being clever at things involves real intellectual effort; it is not effortless second nature. Ryle hardly has anything to put in the place of intellectualism.

(B) Intellectualism, Chess Playing, and Knowing How

I do not think that it is too severe a verdict on Ryle's characterization of intellectualism to say that although it conveys a broad and vague sense of what it is, his characterization leaves very many aspects not properly explained, to such an extent that we have little sense of what we are dealing with or why we are dealing with it. It is also a consequence of the unclarity of intellectualism that certain important questions that need to be faced turn out to be rather difficult to settle. Now, it is only on page 4 that Ryle mentions knowing how (aside, that is, from the paper's title!). This brings us to the central mystery of Ryle's approach. What is the relation between the debate about intellectualism and the debate about the nature of know how? One aspect of this question is: what is Ryle's primary topic, intellectualism (and its ills) or the nature of knowing how? The answer is, I believe, that intellectualism is the primary topic, and the insights about knowing how are side effects of that. The title of the article indicates otherwise, but the preamble surely directs us to Ryle's main interest—intellectualism. So the central question for us is whether Ryle's treatment of intellectualism generates *any* insights into the nature of knowing how.

To consider this, I want to investigate the two central and very interesting examples that Ryle uses in his debate with intellectualism. The first is the example of the good chess player (5–6), and the second is the example of the defective reasoner (6–8).

When considering the chess player case, Ryle's point is that the difference between the clever player and the stupid player cannot be that the clever player knows information that the stupid player lacks, because if the clever player were to tell the stupid player all that he knows as he approaches a choice of moves, and the stupid player were to learn it all, that would not guarantee that the stupid player plays well. As Ryle puts it, "He might…be unable intelligently to apply the maxims, etc." (Ryle 1945, 5).

Ryle's conclusion seems clearly correct. If two people arrive at a problem with the same antecedent information INF, that does not guarantee that they will engage with the problem with the same degree of intelligence, and so solve it equally intelligently.

However, there are three reservations to express about the way Ryle makes this point:

> 1. Neither Ryle nor we really know what in fact belongs in what I have called INF. We have little idea what antecedent information a good chess player draws on in playing chess. (Fairly obviously, in fact, there is no such collection of information shared by all intelligent chess players.) So it is not that we can envisage giving *that* information to a stupid player. We do not know what to give him. Our conviction that Ryle's negative conclusion is correct draws on our belief that whatever INF is giving, it does not guarantee cleverness. In realizing that, we simply draw on an obvious feature of intelligence: having information (at the start of problem solving) does not guarantee intelligence.
>
> 2. Ryle's form of argument encourages a misconception. We envisage the clever chess player arriving with INF, and we imagine the stupid player given INF as well. We then ask, what is the difference? Ryle is clearly inclined to say that the clever player knows "how to apply the truths" (6) in INF, whereas the

stupid player does not how to apply them. But obviously our contrasting judgments about the clever player and the stupid player who share the same antecedent information does not license *that* conception of the difference between them. We have no right to assume that the difference between the clever player and the stupid player is a matter of what they *do with* INF.

3. Not only is the description of the difference that Ryle seems tempted by quite unjustified but also it is rather hard to understand. The Rylean slogan is that the stupid player does not "know how to apply the truths." But what can that possibly mean? Let us suppose, to facilitate engagement with this issue, that the truth in question is that one must never move one's queen before the fifth move. If we asked the stupid player how one could apply that principle, the stupid player would surely know—by not moving one's queen before the fifth move. There is therefore no plausibility in describing him as *not* knowing how to apply the truths. Ryle's diagnosis, unjustified as it is, is also simply inappropriate.

(C) Learning from the Chess Example

I want now to suggest three more substantial observations.

1. Let us assume that Ryle is right to reject the view, which he seems to take to be intellectualism, that the difference between the clever chess player and the stupid one is that the clever one knows more. What does this show us about knowing how? Ryle's argument, I suggest, is that the agreed difference is that the clever player knows how to apply truths, which the stupid player does not know how to apply, but it has also been agreed that the difference is not in what facts are known, so knowing how is not the same as knowing that. That is the line of thought that Ryle thinks reflection on the intellectualist mistake provides us with to draw a conclusion about knowing how. But I have suggested that it is a complete mistake to say that the clever player can be characterized as someone who knows how to apply truths that the stupid player does not know how to apply. If my claim on that point is correct, Ryle's reflection on chess playing reveals nothing about the relation between knowing how and knowing that.

2. If we view the basic problem in the way that Ryle does, as the task of analyzing the concept of (roughly) an intelligent action, the most obvious suggestion is that for an agent to do F intelligently is for the agent to do F in the manner that someone who is intelligent would do F. (By manner here is meant not solely the outer action but the manner of choice and deliberation and thinking linked to intelligence.) Mutatis mutandis the same goes for doing F stupidly. This is, of course, only the sketch of an

approach, but I want to assume that it is on the right lines and to develop it a little. The idea is that we sort people into the clever and the not so clever, plainly on the basis of their relative capacities to problem solve. We then extend that to classifying ways of acting—that is, problem solving in the domain of action—into ways of so doing that depend on the presence of intelligence and those that can be present without intelligence. That is, I want to suggest, about as far as conceptual analysis can take us. There is then, as one might say, a gap in this concept—namely, that it is to be empirically determined what the manners of acting are that are associated with intelligence. Determining that is the main problem in the psychology of intelligent action. My suggestion, then, is that the conceptual problem that Ryle focuses on can be solved (or the direction of its solution indicated) in this fairly simple way, and the analysis simply opens up an important empirical question.

3. As well as classifying actions as intelligent or stupid, we also classify agents in relation to domains of action as expert or inexpert. In this sort of classification, we are not assuming that experts have to be intelligent; rather, they have acquired an expertise through training and performance. Conceptually speaking, this amounts (roughly) to being better at doing certain tasks than normal people. But again there is a real empirical question—what is the real grounding in agents of this expertise?

I suggest then that reflection on the chess case indicates a direction to solve Ryle's conceptual problem and the central empirical problem that intelligent action, or expert action, raises.[6]

(D) The Defective Reasoner

Ryle's second example, which clearly interested him greatly and which is, indeed, very perplexing, is that which we might call the defective reasoner. The basic case is that of a pupil who accepts, say, that P and that if P then Q, but who does not infer Q, and who shows no inclination to infer Q. Ryle envisages that the teacher tells him as a way of unlocking the inference that if P and (if P then Q) then Q. The pupil accepts that but still draws no inference. The teacher then reacts by telling him the next conditional in the series, with, however, the same negative result.

---

6. I am very grateful to Dr. Mark Addis for conversations that helped me to see some of this.

What does Ryle think this case shows? Ryle takes it that we should say that the pupil does not know how to reason. Given that, Ryle draws two conclusions. The first is that since the pupil does accept any proposition that the teacher gives him but still does not know how to reason, it follows that knowing how to reason is not knowing that P (for any P). Second, to know how to reason is to be "able to perform an intelligent operation" (Ryle 1945, 7). This is to see the reasoned case as supporting both of Ryle's central ideas—that knowing how is not knowing that, and that the presence of knowing how is a matter of the presence of an ability.

The counter to Ryle's inference here starts from querying whether Ryle has described the case correctly. There are two points to stress. The first is that talk of knowing how to F is appropriate only where F represents a genuine action. We do not know how to digest food, faint, or sweat. We simply are able to and do these things (in a nonactional sense of 'do'). The second point is that forming a belief (by inference) is not an action, but is, rather, a cognitive development or change. A reasoner moves from a cognitive position in which he or she has a complex of beliefs to a new cognitive position in which a belief (related in certain ways to those present in the previous stage) is added. That precisely is the process of forming beliefs by inference. If inference is not an action, then there is no such thing as knowing how to do it. Its presence is a matter of there being a pattern of cognitive response. If so, this fascinating example shows nothing about knowing how at all.

What does emerge from the defective reasoner case is that we must allow that psychological states have causal powers that are not equivalent to the presence of other psychological beliefs. This emerges because in the thought experiment, the subject's inferential powers remain nil; however, many further beliefs are acquired by the subject. The only way to unlock the defect is for the extant bunch of psychological states to acquire causal powers, not for more cognitive states to enter the picture.

What we learn from this consideration of the two main cases that Ryle discusses is that they reveal nothing about knowing how: the defective reasoner case reveals that psychological states have dynamic and causal properties not corresponding to further psychological states; the chess case helps us generate a conceptual analysis of (some) intelligence concepts and indicates the empirical psychological enquiries that remain.

3. *Wiggins's Defense of Ryle*

I have tried so far to analyze some central aspects in Ryle's first presentation of his views about knowing how. Given the background observations about what we should expect an account to be like and the (according to me) weaknesses in Ryle's own arguments, the verdict I am proposing is that Ryle's approach is unacceptable. In the second part of this chapter, I want to consider an attempt by Professor Wiggins to show that Ryle is basically right.

(A) Ryle's Thesis According to Wiggins

Wiggins's attitude to the debate is that Ryle proposed the thesis that he, Wiggins, puts in these words: "knowing how [to V] and knowing that [p] (are) distinct, not the same thing" (Wiggins 2009, 263). Let us call this the *distinctness thesis*. Wiggins, as he avers, believes this thesis is true; Ryle, according to him, was right to claim this. Wiggins evidently feels, though, that some care needs to be taken over the *interpretation* of the distinctness thesis, and in the earliest sections of his recent essay, Wiggins indicates both what Ryle is claiming and what he is not claiming.

Let me start with the basic clarifications (presented in §§1–2). Wiggins's simplest formulation of the Rylean thesis is "that knowing how [to V] and knowing that [p] (are) distinct, not the same thing" (Wiggins 2009, 263). Now, no one is inclined to say that knowing [that p] is always the same as knowing how [to V]. So no one is inclined to say that they are the same thing. Rather, Ryle's opponents are inclined to say that knowing how [to V] is one *sort* of knowing [that p]; it is one genus of that species. Since a species is not the same thing as the genus, even Ryle's opponents can agree with Ryle as characterized by Wiggins in some of the words of this passage.

Wiggins adds a further point of clarification. He says:

> At the risk of labouring the obvious, let us be as clear as possible about this. If I say that being a baker and a life-boat pilot are distinct occupations/avocations, I do not mean that nobody is both. (2009, 264)

Before grappling with what Wiggins means, we can note that this claim is less strong than it might have been. In agreeing that being a baker and being a life-boat pilot are distinct occupations, I am not even ruling out that everyone who is a baker is a life-boat pilot and vice versa. The question, though, is what Wiggins's point is. Is Wiggins inviting us to entertain the thought that although knowing how to V and knowing that p are distinct states, a single thing can *be* both? That is parallel to the way he speaks about being a baker and life-boat pilot. The reason, though, that this cannot be his point is that we think of objects as bakers and pilots, but we do not similarly think of some item being a knowing that or a knowing how. Rather, we think of objects as knowing how or as knowing that. It cannot be Wiggins's point either that although knowing how and knowing that are distinct states, a single thing can both know how and know that. Wiggins cannot suppose that anyone thought that Ryle's view implied that that is incorrect. We are, then, so far left unclear as to what Wiggins's point is. There is, we should agree, something in this area in need of clarification. The issue can be approached in the following way. Suppose that we want to say something like this: in a certain particular case, what makes it true that S knows how to V simply is that S knows that p (for some value of p). The question is: is it consistent with Ryle's distinctness thesis, as we should understand it, to say this? It seems obvious that there is a natural way of understanding the distinctness claim in which it is not consistent, that is, to understand it as claiming that it is never the case that knowing how is, or consists solely in, knowing that. But it is also true that one can understand the distinctness thesis in a way with which this is consistent. That would be to understand the distinctness thesis as claiming that there are (some) cases of knowing how that are not, or do not consist in, knowing that. There are, in effect, two distinctness theses. The question then is: which does Ryle subscribe to? This is a substantive question of interpretation, and it cannot rank as primarily a matter of clarification.

On the question that we have now arrived at of how to interpret Ryle's view, I wish to make two points. First, it seems to me fairly clear that Ryle did endorse the stronger distinctness thesis. This is based on the fact that he stresses the independence of knowing how from knowing that and the fact that he shows no inclination to moderate the contrast. Second, it is not totally satisfactory to represent Ryle as solely affirming the (negative) distinctness thesis. He surely offers a positive conception. He stresses that the presence of knowing how is the presence of a disposition (Ryle 1945, 7).

(B) The Interdependence of Knowing How and Knowing That

Wiggins moves on to the task of counseling against some further alleged implications of Ryle's view. The basic message is that Ryle can allow that "knowing how to and knowing that need one another" (Wiggins 2009, 265). As he later puts it, there is a "constant back-and-forth between knowledge that rests upon the practical and knowledge which rests on the propositional" (Wiggins 2009, 265).

What does Wiggins mean by this? He gives as an example of this sort of dependence in one direction the following:

> We may be unable to exercise practical knowledge without some piece of propositional knowledge (where the fuse box or trip switch is located, ... or the stop-cock). (2009, 265)

This charming illustration seems to be understood by Wiggins as a matter of what he calls the exercise of practical knowledge depending on propositional knowledge. But understood in this way, it is not an illustration of how knowing how depends on propositional knowledge, but rather of how acting out of know-how can depend on propositional knowledge. It is like the following case: a safecracker might say, "I certainly know how to open Dave's safe, but I cannot do so at the moment because they have moved it and I don't know where it is."

He also offers an alleged example of the opposite dependence, that of knowledge that on practical knowledge. His example is this:

> A ship's pilot who is retained to bring large ships safely to anchorage in a difficult harbour can say, on the basis of his experience, that, when the wind is from the north and the tide is running out, the best way to avoid the hazardous sandbank is to steer straight for such and such a beacon.... Here propositional knowledge reposes upon practical knowledge. (2009, 265)

This is again a charming illustration, but it seems misconceived. Of course, the pilot knows that the best procedure is to do X on the basis of what he has learned from his experiences of steering such ships. But having steered such ships and had such experiences is not itself know-how; it is, rather, that the pilot has learned that X is the best way to steer the ship from observing the ways that he and perhaps others have tried and what results they achieved. So the example does not illustrate a dependence of knowing that on knowing how. Indeed, rather oddly, the sort of knowledge that Wiggins here calls propositional itself seems very close to what most people would call know how. The pilot knows how to best steer ships in these circumstances. Those inclined to be skeptical of Ryle's sharp know how–know that distinction would draw comfort from something this example seems to illustrate—namely, that one can sometimes reexpress know how very easily as know that. In other words, in precisely this sort of case, the Rylean sense of distinctness between know how and know that does not seem plausible.

What I suggest these examples bring out very well is that there are *three* elements that need comparing and linking. One is knowledge that, the second is knowledge how, and the third is practice (what we do). When we say that practice has improved, we are, strictly, predicating an improvement or change in a type of *activity*. Such an ascription is not about knowing how or knowing that. It is, as one might say, about *doing*!

(C) The Alleged Support for Ryle

What reason is there, according to Wiggins, to accept the distinctness thesis? Wiggins endorses Ryle's claim on the basis of the following assertion. Wiggins claims that

> among the huge variety of things human beings do there have to be some that they come to do otherwise than on the basis of learning that such and such is the way they are done. (2009, 268)

He adds that

> He [i.e., Ryle] might have said that these are among the things we learn to do by habituation and practice: and that when we do them, we do them directly and not on the basis of information how they are done. (2009, 268)

Before investigating whether the general claim here is true and what, if it is, it implies about know how, there is an aspect of this remark that needs scrutinizing. The question that this brief passage raises is why Wiggins seems to think that the things that we can do 'otherwise than on the basis of learning that such and such is the way they are done' will be ones one has to learn to do by "habituation and practice." Of course, we can allow that some things we can do but not on the basis of knowledge of a way to do them are ones that one becomes able to do by practicing, but why should we suppose that is true of all or even most of them? There is, further, a problem with supposing this. To so much as practice something, we must be able to do something, since practice is acting. Similarly, when Wiggins speaks of 'habituation,' he presumably means repeatedly doing something, and in that sense, 'habituation' is a form of action. This means that not all things we can simply do are things *we acquire the ability to do by practice*. Practice presupposes the ability to do things. It seems to follow that not all things we can do without a recipe informing us what the way to do them is can be things we have to learn to do *by practice*.

Leaving that aside, there are two questions that obviously arise about Wiggins's argument. The first is why we should accept the quoted claim that there are things we do but not on the basis of "learning that such and such is the way they are done"? Wiggins's reason for saying this is contained in a longish quotation from Jennifer Hornsby. Putting her argument in my own words, she points out that if everything we do is done on the basis of knowing that a certain way is the way to do them, then we would not be able to act at all. To do H, I rely on my knowledge that the way to do H is to do I in circumstance G. However, to do I, I need to rely on my knowledge that doing J in circumstance H amounts to doing I. But to do J, I would need more knowledge, and so on. It looks as if this chain of dependence generates an infinite regress, and action would be impossible. The way to break the chain is to allow that we can simply do certain (basic) things without dependence on knowing a way to do them. Wiggins points out that there may be some resistance to accepting this argument, a resistance as he conceives of it that I shall explore shortly. But the second question that arises is what the quoted claim shows about the relation between knowing how and knowing that, which is, after all, the target of our investigation.

As the argument is presented, the reader has to do some reading between the lines to work this out. The problem is that the central claim is that there are things we do directly 'and not on the basis of information about how they are done.' The way these basic cases are characterized in terms of the absence of information about how they are done is presumably intended to rule out that there is any fact such that the agent can count as knowing that that fact obtains that is involved in their being able to so act. So let us allow that there is no relevant knowing that in such cases. This is, however, irrelevant to the central issue unless knowing how counts as being present. If that is absent and knowing that is also absent nothing at all has been revealed by this argument about their relation.

Now, in the exposition of the basic argument by Jennifer Hornsby that Wiggins quotes (Wiggins 2009, 268–269), she simply says of these that

> We can do…a very great deal more than we are able to simply do; but our doing these other things requires procedural knowledge that we can put into practice. Practical knowledge, when it has been learned and not forgotten, is what enables us to get started as it were. (Hornsby 2005, 113–115)

What, I believe, stands out about this comment is that Hornsby simply assumes, at least as far as the quoted passage on which Wiggins is relying is concerned, that it is right to say that there is practical knowledge possessed by the agents who can do these things without knowing that "such and such is the way they are done." In Hornsby's way of speaking, there just is practical knowledge that does not consist in procedural knowledge. Now, Hornsby's way of speaking does not, presumably, represent a philosophical conviction that we should speak of 'practical knowledge' here. It rests, rather, I assume, on the claim that people with such capacities independent of procedural knowledge properly count as knowing how to do the acts in question. The crucial issue, then, is whether that claim about knowing how ascriptions is correct. This is, in fact, quite a hard question because although there is a general argument provided by Hornsby, which strikes me as plausible, that there must be cases of capacities not resting on procedural knowledge, given that we do have capacities to act, the argument does not help us identify which cases they are, and so we cannot easily decide whether they are cases where there is actually know how.

What I want to argue is that it would not be correct to say that in all the cases where someone can act but without knowledge of a recipe for doing the act, there is know how. Consider this simple case: someone can blink with his left eyelid. Does he rely on a recipe as to how to blink? We can say that he knows what blinking is, but there is, it would seem, no recipe to perform that act. Let us assume so. Now, it seems to me, that it is not true to describe the agent as knowing how to blink. That is not a knowledge ascription we would make. The proper ascription is that the subject can blink and has the ability to blink. At least that is how it seems to me. This means that there are among the sort of cases that Hornsby's argument indicates must exist, cases where know how should count as absent. Now, if that is true, the interesting argument constructed by Hornsby and endorsed by Wiggins in itself shows nothing about the relation between know how and knowledge that. It may, of course, be that there are indeed such cases where there is know-how, but the argument itself shows no such thing.

Wiggins's conception of the debate raised by the argument is that Ryle's opponents will respond by postulating tacit or implicit knowledge in the cases under consideration. Against this, Wiggins raises some objections. But if I am right, this overlooks that the anti-Rylean can respond in a different way.

(D) Further Alleged Support for Ryle

In §§8–10, Wiggins adds what he describes as one "larger and even more important point that needs to be made on Ryle's behalf" (Wiggins 2009, 270). What is it? Wiggins starts with a proposal made some time ago by the ever ingenious A. R. White. White proposed that to know how to F is to know (a) way to F, and that "knowing the way to V was knowing propositionally that such and such is the way to V" (Wiggins 2009, 270). Now, this proposed equivalence has occurred to many people without realizing they were repeating a suggestion of White, and it is not unattractive, even though in need of some modification. Wiggins assumes that the opponents of Ryle must claim that all knowing how is knowing that so and so is the way to do something. In fact, something like that is what opponents of Ryle have said, so the target is appropriate. However, Wiggins takes over something that White says as the background for his criticism. He takes it that if someone knows that so and so is the way to F, that requires them to be able to "say or show" (to another, presumably) the way to F. Whether that is right is a further question, amounting in fact to the issue of what implications ascriptions of so-called propositional knowledge have. Noting that this is a substantial assumption—not directly discussed by Wiggins—about propositional knowledge, the question facing us is how Wiggins creates an argument for Ryle on the basis of it.

Here is what he initially says, employing the example of the ship's pilot again:

> Consider the advice the pilot offers for the case where the wind is from the north and tide is running out. The advice does not purport to be complete; it is gathered from the pilot's own competence and experience; and its usefulness presupposes an existing competence of some kind in any recipient who will deploy it. (2009, 271)

I want to work backward through these points. We are to imagine the pilot says something like: "if the tide is going out and the wind is from the north, you should steer the ship in the so and so direction at so and so speed." Now, we can agree that this is not useful advice unless the person hearing it can steer the ship in the right direction and the right speed. Its usefulness depends on a battery of preexisting competences. But in this, the case resembles the usefulness of information in general. If I am told that the delivery will be at five o'clock, that will not be of much use unless I can tell when it is five o'clock (or approaching five o'clock). So we can describe imparting information to the audience as telling them how to steer in certain conditions, where that information is passed onto them and learned, but where the usefulness of their knowing it depends on their possession of certain related competencies. The agreed dependence of usefulness in no way shows that what was imparted and learned was not factual information about the way to do something in certain circumstances. Wiggins says that the advice is gathered from the agent's competence and experience. Now, in saying the advice comes from the agent's experiences, nothing is being said that counts against regarding it as expressing what the agent knows and in virtue of which he counts as knowing how to steer a ship in those conditions. How else would he have learned that information? If, rather, Wiggins is stressing that it is drawn from a competence, and by that, he has in mind a picture according to which the pilot has developed a mode of response when in charge of the boat in such circumstances, which is to say that is his competence, and only afterward does he acquire any impartable information as to what he is doing, then he needs to say why he thinks that that is the correct description of a case such as this. Does Wiggins mean that that has to be the correct description of the source of a pilot's advice, or rather that at least it might be? As far as I can see, the sketched case does not force us to accept his description.

Among the points that he makes, the one that seems to impress Wiggins most is the first one—that the agent's advice is not "complete." He adds:

> Why should we suppose that such a procedure could ever be spelled out and set forth in the way required for there to be a propositional knowable in the form '*w* is the way to V'? (2009, 271)

What does Wiggins mean by describing the advice as not complete? One might say that as far as direction and speed in such circumstances are concerned, it is complete. So relative to what, is it incomplete? If someone said, "Convey to me everything that you knew how to do and the knowledge you drew on there and then in steering that boat into port," then the answer is incomplete. Obviously, the agent did not draw solely on the knowledge that the way to steer the boat was in a certain direction and at a certain speed in performing that highly complex action. The question, though, now is: what does *that* incompleteness imply or show? The answer is that it does not show anything. In particular, it does not show that the advice does not represent a piece of information that the pilot knew and that he drew on in steering the ship in those circumstances. That would be like saying to someone when they told you that the Battle of Hastings was fought in 1066, that since that does not express all they know about the battle, and hence is incomplete from that point of view, that it is not something that the subject knew. We need to go back, at this point, to something that Wiggins introduced earlier and that he seems to be relying on here. That is the remark from A. R. White that the anti-Rylean who thinks that know how is know that is committed to supposing that the agent who knows how to F can "say or show" or show how to F. Wiggins seems to be thinking that his example reveals that this condition is not met in the know how case. There are three comments to make here.

1. Although it looks plausible to think that there is some sort of expressibility implication of propositional knowledge, White's particular version, involving the ability to say or show, seems too strong. Those who are completely paralyzed do not lose their propositional knowledge, but they cannot say or show anything.

2. It is important to realize that any expressibility implication of propositional knowledge applies at most to what might be called individual pieces of information. Thus, if S knows that p, then (maybe) S must be able to express p, and if S knows that q, then S must be able to express that q, but S can possess both those pieces of knowledge without being able to express both of them. The reason is that joint expression of what S knows might be impossible since there is simply too much of it. It is, therefore, a plausible claim that in one

sense all expression will be incomplete; one will never be able to express all one knows—in which case, the incompleteness of expression does not reveal anything about the status of what is expressed.

3. If one thinks quite what is imparted or signified by saying of someone that he knows how to pilot boats safely in a particular harbor, it seems reasonable to suppose that the simplicity of the ascription hides what anyone hearing would realize is a complex battery of interrelated pieces of know how. If we think that know how is a species of know that, then we can allow, it seems to me, that a simple know how ascription conveys the presence of a battery or multiplicity of factual information. I am not here making a proposal about the grammatical structure or logical form of know how ascriptions but about what people hearing them can in certain cases take to be the knowledge structures that we should count as making the ascription true.

If these comments are combined and seem reasonable, then Wiggins's incompleteness observation seems to imply nothing about the nature of what the truth of a knowing how ascription requires.

4. Conclusion

There is no single conclusion that I have aimed to support, but I hope that the cumulative effect of these reflections is to lessen the appeal of the Rylean 'paradigm.' I have picked on various elements in Ryle's discussion and in the attempt by Wiggins to support him, and I tried to both disarm the support and learn what there is to learn from their points.

3

Ryle's Knowing-How, *and Knowing How to Act*

Jennifer Hornsby

I THINK THAT there is a way of understanding Gilbert Ryle's main point against those he called intellectualists that is missed in the literature on 'knowing how to.' And I shall suggest that one won't have a correct account of agency if one doesn't grasp Ryle's point.

Ryle first gave his reasons for rejecting "the intellectualist legend" in an essay with the same title as chapter 2 of *The Concept of Mind*, 'Knowing How and Knowing That.' The essay (1945), like the chapter (1949), is concerned with how "thinking affects the course of practice," but it treats a more compendious category of *practice* than the chapter does, and an understanding of Ryle's argument should take this into account. I shall suggest that Ryle's central claim in both places was that the use of propositional knowledge requires a sort of knowledge that could not itself be propositional. This claim is rejected by those of Ryle's opponents who maintain that propositional knowledge is ascribed whenever someone is said to know how to do something. I shall argue against the account they give of knowing how. And I shall explain why these opponents may be seen as complicit in a sort of Cartesianism which it was the purpose of *The Concept of Mind* to trounce.

I

1.1

According to many, there is, in Ryle's view, "a fundamental distinction between knowing that something is the case and knowing how to do something," the former being a relation to a proposition, the latter an ability.[1] This cannot be quite

---

1. See the start of Stanley and Williamson (2001) for attribution of this view to Ryle. Snowdon (2003) comes close to making the attribution, and he is right at least in thinking that those who hold what he calls 'The Standard View' have been influenced by Ryle.

right. Ryle thought that the possession of knowledge—whether it belongs under the head of knowledge-that or of knowledge-how—was "a mark of intelligence." And when he spoke of 'know' as a "determinable dispositional word...signify[ing] abilities...to do things of many different kinds," he made no distinction between possible objects of knowledge.[2] In his view, both knowledge-how and knowledge-that are connected with abilities of certain sorts, as indeed are knowledge of a language or a tune or knowledge of syntax.

Why then should Ryle have insisted on the importance of his distinction between two species of knowledge? To understand this, one needs to see what role the distinction plays in his arguments. Ryle said that the main object of *The Concept of Mind* chapter was "to show that there are many activities which directly display qualities of mind, yet are neither themselves intellectual operations nor yet effects of intellectual operations" (1949, 26). He surely thought that a conception of knowledge that obliterates a distinction between two species of knowledge stands in the way of his object.

Ryle characterizes his opponents, the intellectualists, as having a mistaken conception of knowledge, resulting from a mistaken view about the difference between "intelligent" beings and others. The intellectualists take human beings' superiority to nonhumans to reside in a capacity for theorizing, where the goal of theorizing is knowledge of true propositions (1949, 26). So they treat knowing-that as "the ideal model of all operations of intelligence" (1945, 5), and the model informs their conception of what it is to be rational and to act rationally. To understand, and then correct, the intellectualists' errors, we have to see that their model of intelligence breaks down. We are meant to see that it does by recognizing the work of knowledge-how. Ryle does not think he needs to prove that there is such a species of knowledge: he relies on the fact that a distinction between knowing propositions and knowing how to do something is "quite familiar to all of us" (1945, 7). But the intellectualists are in denial of such a species: they "are apt to try to reassimilate knowing *how* to knowing *that*" and so are forced to introduce acknowledgments of propositions as antecedents of intelligent doings (1949, 28–29).

One might say that, in Ryle's book, knowing how is the knowledge which intellectualists fail to reckon with, and their disregard of it ensures that they treat exercises of qualities of mind as "occult episodes" (1949, 25). If this is right, then Ryle had no need of a general account of what it is to know how to do something—an account of what it is to know how to Φ, for arbitrary Φ. It seems certain that Ryle never had such an account in view. None of his remarks about

---

2. For an account of knowledge-that in terms of abilities, see Hyman (1999).

'knowing how' invites this construal. (Consider, for instance, "Understanding is a part of knowing *how*," 1949, 54.) His short section called "The Positive Account of Knowing How" does not even pretend to start on such an account: it is focused on just one example (1949, 40–41; the example is playing chess). It is true that Ryle introduces a great many examples of things that someone may know how to do. One must assume that the examples are all supposed to provide illustrations of knowledge that goes missing in the intellectualists' vision: they are the sort of examples to which we need to pay attention if we want "to do justice to 'knowing how'" (1945, 4)—to do justice to the species of knowledge that Ryle hopes to persuade us is different from that to which intellectualists restrict themselves.

The idea that Ryle had a definite account to offer of what is meant by 'knowing how to' is shared by some of his detractors and some of his self-styled defenders.[3] Parties to both sides of a debate about knowing-how have attributed to him the view that to know how to Φ is to have the ability to Φ. But this was certainly not Ryle's view. He said that there were many more ways of exercising one's knowledge of how to do something than merely putting to work an ability to do it (1949, 55). And he contrasted someone whose being able to do something on occasion is owed to luck with someone who knows how to do something and can do it reliably (1949, 130). So he did not think that having an ability to do something suffices for knowing how to do it. Moreover, there is no evidence that he would have wished to endorse the converse claim—that knowing how to do something suffices for having the ability to do it. Ryle said nothing that rules out cases that have been offered as counterexamples to this.[4] In connection with knowing-how, he spoke of all of "abilities," "skills," "competences," and "capacities," and one might assume that he used these various terms in part because he recognized that 'knowing how' could not be understood in terms simply of ability.

Ryle is misunderstood, then, if he is taken to have entered any claim about the correct treatment of the schematically given general category—knowing how to Φ. To make his case against the intellectualist, all that he needs (so he thinks) is that there should be knowledge that is not knowledge of any proposition and

---

3. Stanley and Williamson say, "According to Ryle, an ascription of the form '*x* knows how to F' merely ascribes to *x* the ability to F" (2001, 416). Rosefeldt (2004) argues on behalf of Ryle that knowing how to do something is "in one sense" having the ability to do it; Noë (2005) takes Ryle to have equated knowing-how-to with having-the-ability-to.

4. They are examples in which, in order to Φ, one needs some capacity other than the capacity to Φ, and the person who knows how to Φ while lacking the ability to Φ lacks the ability in consequence of lacking that other capacity, needed for Φ-ing. For examples drawn from a number of sources, and some discussion (but not the diagnosis of examples the description I have just given is meant to suggest) see §2 of Fantl (2008).

that may be ascribed when a person is said to know how to do something. This is what I shall defend against Ryle's detractors in part 2.

1.2

Consider now how Ryle makes his case. The "crucial objection to the intellectualist legend," as it appears in *The Concept of Mind*, is stated as follows:

> If for any operation to be intelligently executed, a prior theoretical operation had first to be performed and performed intelligently, it would be a logical impossibility for anyone ever to break into the circle. (1949, 30)

Here there is no mention of knowledge of any sort. The need for knowledge of a sort that intellectualists leave out of account is meant to emerge from the argument. What is impossible, according to Ryle, is that "intelligently executed operations" should always require prior theoretical operations. So there must be operations that belong in the category of the intelligently executed but don't belong there by virtue of the performance of any prior theoretical operation.

Ryle speaks of "knowing how to apply truths" (1945, 6). We might call any operation that is not theoretical 'applied.' Then Ryle's argument will be meant to show that applied operations are among the intelligently executed ones. Assume that knowledge-*that* is exercised in an intelligently executed *theoretical* operation, and knowledge-*how* in an *applied* one. The conclusion will be that it is impossible that knowledge-how should be absent so long as there is an intelligently executed operation.[5] Knowledge-how belongs in *applied* operations and is in play when knowledge-that is put into practice.

People often speak of Rylean knowledge-how as *practical* knowledge. But Ryle does not apply 'practical' to knowledge himself. And it isn't helpful to use the label in trying to understand him.[6] When the practical is distinguished

---

5. This argument is meant to establish that *use* of knowledge-that requires knowledge-how. Ryle also thought that *presence* of knowledge-that requires knowledge-how. He said that he wanted to prove that "Knowledge-how is a concept logically prior to the concept of knowledge-that" (1945, 4–5). He argued that "knowing-that presupposes knowing-how," saying, "To know a truth, I must have discovered or established it. But discovering and establishing are intelligent operations, requiring rules of method, checks,...etc." (1945, 15). There will be no need to be concerned here with the claim about the priority of knowledge-how.

6. Of course, there can be perfectly good understandings of practical knowledge despite Ryle's having no use for the label 'practical knowledge'. G. E. M. Anscombe (1957) has one such understanding, not itself understood, she says, "unless we first understand practical reasoning." Setiya (2009) brings together Anscombe on practical knowledge with Ryle on knowing how.

from the theoretical, one is likely to think of a division between two sorts of activity—a division between activity we think of as going on in people's heads (thought, theoretical) and activity consisting of "audible and visible performances" (action, practical). Some people take this division to correspond to a distinction between the categories of the mental and the physical—between two categories whose exclusiveness Ryle is at pains to deny. Ryle does have a use for the words 'theoretical' and 'practical', but he does not apply these to knowledge. He thinks that knowing anything—whether knowing that so-and-so or knowing how to such-and-such—is a matter of being disposed to *do*. He describes theorizing as "one practice amongst others" (1949, 26). He says, "Effective possession of a piece of knowledge-that involves knowing how to use that knowledge, when required, for the solution of…*theoretical or practical* problems" (1945, 16, my italics). He speaks of reasoning as a "practice" and as a "sort of doing"; he disparages "the idea that 'internal doing' contain[s] some contradiction" (1945, 1).

It will be instructive to see how the argument works for "internal doings," where theoretical reasoning is in question. According to Ryle, knowing how to reason is knowing rules of inference. And he thinks that Lewis Carroll's puzzle of Achilles and the tortoise would be insoluble if knowing such rules were taken to be a matter of knowing propositions. The tortoise "considers reasons, but he fails to reason," Ryle says (1945, 6). I suggest that his idea is that no one could ever reach conclusions that they know if reasoning itself were merely a matter of knowing, or considering, propositions. One might spell this out by thinking about a person who knows some particular thing, having arrived at this knowledge by reasoning from some propositions that they know. Imagine that they know there's fire because they see there's smoke and they know that if there's smoke, there's fire. This is not the condition of someone who knows that there's fire also knowing that there's smoke and that if there's smoke, there's fire. Someone could have this latter knowledge without having gone in for any reasoning. Nor, if the person is to be portrayed as having a sound basis for the knowledge that there's fire, could it help to attribute to the person knowledge of further propositions. They may know not only that there's smoke, and that if there's smoke, there's fire, but also that there's fire if these two propositions are true; they may know that these two propositions constitute a conditional and its antecedent; they may know that these two propositions imply that there's fire. And they may know yet further conditional propositions or further propositions about conditionals or implications. But it is possible for someone to know all these things, and to consider all these propositions, without applying the rule of *modus ponens*—without actually *doing* anything that goes by the name of reasoning.

> Of course the intelligent reasoner is knowing rules of inference whenever he reasons intelligently, but knowing such a rule is not a case of knowing an extra fact or truth; it is knowing how to move from acknowledging some facts to acknowledging others. (1945, 7)

I interpret Ryle as relying on a general point. Someone's reaching a conclusion requires a passage of their thought, which cannot be understood in terms only of the "theoretical operation" of "considering propositions."[7] Merely durative conditions of mind, such as considering the fact that there's smoke or knowing that if there's smoke, there's fire, will never be enough for modifications of mind. The general point could be made about any process that culminates in acceptance of some proposition, regardless of whether the process follows the lines of a deductively valid argument and regardless of whether it begins from or ends in knowledge. But Ryle is interested in a sort of rational process distinctive of the beings he calls 'intelligent.' He appreciated that it is not only reasoning governed by deductive rules that moves from pieces of knowledge to pieces of knowledge (e.g., 1945, 16). And he could have allowed that there can be reasoning of such a kind as to be knowledge-preserving but based in beliefs or suppositions, not in knowledge. Again, Ryle could have allowed that someone might make faulty inferences, so that there can be reasoning that is not of a knowledge-preserving kind at all. Still, if someone knows that q *because* they know propositions that imply q, then their knowledge of those propositions alone is not responsible for their knowing that q. They have applied a rule. And "whatever 'applying' may be, it is a proper exercise of intelligence…not a process of considering propositions" (1945, 4).

The problem, then, for Ryle's intellectualist, in Ryle's view, is that he can have no account of those exercises of intelligence that are applyings of rules. The problem arises because the intellectualist restricts "intelligent operations" to considerings of propositions, so that an application of a rule can be thought of as intelligent only insofar as its intelligence is seen as somehow inherited from considerings of propositions. But since a prior process of considering a proposition cannot do the trick of conferring intelligence upon a process with new knowledge as its upshot, the intellectualist is obliged to introduce another considering of a proposition, and then another—thus the regress of Lewis Carroll's puzzle. And thus it must be that there is knowledge that correct reasoning is the application *of* which is not knowledge of those propositions *to* which the reasoning is applied.

---

7. In 1945, Ryle talks of "*contemplating*" propositions, as well as "considering" them, making it seem as if reasoning were always consciously engaged in. It could be that Ryle thought that his intellectualist opponents were apt to think of reasoning as consciously engaged in, or it could be that he thought of it thus simply in order to talk about it more easily.

When Ryle's argument is understood in this way, his hope is to persuade us that participation in certain processes requires knowledge-how. It helps to confirm that Ryle wants us to think about *processes* of reasoning to notice that he speaks of the intelligent reasoner as someone who "is know*ing* rules of inference." This strikes one as strange, because Ryle would be the first to say that the word 'know' is "not used for an episode" (1949, 116 and elsewhere). Surely, what Ryle should have said is that the reasoner is *exercising knowledge* of rules of inference whenever he reasons intelligently. Presumably, he didn't say this, because it would be compatible with allowing knowledge-how to be a mere accompaniment of reasoning. And of course, Ryle did not think that the exercise of knowledge-how is in play alongside a piece of reasoning; he thought, naturally enough, that reasoning correctly *is* applying one's knowledge.

An objection might be that there is no call to use the word 'knowledge' in connection with an ability to *reason*. But when an ability is an ability to engage in knowledge preserving processes (as I have put it), perhaps we can understand why its possession should be thought of as possession of a sort of knowledge. And without the specter of skepticism, which never haunted Ryle, it could seem obvious that sound reasoning is of a knowledge-preserving kind.[8] At any rate, Ryle was clear that we need to think of abilities to reason in epistemic terms; he wrote that if someone

> is to merit the description of having deduced a consequence from premises, he must know that acceptance of those premises gives him the right to accept that conclusion;...though he would not, of course, be expected to name or to formulate the principle *in abstracto*. (1949, 300)

Allowing that rules of inference may have propositional formulations does not interfere with Ryle's argument. Ryle himself appears to have been uncertain about the status of such rules, sometimes calling them "regulative propositions" that may be "acknowledged in thought," sometimes speaking of them as expressed in "brief formulae or terse orders." But however rules might be expressed when formulated, knowledge of what is then expressed will not be the knowledge-how that his argument invites us to accede to. Indeed, Ryle draws on the fact that one may be ignorant of a proposition that formulates a rule that one uses in reasoning. "Arguing intelligently did not before Aristotle and does not after Aristotle require the...acknowledgment of the truth or 'validity' of the formula" (1945, 7). Given that "application of rules [does] not have to await the work of...codifiers"

---

8. Ian Rumfitt (chapter 15) suggests an argument for a particular instance of the claim—for his deduction principle.

(1946/1971, 233), the knowledge that someone exercises when they operate in accordance with a rule could not be the knowledge that is cited when the rule is cited. The knowledge that ensures that a person can "break into the circle" "is realized in performances which conform to the rule, not in theoretical citations of it" (1945, 7).

When Ryle allows that knowledge-how can sometimes be recapitulated propositionally, he writes, "In respect of many practices, like *fishing, cooking and reasoning*, we can extract principles from their applications by people who know how to fish, cook and reason" (1945, 12, my italics). One may find it curious that fishing and cooking should come under the same head as reasoning. But on the present understanding of Ryle, he has the same point to make in respect of them all: that "there is no gap between intelligence and practice" (1945, 2). In the earlier essay, rejection of "the gap" is at the service of practicalizing philosophers' conception of the intelligence involved in rational doings quite generally, including successful thinking; in *The Concept of Mind*, it is at the service more specifically of exteriorizing philosophers' conceptions of the thinking involved in successful bodily action.

2

2.1

In *The Concept of Mind*, Ryle needed to be concerned with "overt" doings "in the outside world," so as to put across the book's anti-Cartesian message. The Cartesian thinks that the mental is separate from the physical. Ryle wanted it to be clear that the states of mind implicated in intelligent bodily action are inseparable from bodily action itself. He opens chapter 2 saying that he will "try to show that when we describe people as exercising qualities of mind...we are referring to...overt acts and utterances themselves" (1949, 25). The Cartesian does not doubt that we can be referring to acts that are *not* overt when we describe people as exercising qualities of mind. So theoretical reasoning need not be the topic here. (Ryle speaks of "qualities of mind" because he is much concerned with aspects of intelligence that don't come under the head of knowledge.)[9]

---

[9]. I leave out a great deal by thinking only about knowledge-how. Ryle is concerned with 'mental-conduct concepts'—that "family of concepts ordinarily surnamed 'intelligence,' which are attributed when words such as 'clever,' 'sensible,' 'careful,' 'methodical,' 'inventive,' 'prudent,'..." are used (1949, 25; Ryle's own list runs on). There are good questions about the connections between knowing-how on the one hand and capacities to act cleverly, carefully, and so forth, on the other (for discussion, see the state of play essay in this volume and Snowdon chapter 2). Snowdon (2003, 16–17) raises such questions in the course of arguing (a) that Ryle's views

To reason, in the sense that was of concern to Ryle, is to do something rational, but it is not, or at least need not be, to do anything on purpose. To *act*, in the sense of concern to philosophers of action nowadays, is to do something *intentionally*.[10] In turning from reasoning to acting, then, things intentionally done are brought into account. Not that 'intend' and 'intentionally' are words Ryle has much use for himself. But if it is allowed that things are intentionally done in the cases he considers, then Ryle's "intelligent *behaviour*" will mean, near enough, *intentional action*.[11] At any rate, Ryle's own examples of things a person knows how to do are of activities in which a person intentionally engages. Riding a bicycle, although not one of Ryle's own, is of this sort. His own examples of things one may know how to do include, as well as fish and cook, talk grammatically, play chess, swim, play an instrument, tie a clove hitch knot, and prune trees.

A signal feature of many activities is that one may be able to say very little about *how* one engages in them. Someone who is asked how she rides a bicycle may say something about how she place parts of her body in relation to parts of a bicycle, and that she turns the pedals using her legs, but she probably cannot say how she maintains her balance, even though this is something one has to do to ride a bicycle and something that someone who wants to learn how to ride a bicycle will want to come to be able to do. Again, speakers of English know how to pronounce English words and may have something to say about how they do so, but they are unlikely to have enough to say to distinguish the way they sound the end of the word 'dogs' from the way they sound the end of the word 'cats'; indeed, they may be unaware that there is a difference in the way the 's' sounds are made. Here knowledge-how seems to come into its own. Ryle said that someone can know rules that govern reasoning without being able to formulate the rules propositionally. Something similar appears to be true of the knowledge-how of someone who knows how to participate in one or another activity. One knows

---

about knowing-how "do not contribute to the dissolution of the Intellectualist Legend" and (b) that the Legend has no essential link to Cartesian dualism. It is partly because the argumentative course of chapter 2 of *Concept of Mind* is so hard to fathom that I draw on Ryle's earlier essay in my attempt to understand the 'crucial objection.' Then I think one finds an argument that does speak against a kind of dualism: see part 3.

10. Not, of course, that the only things one does intentionally require the use of one's body; there is "mental action," as it is put nowadays. Ryle was interested in mental action (as opposed to reasoning, which is usually *not* intentionally engaged in) only insofar as he wanted to encourage us to think of it as a silent counterpart of what may happen out loud.

11. Indeed, Ryle himself made use of 'intentionally' only in cases in which it might actually be in question whether something was done intentionally. And he took the prevailing view to have been that the category of human action is marked out with an idea of what is done voluntarily, rather than what is done intentionally.

how to do so, but one's knowledge seems not to be, certainly not to be exhausted by, knowledge-that. If no propositions one knows record one's way of doing something, how could one's knowledge how to do the thing be propositional?

Stanley and Williamson give an account of the construction <'know' + 'how' + infinitive> that purports to answer this. I showed that Ryle would be misunderstood if taken to be offering any contrary account himself. But inasmuch as Stanley and Williamson's account would corroborate the intellectualists' assimilation of knowing-how to propositional knowledge, it would certainly be unacceptable to Ryle. I shall outline their account now, and argue that it is untenable—that it cannot actually accommodate the inarticulability of some of our knowledge of how we do things.

2.2

Stanley and Williamson describe their account as following "from basic facts about the syntax and semantics of ascriptions of knowledge-how" (2001, 441). They appeal to an accepted semantics for embedded questions suited for treating 'know whether,' 'know where,' 'know when,' and so on; 'how' is then just one more interrogative particle, they say. 'Know how' might seem to be special when it is followed by an infinitive—'knowing how to Φ.' But the construction with an infinitive is also found with the *wh*-interrogatives. (One may know whether to go to the lecture, where to turn right, and so on.) And on a certain standard treatment, when an infinitive verb follows an interrogative after 'know,' there is a phonologically null pronoun in the subject position of the verb that is obligatorily linked to the subject of the whole sentence. This is written 'PRO.' So, according to Stanley and Williamson, 'A knows how to Φ' can be written 'A$_i$ knows how PRO$_i$ to Φ,' which may be taken to say, roughly, that A knows how A Φs. A's knowing how to Φ is then understood as a matter of there being some way w such that A knows that w is a way for A to Φ.

We can now see how allowance is supposed to be made for the inarticulability of some knowledge how. Stanley and Williamson "take ways to be properties of token events" (2001, 427), and they rely on the use of indexicals. Using an indexical and the device of deferred ostension, it is possible to refer to a property of an event without providing a specification of the property. The way in which A Φ-s—how A Φs—can be conveyed by pointing to an event that is A's Φ-ing and saying, '*That* is a way for A to Φ.'

This tells us how to make reference to a way or ways of Φ-ing without finding descriptive words that fill the blank in 'A Φ-s by…-ing' or '…is how A Φ-s.' But it is not yet an account of what would ordinarily be meant when someone was said to know how to do something. As it is ordinarily meant, 'A knows how to ride a bicycle' is true only if, other things equal, riding a bicycle is something A is able to do: she knows how to ride a bicycle *herself*. Here Stanley and Williamson introduce "practical modes of presentation." They say that the proposition knowledge of which is attributed to a person who knows how to do something *herself* is ascribed, not under a demonstrative mode of presentation but under a *practical* one. Their account of a person's knowing how to Φ (as this would ordinarily be meant), then, is this:[12]

> X knows how to Φ iff for some [contextually relevant] way w which is a way for X to Φ, there is a practical mode of presentation m, such that X knows under m that w is a way for her to Φ.

To see why this account cannot be correct, it will be important to be clear that we have no grip on practically presented ways of Φ-ing except insofar as we know that they are things of such a sort as might be demonstratively presented on occasions of Φ-ing. Just as "first personal" modes of presentation of ways are required to account for the difference between 'A believes that that man is F' and 'A believes that he himself is F,' so "practical" modes of presentation are required to account for the difference between 'A knows that that way is a way for him to Φ' and 'A$_i$ knows [how PRO$_i$ to Φ].' Or so Stanley and Williamson say (2001, 428–429). That is, they introduce practical modes of presentation on the strength of claiming that there is a role for them in the semantics. Now one might start a quarrel at this point. One could draw attention to the fact that their proof that there are practical modes is based in the assumption that 'A$_i$ knows [how PRO$_i$ to Φ]' gets the syntax of 'A knows how to Φ' right and then point out that this assumption is disputed by anyone who takes Ryle's side. But I want to start the quarrel at a different point, because I am interested in seeing where Stanley and Williamson's account goes wrong. My doubts concern whether *ways* can do the work they are supposed to.

Consider first that someone may have a way to do something they want to do without *knowing* how to do it. Suppose that a portion of some Web site is security protected: a password is needed to enter it. Tom thinks that he knows the password, and accordingly he types a particular eight-letter string at the relevant prompt. Luckily, he enters. He was lucky because he'd forgotten the password and tried during the very brief period when typing *any* eight-letter string would have

---

12. The account posits a conventional link between constructions that embed instances of the schema 'X$_i$ knows how PRO$_i$ to Φ' and practical modes of presentation. To keep things simple, I let 'contextually relevant' take care of itself, and I ride over various distinctions that are essential to Stanley and Williamson's full account.

got him in. (During that period, someone was altering the security settings, which had had to be suspended.) Now Tom might think that he had known how to get into the Web site, but he would discover that he hadn't as soon as he tried again. Someone who pointed at the event of Tom's entering his eight-letter string, although they might ostend an instance of a way of getting into the Web site, would not ostend an instance of a way known to someone who knew how to get into the Web site. The ways that could properly belong in an account of knowing how to do something, then, are only those whose being known by A to be ways for A to do something might constitute A's knowledge of how to do the thing.

In order now to see that ways in which A Φ-s on particular occasions could not be constitutive of A's knowledge how to Φ, consider this example. Jim, an accomplished typist, exercises his knowledge how to type when he types the word 'Afghanistan'; this is a word that it so happens he has never typed before. We point at him as he types, saying, 'That's a way for Jim to type,' ostending an instance of a way of typing by using 'that' to refer to a property of which his typing then is an instance. Inasmuch as Jim has never previously typed this word, we may think that this is not a way that Jim has previously deployed. But since Jim is typing in his usual way, which has served him well in the past, presumably we should try to think of the way as somehow more abstract, less specific, than the one we imagine if we focus on the fact that Jim typed only one particular word. But now imagine Joe, who has not yet learned to type but has typed the word 'Afghanistan' a hundred times. (He was told that this is a good word for a learner to start by practicing.) He does it impeccably, using all the right fingers, so that it need not be far-fetched to assume that there is no discriminable difference between Joe's typing and Jim's. But then, if it were allowed that 'that' said as Jim typed, makes reference by deferred ostension to a way of typing such that Jim knows how to type in virtue of his typing thus, we should have to say that Joe also knows how to type. But he doesn't. The difference between the practiced typist and the learner is a difference in what they know how to do but is not apparent in the "token events" they participate in when they exercise their knowledge.

Another sort of example also shows that token events of A's Φ-ing fail to provide what is needed to latch onto what A knows when A knows how to Φ. Consider Clare, an excellent gardener, who is pruning the roses. As she cuts with the secateurs, you say, 'That's a way for Clare to prune roses.' Then, as she is examining a bit of a plant in order to determine where to cut next, you say again, 'That's a way for Clare to prune roses.' The ways you denote with your successive 'that's' evidently have very little in common. When you first say 'that,' Clare's hand is in motion; when you say 'that' a second time, her brow is furrowed as she contemplates the next step. But each of these samples of rose pruning must be supposed to serve equally well to show a way to prune roses that is known by Clare.

If the demonstratives in these examples behaved as they would need to in order to fit an account of what it is to know how to do something, then they would go hand in hand with ways of Φ-ing such that their being known by an agent to be ways for her to Φ amount to her knowing how to Φ. But in the example of typing 'Afghanistan,' two different pieces of knowing how are exercised (Jim's knowing how to type, Joe's knowing how to type 'Afghanistan') and only one such way (the way they both typed). In the second example, only one piece of knowing how is exercised (Clare's knowing how to prune roses), but it is exercised in two evidently different ways (in moving her hand, in determining what to do next). The conclusion must be that A's knowing how to Φ cannot be understood as A's knowing a way to Φ, if ways are constituents of propositions such as might be used in saying how A is Φ-ing on some particular occasion. But then Stanley and Williamson's treatment of 'knowing how to' in a semantics fitted for embedded questions provides no account of the ascriptions of 'knowing how to' that we actually make.

One gets a sense of the character of knowing-how to act by seeing *why* it cannot be propositional. The point against Stanley and Williamson could be put intuitively by saying that what is known by a person who knows how to Φ needs to be somehow *generic*, and that is why it cannot be captured by citing particular instances of the person's Φ-ing. The generic character of what is known explains why Ryle and so many others should have thought that a person is related to something *general* in having knowledge of how to do something. To know how to do something is not to stand in the relation of knowing to any proposition true on the occasion of a particular piece of activity or token action, but to stand in the relation of knowing-how to an activity or a type of action.

This can be put as a linguistic claim—about the attachment of the 'how' to the 'know' in the English 'know how to….' There is then plenty of properly linguistic evidence against Stanley and Williamson's contrary claim. These authors say that "from the perspective of syntactic theory…there is no basis in structure" for the difference that Ryle's supporters suppose there to be between 'Hannah knows how Bill rides a bicycle' and 'Hannah knows how to ride a bicycle.' But really they are entitled only to say that the difference lacks a basis when the particular syntactic theory is applied perfunctorily to sentences of English.[13] And as Rumfitt has amply demonstrated,

---

13. Perfunctory application of the syntactic theory seems out of order, given that Stanley and Williamson themselves allow an ambiguity in, say, 'Hannah knows how to ride a bicycle.' [It has two readings according as it is, or is not, to be interpreted—in their own view—as introducing a proposition presented under a practical mode of presentation.] It is surely a good question at least whether this ambiguity has a structural basis from which superficial structure of English might be a distraction.

English is far from typical in employing an interrogative particle ('how') to ascribe the knowledge that one has when one knows how to ride a bicycle, or to swim, or to speak a language. When a French speaker [for example] ascribes the sort of knowledge-how in which Ryle was interested...he does not use an interrogative construction at all, but instead employs a bare infinitive, [saying, e.g.] 'Elle sait monter à vélo.' (Rumfitt 2003, 160–161)

It should come as no surprise, then, that properties of token events will not serve to identify the knowledge exercised when knowledge-how is exercised. Ryle himself would speak of such knowledge as "a disposition," "the exercise of which is indefinitely heterogeneous" (see Ryle 1949, 44).

I want to conclude by connecting the failure of Stanley and Williamson's account with Ryle's animadversions against dualism.

3

3.1

I suggested that Ryle may be seen as arguing that the applying of knowledge requires a sort of knowledge that is not knowledge of propositions applied, and that his concern with "intelligently executed operations" is a concern with intelligent practice—with intelligent acts quite *generally*. If what goes for his "theoretical acts" goes also for "practical acts," then acting intentionally, like theoretical reasoning, will require nonpropositional knowledge.

The need to bring nonpropositional knowledge into account of action is clear from the examples that showed that knowledge how to cannot always be knowledge of ways. Suppose that Clare decides to spend the next half hour pruning the roses and sets forth accordingly; she will have pruned some roses in half an hour's time unless she has a change of mind or encounters obstacles. So she now has whatever it takes for her to do so. But as yet, it is quite indeterminate exactly what she will do; it may not be possible to specify even what steps she will need to take or, therefore, what propositional knowledge she may need to draw on. As she acts, an account of what she is doing might be given, saying that first she does this, then that, then the other. But such an account could never record the knowledge she has of how to prune roses. *That* knowledge has equipped her to act in different ways, equally appropriate to the roses' coming to have been pruned, on past occasions; and it will equip her on future occasions also. On any particular occasion, her knowledge-how affords her the capacity to come to know such propositions as enable her to see her way through the contingencies that she needs to negotiate to complete the task. But these propositions relate to the particular circumstances in which the task is carried out; she does not come to the task equipped with knowledge of them, as she does with knowledge of how to prune roses.[14]

I trust that it seems rather obvious that, so far as activities on Ryle's list are concerned, know-how plays a role that propositional knowledge could not play. It might be thought that types of action whose instances are plausibly token events are a different matter. But similar sorts of considerations would seem to argue for nonpropositional knowledge in these cases, too. Take Stanley and Williamson's example of opening the door. They say, "I exercise (or manifest) my knowledge *that* one can get the door open by turning the knob and pushing it" (Stanley and Williamson 2001, 415). (They are quoting Ginet when they say this. And they follow Ginet also in their response to Ryle's main argument.)[15] This can be true, but it hardly shows that the knowledge of someone who opens the door

---

14. My argument here echoes what Ryle says following his statement of "the crucial objection" (in a passage that Stanley and Williamson pay no attention to). Ryle's thought there, cast so as to bring it into line with my interpretation, is that the philosopher who denies that there is knowledge-how can have no account of the intelligence of a person's passage through a process of acting. Such a philosopher may try to account for this by bringing in pieces of knowledge-that, namely, considerations the person makes use of. But a consideration introduced into the process must be pertinent at the point at which it enters. And propositional knowledge alone could never account for a capacity to introduce what is pertinent. The paragraph in question is concerned with "some salient points at which [the] regress would arise" (1949, 30–31).

15. Let me contrast Stanley and Williamson's interpretation of Ryle's argument with my own. They take Ryle to invoke the following two premises:

(1). If one Fs, one employs knowledge-how to F; and
(2). If one employs knowledge that p, one contemplates the proposition that p.

They see Ryle as arguing that (1) and (2) combine with the claim that knowing how to do something is propositional to give a regress. But no regress can be generated from (1) and (2), they say, because (1) is plausible only if instances of 'F' are confined to things intentionally done, and (2) then is false: "It is simply false that manifestations of knowledge-that must be accompanied by distinct actions of contemplating propositions" (Stanley and Williamson 2001, 415). Well, inasmuch as Ryle's argument concerns reasoning as well as acting, it isn't likely that he was concerned with conditions on anything's being done *intentionally*. And Ryle does not speak of contemplating propositions in chapter 2 of 1949; his word there is 'consider'. (He uses 'contemplate' sometimes in 1945; see note 7 on this.)

On my reading of Ryle's argument, if it is given the sort of shape that Stanley and Williamson give it, then the scope of premise (1) will be the class of Ryle's 'intelligent performances,' encompassing both reasoning and acting intentionally. So the instances of 'F' are things such that *reason* is at work in doing them. Premise (2) then records Ryle's claim that when a proposition is considered, reason *does no work* (there is no modification of mind, as I put it earlier). There is now a potential regress, because the intellectualist who tries introducing knowledge-that to meet the condition of reason's being at work in doing something fails to meet it; and his only recourse is to introduce further knowledge-that, and then yet more knowledge-that....

is exhausted by propositional knowledge. Suppose that actually you turn the door knob perfectly efficiently but that it might have been that the knob had needed to be turned very slightly further than you would have thought when you started to turn it. Given that you knew how to turn the knob to open the door, you would, in these slightly altered circumstances, have turned it slightly further than actually you did. Rather than enabling your participation simply in the event of your turning the knob that actually there was, your knowledge how to turn a door knob ensures that you would turn the knob in an appropriate way in a range of circumstances. Nonpropositional knowledge-how apparently plays a role even in a case like this, where the idea that someone's doing something is a token event is at its most plausible.

But however this may be, an account of agency can hardly be confined to such actions as are plausibly called token events. A list of events in which a person participated over a period of time would evidently fall far short of saying what the person had been doing over the period. And even something as simple as opening the door is hardly a once-off occurrence. People who open a door typically make their way to the door, position themselves appropriately, reach for the knob and grasp it with a hand, turn the knob, and push or pull as required. And each of these things may make slightly different demands on them in different circumstances. If one has what it takes to open a door intentionally, then one has whatever knowledge is needed to see one through the process of getting a door open in a range of circumstances. Once it is allowed that there is a place for know-how in an account of agency, it comes to seem doubtful that the account should concern itself much with token events.

None of this is to deny that propositional knowledge belongs in a story of human agency. Propositional knowledge very obviously does have a place there, since those who act for reasons know the reason for which they act. And unless there were propositions about ways of doing things, it would be impossible to inform someone about how to do this or that. So of course, there can be nothing wrong with thinking that someone who knows how to open some door may know that one gets it open by (inter alia) turning the knob. But just as it did not interfere with Ryle's argument about reasoning to allow that rules of inference may be formulated propositionally, so it need not interfere with a conception of knowledge-how as exercised in action to allow that one knows plenty of propositions that record one's ways of doing things.

Sometimes a piece of information makes all the difference to whether someone is able to do something. For example, you might know everything you need to know to get the door open, save that one has to turn this knob *counter* clockwise and *pull*. A particular piece of propositional knowledge becomes salient when one thinks about such a case, and then one can easily be misled into thinking that propositional knowledge is what acting requires. One then forgets about everything that enables us to find our way about and to act on objects we encounter everyday. In the ordinary way, we take this all for granted. If people need to know how the door is opened, it can be taken for granted that they already know how to reach out an arm so as to put a hand on the knob. If someone needs to know which stop the bus to the train station goes from, it can be taken for granted that they already know how to make their way to a bus stop, how to board a bus, and so on. We leave out the obvious. So we may forget that pieces of propositional knowledge are not applied in isolation.[16]

There are good questions about how much of what we do we are enabled to do by possessing *knowledge*. I allowed that some will doubt that we *know* how to reason. And it might also be put in question whether there is any call to bring under an *epistemic* head the various abilities—to move parts of one's body, to manipulate objects—that are typically possessed by human adults. But perhaps when one thinks about everything needed in a full account of what we actually rely on as agents, nonpropositional knowledge will appear to be ubiquitous and as ineliminable from an account of action as Ryle held it to be from an account of reasoning. At any rate, the questions here relate to how much nonpropositional know-how we have. Ryle left it in no doubt that at least we all have plenty.[17]

3.2

Ryle confined himself to activities and spoke of *processes* of doing; he said nothing about the types of action on which some philosophers of action have come to tend to concentrate—opening doors, turning on lights, and the like. I've suggested that those who treat actions as token events leave processes out of the picture and that this makes it easier for them to leave knowledge-how out of account. It might then be thought that treating actions as token events would help them in avoiding the anti-Cartesian message of Ryle's argument. But I think that their denial of genuine knowledge-how actually puts them on the side of Ryle's Cartesians.

---

16. For the "manifold relations of interdependence" between knowledge-that and knowledge-how and for a range of much more interesting examples, see Wiggins (2009).

17. Much more would need to be said to settle these questions. And we won't find answers in Ryle. By associating 'theory' closely with 'Reason,' Ryle left no place for *practical reason*. And his disdain of self-knowledge ensures that the knowledge an agent has in acting is left out of account. It is no wonder that his anti-Cartesianism appears so different from Anscombe's; cf. note 6. (Ryle [1949, 177] comes closest to Anscombe's way of thinking when he speaks of someone who is active as "alive to what he is doing.")

Here is Ryle's diagnosis of the errors of his Cartesian opponents.

> [They are] drawn to believe...that the intelligent execution of an operation must embody two processes, one of doing and another of theorizing... Since doing is often an overt muscular affair, it is written off as a merely physical process. On the assumption of the antithesis between 'physical' and 'mental', it follows that muscular doing cannot itself be a mental operation. (1949, 32)

Ryle imagined his opponents as envisaging two processes running in parallel to achieve a separation of "mental" from "merely physical." But the assumption of an antithesis between mental and physical can be in place even when no processes of acting are envisaged.

In the events-based story of action that has informed most analytical philosophy of mind for most of the last sixty years, the token events that are actions are those bodily movements that are caused and rationalized by the agent's beliefs and desires. As the story is standardly told, knowledge does not come in at all.[18] But the contents of the beliefs that belong in the story are exactly those propositions that, according to Stanley and Williamson, are known by someone who knows how to do something: the beliefs are to the effect that one thing may be done by doing another—that this is a way of doing that. Thus the pieces of propositional knowledge that purport to do duty for knowing-how in Stanley and Williamson's treatment are cut out for exactly the job of the standard story's beliefs—the job of mental states that cause bodily, physical movements.

Whereas Ryle's Cartesians thought of propositional knowledge as somehow steering bodily activity, in the events-based conception, pieces of propositional knowledge (or, in a more standard version, beliefs) are presumably to be thought of as somehow triggering bodily movements.[19] In both accounts, the bodily

---

18. Those who tell the story might need to be persuaded that *knowledge* should come in at all, never mind *knowledge-how* specifically. For arguments that it must be brought in, see Gibbons (2001), Hawthorne and Stanley (2008), and Hornsby (2008). And it is in keeping with Williamson's epistemology to suppose that knowledge-*that* will come in.

Some may wish to say that Φ-ing intentionally requires knowledge how to Φ, but Setiya (2008) offers what he takes to be counterexamples. At any rate, something weaker will be enough to make a connection between action and knowledge-how—for example, that Φ-ing intentionally requires knowledge of how to do something that is taken to be a possible means of Φ-ing.

19. Frankfurt says something to show why triggering, rather than steering, would seem apt for the role of mental states in the events-based conception: "Events are caused by preceding states of affairs, but an event cannot be guided through the course of its occurrence at a temporal distance" (1978, 158).

goings-on can safely be taken to be "physical," for they are treated as the activities, or actions, of an intelligent being only insofar as they are steered, or triggered, by states of mind. But then one may want to object to those who adduce properties of token events in order to assimilate knowing-how to propositional knowledge on the same grounds as Ryle objected to his Cartesians. They treat actions as "effects of intellectual operations" rather than as "directly displaying qualities of mind."[20]

---

20. I thank Adrian Haddock, David Ruben, and David Wiggins for helpful discussion of some of the material here.

PART II

Philosophical Considerations

4

Practical Expertise

Julia Annas

HERE ARE TWO examples of activities. We can see a commonsense distinction between them, which I shall argue is of more than commonsense importance.

I drive my car to the university parking garage for which I have a permit. I do this nearly every day and have done so for years; I am familiar with the route I take and so would not hesitate to say that I know how to drive to my parking garage. When I started to drive this route, it was unfamiliar, and I had to think consciously about the best way to do it, balancing factors like directness of route against avoiding traffic, and the like. Gradually, I became used to driving on this route, and it has become habit with me. I no longer have to think about which way to turn at each corner, where to slow down, and the like. My driving has become routine. This does not make it mindless; I am still at some level aware of where I am going, since I stop at red lights, drive at the right speed, and behave cautiously around dangerous drivers. But driving has become detached from my conscious thinking, and my actual conscious thoughts and deliberations may fail to be properly integrated with it. We all recognize the phenomenon of finding yourself at the garage, having started out intending to go somewhere else en route, but not having done so, or finding yourself at the usual entrance, which is closed, although you know perfectly well already that it is closed for construction. A decision to act differently from the usual has not successfully penetrated and affected the patterns of routine, which have carried on unaffected.

Contrast this with a skilled pianist playing a piece. (This, unlike the routine example, is not autobiographical, although I used to play the piano; readers are invited to substitute different examples if these make the point work better for them.) As I learn to play the piano, I need first to work out consciously what is the right thing to do and then do it over and over again. This proceeds from learning notes to learning scales, arpeggios, and so on and eventually learning to play whole pieces. Here there is habituation that results in my coming to be able to do effortlessly and without conscious deliberation what at first had to be explicitly worked out. My fingers now pick out the right notes in the right relation to one another at the right speed, without need for conscious thinking before each action of striking the keys. When we consider the speed with which an expert pianist plays the notes, we might be tempted to think that the original experience has been transformed into routine. But there is a difference from the driving case. While it is true that my ability to play expertly may require that I have developed some physical capacities in my fingers such that certain movements are 'automatic,' the playing itself is not routine or automatic—or rather, if it is, my playing is not expert. For one thing, the expertise is not detached from the person's ability to think and decide consciously; the playing is continually responsive to my thought about the piece, my decisions to speed up or slow down, and the like. If I resolve to play the first movement more feelingly and romantically than usual, I won't find myself at the end of it having played it the usual way or, again, if I do, this is a failure of expertise. Rather, my playing is constantly informed by and sensitive to my thinking in a way that produces, and is in turn responsive to, feedback. The expertise is not a static given; it is dynamic and always developing. It decays, is sustained, or is modified, depending on the conditions of its exercise. Routine, on the other hand, once developed to the point of adequacy, stays where it is.

The key difference here is between habituation that results in mere habit and routine and habituation that results in a dynamic trait that expresses itself in intelligent and selective response. It is central to routine that the reaction to the relevant situation is always the same; this is why routine is predictable and dependable, which is often useful. The second type of habituation, however, results in reactions that differentiate among, and are appropriate to, different situations.

This distinction is not well marked in our ordinary discourse about habits (even the word *habituation* is artificial). It is not respected in contemporary psychological research on automaticity.[1] And it has, as far as I know, made almost no impact on contemporary philosophical debates about practical expertise and reasoning, except in the discussion of Aristotelian themes. Why then press it?

It seems important in itself, once we notice that speed and immediacy of reaction can be found in two such diverse contexts. This should at least arouse our curiosity as to the different kinds of habituation that result in such different abilities as routinization and intelligent response. Further, we can, as I noted, say both that I know how to drive to my garage and that I know how to play the Schubert *Wanderer* fantasy. Given the sharp differences between these kinds of 'knowing how,' we should be curious as to the different notions here of 'know-how.'

---

1. The work of psychologists like John Bargh—as in the influential 'The Unbearable Automaticity of Being' (Bargh and Chartrand 1999)—makes no distinction between the automaticity resulting from routine and the immediate response resulting from developed practical expertise.

In this chapter, I shall be following up one of them, hoping that this makes a contribution to contemporary discussions of know-how. I shall be focusing on the kind of habituation that results in the second kind of case I sketched. Rather than routine, this kind of habituation results in *practical expertise*.

In this account, I have been heavily influenced by the role in ancient epistemology and ethics of what has been labeled 'the skill analogy.' It is a commonplace in study of ancient philosophy that ancient accounts of knowledge and of virtue were influenced by the notion of *techne*, translated 'craft,' 'skill,' or 'expertise.' I shall not, however, be trying to do anything like transpose the ancient notion of skill into a contemporary setting. Apart from the general anachronism of any such proceeding, we have to be aware of the point that practical skills played a very different role in the ancient world from any that they play in an industrial (and postindustrial) world, so that skill no longer seems to us an interesting source of analogy. One mark of this is that the idea of practical skill or expertise in the ancient world centered on a few central and agreed examples: medicine, farming, navigating, shoe making, and so on.[2] For us, these are examples of activities that have either been mechanized or now depend in large part on theoretical scientific knowledge. Our central examples of practical expertise are more likely to come from sports or the arts, and so they are less central to daily living and our employments.[3] This does not lessen the philosophical interest of practical expertise, but it renders it less obvious for us. Moreover, our notion of *skill* has expanded, sometimes in ways that take it far from the idea of practical expertise; we talk of social skills and also of children's skill in tying their shoelaces and so on. We sometimes talk of skill in contexts where natural talent plays a crucial role, as in sporting skills. And the idea of *craft* has become marginalized; we expect craft products and craftspeople to be working in a niche rather than in the center of the economy.[4] For these and other reasons, I will not be trying to capture the ancient notion of skill but rather developing from it an account of practical expertise as one kind of the phenomenon we call 'know-how.' I will then indicate briefly ways in which this has been found to be of philosophical interest.

---

2. Socrates in Plato's 'Socratic' dialogues is constantly using examples of this kind. At *Gorgias* 491, the aristocratic Callicles accuses Socrates of always talking about 'cobblers, fullers, cooks and doctors' (Socrates has just been using the examples of weavers and farmers).

3. This issue, and some others about ancient and modern conceptions of skills, is discussed in my 'Virtue as a Skill' (1995).

4. Perhaps it is worth pointing out that in some cultures this has not diminished the former respect in which craftspeople were held; in Japan, for example, some craftsmen and women in ceramics and textiles are still valued as 'living national treasures.' This seems to be the exception, however.

I will be relying heavily on unpacking, and coming to understand, our everyday conception of practical expertise, and the question can quite rightly be raised of why we should pay any attention to this when we are doing philosophy. One answer is that when we think about practical expertise, we are at an advantage, for we have it to hand. Even if I cannot myself fix the computer, mend the car, plumb in the washing-machine, I know what is needed and understand the difference between it and muddling through, fixing things inexpertly, and hoping for the best. Moreover, most of us do have some kind of practical expertise ourselves. We have a better idea from our own experience of what practical expertise is, then, than we do of the more abstract idea of 'know-how,' still less of the conception of knowledge that interests philosophers, and practical expertise appears to be at least a promising place to start investigating.

What most strikingly characterizes practical expertise is that acquiring it necessitates two factors that might at first sight not go well together. One is the need to learn; the other is the drive to aspire. The need to learn seems obvious enough, but it is worth noting an implication it has, one pointed out by Aristotle.

> What we need to learn to do, we learn by doing; for example, we become builders by building, and lyre-players by playing the lyre. (Aristotle 350 B.C.E./2000)

There is something we lack and have to have conveyed to us by teachers. We don't know what to do and have to learn what to do by doing what somebody else does, someone who does know what to do. We begin to learn by copying them, as we try to do what they do.

But even with a comparatively nonintellectual skill like building, I will have failed to learn if I *just* copy the teacher and take 'doing what he does' to be a matter of routine to be established. The teacher tries to get the learner precisely *not* to establish a routine of doing what the teacher does. A piano student who faithfully copies the teacher's way of playing ends up impersonating the teacher, mannerisms and all, and this is clearly a failure to learn, not a success. The successful learner of a practical skill needs to do three things.

First, he needs to *understand* what in the role model to follow. The mindless learner copies the teacher, mannerisms and all; the successful learner works out what in the teacher's performance is important to the expertise and what is not and copies the former, coming to ignore the latter. This is the point at which expertise becomes divided off from routine performances. We learn to tie our shoelaces as a matter of routine, and we do pick up, harmlessly, the idiosyncrasies of the person who taught us. Shoelace tying is not a matter of sufficient complexity that we need to understand what is crucial in it.

Second, the point of understanding what is crucial to pick up in what the teacher does is that the learner should be able to acquire *for herself* the skill the teacher has. The successful learner goes on to do what is in one sense the same thing the teacher did, but not in a blankly routine way. The apprentice builder learns to do what the expert builder does—that is, to build—but at a more specific and concrete level what he is doing may in many respects be different from the actual steps taken by the teacher, the steps from which she learned to build. This underlines the further point that routine reaches a plateau, beyond which further input and thinking is not needed, whereas this is not true of practical expertise. The moment comes when you have to speak French, bicycle, dance on your own; this is notoriously the moment when it becomes clear whether you have actually learned the skill. Self-direction leads naturally from understanding; you need understanding to be able to carry on for yourself in dancing, speaking French, or building, and understanding enables self-direction rather than remaining on a plateau of routine.

Third, the successful learner strives to improve, to do what he is doing better, rather than being satisfied by taking it over by rote from the teacher. This is what a lot of practice is about; we do what is in some sense 'the same thing' over and over, but not to perfect the routinization of a movement. Rather, we are learning to speak French, skate, or drive, *better*. Again, this distinguishes cases where all that is required is repetition and routine from cases where staying at that level signifies failure to learn. The point about improvement links naturally to the other two points; you can improve because you understand what it is, in what you are learning, that you, rather than the teacher, can improve.

It might be objected that an expertise cannot always continue to demand a drive to improve; doesn't there come a point at which you can speak fluent German, drive, skate, or whatever? At this point, the drive to improve recedes, but with a practical expertise, it never entirely disappears. Expert golfers, tennis players, and flautists continue to practice to maintain and not lose the expertise they have (though they may maintain routine mastery of technical matters needed for the exercise of the skill). A practical expertise is never static in the way that a routine habit is, so even experts face the same issues as learners, though in a modified form.

All three of these points indicate aspects of the drive to aspire, which marks off the acquisition of practical expertise from the development of routine, while both require learning something you previously didn't know. These points about learning may seem commonplace, but their implications are important: there is a kind of 'know-how' for which it is important to note the development from learner to expert, with no plateau at which the ability is routinized.

Other aspects of practical skill converge with this result. One is the role of enjoyment. Intuitively, practical expertise gives us examples of increasing enjoyment as a skill develops. As we begin to learn a practical expertise—learning Italian, tennis, skating—we are held back by not being able to do it very well, and when this happens, we are frustrated and find the activity unpleasant. Who enjoys getting tenses wrong and hitting balls into the net? As we improve at Italian or tennis, we enjoy doing it more because we are less frustrated by inadequacies and mistakes and have fewer occasions when we fail to exercise the expertise. Playing tennis is painful and annoying as long as your performance comes up short of your intentions; speaking Italian is painful and annoying as long as you have to make a conscious effort to find the right words and get the sentence construction right. As we improve in both cases, the skill is exercised more smoothly and successfully, and we come to enjoy its exercise. An indication of this is that conscious thought is no longer required for me to exercise the expertise successfully.

But if conscious thought is no longer required, have we not admitted that the skill has become routine? No. We can begin to see why, by thinking of activities that really are routine, like driving a familiar route, getting dressed and undressed, or tying shoelaces. These are not examples of enjoyable activities. It is indeed a mark of practical expertise, as opposed to routine, that it can become enjoyable. This intuitive point has been supported by the work of the positive psychologist Mihalyi Csikszentmihalyi, who has for many decades studied what makes people experience activity as satisfying and enjoyable.[5]

We perhaps tend to think that we enjoy ourselves most when we are relaxed and not working, at least not engaged in work that requires effort. For us 'leisure,' understood as freedom from work, is desirable. Csikszentmihalyi's research shows, strikingly, that we need to rethink this. What he calls 'optimal experience,' the experience of enjoyment and satisfaction, is experienced not when we are inactive but rather when we are engaged in activity in an intelligent and concerned way. We enjoy what we are doing when we can "focus attention at will…be oblivious to distractions…concentrate for as long as it takes to achieve a goal, and not longer" (Csikszentmihalyi 1991, 31). Mere repetition and rote activities leave us bored and frustrated, whereas we enjoy being engaged in complex activities like puzzle setting and problem solving.

Enjoyment is felt most when we are engaged in goal-directed activities, where achieving the goal typically involves responding to feedback and picking up on new features created by the solution of the previous problem. Enjoyment is threatened, however, by frustration caused by new information the person doesn't know how to deal with. This applies especially to achieving one goal at the cost of others. Enjoyment is most achieved when all the person's relevant goals are

---

5. Csikszentmihalyi (1991), summarizing much previous research.

harmoniously organized and sorted out, so that she is equipped to deal with feedback and new information without having to stop to figure out how it relates to the goal being pursued.

> Every piece of information we process gets evaluated for its bearings on the self. Does it threaten our goals, does it support them or is it neutral?... A new piece of information will either create disorder in consciousness...or it will reinforce our goals, thereby freeing up psychic energy. (Csikszentmihalyi 1991, 39)

So when all the relevant goals are harmoniously structured and the person is focusing on the achievement of a goal that requires engagement with the situation,

> attention can be freely invested to achieve a person's goals, because there is no disorder to straighten our, no threat for the self to defend against. We have called this state the *flow experience*. (Csikszentmihalyi 1991, 39)

This interesting result can be related to the distinction I have been sketching. The routine driving to the parking garage is not something I give my attention to, and it goes on in a way sometimes independent of my actual deliberations. It is not well integrated with new goals, such as going somewhere else on the way, as there is no feedback to keep me aware of the need to drive a different route. It is not an enjoyable experience, as there is nothing to produce flow, in Csikszentmihalyi's sense. We can see how different is the case of the skilled pianist. The skill she exercises is the result of a lot of habituation, but the result is not routine. The way she plays the piece expresses the intelligence of her interpretation of it; the playing is responsive to the interpretation, and the activity has the structure in which flow can be produced. And skilled piano playing, like skilled exercise of golf, skating, translating, and many others, can be, and often is, enjoyable. 'Flow' is perhaps not the best metaphor for what Csikszentmihalyi is talking about here, for it brings to mind passively going with the flow, which suggests activities like my routine driving. What is meant by flow requires the opposite: engagement in a task in a way characteristic of experts,[6] in a way requiring attention and continual modification of activity.

The 'flow' experience has two important features. It is 'autotelic': that is, the activity is experienced as being its own end, enjoyed in itself even where in fact

---

6. Csikszentmihalyi himself is not explicit about dealing with skills, but this is what his examples overwhelmingly show.

the activity produces something further. Here sporting activities produce good examples: actions in some sports can be experienced as enjoyable in themselves even if they do not produce the goal, or whatever. The other feature is that persons engaged in the activity lose awareness of their selves—that is, they cease to be aware of themselves as performing the activity (and so may lose track of the time passing). Again, this lack of self-consciousness is most easily illustrated from trained athletes, who often report a sense of 'loss of ego' as they are engaged in running or throwing the javelin. 'Flow' is produced when we have a combination of intense focus and loss of self-consciousness. Nothing could be further from the blankness experienced in routine activity.[7]

The role of enjoyment in activity, then, gives us a further way in which routine activities differ from practical expertise. Routine activities do not characteristically produce 'flow,' since there is nothing requiring focus and engagement. It is intense engagement in skilled and expert activities that produces the loss of self-consciousness characterizing flow. We have here an interesting empirical confirmation of an intuitive distinction between routine habits and practical expertise, namely, that the latter are characteristically enjoyable, and the former are not.

Another point where an intuitive difference turns out to unpack into a philosophically significant divergence is a difference in the structure of learning between routine habits and practical expertise. When I pick up a routine habit, I need to do nothing but copy my role model, or sometimes just develop my own habit of doing the same thing over and over. There is no content to my learning over and above my being able to repeat the same activity without thinking about it. With practical expertise, more is needed. Something has to be conveyed from the teacher to the learner that cannot be reduced to the teacher's showing the learner something to repeat. What is this? The learner has to come to understand what to emulate in the teacher's activity in order to take it over for herself. We could call this, very generally, the point of the activity. This could just be the obvious aim, or it could be more complex, involving grasp of rules or principles. The more complex the activity, the more is involved in coming to understand its point.

In ancient philosophy, what characterizes skill or expertise, as opposed to merely having a subrational 'knack' or routine, is the ability to 'give an account,' where this means to explain the point of what you are doing, why you are doing this rather than that.[8] Someone who isn't able to do this thereby reveals that he

---

7. A great deal of Csikszentmihalyi's own work is trying to systematize ways of turning boring, frustrating routine work into challenging and flow-encouraging work.

8. For notable examples, see Plato's *Gorgias* (462d–465a and 501–501d) and the opening chapters of Aristotle's *Metaphysics* A.

doesn't understand what he is doing (though he might, of course, still get things right if all that is required is a subrational routine). Does this answer to anything that might be found convincing in contemporary terms? If we think of how practical expertise is actually conveyed, we see at once the importance here of the giving and understanding of reasons. The apprentice builder or plumber needs to know not just *that* you lay the pipe this way, but *why*. Only by being given reasons for laying the pipe this way rather than that will she be able to distinguish relevant from irrelevant factors in the situation in which she has seen the pipe laid, and only if she has a grasp of this will she be able to lay pipe in different situations without doing it in ways relevant to the original situation but inappropriate in the new one. Reasons here are the medium of explanation; the teacher can, by giving reasons for what she does, explain to the learner why she must wire or lay pipe in such and such a way, so that the learner can then go ahead in different situations without routinely doing the exact same thing in all of them. Clearly, in cases above a certain level of complexity, explanation is necessary, or the learner will not get the point at all; there are many ways in which we can focus on irrelevant aspects of what the teacher is doing.

This giving and understanding of reasons implies that practical expertise implies some degree of articulacy. This claim frequently meets with resistance, on the grounds that we recognize cases of expertise or skill where articulacy is not necessary (frequently gardening is proffered as an example) or where it may not seem feasible (people with physical skills are often unable to coach others who wish to acquire those skills). Many of these cases are really cases of natural talent or of mastery of technical matters needed for exercise of the skill. In any case, we have already seen that contemporary usage of the notion of skill or expertise is quite broad, and it is no surprise that it does not cover all and only the kinds of expertise that we have been looking at so far; these are the cases that I am interested in, where we can see a sharp distinction between practical expertise and mere routine, despite some apparent shared characteristics.

The articulacy requirement can appear quite problematic, however convincing it may seem in the context of learning a practical expertise. It can seem especially so if we think in terms of 'knowing how' and 'knowing that.' Obviously, a prominent feature of practical expertise is that it involves a development from the learner to the expert, and so it cannot be thought of as a kind of 'knowing how' that excludes 'knowing that.' It is routine habit that could be thought of as 'knowing how' with no 'knowing that'—precisely what is contrasted with practical expertise. Where expertise is concerned, we are happy to say that the mechanic knows how to fix the car, if he is an expert; if he is not an expert, then he doesn't know how to fix the car, though he might be able to follow the instructions of someone who does know. And the issue of whether he is, in fact, an expert is settled by whether he can give reasons for what he does.

The main problem, however, is that the articulacy requirement seems to sit uneasily with the fact that practical expertise is exercised readily and without hesitation, with an immediacy that seems not to leave psychological room for the entertaining of reasons. Indeed, it is exactly this immediacy that forms the basis for the point that expertise can involve enjoyable activity, when you are so engaged in the complexity of the task that you lose awareness of yourself as performing the activity. How can this immediacy of engagement go with the idea that practical expertise requires the giving and understanding of reasons? The articulacy requirement seems outrageously intellectualist.

The answer to this is obvious by now. The account of practical expertise is a developmental one. At first, the builder or pianist does need to learn by being given reasons for what he does. The pianist acquires skill first by consciously thinking what to do and will at first be running through thoughts about reasons the teacher has given him for playing the arpeggio one way rather than another, adjusting the left-hand speed, and so on; these in fact form the basis for his practicing. If this is not the case, he is merely acquiring a routine habit and will never acquire the skill. Understanding what you are doing is acquired by thinking before acting in ways that incorporate what has been learned, and understanding is increased as it leads to, and is in turn reinforced by, increased self-direction and improvement. This is just a fact of experience, familiar to anyone who learns a practical expertise. An equally familiar fact of experience is that as you improve, you need to think less and less about what you are doing. As the pianist improves, he needs less and less to think what fingering the next chords will require, how to balance what the two hands are playing, and so on. Eventually, the expert pianist will play with a speed and immediacy utterly different from the thought-requiring plodding of the beginner. We have already had underlined the point that the speed and directness of response may seem from the outside comparable to those of habituated routine activity but that there is a huge difference: in the case of practical expertise, the thoughts that have gone into the development of the skill now inform and educate the way the skill is exercised, so that the exercise of piano playing, building, or whatever involves educated rather than mindless response. Moreover, the response, however direct and immediate, is sensitive to situations and thus flexible in the way it reacts to modifications in them. The thoughts required in learning do not get in the way of this. They have, in a useful philosophical term, effaced themselves.

However, does this in turn not leave us with a problem? If the articulacy requirement applies only to the learning of practical expertise, and not its expert exercise, then it seems to play no role in bringing about the actual expert activity, and we might well wonder whether it should enter into an account of what practical expertise itself is. Here again, though, it emerges that a contrast with routine is helpful. The original thoughts about driving on my route clearly play no role now in my driving to my parking garage; this is what makes it a case of routine. Moreover, they are not readily recoverable, either. If someone asks me whether the route I drive is the best, I will have to detach myself from my ongoing practice and work out whether this is the case. It may be that my route no longer is the best, since I have been driving it routinely, rather than in a way sensitive to new input. With practical expertise, on the other hand, the thoughts have effaced themselves, but they have not entirely evaporated. If the expert meets with an unusually stubborn problem, for example, thoughts about the best way to cope with this sort of situation will be available to her without her having to detach herself from the activity and start over with the investigating. Most important, these thoughts become available when the expert teaches a nonexpert or explains the skilled activity to her. A skill taught to one person is conveyable through that person to someone else.

This is a matter of degree, since it is a further commonplace that not everyone is equally good as a teacher. There are also other factors: with physical skills, a large part of the accomplishment may be due to natural talent; the outstanding physical performer may not be a good teacher, since much of his performance is not due to learned factors. Still, if someone is an expert practitioner of a skill, but when asked to explain how to do it or what makes for a good or a bad exercise of the skill can say absolutely nothing helpful, we infer that she is not good at articulating what she knows or that what appears to be expertise may in fact be natural talent or even routine. We don't infer that there is nothing to articulate. A plumber or car mechanic who can explain nothing whatever about the way he has fixed the leak, or the car, soon loses our confidence; we judge that he doesn't know what he is doing. The same is even more strikingly true of a computer help line.

So far, I have sketched a notion that may seem commonplace, one we are all familiar with when we need an expert to fix the computer, translate the Latin, or rebuild the wall. What we want is someone with practical expertise, not with the kind of 'know-how' that is mere routinized habit and brings with it no ability to explain and teach what is being done. Is this philosophically interesting?

First, this notion of practical expertise was extremely influential in two areas of ancient philosophy that have recently made some impact on contemporary philosophizing. One is that of knowledge. It is a commonplace among ancient philosophers that for Plato (to take only one example) the model of having knowledge, at least in the so-called 'Socratic' dialogues, is that of the person with a *techne* or practical skill, who knows what he is doing and can thus 'give an account' of what he says and does. Socrates' interlocutors are shown up time and again as people who make claims to knowledge but lack it because they cannot 'give an account' when challenged of what they say and do. They pontificate about virtue, or piety, but it turns out that they don't know what they are talking about.[9]

Second, accounts in ancient ethics of virtue draw heavily on 'the skill analogy'—the idea, that is, that virtue has the intellectual structure of a practical expertise. Some ethical theorists take the analogy further than others; Aristotle thinks that there are definite limits to it, while the Stoics think of virtue as 'the expertise of living.' What interests them all are the aspects of practical expertise I have highlighted, which turn out to prove illuminating for an account of virtue. There are, of course, aspects of virtue that have no echo in practical expertise, and vice versa; for all that, 'the skill analogy' is central to all ancient accounts of virtue.

I do not have the scope here to follow up these philosophical fortunes of practical expertise, but I think it is interesting that the relevant accounts both of knowledge and of virtue have recently become familiar in contemporary discussions otherwise completely unlike the ancient ones. One important point that we may find more salient if we take practical expertise seriously is that simple talk of 'knowing how,' especially if it is assumed to be opposed to, or always in some kind of contrast with, 'knowing that,' can blind us to the importance of recognizing different kinds of knowing how to do things. In particular, it can lead us to overlook the interesting combination I have claimed that we find in practical expertise. Here we find immediate and direct response, which looks superficially like the immediate and direct response of routine, but which is actually sensitive to modifications in the situation, intelligent and educated. Taking these points about practical expertise seriously may enrich the thoughts we have today about the ways we engage with the world in practice and the different types of ability that we classify together as 'know-how.'

---

9. I discuss this side of the 'skill analogy' in my 'Virtue as a Skill' (1995) and some other aspects in 'Moral Knowledge as Practical Knowledge' (2001).

5

Knowing How without Knowing That

Yuri Cath

WHAT IS KNOWLEDGE-HOW? One prominent view, often known as *intellectualism*, is that knowledge-how is a species, kind, or sort of knowledge-that. More precisely, intellectualists hold that one knows how to ϕ if and only if one stands in the knowledge-that relation to some relevant proposition, and (on some variations of this view) one may also have to satisfy some further condition. In what follows, I present and then examine three new arguments by counterexample against intellectualism, so understood. Each putative counterexample is intended to be a scenario where a subject knows how to ϕ and yet fails to know that p, for any proposition p such that their knowing how to ϕ might plausibly be equated (partly or wholly) with their knowing that p. More cautiously, the subject in each scenario fails to possess the relevant knowledge-that if a standard assumption about the nature of knowledge-that is correct. The scenarios differ with respect to the assumption in question.

1. Three Putative Counterexamples

To see why the cases I will discuss are putative counterexamples, it will help to have an actual intellectualist account of knowledge-how in mind. I shall focus on Stanley and Williamson's influential account of knowledge-how as "simply a species of propositional knowledge" (Stanley and Williamson 2001, 441). Stanley and Williamson (henceforth S&W) argue that the truth conditions of 'S knows how to ϕ' ascriptions conform to the following schema:

> 'S knows how to ϕ' is true in a context *c* if and only if there is some contextually relevant way *w* for S to ϕ such that:
> (a) S stands in knowledge-that relation to the proposition that *w* is a way for S to ϕ, and
> (b) S entertains the proposition that *w* is a way for S to ϕ under a practical mode of presentation.[1]

On the basis of this analysis of knowledge-how ascriptions, S&W (2001, 435) adopt an intellectualist view of knowledge-how, according to which "knowing how to F is a matter of knowing that p, for a certain proposition p (as well as entertaining it under the right mode of presentation)." For example, on S&W's view, Shane Warne knows how to bowl a googly if and only if there is some way w such that Shane knows, under a practical mode of presentation, that w is a way for him to bowl a googly.

With S&W's account in mind, I can introduce our three putative counterexamples to intellectualism. I take each example to be a case where knowledge-how *comes apart* from knowledge-that, that is, a case where someone knows how to ϕ, but there is no proposition p concerning a way to ϕ such that their knowing how to ϕ might be plausibly equated (partly or wholly) with their knowing that p. The first example is a case where intuitively someone knows how to ϕ, but they do not possess the kind of knowledge-that that such knowledge-how might be plausibly equated with, because their relevant beliefs are only *accidentally true*. S&W (2001, 435) and Poston (2009) discuss similar cases. But neither author discusses the possibility that such cases might constitute *counterexamples* to intellectualism (a point I will return to).[2]

The second and third cases are each of a kind that has not been discussed before. The second case is a scenario where intuitively someone knows how to ϕ,

---

1. Conditions (a) and (b) accurately reflect S&W's most explicit statement of their view (see 430). However, I think S&W should actually state (b) as something like: (b*) *In standing in this relation* S entertains the proposition that w is a way for S to ϕ under a practical mode of presentation. The reason is that there will likely be possible cases where a subject S only stands in the knowledge-that relation to the proposition that w is a way for S to ϕ under a nonpractical mode of presentation, but S does entertain this proposition under a practical mode of presentation when they stand in some other intentional relation to it. (I assume this because it is easy to describe cases with this structure for other modes of presentation.) And presumably, S&W would not want to say that one knows how to ϕ in such a scenario. This is why I think S&W are best interpreted as not actually making the conjunctive claim: 'S knows how to ϕ' is true in a context c iff there is some contextually relevant way w such that S knows that w is a way for S to ϕ *and* S entertains this proposition under a practical mode of presentation. Rather, S&W should only be interpreted as making the claim: 'S knows how to ϕ' is true in a context c iff there is some contextually relevant way w such that Hannah *knows, under a practical mode of presentation*, that w is a way for S to ϕ. (S&W use both claims to describe their view at different points, which suggests that they assume them to be equivalent. But if the kind of scenario just described is possible, then the latter claim can be false even when the former claim is true.) And I think what the latter claim amounts to is the claim we get when we replace (b) with something like (b*).

2. Aidan McGlynn (2007), on his blog *The Boundaries of Language*, makes a similar point with respect to S&W's discussion of this first kind of case.

but they do not possess the kind of knowledge-that that this knowledge-how might be plausibly equated with because their relevant beliefs are *defeated*. The third case is a scenario where intuitively someone knows how to φ, but in this case they do not possess the kind of knowledge-that that this knowledge-how might be plausibly equated with because they *lack* the relevant beliefs.[3] Here, then, are our three putative counterexamples:

> *The Lucky Light Bulb*: Charlie wants to learn how to change a light bulb, but he knows almost nothing about light fixtures or bulbs (as he has only ever seen light bulbs already installed, and so he has never seen the end of a light bulb or the inside of a light fixture). To remedy this situation, Charlie consults *The Idiot's Guide to Everyday Jobs*. Inside, he finds an accurate set of instructions describing the shape of a light fixture and bulb and the way to change a bulb. Charlie grasps these instructions perfectly. And so there is a way, call it 'w_1' such that Charlie now believes that w_1 is a way for him to change a light bulb, namely, the way described in the book. However, unbeknownst to Charlie, he is extremely lucky to have read these instructions, for the disgruntled author of *The Idiot's Guide* filled her book with misleading instructions. Under every entry, she intentionally misdescribed the objects involved in that job and described a series of actions that would not constitute a way to do the job at all. However, at the printers, a computer error caused the text under the entry for 'Changing a Light Bulb,' in just one copy of the book, to be randomly replaced by new text. By incredible coincidence, this new text provided the clear and accurate set of instructions that Charlie would later consult.
>
> *The Dogmatic Hallucinator*: Lucy occasionally suffers from a peculiar kind of hallucination. On occasion, it seems to her that she remembers events of learning how to φ, when in fact no such event occurred. Furthermore, the way Lucy 'remembers' as being the way to φ is not a way to φ at all. On Saturday, a clown teaches Lucy how to juggle. By the end of the class, she knows how to juggle and is juggling confidently. And so there is a way, call it 'w_2,' such that Lucy now believes that w_2 is a way for her to juggle, namely, the way the clown taught her to juggle. On Sunday, Lucy is about to tell a friend the good news that she knows how to juggle. However, as she begins, the alarm goes off on her false

---

3. The three arguments by counterexample I give against intellectualism are closely related in form to arguments that Pettit (2002) has given for a different conclusion, namely, that linguistic *understanding* is not a kind of knowledge-that. The first of the arguments I give is also related to an argument by Kvanvig (2003, ch. 8) that what he calls 'objectual understanding' is not a kind of knowledge-that.

memory detector (or FMD), a remarkable device that is a superreliable detector of her false memories. This indicates to Lucy that her apparent memory of learning how to juggle is not only a false memory but also misleading with respect to the way to juggle. Normally, Lucy would revise her beliefs accordingly, and this is what she believes she ought to do now. However, on this occasion, she is unable to shake the beliefs she believes she ought to revise. So, Lucy continues to believe that she knows how to juggle and that w_2 is a way for her to juggle. Of course, Lucy did learn how to juggle yesterday, so her FMD has made an error, albeit one that was highly unlikely.

The Non-Dogmatic Hallucinator: Jodie occasionally suffers from a peculiar kind of hallucination. On occasion, it seems to her that she remembers events of learning how to ϕ, when in fact no such event occurred. Furthermore, the way Jodie 'remembers' as being the way to ϕ is not a way to ϕ at all. On Saturday, a clown teaches Jodie how to juggle. By the end of the class, she knows how to juggle and is juggling confidently. And so there is a way, call it 'w_3,' such that Jodie now believes that w_3 is a way for her to juggle, namely, the way the clown taught her to juggle. On Sunday, Jodie is about to tell a friend the good news that she knows how to juggle. However, as she begins, the alarm goes off on her false memory detector (or FMD), a remarkable device that is a superreliable detector of her false memories. This indicates to Jodie that her apparent memory of learning how to juggle is not only a false memory but also misleading with respect to the way to juggle. Normally, Jodie would revise her beliefs accordingly, and this is exactly what Jodie does. So, she no longer believes that she knows how to juggle or that w_3 is a way for her to juggle. Of course, Jodie did learn how to juggle yesterday, so her FMD has made an error, albeit one that was highly unlikely.

The conclusion that these examples are all counterexamples to S&W's account of knowledge-how rests on two premises. The first premise is that the subjects in these cases each possess the relevant knowledge-how. More precisely, the premise is that the following claims are all correct, where 't_1' refers to a moment just after Charlie has grasped the instructions in *The Idiots Guide*, 't_2,' a moment just after Lucy has resisted revising her beliefs, and 't_3,' a moment just after Jodie has revised her beliefs:

The Knowledge-How (KH) Claims
(KH1) At t_1 Charlie knows how to change a light bulb
(KH2) At t_2 Lucy knows how to juggle
(KH3) At t_3 Jodie knows how to juggle

The second premise is that the subjects do not possess the kind of knowledge-that which S&W would identify their knowledge-how with. More precisely, the premise is that the following claims are all correct:

The No Knowledge-That (NKT) Claims
(NKT1) At t_1 Charlie does not know that w_1 is a way for him to change a light bulb
(NKT2) At t_2 Lucy does not know that w_2 is a way for her to juggle
(NKT3) At t_3 Jodie does not know that w_3 is a way for her to juggle

The KH claims, I submit, are all intuitively correct. The fact that Charlie is extremely lucky to read accurate (as opposed to misleading) instructions just seems irrelevant to whether he comes to know how to change a light bulb on the basis of reading those instructions. The fact that a number of Lucy's beliefs about juggling are defeated does not seem to be a reason to think that she has lost her knowledge how to juggle. Indeed, the intuitive thing to say with regard to Lucy's belief at t_2 that she knows how to juggle is that while this belief is unjustified, it is nonetheless true. Finally, the fact that at t_3 Jodie no longer believes that she knows how to juggle, or that w_3 is a way for her to juggle, does not seem to be a reason to conclude that Jodie has lost her knowledge how to juggle. Indeed, while Jodie's belief at t_3 that she does not know how to juggle is justified, it is also intuitively false.

Moving to the NKT claims, recall that according to S&W an ascription of the form *S knows how to* ϕ is true only if there is some contextually relevant way *w* such that S knows that *w* is a way for S to ϕ under a practical mode of presentation. But this putative necessary condition for knowing how to ϕ fails to hold in any of our three scenarios.[4] The contextually relevant ways in these three scenarios

---

4. The editors of this volume suggested to me that one might try to resist NKT1 by arguing that at t_1 Charlie would have access to a new source of evidence for w_1 being a way for him to change a light bulb that would be independent of the testimony of the book and would suffice for his knowing that w_1 is a way for him to change a light bulb. The suggestion was that now that Charlie can entertain the proposition that w_1 is a way for him to change a light bulb, he would be able, simply with the aid of his imagination, to see that w_1 is a way for him to change a light bulb. In response, I have made explicit in my description of the case the detail that Charlie has previously never seen the end of a light bulb or the inside of a light fixture. This is to make clear that the instructions Charlie reads are not only meant to be the source of his true beliefs about the series of actions he has to follow in order to change a light bulb but also the source of his true beliefs about the shape of light bulbs and fixtures. Now, suppose that prior to t_1 Charlie had just happened to entertain the proposition that w_1 is a way for him to change a light bulb, as well as all the other true propositions about the shape of light bulbs and fixtures expressed by the instructions he will later read (these thoughts all just pop into his head). And we can also stipulate that he entertains each of these propositions under a practical mode of presentation.

are clearly just w_1, w_2, and w_3. Now, each subject presumably entertains the relevant way under a practical mode of presentation. The problem is that they do not know that it is a way for them to perform the action in question. At t_1, Charlie does believe that w_1 is a way for him to change a light bulb, and this belief is both true and justified. But this belief does not constitute knowledge, for it is only accidentally true, or true only as a matter of mere luck. And it is a familiar lesson from the Gettier literature that knowledge-that is incompatible with the kind of epistemic luck present in this scenario.

Similarly, at t_2, Lucy does believe that w_2 is a way for her to juggle. But again, this belief does not constitute knowledge, for Lucy knows that her FMD is a superreliable detector of her false memories and that these false memories are misleading with respect to the way to perform the relevant action. Lucy believes then that her belief that w_2 is a way for her to juggle is not reliable or epistemically responsible. Furthermore, she is justified in this higher-order belief. In such a situation, Lucy's first-order belief that w_2 is a way for her to juggle, while true, does not possess the justification or warrant necessary for knowledge.[5] Finally, at t_3, Jodie clearly does not know that w_3 is a way for her to juggle, for she does not even believe that w_3 is a way for her to juggle.

I submit that the KH and NKT claims are all correct. If this is correct, it follows that each of our three examples is a scenario where a subject knows how to do something but fails to possess the kind of knowledge-that that S&W would equate their knowledge-how with. In other words, each case is a counterexample to S&W's account of knowledge-how.

Furthermore, I submit that these examples will also be counterexamples to any plausible account of knowledge-how whereby one knows how to ϕ only if one stands in the knowledge-that relation to some relevant proposition p. On any

---

Perhaps, with the aid of his imagination, Charlie would thereby be able to reflect on these propositional contents and come to know that *if* light bulbs and fixtures are shaped in that way, then w_1 is a way for him to change a light bulb. But given that Charlie has no reason to think that light bulbs and fixtures are actually shaped like that, he clearly would not be able to know that w_1 is a way for him to change a light bulb. The moral is that mere reflection on the contents of the instructions he reads would not provide Charlie with a source of evidence at t_1 that would suffice for him to know that w_1 is a way for him to change a light bulb.

5. I assume that the defeater for Lucy's belief that w_2 is a way for her to juggle is her higher-order belief that her belief that w_2 is a way for her to juggle is not reliable or trustworthy. However, this assumption is not essential to my argument. It could be that the defeater is Lucy's experience of seeing the readout on her FMD or some relevant proposition. For our purposes, all that matters is that Lucy's belief that w_2 is a way for her to juggle does not constitute knowledge-that in this scenario. Similarly, for ease of exposition, I assume that what gets defeated is Lucy's belief that w_2 is a way for her to juggle. But my argument is perfectly consistent with views according to which it is Lucy's reasons for believing that w_2 is a way for her to juggle that are defeated, rather than the belief itself.

plausible version of such an account, this proposition p will concern something like a way, method, or procedure for φ-ing. If so, it will be an easy exercise to redescribe our three examples to emphasize the fact that Charlie's belief that p is only accidentally true, that Lucy's belief that p is defeated, and that Jodie does not believe that p. That is, for any such account of knowledge-how, we will be able to provide parallel arguments for the corresponding NKT claims of the form: *At t_n S does not know that p.*[6]

To clarify these three arguments against intellectualism, it may help to contrast the first of them with a related but weaker form of objection to intellectualism examined by S&W and Poston (2009). S&W (2001, 435) imagine that someone might object to their account of knowledge-how by appealing to a supposed disanalogy between knowledge-how and knowledge-that:

> On the analysis we presented... knowing-how is straightforwardly analysed in terms of knowing-that. But one might worry that significant disanalogies still remain between knowing-how and other kinds of knowing-that. One potential source of disanalogy involves Gettier cases. We can imagine cases of justified true belief that fail to be knowledge-that, because they fail to satisfy some extra condition. It may appear difficult to conceive of Gettier-cases for knowledge-how. But if knowledge-how is really a kind of knowledge-that, there should be such cases.

S&W dismiss this disanalogy objection by disputing the claim that there are no Gettier cases for knowledge-how.[7] In response, Poston defends this objection by defending the claim that there are no Gettier cases for knowledge-how. And both S&W and Poston discuss cases like the *lucky light bulb* when evaluating this objection.

However, this disanalogy objection and my argument are importantly different. Suppose we could demonstrate that Poston is right, and there are no Gettier

---

6. The arguments given here can clearly be extended to other existing intellectualist accounts of knowledge-how, including those suggested by Bengson and Moffett (2007) and Brogaard (2008, 2009). Bengson and Moffett (2007) state their view so that one knows how to φ only if there is some way *w* such that one knows that *w* is a way to φ. (However, in Bengson and Moffett (chapter 7) and in Bengson, Moffett, and Wright (2009, n. 5), the proposal is broadened to explicitly allow for the possibility that knowledge how is grounded in propositional attitudes other than knowledge that.) And Brogaard is committed to the claim that one knows how to φ only if there is some way *w* such that one knows that *w* is how to φ.

7. As we will see in §2, S&W also give another reason for rejecting this disanalogy objection; namely, they reject the assumption that all kinds of knowledge-that are susceptible to Gettier cases.

cases for knowledge-how, that is, no cases where one fails to know how to ϕ for the same kind of reason one fails to know that p in a standard Gettier case. This alone would not establish that intellectualism is false, for it could be the case that knowledge-how is a kind of knowledge-that that is merely disanalogous, in this respect, to other kinds of knowledge-that. That is, for all that we have shown, it could be the case that in any Gettier-like scenario where someone knows how to ϕ, they will also possess the kind of knowledge-that that intellectualists would identify their knowledge-how with.

On the other hand, my argument claims that there is at least one Gettier scenario where someone knows how to ϕ and also fails to possess the kind of knowledge-that that this knowledge-how might be plausibly identified with. If this is correct, it does follow that knowledge-how is not a species of knowledge-that. Furthermore, the existence of such a Gettier scenario is consistent with the existence of other Gettier scenarios where knowledge-how and knowledge-that go together. This argument does not require then that knowledge-how is never susceptible to the kind of epistemic luck found in Gettier cases. Nor, for that matter, does it require that knowledge-that is always susceptible to such luck.

The crucial issue then is not whether there is some disanalogy between knowledge-how and knowledge-that with respect to Gettier scenarios. Rather, the crucial issue is whether knowledge-how and knowledge-that *come apart* in any such scenarios. The more general moral is that to respond to any of my putative counterexamples, it will not suffice for the intellectualist to merely argue that there are other similar cases where knowledge-how and knowledge-that go together. Rather, the intellectualist must dispute the evaluation offered of these particular examples. There are obviously two ways they could do this. For each case, the intellectualist could deny the relevant KH claim or deny the relevant NKT claim. I will examine each response separately.

2. *The No Knowledge-That Claims*

The first form of response I will consider is that which disputes the NKT claim. If we start with the *lucky light bulb* case, the question is whether the intellectualist can reasonably deny NKT1. Recall that the reason for thinking that Charlie's belief that w_1 is a way for him to change a light bulb does not constitute knowledge-that is that this belief is only accidentally true.[8] If the intellectualist is to

---

8. One might point out that at t_1 Charlie is better positioned with respect to knowing that w_1 is a way for him to change a light bulb than he was before t_1. For example, if he now attempts to change a light bulb, he will come to know that w_1 is a way for him to change a light bulb more easily than he would have if he did not already believe that this was the case. This is true but

claim that at t_1 Charlie does know that w_1 is a way for him to change a light bulb, they will have to deny the standard view that knowledge-that is subject to an anti-luck condition, namely, that if one knows that p, then it is not a matter of mere luck or accident that one's belief that p is true. Denying NKT1 is an unattractive response to the *lucky light bulb* case because it commits the intellectualist to a major revision of our conception of knowledge-that.

The intellectualist might respond that all that is needed is a 'localized' rejection of the idea that knowledge-that is subject to an anti-luck condition. S&W (2001, 435) themselves could be interpreted as suggesting this kind of response in their discussion of the disanalogy objection:

> We doubt that every kind of knowledge-that is susceptible to Gettier cases. So it would not worry us if it were not possible to come up with a Gettier case for knowledge-how.

On one interpretation of this passage, S&W are claiming that they would be unconcerned if they had to deny that knowledge-how is subject to an anti-luck condition because they think that there are other kinds of knowledge-that that are also not subject to such a condition.[9] And the claim that knowledge-how is not subject to an anti-luck condition is consistent with the claim that other kinds of knowledge-that are subject to such a condition. S&W might then point out that in claiming that Charlie knows that w_1 is a way for him to change a light bulb, they need only commit themselves to the claim that one particular kind of knowledge-that is not subject to an anti-luck condition.

However, S&W cannot simply assert that knowledge-how is a distinctive kind of knowledge-that that is not susceptible to Gettier cases. Rather, what they would need to establish is that S's standing in the knowledge-that relation to a

---

beside the point, as it does not alter the fact that *at t_1* Charlie does not know that w_1 is a way for him to change a light bulb.

9. This claim, that not all kinds of knowledge-that are susceptible to Gettier cases, can be interpreted in at least two ways. As interpreted here, the idea is that there is at least one kind of knowledge-that such that one can possess this kind of knowledge-that even when one's relevant justified true beliefs are only accidentally true. If this were the case, then this kind of knowledge-that would not be susceptible to Gettier cases because it is not subject to an anti-luck condition. However, it may be that S&W's idea is that there are some kinds of knowledge-that such that one simply cannot describe any scenario where one has the relevant justified true beliefs but they are only accidentally true. If this were the case, then this kind of knowledge-that would not be susceptible to Gettier cases, but it would still be subject to an anti-luck condition, for it would trivially satisfy such a condition. I have focused on the former idea here for the simple reason that we obviously can describe scenarios where someone has a justified true belief of the form *w is a way for me to ϕ* that is only accidentally true.

proposition of the form *w is a way for S to ϕ* is a distinctive kind of knowledge-that that is not susceptible to Gettier cases. But why should we think that this is the case? There is nothing obviously special about propositions concerning ways to perform actions such that S could know that p, even though S's belief that p is merely accidentally true, whenever p happens to be a proposition of the form *w is a way for S to ϕ*.

Perhaps S&W might argue that the relevant kind of knowledge-that that is not susceptible to Gettier cases is the knowledge-that S has when S stands in the knowledge-that relation to some proposition of the form *w is a way for S to ϕ* and, in addition, S entertains that proposition under a practical mode of presentation. That is, S&W could claim that the fact that Charlie's belief that w_1 is a way for him to change a light bulb is accidentally true is irrelevant to whether he knows that w_1 is a way for him to change a light bulb *under a practical mode of presentation*.

But note how odd this suggestion would be. No one ever tried to defend the tripartite analysis of knowledge by claiming that while the subjects in Gettier cases do not come to know that p under such-and-such mode of presentation, they do come to know that p under some other mode of presentation. And there is a good reason why not. The fact that someone's belief that p is merely accidentally true is surely a reason to think that they do not know that p *simpliciter*, regardless of what mode of presentation they happen to entertain that proposition under.

At the very least, if S&W were to adopt this response, they would owe us an explanation of why knowledge of propositions of the form *w is a way for one to ϕ* is resistant to Gettier influences in the special case where one entertains that proposition under a practical mode of presentation. And this explanation cannot simply consist in the claim that knowing that *w* is a way for one to ϕ under a practical mode of presentation is knowledge-how, and knowledge-how is resistant to Gettier influences.

The problem is that modes of presentation look like the wrong kind of thing on which to base such an explanation. Consider the sorts of reasons that are typically offered to explain why S fails to know that p in a given Gettier scenario: that the truth of S's belief that p is not appropriately related to S's reasons for holding that belief, or that the source of S's belief that p is unreliable, and so on. Such reasons for thinking that S fails to know that p do not seem even to be addressed—let alone outweighed or undermined—by the extra information that S happens to entertain p under such-and-such a mode of presentation. It is very difficult to see then how the intellectualist could motivate the claim that in denying NKT1, they need only endorse a localized, rather than wholesale, rejection of the idea that knowledge-that is subject to an anti-luck condition. This is because the kind of knowledge-that that intellectualists equate knowledge-how with has no distinctive features that would support such a claim. In this case, denying NKT1 still commits the intellectualist to a major revision of the standard conception of knowledge-that.

And if anything, the situation with regard to NKT2 and NKT3 is worse. Recall the reasons given in §1 for accepting these two claims: NKT2 was supported by the claim that at t_2 Lucy's belief that w_2 is a way for her to juggle is defeated and hence does not possess the justification or warrant necessary for it to constitute knowledge; NKT3 was supported by the claim that at t_3 Jodie does not believe that w_3 is a way for her to juggle. If we accept the defeat and no-belief claims, the consequences of denying NKT2 and NKT3 are severe. If the defeat claim is true, to deny NKT2 is to deny that having justification or warrant for one's belief that p is a necessary condition for knowing that p. And if the belief claim is true, to deny NKT3 is to deny that believing that p is a necessary condition for knowing that p.

If the intellectualist is to deny NKT2 and NKT3 while avoiding these consequences, they must establish that the defeat and belief claims are false. But can one plausibly deny either of these claims? Perhaps, against the defeat claim, the intellectualist might argue that when one entertains a proposition p under a practical mode of presentation, then one's belief that p can be justified even when one has a justified belief that the belief that p is unreliable. But again, I think the intellectualist would be hard-pressed to justify this 'localized' rejection of what clearly looks like a necessary condition for knowledge-that in general, namely, that if one knows that p, then one does not have a justified belief that one's belief that p is unreliable, or epistemically inappropriate.[10] The fact that Lucy has a justified belief that her belief that w_2 is a way for her to juggle is unreliable is surely a reason to conclude that she does not know that w_2 is a way for her to juggle *simpliciter*. It is not merely a reason to conclude that Lucy does not know that w_2 is a way for her to juggle, if she happens to entertain this proposition under a nonpractical mode of presentation.

What of the no-belief claim? Could one not argue that at t_3 Jodie still *implicitly* or *tacitly* believes that w_3 is a way for her to juggle? And if so, could one not argue that Jodie still implicitly or tacitly knows that w_3 is a way for her to juggle? Undoubtedly, there is a good sense in which at t_3 it will still *seem* to Jodie that w_3 is a way for her to juggle. For example, if Jodie imagines w_3, this way will still strike her as being a way to juggle. But we should not confuse mere seemings with beliefs.

---

10. This kind of condition is widely accepted as a necessary condition for knowledge-that by both internalists and externalists; for discussion, see Bergman (1997). There is a debate about whether one's second-order belief that one's belief that p is not reliable must itself be justified for it to defeat one's first-order belief that p. However, this debate is not relevant here, given that Lucy's higher-order belief is justified.

Even if one knows that the two lines in a Müller-Lyer figure are of the same length, it will still seem to one that they differ in length. And as Bealer (1993) has pointed out, the same point applies not only to perceptual but also to intellectual seemings; it can still seem to one that the naïve axiom of set theory is true, even though one does not believe that it is true, because one knows that it leads to a contradiction. Similarly, while it seems to Jodie that w_3 is a way for her to juggle, I think it is clear that she fails to believe that w_3 is a way for her to juggle.

Furthermore, Jodie has consciously reflected on the question of whether w_3 is a way for her to juggle, and she has concluded on the basis of her relevant evidence that w_3 is not a way for her to juggle. If someone has consciously reflected on the question of whether p and concluded on the basis of the relevant evidence that not-p, this is normally a strong indicator that they do not believe that p. There are difficult cases (including ones involving delusional beliefs) where one might think that someone has both the belief that p and the belief that not-p at the same time. But I see no reason to regard the *non-dogmatic hallucinator* as such a case. Suppose, however, that one did want to say (implausibly) that Jodie both believes that w_3 is not a way for her to juggle *and* that she also believes that w_3 is a way for her to juggle. I think it is clear that in such a situation the latter belief would not possess the justification or warrant required for it to constitute knowledge. In this case, NKT3 would still be true; all that would have changed is the diagnosis of why Jodie fails to know that w_3 is a way for her to juggle.

Denying the relevant NKT claim does not look to be an attractive response for the intellectualist to any of our putative counterexamples. In each case, denying NKT1, NKT2, or NKT3 forces the intellectualist to reject a plausible and widely accepted assumption about the nature of knowledge-that, namely, that knowledge-that is subject to an anti-luck condition, a justified or warranted belief condition, and a belief condition, respectively. Perhaps some intellectualists would be prepared to radically revise our conception of knowledge-that just to maintain the thesis that knowledge-how is a kind of knowledge-that. I am skeptical that such a position could be made plausible, but my main concern here is simply to highlight these substantial costs involved in denying the NKT claims. However, there is still another form of response available to the intellectualist that we need to consider.

3. *The Knowledge-How Claims*

The second possible form of response to our putative counterexamples is to contest the KH claim. There is reason to think that S&W would at least reject KH1. Consider what S&W (2001, 435) say about the following example they offer as proof that there can be Gettier cases for knowledge-how:

> Bob wants to learn how to fly in a flight simulator. He is instructed by Henry. Unknown to Bob, Henry is a malicious imposter who has inserted a randomising device in the simulator's controls and intends to give all kinds of incorrect advice. Fortunately, by sheer chance the randomising device causes exactly the same results in the simulator as would have occurred without it, and by incompetence Henry gives exactly the same advice as a proper instructor would have done. Bob passes the course with flying colors. He has still not flown a real plane. Bob has a justified true belief about how to fly. But there is a good sense in which he does not *know* how to fly....

So S&W think that this example—I will call it *the flight simulator* case—is a case where someone fails to know how to ϕ for the same kind of reason one fails to know that p in a Gettier scenario. Now, for the reasons discussed at the end of §1, if S&W's evaluation of this case is correct, it does not follow that KH1 is false. Nevertheless, given the obvious similarities between the *flight simulator* and *lucky light bulb* cases, one might reasonably expect that our verdicts about whether Bob knows how to fly and whether Charlie knows how to change a light bulb should be the same. If S&W are right then in claiming that Bob does not know how to fly, this would at least give us some reason to reconsider KH1.

But are S&W right? Is there a good sense in which Bob does not know how to fly? Clearly, Bob has justified and true beliefs about flying that do not constitute knowledge-that because they are only accidentally true. However, I think S&W are simply wrong that the intuitive thing to say of this case is that Bob does not know how to fly. As Poston (2009, 744) says, "As far as intuition goes this does not seem correct. There is a good sense in which Bob *does* know how to fly."

To make the intuition vivid, compare Bob with his near-perfect counterpart Joe. The only salient difference between Bob and Joe is that in Joe's world, his simulator not only operates correctly but also has not been interfered with, and his instructor not only gives him the correct advice but also intended to do so. So when Joe exits his simulator, we can safely assume that he knows how to fly. But on what grounds, then, could we deny that Bob knows how to fly? The fact that Bob, unlike Joe, is extremely lucky to receive the very same feedback from his simulator and instructor does not seem to be a reason to conclude that only Joe comes to know how to fly on the basis of receiving this feedback.[11]

---

11. Note that we could have used a similar comparison to support the intuition for KH1. Compare Charlie with his near-perfect counterpart Jack. Jack's world is just like Charlie's in all but one salient respect, namely, in Jack's world *The Idiots Guide*" was written by a nonmalicious author who intended to fill her book with helpful descriptions of ways to perform everyday

Someone might try to argue that there is both a good sense in which Bob knows how to fly and a good sense in which he does not know how to fly. I doubt that this is the case, but two points are worth mentioning about this idea. First, it is clear that S&W themselves do not take knowledge-how ascriptions to be ambiguous in this way. Second, as S&W acknowledge, Bob's relevant belief of the form *w is a way for Bob to fly* does not constitute knowledge-that in this scenario. If so, then if there is a good sense in which Bob knows how to fly, it follows that there is a good sense in which knowledge-how comes apart from knowledge-that in the *flight simulator* case. In other words, it would follow that there is a good sense in which knowledge-how is not a kind of knowledge-that.[12]

S&W's interpretation of this case is also strange, given that their own account of knowledge-how tells us that Bob knows how to fly. Let me explain. The core of S&W's account of knowledge-how was stated earlier in §1. But S&W also make two further, and important, claims about the nature of knowledge-how. First, S&W (2001, 442–443 and 415–416) hold that all intentional actions "are employments of knowledge-how." That is, they accept the following claim:

(1) If S φs intentionally, S knows how to φ

Second, S&W (2001, 442–443) infer from (1) a further claim concerning abilities, as their discussion of the ability hypothesis reply to the knowledge argument[13] reveals:

---

jobs (and there were no errors during printing, etc.). The text in Jack's copy of *The Idiot's Guide* is the same as the text in Charlie's copy of *The Idiot's Guide*. So Jack reads the exact same description of how to change a light bulb that Charlie reads. And Jack, like Charlie, comprehends these instructions perfectly. Obviously, it is safe to assume that Jack knows how to change a light bulb after reading these instructions. This is an ordinary way of gaining knowledge-how. But how could we deny that Charlie comes to know how to change a light bulb after reading the very same instructions? The fact that Charlie, unlike Jack, is extremely lucky to read these instructions does not seem to be a reason to conclude that only Jack comes to know how to change a light bulb.

12. Stanley (2005, 131) explicitly denies that knowledge-how ascriptions are ambiguous between a sense in which they attribute knowledge-that and a sense in which they do not. Bengson and Moffett (2007, 38–40) deny that knowledge-how ascriptions are ambiguous at all. Brogaard (2008, 175) does hold that 'S knows how to φ' ascriptions are ambiguous, as she claims that 'John knows how to play the piano' can be read as "saying that there is a *w* such that John knows that *w* is how JOHN may play the piano, or as saying that there is a *w* such that John knows that *w* is how ONE may play the piano." But clearly, on either disambiguation, knowing how to play the piano is still a kind of knowledge-that.

13. S&W claim that their account of knowledge-how is inconsistent with the ability hypothesis reply to Jackson's (1982, 1986) knowledge argument. I dispute this claim in Cath (2009).

For the ability to imagine an experience of red is clearly an ability to perform an intentional action. And we do find it very plausible that intentional actions are employments of knowledge-how...But if intentional actions are employments of knowledge-how then Mary's acquisition of an ability to imagine an experience of red brings with it knowledge how to imagine red.

So S&W hold that if one has the ability to perform an action intentionally, then one knows how to perform that action. That is, they accept the following claim:

(2) If S has the ability to ϕ intentionally, S knows how to ϕ.[14]

But then it is a necessary consequence of S&W's full account of knowledge-how—and a plausible assumption—that Bob does know how to fly. The assumption is that Bob has the ability to fly a plane intentionally. And this is very plausible. After all, Bob passes the course that imparts this ability with "flying colors." To emphasize the point, note that Joe has the ability to fly a plane intentionally as he exits his simulator. But then we must conclude that Bob also has this ability, for Joe and Bob are clearly equivalent with respect to their abilities to fly a plane.

The issue here can be illustrated by noting that the following three claims form an inconsistent triad:

(2) If S has the ability to ϕ intentionally, S knows how to ϕ
(3) Bob has the ability to fly intentionally
(4) Bob does not know how to fly

S&W claim both that Bob does not know how to fly and that having the ability to ϕ intentionally entails knowing how to ϕ; that is, they endorse both (2) and (4). However, (3) is true. It must be the case, then, that either (2) or (4), or both (2) and (4), are false. So to maintain that Bob does not know how to fly, S&W would have to deny (2), thereby denying a key commitment of their full account of knowledge-how.

Furthermore, if S&W are right that having the ability to ϕ intentionally entails knowing how to ϕ, this is highly important in this context, given that the following ability ascriptions are very plausible:

---

14. This claim is consistent with S&W's opposition to the idea that S know how to ϕ iff S possesses the ability to ϕ, for S&W (2001, 416) explicitly deny the entailment in the other direction: "ascriptions of knowledge-how do not even entail ascriptions of the corresponding abilities."

(5) At t_1 Charlie has the ability to change a light bulb intentionally
(6) At t_2 Lucy has the ability to juggle intentionally
(7) At t_3 Jodie has the ability to juggle intentionally

If S&W are right that (2) is true, then (5), (6), and (7) each entail the corresponding knowledge-how ascription; that is, they entail KH1, KH2, and KH3, respectively. At this point, there are only two choices available to an intellectualist who wishes to deny any one of the KH claims: they could deny (2), that is, they could reject S&W's idea that having the ability to ϕ intentionally entails knowing how to ϕ; or they could deny the corresponding ability claim (5), (6), or (7), that is, they could deny that the subject in the putative counterexample possesses the ability to perform the action intentionally.

Some intellectualists have offered what could be regarded as counterexamples to (2) when arguing against the view that to know how to ϕ is to simply possess the ability to ϕ—a view that is often attributed to Ryle that I will call *neo-Ryleanism*.[15] For example, Bengson and Moffett (2007, 46) present the following scenario—I will call it the *salchow* case—where intuitively someone has the ability to ϕ but does not know how to ϕ:

> Suppose that Irina is seriously mistaken about how to perform a salchow. She believes incorrectly that the way to perform a salchow is to take off from the front outside of her skate, jump in the air, spin, and land on the front inside edge of her skate. (The correct sequence is to take off from the *back inside edge* and land on the *back outside edge* of the opposite foot after one or more rotations in the air.) However, Irina has a severe neurological abnormality that makes her act in ways that differ dramatically from how she actually thinks she is acting. Whenever she actually attempts to do a salchow (in accordance with her misconceptions) this abnormality causes

---

15. My use of this term is borrowed from Bengson and Moffett (2007). I use this term rather than 'Ryleanism' because while it is clear that Ryle (1945, 1949) identified knowing how to ϕ with the possession of a complex of dispositions, I think it is not actually clear that he endorsed neo-Ryleanism. S&W (2001, 411) attribute both the complex disposition view and neo-Ryleanism to Ryle, as they claim that according to Ryle, "knowledge-how is ability, which is in turn a complex of dispositions." That is, they take Ryle to be committed to both of the following identity claims: (i) to know how to ϕ is to possess the ability to ϕ; and (ii) to know how to ϕ is to possess a complex of dispositions. This is why S&W take the counterexamples they offer to (i) to be counterexamples to Ryle's account of knowledge-how. Brian Weatherson, on his blog *Thoughts Arguments and Rants* (Weatherson 2006), argues that such counterexamples do not apply to Ryle on the grounds that he is only committed to (ii) and not (i). Like Weatherson, I am not convinced that Ryle is committed to (i), but even if he is, it seems to me that Ryle would lose little if, in response to the standard counterexamples to (i), he were to simply reject (i) while retaining (ii).

her to reliably perform the correct sequence of moves. So, although she is seriously mistaken about how to perform a salchow, whenever she actually attempts to do a salchow (in accordance with her misconceptions) the abnormality causes Irina to perform the correct sequence of moves, and so she ends up successfully performing a salchow. Despite the fact that what she is doing and what she thinks she is doing come apart, she fails to notice the mismatch. In this case, it is clear that Irina is (reliably) able to do a salchow. However, due to her mistaken belief about how to perform the move, she cannot be said to know how to do a salchow.

Does Irina also have the ability to perform the salchow *intentionally*? Bengson, Moffett, and Wright (2009, n. 22) seem to suggest that she does, and on this basis they reject S&W's claim that having the ability to ϕ intentionally entails knowing how to ϕ. But Stanley (2011, 218) disputes the idea that the *salchow* is a counterexample to (2):

> Irina has a false belief about how to do the Salchow, and she is lucky enough that whenever she intends to do the Salchow, she succeeds. Though she intelligently and successfully performs the Salchow, she does not *intentionally do the Salchow* when she succeeds, anymore than it follows that I *intentionally win the lottery* when I win the lottery after buying a lottery ticket intending to win. Of course, when Irina performs the salchow, she does it with the intention of performing the Salchow, and there is a causal connection between her intention to perform the Salchow and performing the Salchow. But as we have learned from Davidson, F-ing with the intention of F-ing does not entail intentionally F-ing, even when there is a causal connection between one's intention to F and one's F-ing. In order to intentionally F there must be the *right kind* of causal relations between one's intention to F, and one's F-ing, and those are lacking in Irina's case.

Stanley (2011, n. 8) also claims (in response to an earlier draft of this paper) that, faced with the inconsistent triad I presented, S&W would reject (3) on similar grounds. I agree with Stanley's reasons for concluding that Irina would merely have the ability to perform the salchow, and not to do so intentionally. But the *flight simulator* case is importantly different from the *salchow* case. Bob's success in flying is not lucky in the way that Irina's success in performing the salchow is. Of course, Bob is very lucky to have true, rather than false, beliefs about how to fly. But how Bob came to possess these beliefs is irrelevant. What matters, as Stanley says, is whether the causal relation between Bob's intention to fly in accord with these beliefs and his flying is the *right kind* of causal relation, and it clearly is. Unlike Irina and the salchow, Bob does have an accurate conception of how to fly, and so he needs no lucky abnormality, or other fortuitous intervention, to succeed in flying when he forms the intention to fly. And the exact same kind of point can be made in support of (5) and (6).

Perhaps with regard to (7), one might argue that Jodie does not have the ability to juggle intentionally because she does not believe that w_3 is a way for her to juggle. However, as mentioned earlier, at t_3 it would still seem to Jodie that w_3 is a way for her to juggle. Suppose one convinced Jodie to try to juggle that way that merely seems to her to be a way to juggle. If she did try, she would probably succeed as a result of this intention, and it would be no lucky accident that her intention caused this success. In this case, I think the right thing to say would be that Jodie not only juggled but also did so intentionally.

Anyway, even if one could resist (7) on such grounds, (5) and (6) seem straightforwardly true. It may be a necessary condition of S's having the ability to ϕ intentionally that there be some way w that is a way for S to ϕ such that S believes that w is a way for S to ϕ. But it is surely not a necessary condition of S's having the ability to ϕ intentionally that such a belief must also be nonaccidentally true and/or justified.[16]

If the intellectualist is to deny any of the KH claims (or at least KH1 and KH2), then they must deny (2); that is, he must deny that having the ability to ϕ intentionally entails knowing how to ϕ. Whether the intellectualist can justify denying this entailment thesis is another matter. As Stanley shows us, examples like the *salchow* are not convincing counterexamples to (2). But suppose that the intellectualist could establish that (2) is false. This would show us that one can *consistently* deny KH1, KH2, and KH3 while accepting (5), (6), and (7). However, this is not yet a reason to think that any of the KH claims are false.

I think it is clear that in practice many subjects would share the intuition that the KH claims are correct. One line of response available to the intellectualist is to claim that while the KH claims are intuitive, they are nonetheless false. But if they are to deny these intuitive claims, the intellectualist owes us some explanation of why our intuitions about these cases are so systematically misleading.

Probably the most obvious explanation would be to claim that we somehow confuse the fact that the subjects in our putative counterexamples possess the relevant ability with their possessing the corresponding knowledge-how. Appealing to the idea that ability ascriptions implicate, but do not entail, the corresponding knowledge-how ascription would be one way to develop such an argument. The

---

16. See Bengson, Moffett, and Wright (2009, n. 22) for a related concern with S&W's commitment to (2).

explanation then of our intuitions regarding KH1, KH2, and KH3 would be that we confuse a conversational implicature with an entailment. For example, our intuition that Charlie knows how to change a light bulb is explained by the fact that we know that Charlie has the ability to change a light bulb, and we mistakenly think that 'S has the ability to φ' entails 'S knows how to φ.'

This strategy for explaining away our intuitions regarding the KH claims may appear promising.[17] Even if there is no entailment from 'S has the ability to φ' to 'S knows how to φ,' it would still presumably be true that in stereotypical cases of someone's having the ability to φ, they will also know how to φ, in which case it seems reasonable to suppose that 'S has the ability to φ' implicates 'S knows how to φ.'

However, note that there is an inherent tension in this kind of response to our putative counterexamples. To establish that having the ability to φ does not entail knowing how to φ, the intellectualist needs there to be clear cases where someone intuitively has the ability to φ but does not know how to φ. And there are such cases. But then why does our familiarity with the relevant implicature lead us to mistakenly have the intuition that KH1, KH2, and KH3 are true, when it obviously does not lead us to make the parallel mistake with regard to examples like the *salchow* case? In such cases, the relevant subject has the ability to φ and, according to the intellectualist, does not know how to φ. The intellectualist then would have to provide a plausible explanation of this asymmetry that is also consistent with his interpretation of these cases. Perhaps there is some such explanation, but I am not sure what it would be.

On the other hand, we can offer a natural explanation of this asymmetry in our intuitions, namely, that the subjects in the *lucky light bulb*, *dogmatic hallucinator*, and *non-dogmatic hallucinator* cases know how to perform the relevant actions, whereas the subjects in the *salchow* and *man in a room* cases do not.

I also doubt that it is an essential feature of the counterexamples offered here that the subjects in these scenarios possess the ability to perform the relevant action. As intellectualists often point out, one can know how to φ without possessing the ability to φ. For example, S&W (2001, 416) offer the case of "a master pianist who loses both her arms in a tragic car accident." Intuitively, the master pianist would still know how to play the piano, even though she has lost her ability to do so. Again, such examples are cited by intellectualists as evidence against neo-Ryleanism, for they suggest that having the ability to φ is not a necessary condition for knowing how to φ.

---

17. Bengson and Moffett think that there is a stereotypical implicature in the other direction, from knowing how to φ to having the ability to φ. For further discussion of the notion of a stereotypical implicature, see Bengson and Moffett (2007, 35).

Bearing this point in mind, let us add an unfortunate twist to the *lucky light bulb* case. Namely, just after Charlie grasps the instructions in *The Idiot's Guide* at t_1 his arms are removed (I will spare you the details of how this happens). Otherwise, the case remains exactly the same. Does Charlie still know how to change a light bulb? As with S&W's *pianist* case, I take it that the intuitive answer is yes. In this case, we still have a scenario where intuitively Charlie knows how to ϕ, and the same reasons are still present for thinking that Charlie does not possess the kind of knowledge-that that such knowledge-how might be plausibly equated with. But in this modified scenario, Charlie also lacks the ability to change a light bulb. So the intellectualist cannot dismiss the knowledge-how intuition here by claiming that we are merely confusing the fact that Charlie has the ability to change a light bulb with his knowing how to change a light bulb. And I think one could modify the *dogmatic hallucinator* and *non-dogmatic hallucinator* cases to achieve the same kind of result.

However, the more important point here is simply that there are good reasons to be suspicious of this kind of strategy for dismissing our intuitions regarding the KH claims. Consider the very examples intellectualists appeal to when arguing against neo-Ryleanism—like the *salchow* and *pianist* cases. As counterexamples to neo-Ryleanism, these cases are compelling. But the intuitive force of such examples suggests that we are quite capable of discerning the difference between knowing how to ϕ and possessing the ability to ϕ. It seems implausible, then, to suppose that our intuitions about the KH claims are merely the result of our confusing the fact that a subject has the ability to ϕ with the subject's knowing how to ϕ.

There is no simple way to dismiss our intuitions that the KH claims are true. But we saw in §2 that intellectualism requires that we deny the KH claims if we are to avoid radically revising our conception of knowledge-that. In the absence of some good argument for dismissing our intuitions regarding the KH claims, I submit that that we should reject intellectualism or revise our conception of knowledge-that.

4. *What These Arguments Do Not Establish*

I have argued that intellectualism is false if certain standard assumptions about the nature of knowledge-that are correct. But what is knowledge-how if not a kind of knowledge-that? This question cannot be answered here, but I do want to show that the arguments given in §1 should not be regarded as arguments for the most prominent alternative to intellectualism, namely, neo-Ryleanism. The reason is that even if these arguments succeed, it might still be reasonable to hold that knowing how to ϕ is a matter of standing in an intentional relation to a proposition *other than* the knowledge-that relation.

This claim may appear implausible. After all, if my evaluation of the *non-dogmatic hallucinator* case is correct, knowledge-how cannot even be analyzed in terms of the *belief* relation to a proposition. To support this claim then, it may help to consider a possible alternative to both the standard intellectualist and neo-Rylean views of knowledge-how. According to this view, knowing how to φ is a matter of standing in the relation to a proposition that S stands in when it *seems* to S that p is the case. Importantly, this is not the belief relation. As mentioned earlier, it can seem to one that p even when one fails to believe that p. In this case, seemings cannot be understood as simply a kind of belief.[18] Bearing that in mind, here is our alternative analysis of knowledge-how:

The Seeming Analysis
S knows how to φ if, and only if, there is some way w to φ such that:
(c) S stands in the seeming relation to the proposition that w is a way to φ, and[19]
(d) S entertains the proposition that way w is a way to φ under a practical mode of presentation.[20]

---

18. Note that this claim is consistent with the common idea that seemings are a kind of inclination or disposition to believe. I am inclined, however, to agree with Tolhurst (1998, 297) when he claims that when it seems to one that p, one is not merely inclined to believe that p but one also "experiences believing [that p] to be demanded or required."

19. As indicated earlier, Bealer (1993) and others like Huemer (2005) and Pust (2000) distinguish perceptual from nonperceptual seemings, including intellectual seemings. Assuming that such distinctions can be made, I think one would want to restrict (c) to a nonperceptual seeming relation. Also, with regard to (c), one can obviously know how to φ even when it does not *occurrently* seem to one that some way *w* is a way to φ, for example, when one is asleep. The seeming analysis will not be plausible then unless one can satisfy (c) even when it does not occurrently seem to one that *w* is a way to φ. But I think there is a natural interpretation of 'It seems to S that p' ascriptions, whereby they can be satisfied by nonoccurrent states. Suppose that during a conversation about the intuitions of our friends, I assert, 'It still seems to Bill that the naïve axiom of set theory is true even though he knows it to be false.' In such a context, it is no objection to my claim to point out that Bill is currently in a deep dreamless sleep. My claim is naturally interpreted as being satisfied by some standing, or nonoccurrent, state of Bill, rather than some occurrent state of it seeming to Bill that the naïve axiom of set theory is true. Presumably, a nonoccurrent state that consists (at least partly) in the disposition for it to occurrently seem to Bill that the naïve axiom of set theory is true, in certain relevant conditions. Likewise, (c) should be understood in such a way that to satisfy (c) it suffices that it seem to one that *w* is a way to φ, in this nonoccurrent sense of 'It seems to S that p.' See Hunter (1998) for a structurally parallel distinction between states of occurrent understanding and dispositions to be in occurrent states of understanding.

20. Why include the parallel of S&W's condition (b) here as condition (d)? S&W include (b) because without it their analysis would clearly not describe a sufficient condition for knowing how to φ. Intuitively, there can be contexts in which one fails to know how to φ even though there is some way *w* such that one knows that *w* is a way for oneself to φ. Likewise, one could

The seeming analysis is consistent with the arguments given in §1 because in all of my putative counterexamples, there is still some way w for the subject to perform the relevant action ɸ such that it *seems* to the subject that w is a way to ɸ. It seems to Charlie that w_1 is a way to change a light bulb even though his belief that w_1 is a way for him to change a light bulb is only accidentally true. It seems to Lucy that w_2 is a way to juggle even though her belief that w_2 is way for her to juggle is defeated. And as noted earlier, it still seems to Jodie that w_3 is a way to juggle even though she does not believe that w_3 is a way to juggle.

The seeming analysis also accords with our intuitions about examples like the *salchow* and *pianist* cases. There is a series of actions such that it seems to Irina that that series of actions is a way to perform the salchow. But this series of actions is not a way to perform the salchow. The seeming analysis rightly predicts, then, that Irina does not know how to perform the salchow. Even after her accident, it will still seem to the pianist that that way she used to play the piano is a way to play the piano. Across a diverse range of cases, then, the seeming analysis accords with our intuitions better than both intellectualism and neo-Ryleanism. Unlike intellectualism, it accords with our intuitions about the *lucky light bulb*, *dogmatic hallucinator*, and *non-dogmatic hallucinator* cases. And unlike neo-Ryleanism, the seeming analysis accords with our intuitions about the *salchow* and *pianist* cases.

Obviously, I am not claiming to have thereby shown that the seeming analysis is a serious rival to intellectualism and neo-Ryleanism. The role of the seeming analysis here is simply to illustrate the possibility of promising alternatives to both intellectualism and neo-Ryleanism.[21] In the literature, intellectualism and

---

presumably fail to know how to ɸ even though there is some way w such that it seems to one that w is a way to ɸ. S&W's condition (b) is intended to be a solution to this problem. Insofar as this fix works for their intellectualist account of knowledge-how, the same fix should work for the seeming analysis. If practical modes of presentation cannot solve this problem, one could appeal to other intellectualist strategies for addressing the same issue. For example, Bengson and Moffett (2007, 50–53) attempt to address this problem by requiring that to know how to ɸ, not only must there be some way w such that one knows that w is a way to ɸ but also one must *minimally understand w*. Also, the kind of qualification I made in note 1 about (b) and (b*) should also be made here with respect to (d).

21. I hope to examine the seeming analysis and other alternative analyses of knowledge-how in future work. I should note that Ryleans would presumably still regard the seeming analysis as being 'intellectualist,' given that it analyzes knowledge-how in terms of an intentional relation to a proposition. Bengson, Moffett, and Wright (2009, n. 5) suggest that intellectualism should be understood in a broad way such that any view that analyzes knowledge-how in terms of a propositional attitude is a form of intellectualism. Bengson and Moffett (chapter 7) and the state of play chapter in this book usefully distinguish an even broader understanding of intellectualism that includes accounts on which knowledge-how is an objectual state or attitude. If we were to define 'intellectualism' in either of these broad ways, then my point would be that the arguments I have given only undermine those intellectualist accounts that analyze knowledge-how in terms of the knowledge-that or belief relation. See also Glick (forthcoming) for a

neo-Ryleanism are normally the only accounts of knowledge-how that are discussed. This situation can lead to a tendency to regard arguments against either account as being arguments, by default, for the other. The seeming analysis emphasizes the point that we should not regard the arguments against intellectualism given here as being arguments for neo-Ryleanism. Furthermore, it shows us that even if knowledge-how is not a kind of knowledge-that, it could still be the case that knowledge-how is propositional in nature. In looking beyond the standard dichotomy of intellectualism and neo-Ryleanism, we may just find a more adequate account of knowledge-how.[22]

---

useful distinction between weak and strong intellectualism; in his terminology (as I understand it), the seeming analysis would be a version of weak but not strong intellectualism.

22. I would like to thank audiences at the Australian National University and the University of St Andrews for their criticisms and suggestions. This chapter has existed in one form or another for some time. Special thanks to the editors of this volume, Berit Brogaard, Andy Egan, Jonathan Ichikawa, Jonathan Schaffer, Nicholas Silins, Jason Stanley, Daniel Stoljar, and, in particular, David Chalmers, for helpful feedback on various drafts of this paper.

6

Knowledge-How

A UNIFIED ACCOUNT

Berit Brogaard

THERE ARE TWO competing views of knowledge-how: intellectualism and anti-intellectualism. According to the reductionist varieties of intellectualism defended by Jason Stanley and Timothy Williamson (2001) and Berit Brogaard (2007, 2008, 2009), knowledge-how simply reduces to knowledge-that. To a first approximation, s knows how to A iff there is a w such that s knows that w is a way to A. For example, John knows how to ride a bicycle if and only if there is a way w such that John knows that w is a way to ride a bicycle. John Bengson and Marc Moffett (2007, chapter 7) defend an antireductionist version of intellectualism that takes knowledge-how to require, in addition to a propositional attitude, that s understands the concepts involved in her attitude.

According to the anti-intellectualist accounts originally defended by Gilbert Ryle (1945) and many others after him, knowledge-how requires the possession of a practical ability and so knowing that w (for some w) is a way to A does not suffice for knowing-how. For example, John knows how to ride a bicycle only if John has the ability to ride it; if John merely knows that w (for some w) is a way to ride a bicycle, John does not know how to ride a bicycle.

Here I argue for a conciliatory position that is compatible with the reductionist variety of intellectualism: knowledge-how is reducible to knowledge-that. But, I argue, there are knowledge states that are not justification entailing and knowledge states that are not belief entailing. Both kinds of knowledge state require the possession of practical abilities. I conclude by arguing that the view defended naturally leads to a disjunctive conception of abilities as either essentially involving mental states or as not essentially involving mental states. Only the former kind of ability is a kind of knowledge-state, that is, a knowledge-how state.

1. Intellectualism versus Anti-Intellectualism

On the anti-intellectualist view of knowledge-how, originally due to Gilbert Ryle (1945, 1949, ch. 2), one knows how to A only if one has the practical ability to A.[1] On the face of it, this view is exceedingly plausible. Tim (a distinguished philosophy professor and devout defender of the intellectualist view of knowledge-how) is going on a skiing vacation. In preparation for the trip, he carefully studies two renowned skiing 101 books. But on his arrival at his destination, he finds, to his surprise, that he doesn't know how to ski. Fortunately, the ski holiday resort is full of able skiing instructors who are more than willing to teach Tim how to ski.

As Tim is an excellent scholar, Tim was, prior to his skiing vacation, in the possession of a vast amount of knowledge-that concerning skiing. Tim knew that to slow your speed as a beginner, you should use the snowplow position, that to snowplow you must stand with the tips of the skis closer together than the tails, that to turn right your head should move toward the tip of your right ski, and so on. But he still didn't know how to ski. After ten days on the slope with his private skiing instructor, Tim had acquired the ability to ski. Only then could Tim claim to know how to ski.

Consider further examples. Suppose I have never practiced playing the piano but have taken numerous theory lessons. There is then a way w such that I know that w is a way for me to play the piano. Still, it would seem that someone could correctly claim that I don't know how to play the piano. Likewise, if Mary—a monolingual speaker of English—sees Danny curse out his cousin in Italian, she might correctly say (while pointing), "*That* is how to curse out someone in Italian." Yet someone could correctly say, "Mary doesn't know how to curse out someone in Italian." After all, Mary doesn't even speak Italian.

In all of these cases, we are willing to treat the relevant knowledge-attribution as correct only if the subject possesses the relevant practical ability.

However, despite the initial plausibility of the anti-intellectualist view, the view cannot ultimately be correct. The view raises the following two related worries. First, it is plainly obvious that there are cases in which one can know how to A without having the ability to A. Here is an example from Bengson and Moffett (2007): the Olympic figure skater Irina Slutskaya cannot perform a quintuple salchow. Still, it makes good sense to say that Irina knows how to perform a quintuple salchow. She knows exactly what one ought to do to perform one; she just can't do it.

Second, it is uncontroversial that some forms of knowledge-how do *not* require practical abilities. John knows that Mary caught a ride home with Peter. So John knows how Mary got home. Yet John's knowledge of how Mary got

---

[1]. For defenses of this and related views, see also Bechtel and Abrahamsen (1991, 152), Brandom (1994, 23), Braddon-Mitchell and Jackson (1996, 131), Haugeland (1998, 322), Hawley (2003), Noë (2005), and Cath (chapter 5).

home does not require any practical abilities on John's part. So the anti-intellectualist view cannot handle the full range of knowledge-how attributions.

Of course, defenders of the anti-intellectualist view could reply to this latter objection by insisting that their view applies only to constructions of the form 's knows how to A.' Since John's knowledge of how Mary got home is not of this form, the example does not run counter to the anti-intellectualist view. But this reply is idle. It is idle because it presupposes that 'knowledge-how' means different things depending on whether it occurs with an infinitive clause or an indicative clause. Yet there is no evidence for this being the case. There is certainly no lexical ambiguity in play here. 'Know' is, familiarly, lexically ambiguous. The objectual 'know,' which occurs in constructions such as ' John knows Peter,' and the nonobjectual 'know,' which occurs in know-how and know-that constructions, have different lexical meanings. This can be seen from the fact that the two occurrences of 'know' translate into different words in languages such as German and Italian. In German the objectual 'know' translates as 'kennen,' whereas the nonobjectual 'know' translates as 'wissen.' Likewise, 'how' is lexically ambiguous. In some languages (e.g., Danish) 'how' translates one way when it occurs in scalar constructions such as 'John knows how tall Mary is' and another when it occurs in nonscalar constructions such as 'John knows how to ski' or 'John knows how Mary got home.' But the occurrences of 'know how' in 'Tim knows how to ski' and 'John knows how Mary got home' do not translate into different expressions in other languages. As the relevant occurrences of 'know how' are not lexically ambiguous, the fact that practical abilities are required for Tim to know how to ski but not for John to know how Mary got home presents a serious problem for the anti-intellectualist view.

In view of these difficulties, it is fair to conclude that the anti-intellectualist account cannot be quite right. Several thinkers have thus turned to an intellectualist account of knowledge-how.[2] Reductionists take knowledge-how to be reducible to knowledge-that. According to Stanley and Williamson, for example, s knows how to F iff for some contextually relevant way w which is a way for s to F, s knows that w is a way for her to F.

Stanley and Williamson are well aware of potential counterexamples to their account. Recall the case of Tim. It is fair to say that, prior to Tim's skiing vacation, there was a contextually relevant way w such that Tim knew that w was a way for him to ski. But in some very salient sense, Tim didn't know how to ski until he hit

---

2. See Stanley and Williamson (2001), Brogaard (2007, 2008, 2009), and Bengson and Moffett (2007). Stanley and Williamson (2001) and Brogaard (2007, 2008, 2009) defend reductionism. Bengson and Moffett (2007) argue for an antireductionist variation on the intellectualist view that amends the views of Stanley, Williamson, and Brogaard.

the slopes and acquired the ability to ski. To avoid these kinds of counterexamples, Stanley and Williamson argue that knowledge-how sometimes requires having the knowledge in question under a certain practical guise. Prior to his skiing vacation, Tim had knowledge of how to ski, but he didn't have the knowledge under a practical guise. So, it was only once he acquired the ability to ski that he knew how to ski. This, of course, is not to say that we couldn't have truly uttered 'Tim knows how to ski' before Tim hit the slopes but only that in the envisaged context of utterance, our utterance of 'Tim knows how to ski' requires for its truth that Tim had the relevant knowledge under a practical guise. Since Tim didn't have the knowledge under a practical guise, what we said was false.

2. *The Predicate View*

My own sympathies lie with the intellectualist account. However, on my view, the analysis of knowledge-how is a special case of the analysis of knowledge-*wh* (Brogaard 2007, 2008, 2009). On the standard account of knowledge-*wh*, *wh*-clauses that occur as the complements of verbs that take both that-clauses and *wh*-clauses are (implicit) questions that denote their true answers.[3] Following Higginbotham (1996, 381), knowledge-*wh* sentences may be assigned the following *metalinguistic* truth-conditions:[4] There is a proposition p such that s knows that p, and p is a true and contextually appropriate answer to the indirect question of the *wh*-clause.

> Knowledge-*wh*: s knows-*wh* iff there is a proposition p such that s knows p, and p is a true and contextually appropriate answer to the indirect question of the *wh*-clause.

The standard account yields the following predictions for 'Maggie knows what to do to get her mother's attention.' The indirect question of the *wh*-clause 'what to do to get her mother's attention' is 'what should Maggie do to get her mother's

---

[3]. For a defense of the disguised-questions approach to wh-complement clauses, see Hintikka (1975), Boër and Lycan (1986), Higginbotham (1996), Bach (2005), Braun (2006, forthcoming), and Kallestrup (2009, 2010). For a variation on this view, see Schaffer (2007).

[4]. The metalinguistic truth-conditions are also sometimes called the 'truth-maker truth-conditions.' They specify what the world (or logical space) must be like for the sentence in question to be true. But they do not specify which proposition is expressed by the sentence. For example, 'it is possible that there are blue swans' can be given the following metalinguistic truth-conditions: 'it is possible that there are blue swans' is true iff there is a world in which there are blue swans. But if 'it is possible that' functions as a sentential operator rather than as an object-language quantifier over worlds, 'it is possible that there are blue swans' does not express the proposition that there is a world in which there are blue swans.

attention?' So on the standard account, Maggie knows what to do to get her mother's attention iff she knows a true and contextually appropriate answer to 'what should Maggie do to get her mother's attention?' If 'Maggie should scream to get her mother's attention' is a true and contextually appropriate answer to 'what should Maggie do to get her mother's attention?' and Maggie knows that she should scream to get her mother's attention, then she knows a true and contextually appropriate answer to the indirect question of the *wh*-clause in 'Maggie knows what to do to get her mother's attention.' So the sentence is true in the envisaged circumstances.

Likewise, the indirect question of the *wh*-clause 'where her binkie is' is 'where is Maggie's binkie?' So Maggie knows where her binkie is iff she knows a true and contextually appropriate answer to 'where is Maggie's binkie?' If 'Maggie's binkie is on the kitchen table' is a true and contextually appropriate answer to 'where is Maggie's binkie?' and Maggie knows that her binkie is on the kitchen table, then Maggie knows a true and contextually appropriate answer to the indirect question of the *wh*-clause in 'Maggie knows where her binkie is.' So the sentence is true.

The standard account seems to yield the right result in a significant number of cases. However, it runs into trouble with respect to iterated knowledge claims. Consider, for instance:

(1) Bart knows that Maggie knows what to do to get her mother's attention.

(1) can be true even if Bart does not know that Maggie will get her mother's attention if she screams. Yet this is not the result delivered by the standard account. On the standard account, 'what to do to get her mother's attention' denotes the proposition 'Maggie will get her mother's attention if she screams.' So (1) is true just in case (2) is true:

(2) Bart knows that Maggie knows that Maggie will get her mother's attention if she screams.

But (we may suppose) Bart knows that knowledge is factive, and so he knows that if Maggie knows that she will get her mother's attention if she screams, then she will get her mother's attention if she screams. So, as knowledge is closed under known consequence (if *s* knows *p*, and *s* knows that *p* entails *q*, then *s* knows *q*),[5] (2) entails:

---

5. Some prefer the following closure principle for knowledge: if *s* knows *p*, and *s* competently deduces *q* and thereby comes to believe *q* while retaining knowledge of *p*, then *s* knows *q*. But if this is the preferred principle, we can assume that Bart comes to believe 'Maggie will get her mother's attention if she screams' by competently deducing it from 'Maggie knows that she will

(3) Bart knows that Maggie will get her mother's attention if she screams.

But, ex hypothesi, Bart doesn't know this.

One could reply to this objection by rejecting Closure. This move has a considerable degree of initial plausibility. Fred Dretske and Robert Nozick familiarly disallow corollaries of Closure where *p* is an ordinary light-weight proposition and *q* is the negation of a heavy-weight skeptical hypothesis (Dretske 1970; Nozick 1981).[6] For example, they disallow the inference from 'I know I have hands' to 'I know I am not a disembodied brain in a vat.' Someone sympathetic to Dretske/Nozick considerations might thus suggest that we reject the instance of Closure utilized in the argument. However, Dretske/Nozick considerations do not lend support to a rejection of the instance of Closure utilized in the argument. That instance does not license inferences from light-weight propositions to the negation of heavy-weight skeptical hypotheses. It licenses inferences from '*s* knows that *r* knows that *p*' to '*s* knows that *p*.'

It may also be objected that the substitution of 'that Maggie will get her mother's attention if she screams' for 'what to do to get her mother's attention' is illegitimate. Following the standard account, 'what to do to get her mother's attention' denotes the true answer that Maggie will get her mother's attention if she screams, but, it may be said, 'that Maggie will get her mother's attention if she screams' does not denote a proposition; following Frege, it denotes a truth-value.

However, this reply is amiss. As the that-clause 'that Maggie will get her mother's attention if she screams' occurs in an attitude context, it does not denote a truth-value. If it denoted a truth-value, its truth-value would matter to the truth-value of the whole. But the truth-values of sentences embedded under an attitude verb do not matter to the truth-value of the whole (except when the attitude verb is factive).[7] 'Fermat's last theorem is true' cannot be substituted for '2 + 2 = 4' in 'almost everyone believes that 2 + 2 = 4.' When embedded under an attitude verb, '2 + 2 = 4' denotes the proposition that 2 + 2 = 4. Likewise, when embedded under an attitude verb, 'that Maggie will get her mother's attention if she screams' denotes the proposition that Maggie will get her mother's attention if she screams. So when embedded under 'know,' the *that*-clause 'that Maggie will

---

get her mother's attention if she screams' while retaining knowledge of 'Maggie knows that she will get her mother's attention if she screams.'

6. The terms 'light-weight proposition' and 'heavy-weight skeptical hypothesis' are borrowed from Hawthorne (2005).

7. Of course, the truth-value of the that-clause matters when the attitude verb is factive, but the point still stands that the truth-value of the whole is not determined by the truth-value of the that-clause. Factivity is a property of the attitude verb.

get her mother's attention if she screams' and the *wh*-clause 'what to do to get her mother's attention' denote the same proposition. As they denote the same proposition, they are intersubstitutable *salva veritate*.

It may also be urged that the substitution of 'that Maggie knows that she will get her mother's attention if she screams' for 'that Maggie knows what to do to get her mother's attention' is illegitimate. However, it is difficult to see what could possibly be the cause of this sort of substitution failure. As we have just seen, when embedded under 'know,' the *that*-clause 'that Maggie will get her mother's attention if she screams' and the *wh*-clause 'what to do to get her mother's attention' denote the same proposition. Moreover, blocking substitution is unlikely to help. If the standard account does not generalize to iterated knowledge ascriptions, then it does not offer a fully general account of *wh*-clauses.

I have elsewhere defended an alternative to the standard view, the so-called *predicate view* (Brogaard 2008, 2009). On the predicate view, *wh*-complement clauses and how-complement clauses (e.g., 'what to do when assaulted by a bully' or 'how to juggle') function as predicate nominals much like 'a man,' as it occurs in 'John met a man,' or 'a philosopher I met in graduate school,' as it occurs in 'I went out with a philosopher I met in graduate school' (Brogaard 2009). In truth-functional contexts, predicate nominals denote sets whose elements are the entities that satisfy the properties expressed by the predicates. 'A man' denotes the set of men, and 'a philosopher I met in graduate school' denotes the set of philosophers I met in graduate school. In attitude contexts, predicate nominals denote the properties they express. On the predicate view, then, the complement clause 'what to do to get her mother's attention' denotes the property of being a (salient) thing Maggie can do to get her mother's attention rather than a true answer to the implicit question of the *wh*-clause. The sentence structure of 'Maggie knows what to do to get her mother's attention' provides a wide-scope existential quantifier. The sentence is true iff for some way w, Maggie knows that w is what to do to get her mother's attention. That is, 'Maggie knows what to do to get her mother's attention' is true iff for some entity w, Maggie knows that w is a (salient) thing she can do to get her mother's attention.

On the predicate view, then, knowledge-how comes out as a special case of knowledge-*wh*. We can articulate the analyses as follows:

(Knowledge-Wh) s knows-*wh*-F iff there is an x such that s knows that x is *wh*-F
(Knowledge-How) s knows how-F iff there is an x such that s knows that x is how-F

'F' is the remainder of the 'how' clause (e.g., 'to walk' or 'Mary got home'). So the predicate view predicts that Maggie knows what to do to get her mother's attention iff there is an x such that Maggie knows that x is what to do to get her mother's attention. Likewise, Maggie knows how to get her mother's attention iff there is an x such that Maggie knows that x is how to get her mother's attention.

The predicate view has the advantage over the standard view that it avoids the problem of iterated knowledge attributions. John knows that Maggie knows how to get her mother's attention iff John knows that there is an x such that Maggie knows that x is how to get her mother's attention. From this, we cannot infer that John knows that Maggie will get her mother's attention if she screams.

The predicate view also has the advantage over the standard view that it extends to other categories of knowledge-how besides knowledge-how-to, including scalar constructions, for instance, 'Jim knows how many graduate students landed a job this year,' 'Amy knows how sensitive Bob is,' 'Maria knows how much wine she can drink without acting silly,' and 'Rachel knows how Shiraz tastes.' The predicate view predicts that 'Jim knows how many graduate students landed a job this year' is true iff there is an n such that Jim knows that n is how many graduate students landed a job this year, that 'Amy knows how sensitive Bob is' is true iff there is an n such that Amy knows that n is how sensitive Bob is, and so on. As it stands, Stanley and Williamson's intellectualist account does not have this virtue, as it takes knowledge-how attributions to quantify over ways.

3. *Gettier Problems*

The intellectualist accounts offered by Stanley, Williamson, Brogaard, Bengson, and Moffett have a certain degree of initial plausibility. As they stand, however, they cannot be quite right. Consider the following kind of counterexample, originally due to Yuri Cath (chapter 5).[8] The faucet in Jason's apartment leaks. Jason finds a faucet manual in the kitchen drawer and fixes it. However, unbeknownst to him, the manual was created by the previous owner's parrot, who liked to step dance on the keyboard of the owner's old typewriter. Over the fifty years of step dancing, the parrot had created a lot of nonsense, but there was this one time when the parrot happened to hit the right keys and created something that made

---

8. Stanley and Williamson offer a Gettier counterexample as an illustration of the parallel between knowledge-that and knowledge-how. In a footnote, however, they say, "Of course, I may learn how to swim by [a faulty] method. Suppose I were thrown in the water, and started to swim by the envisaged method. Then, I would acquire evidence of a practical sort the method is a way for me to swim, evidence that would then suffice for knowledge-how." It is this sort of response that is developed here.

sense: "the faucet manual." The owner never looked at it but had left it in the kitchen drawer, where Jason found it. Under these circumstances, it seems odd to say that there is a way w such that Jason knows (in the standard sense in which knowledge requires nonaccidentally acquired belief) that w is a way to fix the faucet. There is admittedly a way w such that Jason *believes truly* that w is a way to fix the faucet, but the belief is acquired via a faulty method. So Jason cannot claim to have the relevant knowledge. Even so, it seems all right to say that Jason knows how to fix the faucet. In fact, Jason's neighbors often talk about what a handyman he is. Jason knows how to fix the faucet in virtue of having the ability to fix the faucet, but there is no way w such that Jason *knows* (in the standard sense) that w is a way for him to fix the faucet.

Cath offers two further objections to the intellectualist accounts. One can know how to A, Cath says, if one's belief that w (for some w) is a way for one to A is defeated, or if there is no w such that one believes that w is a way to A. He offers two examples in support of these claims. In the first case, Lucy suffers from memory hallucinations. It often seems to her that she remembers learning how to A in spite of the fact that she never learned it. Lucy learns how to juggle on a Saturday, but on Sunday her false memory detector accidentally goes off. However, despite the fact that Lucy knows that she ought to revise her belief that w (for some w) is a way for her to juggle, she continues to hold onto the belief. As Lucy's belief is defeated, there is no way w such that Lucy knows (in the standard sense) that w is a way to juggle. Nonetheless, it seems intuitively clear that Lucy knows how to juggle. She will show you if you ask her.

The second case is similar. Jodie, too, suffers from memory hallucinations and learns how to juggle on Saturday. On Sunday, her false memory detector goes off. Unlike Lucy, however, Jodie revises her belief that w (for the way w, which she was taught was a way to juggle) is a way for her to juggle. So there is no w such that Jodie knows that w is a way for her to juggle. Nonetheless, it seems initially plausible that Jodie still knows how to juggle. She certainly has the ability to do it.

The examples just outlined are counterexamples to the intellectualist views of knowledge-how. Unlike Gettier counterexamples, the know-how counterexamples do not show that the agent lacks knowledge, in spite of the fact that all the posited constraints on knowledge are satisfied. Rather, they show that the agent has knowledge in spite of the fact that some of the posited constraints on knowledge are not satisfied. So the counterexamples show that standard knowledge is not necessary for knowledge-how. As the intellectualist accounts, as originally formulated, entail that standard knowledge is necessary for knowledge-how, the intellectualist accounts must be rejected. Or so the argument goes.

How might the intellectualist reply to this objection? One possible reply is to say that knowledge-how does not require the kind of solid grounding that is required for knowledge-that. This route is taken by Cath. Cath argues that one can have knowledge-how without having a nonaccidentally acquired belief. On Cath's account, s knows how to A if it intellectually seems to s that w (for some w) is a way to A, and w is a way to A. So on Cath's account, knowledge attributions represent belief- and justification-entailing knowledge states in some contexts and intellectual seemings in others.

    I am sympathetic to this sort of reply. As we will see, I think Cath is quite right in thinking that knowledge attributions do not always represent standard belief- and justification-entailing knowledge states. However, I do not think there is good reason to treat 'know' as ambiguously denoting sometimes a knowledge-state and sometimes an intellectual seeming-state. The right conclusion to draw is not that 'know' ambiguously denotes but rather that not all knowledge states are standard knowledge states. Some knowledge states are belief-entailing states that are grounded in the agent's practical abilities. Other knowledge states are not belief-entailing states but are perceptual states or ability states. I begin by arguing that knowledge sometimes is grounded in the agent's practical abilities. I then argue that not all knowledge states are belief-entailing states.

4. *Practical Grounds*

The key to a solution to the problem of how to account for knowledge-how uniformly is to note that the exact same kind of apparent ambiguity that resides in knowledge-how constructions resides also in other knowledge constructions. Consider the following examples.

(4) Bart knows what to do if he is assaulted by a bully.
(5) Maggie knows what to do to get her mother's attention.
(6) There is a way w such that Maggie knows that w is a way to get her mother's attention.

Each of these knowledge attributions has two readings: an ability reading that requires that the agent possess a practical ability and a nonability reading that requires merely that the agent know that w (for some w) is a way to A but that does not require that the agent have the corresponding practical ability. Even if Bart does not have the ability to kick (perhaps he has no legs), Bart may still know in the nonability sense that kicking a bully in the family jewels is what one ought to do if one is assaulted by one. The more natural reading, of course, is the ability reading. On this reading, (4) requires for its truth that Bart has the practical ability to kick. Likewise, on its nonability reading, (5) may be true even if Maggie does not possess the practical ability that is required to get her mother's attention.

What is required on this reading is that Maggie knows that w (for some w) is a way to get her mother's attention. On the ability reading, on the other hand, (5) requires for its truth that Maggie has the ability to get her mother's attention.

Note that even the knowledge-that construction in (6) admits of these two readings. On its nonability reading, it may well be that Maggie knows what to do to get her mother's attention, even if she is unable to do what it takes (perhaps she has lost her voice). On the ability reading, on the other hand, (6) requires for its truth that Maggie has the corresponding practical ability.

More importantly, one can easily conjure up Gettier-style counterexamples for all of these cases. Consider the following scenario: Bart is told by an unreliable witness that if he is ever assaulted by a bully, he ought to kick the bully in the family jewels. The witness is right. If Bart is ever assaulted by a bully, then he ought to kick him in the family jewels. Despite the unreliability of the witness, Bart thus acquires knowledge of what to do if assaulted by a bully. However, it is not the witness's story that grounds his knowledge of what to do if assaulted.

Consider a further scenario. Bart thinks the only way *not* to get his mother's attention is to scream. However, Bart, wanting to deceive his little sister, tells Maggie that the only way to get their mother's attention is to scream. Unbeknownst to Bart, however, their mother, who has just attended a pioneering child-rearing course, believes that one ought to give one's full attention to children who scream. So unbeknownst to Bart, Maggie's screaming will indeed get their mother's attention. Even so, Bart's story is not what grounds Maggie's knowledge of what to do to get her mother's attention.

Cath's Lucy and Jodie cases also carry over to knowledge-*wh*. If Lucy and Jodie know how to juggle, then plausibly they also know what to do to begin juggling and what to do to keep the ball in the air. So Lucy knows what to do to begin juggling in spite of the fact that her belief that w (for some w) is a way for her to begin juggling is defeated, and Jodie knows what to do to begin juggling in spite of the fact that there is no w such that she believes that w is a way for her to begin juggling.

So what is going on? Here is a tentative hypothesis. If the very same problems that arise for the intellectualist accounts of knowledge-how arise also for a reductionist account of knowledge-*wh* and for the corresponding knowledge-*that* constructions, then the problem we have been encountering does not lie with the intellectualist accounts of knowledge-*how*. Rather, it plausibly lies with our standard conception of what can ground practical knowledge.

As epistemic externalism gained popularity in the post-Gettier era, it became widely accepted that one can gain knowledge by acquiring one's belief in the right way. According to reliabilism, one can gain knowledge by acquiring one's belief via a reliable belief-forming method. More recently, a special brand of reliabilism—virtue epistemology—has become the more widely accepted form of externalism. On this view, one does not gain knowledge by acquiring a belief via just any old reliable method. The method in question must be internal to the agent: it must be a cognitive capacity or virtue.

However, the case of practical knowledge illustrates that virtue epistemology, as it stands, cannot be the whole story about what can ground knowledge states. One can possess knowledge in virtue of possessing the right sort of cognitive capacities and exercising them in the right sort of way in the right sort of environment. Beliefs formed in this way are safe. They could not easily have been false. Further, a belief is reliable iff beliefs formed via the same method in the same sort of environment tend to give rise to safe beliefs. So beliefs acquired through the exercise of an intellectual virtue are reliable. But practical belief accompanied by the right sort of practical abilities also satisfies safety and reliability. Abilities are stable traits. If you have the ability to A by doing P in S, then doing P in S is a way for you to A in worlds in which you are sufficiently physically similar to the way you actually are.[9] So if you believe that doing P in S is a way for you to A, and you have the ability to A by doing P in S, then your belief is safe. In the closest worlds in which you believe that doing P in S is a way for you to A, doing P in S is a way for you to A.[10] So in those worlds your belief is true. Moreover, your belief is reliable. Beliefs with the same sort of ground as your actual belief tend to be safe. Practical belief can thus be safe and reliable without being intellectually grounded.

We can thus distinguish two ways in which a knowledge state may be grounded: practically and cognitively. A cognitive ground, as envisaged here, is whatever makes the difference between mere true belief that p and cognitive knowledge that p, for instance, the fact that the belief was formed via a reliable and virtuous belief-forming method in the right sort of environment. A practical ground is whatever makes the difference between mere true belief that doing P in S is a way for one to A and knowing how to A, for instance, the ability to A. Let us refer to both kinds of grounds as 'justificatory grounds.'

Given this notion of a justificatory ground, let us now return to our Gettier cases. Jason knows how to fix the faucet because there is a way w such that Jason knows that w is a way for him to fix the faucet in the right sort of environment. But what grounds his belief that doing P in the right sort of environment is a way for

---

9. I don't succeed in swimming by making swimlike movements if I am not submerged in enough water. So I don't have the ability to swim by making swimlike movements. But I have the ability to swim by making swimlike movements while sufficiently submerged in water.

10. At least assuming that the closest worlds in which you believe that doing P in S is a way for you to A are worlds in which you are sufficiently similar physically to the way you actually are.

him to fix the faucet is not the fact that his belief was acquired via a faulty method but rather the fact that he has an ability that he acquired by reading the manual: the ability to fix the faucet by doing P in S. One cannot acquire knowledge by using methods that yield the right result only accidentally. However, one can acquire a practical ability by using such a method. Thus, one can acquire the ability to A by relying on a method that yields the right result accidentally, and once one has the ability, it can then serve as a justificatory ground for one's true belief that doing P in S is a way for one to A. By reading the fake manual, Jason acquires the true belief that doing P in S is a way for him to fix the faucet, and he acquires the ability to fix the faucet by doing P in S. The ability then serves as a justificatory ground for his true belief that doing P in S is a way for him to fix the faucet.

The case of Maggie is a bit different. Prior to Bart telling her that screaming while being appropriately situated is a way to get her mother's attention, Maggie already has the ability to scream while being appropriately situated. But prior to hearing Bart's story, Maggie doesn't have a belief to the effect that screaming while being appropriately situated is a way for her to get her mother's attention, and so she does not have the ability to get her mother's attention by screaming while being appropriately situated. Bart's story about their mother, of course, does not serve as a cognitive ground for Maggie's true belief that screaming in a certain kind of situation S will get her mother's attention. But the story, together with her ability to *scream* in S, puts her in a position *to get her mother's attention by screaming in S*. It is this newly acquired ability that grounds Maggie's true belief that screaming in S is a way for her to get her mother's attention. That is, it is not the ability she already possesses, the ability to scream in S, that grounds her true belief, but rather the ability to get her mother's attention by screaming in S, an ability she acquires partially on the basis of Bart's story. So Maggie's ability to get her mother's attention by screaming in S, an ability she didn't possess prior to her encounter with Bart, serves as a justificatory ground for her true belief that screaming in S is a way for her to get her mother's attention.

Here is a further example to illustrate, a variation on Alvin Goldman's barn case. Henry is driving in the country and stops in front of a barn. Unbeknownst to Henry, he is looking at one of few real barns in an area with many facsimiles. The facsimiles are so realistic that if he had stopped in front of any of them, he would have been tricked into thinking that he was looking at a real barn. The standard intuition is that Henry does not know that he is looking at a barn, because he could easily have had the same belief while looking at a facsimile. In the variation, Henry truly believes that w (for some w) is a way for him to get to a barn. As in the original example, Henry's belief could easily have been false. If Henry had stopped anywhere else in barn country, which he could easily have done, he would have stopped in front of a fake barn. As Henry doesn't know that he is in an area full of barn facades, he would still have formed the belief that w (for some w) is a way for him to get to a barn. Yet his belief would have been false. Since Henry's belief that w (for some w) is a way for him to get to a barn could easily have been false, Henry fails to know (in the standard sense) that w is a way for him to get to a barn. Nonetheless, there is a strong feeling that Henry knows how to get to a barn. All he has to do is walk for five minutes in the right direction.

If we allow that knowledge can be grounded in practical abilities, then we have a straightforward explanation of how Henry can have knowledge of how to get to a barn in spite of the fact that there is no way w such that Henry knows (in the standard sense) that w is a way for him to get to a barn. What grounds Henry's knowledge of how to get to a barn is his ability to get to a barn by walking for five minutes toward a barn. In the closest worlds in which Henry believes that walking for five minutes toward a barn is a way for him to get to a barn, Henry's belief is true. So Henry's belief that walking for five minutes toward a barn is safe.

The proposed solution to the Gettier-style counterexamples carries over to Cath's Lucy case. Acquiring the ability to A by doing P in S provides a justificatory ground for one's belief that doing P in S is a way for one to A. The fact that Lucy ought not to have believed that doing P in S is a way for her to juggle is irrelevant. She does believe this, and her belief is safe and reliable. In the closest worlds in which she believes that doing P in S is a way for her to juggle, doing P in S is indeed a way for her to juggle.

A somewhat similar response can be given to an objection offered by Bengson and Moffett (2007) to the reductionist intellectualist accounts defended by Stanley and Williamson (2001) and Brogaard (2007, 2008, 2009). According to them, there are cases in which s knows that w (for some w) is a way for s to A but in which s fails to know how to A because s lacks sufficient understanding of the concepts involved in her belief. They offer the following example as an illustration. Irina knows a way of doing a salchow: to do a salchow, she must take off from the back inside edge of her skate, jump in the air, spin, and land on the back outside edge of her skate. But she is confused about the concepts back inside edge and back outside edge. She takes her back inside edge to be her front inside edge and her back outside edge to be her front outside edge. However, Irina has a neurological disorder and acts in ways that differ from how she takes herself to be acting and is therefore able to perform a salchow in spite of her confusion. In this case, Bengson and Moffett say, Irina does not know how to perform a salchow in spite of the fact that she possesses the ability to perform one. Bengson and Moffett conclude that for one to know how to A, it does not suffice that one has a true and justified belief to the effect that w (for some w) is a way to A; one must also have minimal understanding of the concepts involved in the beliefs one has about the relevant way to A.

My intuitions differ from those of Bengson and Moffett. How odd it would be to say 'Irina performs at least one salchow every day but she doesn't know how to do it; she simply has no clue.' Here is one possible explanation of why it is odd to say this: if Bengson and Moffett are right that there is a *w* such that Irina truly believes that *w* is a way for her to perform a salchow, then the fact that she has the practical ability to perform a salchow suffices to turn her true belief into knowledge. Owing to the stability of her ability to A by doing P in S, her belief that doing P in S is a way for her to A is safe and reliably formed.

Cath's Jodie case is potentially more devastating. Acquiring the ability to A may suffice for acquiring a justificatory ground for one's true belief that *w* (for some *w*) is a way for one to A, but it does not seem sufficient for acquiring the belief that *w* (for some *w*) is a way for one to A.

Here is a possible reply to this case. Some abilities are acquired as a result of acquiring a belief of the right sort. For example, Jason didn't have the ability to fix the faucet by doing P in S before he acquired the belief that doing P in S is a way for him to fix the faucet. Likewise, Maggie didn't have the ability to get her mother's attention by screaming while being appropriately situated until she acquired the belief that screaming while being appropriately situated is a way for her to get her mother's attention. It is plausible that when Jodie acquires the ability to juggle, she also acquires the belief that *w* (for some *w*) is a way for her to juggle. But then if Jodie really has the ability to juggle, arguably she also has a belief to the effect that *w* (for some *w*) is a way for her to juggle. The belief may not be an occurrent belief. Jodie may even deny that she knows how to juggle (and hence also that *w* is a way for her to juggle). But she might nonetheless have acquired the belief that *w* (for some *w*) is a way for her to juggle when she acquired the ability to juggle.

Of course, it may be denied that when Jodie acquired the ability to juggle, she also acquired the belief that *w* (for some *w*) is a way for her to juggle. But there is then a different reply to these sorts of cases. When one has the ability to A, and that ability intuitively suffices for knowledge of how to A, then one is in an ability state that carries information about the procedure that will lead one to A. Such ability states, I will argue, are primitive knowledge states that are not belief entailing. So one can be in them without being in a corresponding belief-state. On this view, then, it could be that even if Jodie does not believe that *w* (for some *w*) is a way for her to A, she has primitive knowledge that *w* (for some *w*) is a way for her to A. I will now offer arguments for thinking that some ability states are (primitive) knowledge states.

5. *Primitive Knowledge*

One argument for the existence of primitive knowledge states is what I will call the 'argument from animal knowledge.' We sometimes say of infants and nonhuman individuals that they know how to A in spite of the fact that we would hesitate to attribute substantive belief states to them. For example, it seems all right to say that my hamster knows how to find his food tray and that baby Bob knows how to touch his feet. But it is quite plausible that to have the capacity for belief in the full sense, one must have the capacity for thought. Yet infants and nonhuman individuals do not have the capacity for thought. So it is plausible that they do not have the capacity for belief either. As the standard intellectualist accounts state that s knows how to A just in case s knows that w (for some w) is a way for s to A, and standard knowledge-that entails belief, the standard intellectualist accounts make the wrong predictions in these cases.

One could perhaps explain away the appeal of attributions of knowledge-how to infants and nonhuman individuals pragmatically. This strategy has some degree of initial plausibility, especially since the problem arises also for knowledge-that. For example, if my hamster Harry sees me fill his food tray and waddles toward it, it seems all right to say that Harry knows that there is food in his tray, and if I hand baby Bob his binkie and he reaches for it, it seems all right to say that Bob knows that his binkie is in front of him.

However, while it is tempting to offer a pragmatic explanation of these cases, I think the strategy ultimately fails. There is a more compelling argument for the thesis that infants and nonhuman individuals can have knowledge. For Williamson, knowledge is the most general factive mental state because any other factive mental state entails it. More precisely, where 'Φ' is a factive attitude verb (e.g., seeing or realizing), 's Φs that p' entails 's knows that p.' For example, "John realized that Mary was in love with him" entails "John knew that Mary was in love with him," and "John saw that there was food on his plate" entails "John knew that there was food on his plate."

Suppose for the moment that Williamson is right about the generality of knowledge. It then follows that necessarily, if s sees that p, then s knows that p. But most of us would be quite happy to grant that infants and nonhuman individuals have the capacity to see. For example, it should be quite uncontroversial to venture that Fido can see that the gate is open and that baby Bob can see that his binkie is in front of him. But if seeing-that entails knowing-that, then it follows by the generality assumption that Fido knows that the gate is open and that baby Bob knows that his binkie is in front of him. So if the generality assumption is correct, then either infants and nonhuman individuals have the capacity for belief, or knowledge is not always belief entailing.

One way to avoid the objection from animal knowledge is thus to argue either (i) that infants and nonhuman individuals have the capacity for belief or (ii) that knowledge is not belief entailing. If indeed belief requires the capacity for thought, which it plausibly does, then the first line of response is not very plausible. The first line of response also does nothing to address other cases of knowledge-that in which the agent has knowledge but not belief. Consider, for example, the problem of the timid student (see Woozley 1953, Radford 1966, and Lewis 1996). The timid student knows the answer to the teacher's question, but he doubts his own abilities and hence fails to believe what he knows. The problem of the timid student is exactly that of explaining how knowledge can be possible without belief.

However, the second strategy, which is that of denying that knowledge is belief entailing, holds some promise. We can interpret Williamson's generality claim as follows: knowledge need not be a belief state that satisfies certain epistemic constraints. Rather, knowledge is a determinable of which other mental states are determinates. Perceptual states, standing belief states, judgments, realizations, recollections, ability states, introspective states, and so on are all determinates of knowledge, as long as they satisfy certain epistemic constraints. Some of these, for example, seeings, are primitive knowledge states; others are standard knowledge states.

We can shed further light on the nature of primitive knowledge states by turning to Ernest Sosa's (2007) distinction between what he calls 'animal knowledge' and 'reflective knowledge.' For Sosa, reflective knowledge requires a reliable second-order belief, whereas animal knowledge requires only a reliable first-order belief. For an individual s to have animal knowledge, s's belief must be apt, that is, correct in a way creditable to the believer (the belief must be accurate in virtue of having been formed on the basis of s's exercise of an epistemic competence). For s to have reflective knowledge, s must in addition aptly believe that she aptly believes that p. Sosa thus takes both of these kinds of knowledge to require belief. But one could spell out the distinction between animal knowledge and reflective knowledge in other ways. For example, instead of saying that s has animal knowledge just when s has an apt belief, one could say that s has animal knowledge that p when s is in some state with the content of 'p' that is apt (e.g., a perceptual state, a memory state, an introspective state, a belief state, and so on). For simplicity, let us take aptness to be analyzable in terms of safety and reliability.

A word on safety and reliability as applied to perceptual states is here in order. To a first approximation, we can say that s is in a safe perceptual state with the content of 'p' iff in the closest worlds in which s is in a perceptual state with the content of 'p', p is true. Likewise, we can say that s's perceptual state that p is reliably formed in a given environment iff perceptual states formed via the same method in the same kind of environment tend to give rise to safe perceptual states.

One virtue of taking perceptual states that satisfy certain epistemic constraints to be primitive knowledge states is that this hypothesis can explain the difference between good and bad perceptual states. Consider the following scenario: Mike is looking at a blue ball right in front of him and sees that the ball is blue and is right in front of him. But after a few minutes, Mike is given a palinopsia-inducing hallucinogenic drug. The drug causes his experience to persist after the corresponding stimuli have left and prevents his visual system from processing new visual information.

If we suppose, for the moment, that perception is a mental state with a Russellian content that consists of properties and/or physical objects, then the content of Mike's initial perceptual state consists of the blue ball o, the reflectance type blue, and the property of being right in front of Mike. But it is plausible that the content of Mike's experience continues to be a conglomeration of the blue ball o, the reflectance type blue, and the property of being right in front of Mike even after the drug takes effect. After all, advocates of the thesis that mental states have Russellian content will be happy to grant that one can have a belief directly about an object even when the object is not present. So given a Russellian view of content, there shouldn't be any principled reason for denying that the blue ball can be a constituent of Mike's experience even after the drug takes effect. Of course, for one to have a belief directly about an object, one must be in some sort of causal contact with the object. But Mike is in causal contact with the blue ball. The blue ball is a cause of his experience. It is thus plausible that the content of Mike's perceptual experience consists of the blue ball o, the reflectance type blue, and the property of being two feet away from Mike. So Mike's hallucination is veridical.

Now, few would be happy to grant that the content of perceptual experience is exhausted by its Russellian content. David Chalmers (2004a) suggests that the content of perceptual experience has a Russellian and a Fregean component.[11] The Fregean component is the phenomenal content of the experience and is the same regardless of what the environment is like. The Fregean content yields a Russellian content in a particular environment. Roughly, the Fregean content of Mike's experience as of the blue ball o consists of the property of being the object that is causing the current experience, and the property of being the property that normally causes phenomenally blue experiences. In the best of cases, the Fregean content yields a Russellian content that consists of the blue ball o and the reflectance type blue. In normal cases of hallucination, there is no external object. So the Fregean content yields a gappy Russellian content, and so the hallucination fails to be veridical.

---

11. Chalmers (2006) argues that perceptual experiences also have edenic content, which consists of primitive nonphysical properties. The edenic content of perceptual experience is (imperfectly) veridical just in case it matches the Russellian content, which it does if it is the sort of content normally caused by the properties and objects constituting the Russellian content.

However, even on the Fregean account of perceptual content, the possibility of veridical hallucination arises. Suppose again that Mike is given a palinopsia-inducing hallucinogenic drug that causes his blue ball experience to persist and prevents his visual system from processing new visual information. We might imagine that Mike's experience remains the same for at least a few minutes following the administering of the drug. But Mike's experience was caused by the blue ball *o*, so arguably the Fregean property of being the object that caused Mike's experience yields *o* in our envisaged circumstances. But Mike's hallucination then is veridical.

It may, of course, be thought that while Mike is under the influence of the drug, Mike's experience is not *appropriately* caused by the blue ball. One could, for example, say that even though there once was a causal chain leading from the blue ball to Mike's experience, such a causal chain no longer obtains. But this can't be right. Causation is never instantaneous. So it cannot be the time lag between the ball's reflectance of light and the experience taking place that stands in the way of causation. In fact, we can even stand in appropriate causal connections to objects that are no longer present. For example, it is quite plausible that I am not hallucinating when I am stargazing. But if we can stand in appropriate causal relations to objects that are no longer present, then it is plausible that Mike can also stand in an appropriate causal relation to the blue ball in the envisaged circumstances. Of course, Mike's perceptual system mistakenly allows his past experience of the blue ball to persist when it ought to have allowed for the receipt of new visual information. But this only shows that Mike's experience is defective in some way, not that it fails to be properly caused by the object the experience is about.

If veridical hallucination is possible, then we cannot take veridicality to be a mark of good perceptual experiences and falsidicality to be a mark of bad perceptual experiences. If, however, good perceptual states are primitive knowledge states, then we have a straightforward explanation of the difference between good and bad perceptual states. Bad perceptual states fail to be primitive knowledge states. Of course, not all safe and reliable perceptual states are primitive knowledge states. Suppose the hallucinatory drug prevents Mike from moving. Then in all the closest worlds in which Mike has an experience as of the blue ball being right in front of him, the blue ball is right in front of him. So Mike's hallucination is safe. Moreover, experiences formed in the same way as Mike's in the same type of environment will tend to be safe. So Mike's hallucination is reliably formed. It is, however, well known that knowledge cannot be analyzed in terms of safety and reliability. Some think knowledge states are sensitive, where *s* is in a sensitive S-state with the content '*p*' iff if *p* were false, then *s* wouldn't be in an S-state with the content of '*p*.' Mike's hallucination fails to be sensitive. In some of the closest worlds in which the blue ball *o* is no longer in front of Mike, Mike would still have an experience as of the blue ball *o* being right in front of him. So one could say that Mike's hallucination fails to be a primitive knowledge state because it fails to satisfy sensitivity.

Of course, appealing to sensitivity will not explain the defect of all cases of veridical hallucination. Suppose Alice is told to give Mike a drug that instantly neutralizes the effects of the hallucinatory drug just if the blue ball *o* is no longer right in front of Mike. Then in the closest worlds in which the blue ball *o* is no longer right in front of Mike, Mike does not have an experience as of *o* being right in front of him. So Mike's hallucination satisfies sensitivity. But this does not show that good perceptual states are not primitive knowledge states but only that knowledge cannot be analyzed in terms of safety, reliability, and sensitivity, which of course is already well known.

Treating perceptual states that satisfy certain epistemic constraints as determinates of knowledge thus has the advantage that we can account for the difference between good and bad perceptual states. A further advantage of treating a wider range of mental states that satisfy certain epistemic constraints as knowledge states is that this gives us a straightforward way of explaining why it seems all right to attribute knowledge to individuals who do not have the capacity for belief. One can be in a primitive knowledge state without being in a corresponding belief state. So one can have primitive knowledge even if one does not have the capacity for belief. For example, my hamster Harry might know that there is food in his tray in virtue of being in a good perceptual state with the representational content of "there is food in my tray," Fido might know the gate is open in virtue of being in a good perceptual state with the representational content of 'the gate is open,' and baby Bob might know that his binkie is in front of him in virtue of being in a good perceptual state with the representational content of "my binkie is in front of me."

The concerns about animal knowledge-how can be addressed in the same way. Even if infants and nonhuman individuals do not have the capacity for belief, it is plausible that they can be in representational ability states. If *s* knows how to A but does not have a belief to the effect that doing $P_1, P_2, P_3, \ldots$ in S is a way for *s* to A, then it is plausible that *s*, at least at some level of information processing, has information to the effect that doing $P_1, P_2, P_3, \ldots$ in S is a way for *s* to A. But if *s* must have this sort of information in order to know how to A, then it is plausible that some knowledge-how states are pairs of a representational informational state and a bodily ability state. This sort of informational-ability state is not a belief-like state but is a quite distinct state, which we might simply call an 'ability state.' Let us stipulate that if one is in such a state, then the state represents the world correctly, and one has the ability to A. One can, of course, have a belief with the representational content of 'doing $P_1, P_2, P_3, \ldots,$ in S is a way for me to A' without being in an ability state. Like the corresponding belief states, ability states are representational states, but unlike the corresponding belief states, they are not pure mental states. Like emotions, they have a mental and a bodily component.

In spite of being psychosomatic states, however, ability states are much more like knowledge states than belief states. Being in a knowledge state with the content of 'p' suffices for p to be true. Likewise, being in an ability state suffices for having the corresponding ability. Moreover, like knowledge states, ability states tend to be reliable, safe, and sensitive. First, if s is in an ability state with the information content of 'doing $P_1, P_2, P_3, \ldots$, in S is a way for s to A,' then in all the closest worlds in which s is in an ability state with the information content of 'doing $P_1, P_2, P_3, \ldots$, in S is a way for s to A,' doing $P_1, P_2, P_3, \ldots$, in S is a way for s to A. Second, in the closest worlds in which $P_1, P_2, P_3, \ldots$, in S is not a way for s to A, s is not in an ability state with the content of 'doing $P_1, P_2, P_3, \ldots$, in S is a way for s to A.' So ability states are sensitive. Third, ability states acquired in the same way as s's ability state by agents physically similar to s tend to be safe. So ability states are reliable. These analogies between standard knowledge states and ability states give us some reason to treat ability states as kinds of knowledge states.

This is good news for the intellectualists. If we do not allow that ability states can be knowledge states, then the best we can do, it seems, is to posit a disjunctive account of knowledge-how: s knows how to A iff s has the ability to A, or there is a w such that s knows that w is a way for s to A. This yields the right result in a number of cases. I know how to get to New York in spite of lacking the ability to get there because there is a way w such that I know that w is a way for me to get to New York. Likewise, because Jodie has the ability to juggle, Jodie knows how to juggle in spite of the fact that there is no way w such that she knows (in the standard sense) that w is a way for her to juggle.

However, the disjunctive account of knowledge-how is not very satisfying. Here are two considerations against it. Disjunctive analyses, while they may be good first approximations, often leave something to be desired. They fail to offer an explanation of why the analysandum obtains just when one of the disjuncts does. This is not to say that there aren't any genuinely disjunctive concepts. There are. 'Sibling' is a case in point. To satisfy this concept, one must be a brother or a sister. However, in this case the disjuncts have important features in common. They both denote one of several offspring of the same parents. Things are different when it comes to a disjunctive account for knowledge-how. On the face of things, having the ability to A and having the knowledge (in the standard sense) that w (for some w) is a way to A are two entirely different things with no interesting features in common. There may, of course, turn out to be interesting commonalities between having the ability to A and having the knowledge that *w* (for some *w*) is a way for one to A. But even if this should turn out to be the case, the disjunctive account is inadequate because it fails to explain what these features are.

Here is a second consideration against the disjunctive account of knowledge-how. If a disjunctive account is required for knowledge-how, then a disjunctive account is required also for knowledge-*wh*, for the problems that threaten to undermine the intellectualist accounts of knowledge-how also threaten to undermine a reductive account of knowledge-*wh*. First, we find it just as natural to attribute knowledge-*wh* to infants and nonhuman individuals as we do attributing knowledge-how. For example, it seems all right to say that baby Bob knows where his binkie is, that Fido knows where his bone is, and that the canary knows what to do to get from point A to point B. Second, one can possess knowledge-*wh* even when one's belief is not reliably formed in the standard way. Maggie knows what to do to get her mother's attention even if she acquired her belief that screaming while being appropriately situated is a way for her to get her mother's attention on the basis of unreliable testimony. Third, one can possess knowledge-*wh* even when one does not have any corresponding beliefs. For example in the Jodie case, if Jodie knows how to juggle, then plausibly she also knows what to do to begin juggling and what to do to keep the balls in the air.

The reductionist account of knowledge-*wh* is thus subject to the same range of problems as the intellectualist accounts of knowledge-how. So if we need a disjunctive account for knowledge-how, then we also need one for knowledge-*wh*. But it is generally agreed that knowledge-*wh* is reducible to knowledge-that. For example, John knows what the capital of Vermont is iff he knows that Montpelier is the capital of Vermont, and Lisa knows who the author of *Naming and Necessity* is iff she knows that Saul Kripke is the author of *Naming and Necessity*.

The hypothesis that one can have knowledge-how by being in a mental state (e.g., an ability state or a belief state) that qualifies as a kind of knowledge state has a number of virtues compared with the disjunctive and standard intellectualist accounts of knowledge-how. First, if both ability states and belief states can be knowledge states, then we have a more unified account of knowledge-how. If *s* is in an ability state with the content of 'doing $P_1, P_2, P_3, \ldots$, in S is a way for *s* to A,' and ability states are knowledge states, then there is a way *w* (namely, doing $P_1, P_2, P_3, \ldots$ in S) such that *s* knows that *w* is a way for *s* to A. For example, it is plausible that my hamster Harry is in an ability state with the representational content of 'doing $P_1, P_2, P_3, \ldots$, in S is a way for me to find my food bowl.' So if ability states are knowledge states, then there is a way *w* such that my hamster Harry knows that *w* is a way for him to find his food bowl. The fact that nonhuman individuals can have knowledge-how then does not give us reason to opt for a disjunctive analysis of knowledge-how. An intellectualist analysis will suffice.

Second, the hypothesis that both belief states and ability states are knowledge states allows for a more unified account of knowledge-*wh*. The kinds of knowledge-*wh* that we most frequently attribute to less cognitively capable individuals are knowledge-where and knowledge-what-to-do. For example, we might say that Fido knows where his bone is or that the canary knows what to do to get from point A to point B. In both of these cases, it is plausible that we attribute ability states to the individuals in question. For example, it is plausible that our attribution of knowledge-where to Fido represents an ability state with the content of 'doing $P_1, P_2, P_3, \ldots$, in S is a way for Fido to find his bone' and that our attribution of knowledge-what-to-do to the canary represents an ability state with the content of 'doing $P_1, P_2, P_3, \ldots$, in S is a way for the canary to get from point A to point B.' So if ability states are knowledge states, then when *s* is in an ability state with the content of 'doing $P_1, P_2, P_3, \ldots$, in S is a way for *s* to A,' there is a way *w* (namely, doing $P_1, P_2, P_3, \ldots$, in S) such that *s* knows that *w* is a way for *s* to A. So if ability states are primitive knowledge states, then there is no need for a disjunctive analysis of knowledge-*wh*.

Third, if Jodie stops believing that *w* (for some *w*) is a way for her to juggle but she still has the ability to juggle, and this ability intuitively suffices for knowledge-how, then plausibly Jodie is in an ability state that represents that a certain way is a way for her to juggle. So if ability states are knowledge states, then there is a *w* such that she knows that *w* is a way for her to juggle. So the Jodie objection then does not present a threat to an intellectualist account.

Fourth, if ability states can be primitive knowledge states, then we have a straightforward way of addressing the problem of the timid student. The timid student knows the answer to the teacher's question but doubts his own abilities and hence fails to believe what he knows. The timid student will answer the teacher's question correctly if asked but will refuse to raise his hand or admit that he believes what he knows (at least prior to answering the teacher's question). The problem of the timid student is that of explaining how the student can have knowledge without belief. One possible solution is to say that the student has a dispositional belief and hence dispositional knowledge. Another, and in my opinion superior, solution is to say that the student has standing knowledge but that the knowledge in question is a kind of primitive knowledge. Although the timid student doesn't believe what he knows, he has the ability to answer the teacher's question correctly. Plausibly, he is in an ability state to the effect that expressing P is a way for him to answer the teacher's question. So if ability states are knowledge states, then the timid student plausibly has knowledge of the answer.

It is plausible, then, that one can have knowledge-how without having a corresponding belief. Being in an ability state with the content of 'doing $P_1, P_2, P_3, \ldots$, in S is a way for me to A' suffices for knowing how to A.

An objection here arises. It may be argued that possessing the ability to A does not always suffice for knowing how to A. Paul Snowdon presents the following counterexample:

> A man is in a room, which, because he has not explored it in the least, he does, as yet, not know how to get out of. In fact, there is an obvious exit which he can easily open. He is perfectly able to get out, he can get out, but does not know how to (as yet). (2003, 11)

It seems perfectly all right to say that the man has the ability to get out of the room (he just has to look around), and yet it seems highly plausible that he doesn't know how to get out. He doesn't know how to get out because at present there is no way *w* such that he knows that *w* is a way to get out. Despite the initial plausibility of this objection, I don't think it succeeds in undermining the thesis that knowledge-how attributions sometimes attribute primitive knowledge.

The example trades on an ambiguity in the word 'ability.' In one sense of the word, *s* has the ability to A just in case *s* is in an ability state with a content that represents a certain procedure for how to A, and *s* has the bodily capacities for carrying out the procedure. In another sense, *s* has the ability to A just in case *s* has certain bodily capacities that, if combined with the right sort of procedural information, will put *s* in a position to A. The man in Snowdon's example is not in a state with a content that represents a procedure for getting out. There is a procedure (namely, looking around) that, when internalized by the man, will put him in a position to get out. Only the first kind of ability is of the sort possessed by agents in ability states.

'Ability,' of course, is frequently used in the latter sense in ordinary language. For example, we might say, "Of course, you can swim, everyone can swim, you just have to learn it first" or "of course, she is perfectly able to walk, she just doesn't know how to yet, she is only eleven months old." Or consider a variation on the man-in-the-room example. To get out, one must press a button behind the bookshelves, step on a particular floor plank, and yell 'out' three times. Even so, saying the following seems perfectly fine: "Of course, the man is perfectly able to get out. He just has to press a button behind the bookshelves, step on a particular floor plank, and yell 'out' three times." However, in neither the original case nor the variation can we attribute to the agent an ability state with a content that represents a procedure for achieving the intended result. Hence, the agents in these scenarios do not know how to get out (as yet). They have not yet internalized the relatively simple procedures that will lead to their escape. The sorts of abilities that are relevant to knowledge-how are abilities that correspond to ability states, that is, abilities that correspond to procedures that have been internalized by the agent. Rather than being a counterexample to our account, Snowdon's example thus turns out to support it. His example shows that it is only the possession of abilities of a special kind that can constitute ability states, namely, abilities that correspond to step-by-step procedures that have been fully internalized by the agent in question.

The view that mental-state-involving abilities are knowledge-how states thus naturally leads to a disjunctive theory of abilities as either (a) states that are constituted by bodily capacities and procedures that have been internalized by the agent and are therefore essentially mind involving or (b) bodily capacities that, if combined with the right sort of procedural information, will put the agent in a position to achieve the relevant end. The former kind of ability is fundamentally a knowledge state, that is, a knowledge-how state.

6. Conclusion

The two predominant views of knowledge-how are the intellectualist and the anti-intellectualist views. On the intellectualist views defended by Stanley and Williamson (2001) and Brogaard (2007, 2008, 2009), one knows how to A just if one knows that w (for some w) is a way for one to A. On the anti-intellectualist view, originally defended by Ryle, one knows how to A just if one has the ability to A. The two views are normally thought to be in conflict. However, I have argued that the conflict is only apparent. The conflict can be partially resolved by noting that there are two ways in which a knowledge state can be grounded. A knowledge state can have either cognitive abilities or practical abilities as its justificatory ground. Whereas knowing that snow is white requires a cognitive ability as its justificatory ground, knowing how to fix the faucet or what to do to get your mother's attention requires a practical ability as its justificatory ground. The really problematic cases of knowledge-how are cases in which the agent does not have a belief that w (for some w) is a way for her to A. I concluded by arguing that there are primitive knowledge states that one can be in without being in corresponding belief states and that knowledge-that and knowledge-how attributions sometimes represent such states. The view defended naturally leads to a disjunctive conception of abilities as either essentially involving mental states or as not essentially involving mental states. Only the former kind of ability is a kind of knowledge state, that is, a knowledge-how state.[12]

---

12. Thanks to Kent Bach, David Braun, Yuri Cath, David Chalmers, Bruce Russell, Jonathan Schaffer, and Daniel Stoljar for discussion of these and related issues.

7
Nonpropositional Intellectualism

John Bengson and Marc A. Moffett

Understanding is a part of knowing how.
GILBERT RYLE, *The Concept of Mind*

THERE ARE MANY things we know how to do: cycle, play chess, do a headstand, tell the truth, assess arguments for validity, and so on. On one hand, such knowledge how seems to be *practical*—unlike mere knowledge that, which can be possessed even by incompetent, impractical "fools". On the other hand, knowledge how seems to be a genuinely *cognitive*, even if not a ratiocinative or discursive, achievement—unlike mere abilities or dispositions to behavior, which can be enjoyed even by mindless entities or automata, such as simple machines and plants.[1] The goal of this chapter is to develop a view of knowledge how that has the resources to account for its simultaneously practical and cognitive character.

Section 1 begins to make room for this view by distinguishing between two debates about knowledge how: a debate about the *grounds* of knowledge how versus a debate about what knowledge how really *is*. Section 2 argues that the grounds of knowledge how must be intellectualist. Section 3 maintains that, nevertheless, there remains a substantive connection between knowledge how and action (although this connection does not motivate anti-intellectualism). Subsequently, section 4 explores the possibility that knowledge how is an *objectual*, rather than propositional, state or attitude. Finally, section 5 advances a view we call *objectualist intellectualism*: to know how to act is to understand a way of so acting, where such objectual understanding involves grasping a (possibly implicit) conception that is poised to guide the successful, intentional performance of such an act—hence, to possess a cognitive state with a distinctively practical character.

---

1. Cf. Ryle (1945, 8) and Descartes (1637/1984, part V), respectively. These two observations are not meant to prejudge the relation between knowing how and knowing that. We use 'cognitive' in a traditional sense that opposes the cognitive to the sensory. Thus, for example, even Ryle allowed that knowledge how is a "*cognitive* disposition" (1949, 44), which is not possessed by, e.g., unintelligent parrots, "louts" (1949, 32), and "fools" (1945, 8); as discussed later, he simply denied that knowledge how is a *propositional* (intellectual, representational) affair.

1. Two Debates

Is knowing how to perform (execute) some action or behavior φ a matter of having certain propositional attitudes regarding φ, or is it instead a matter of having a certain type of power—for instance, ability or disposition—to φ? This question can be understood as dividing "intellectualists" and "anti-intellectualists" about knowing how:[2]

Intellectualism
x knows how to φ in virtue of x's having some propositional attitude(s) regarding φ-ing.[3]

Anti-intellectualism
x knows how to φ in virtue of x's having some power—some ability or disposition—to φ, rather than propositional attitudes.[4]

Here we find disagreement about the *grounds* of knowing how to φ—that is, disagreement regarding that in virtue of which one knows how to φ, when one does.[5]

---

2. To our knowledge, the use of the term *intellectualist* as a label for a view of knowledge how is due to Ryle (1945). These theses about knowing how to φ (hereafter, simply 'knowing how') may be understood as specific instances of more general views about the nature of mind and action; see the state of play chapter in this book for further discussion.

3. Throughout, the 'in virtue of' locution should be understood as invoking a relation of partial or full grounding (asymmetric determination or dependence), not mere necessitation or supervenience (see, e.g., Kim 1974, 1994; Fine 1995; Correia 2005, chs. 3–4; and Schaffer 2009a). Thus the intellectualist claims that knowledge how to φ is grounded in propositional attitudes regarding φ-ing—plus, perhaps, facts about the mode in which one entertains the relevant propositions (Stanley and Williamson 2001) or facts about one's conceptual situation (Bengson and Moffett [BM] 2007; see also §5.1). See note 7 for a characterization of propositional attitudes.

4. We will understand a power to be a feature of agents typically expressed by a modal auxiliary such as 'can', 'could', or 'would'. We will concentrate on abilities and dispositions.

5. Although theorists standardly focus on these intellectualist and anti-intellectualist end points, there are other possible views. For example, a *primitivist* view holds that knowledge how is not grounded in any further state, whether a propositional attitude or power or anything else. It is also worth mentioning two hybrid strategies: a *conjunctivist* view holds that knowledge how is grounded *both* in propositional attitude(s) regarding φ-ing *and* in an ability or disposition to φ (cf. Carr 1979); a *disjunctivist* view holds that knowledge how is grounded *either* in some propositional attitude(s) regarding φ-ing *or* in an ability or disposition to φ (cf. Williams 2008). To the extent that they hold that knowledge how is at least partially grounded in propositional attitudes, conjunctivism and disjunctivism qualify as versions of intellectualism. Later we argue that having the ability or disposition to φ is neither necessary nor sufficient for knowing how to φ (see §2), yet knowing how need not be primitive (see §5). If those arguments are correct, they undercut conjunctivism, disjunctivism, and primitivism, respectively. As far as we can tell, all other plausible alternatives are susceptible to similar arguments. Consequently,

A second, distinct but closely related debate concerns the *nature* of knowing how to φ (or, if you prefer, what it *is*: its analysis, definition, or essence). Suppose that

x knows how to φ

where *x* is an agent and φ is some action or behavior. Here it seems that *x* stands in some relation—a *knowing* or *knowing-how* relation—to something else—φ or *how to* φ.[6] We can then ask, first, what is the relation? Second, what is the second relatum or the object of the relation (i.e., that to which *x* is related in knowing how to φ)? The orthodox answers to these questions can be formulated as follows:

Propositionalism
The relation is a propositional attitude relation (e.g., a *knowing-that* relation), and the second relatum is a proposition (e.g., an answer or set of answers to the question of how to φ).[7]

Dispositionalism
The relation is a behavioral-dispositional relation (e.g., a *being-able-to* relation), and the second relatum is an action-type or some other nonpropositional item (e.g., φ-ing itself).

This second debate is not focused on that in virtue of which one knows how to φ, when one does. Rather, the disagreement concerns the *nature* of knowing how: it is disagreement about what knowing how to φ really *is*. What is the relation, and what is the second relatum?

Traditionally, propositionalism and dispositionalism have gone hand-in-hand with intellectualism and anti-intellectualism, respectively. But an intellectualist

---

because it greatly simplifies the presentation of the material, we will follow tradition in focusing on the indicated end points.

6. Introducing the second debate in terms of relations need not prejudge any substantive questions. We can—and sometimes will—speak in terms of states (the state of knowledge or knowledge-how) or attitudes (the attitude of knowledge or knowledge-how).

7. We will understand a propositional attitude to be a truth-evaluable, possibly externalistically individuated mental state that relates a subject to a proposition, where a proposition is that which is or may be the semantic value of a full indicative sentence. Propositionalists reduce knowing how to such a propositional attitude (or at least a "species" of propositional attitude; Stanley and Williamson 2001, 433–434). Incidentally, the relation expressed by 'knowledge that' attributions is arguably a relation to facts, rather than propositions (Moffett 2003); it is a *factual* attitude. Nevertheless, for ease of exposition we will ignore this subtlety and use the term 'propositional attitude' so as to include such factual attitudes.

need not accept propositionalism, and an anti-intellectualist need not accept dispositionalism. The two debates (however they are labeled) are conceptually distinct.[8]

Thus one might accept anti-intellectualism, thereby holding that one knows how to φ in virtue of having the ability (or disposition) to φ, but reject dispositionalism, thereby denying that knowing how to φ is *reducible* to such ability. For instance, one might hold that knowledge how to φ is a *non-behavioral-dispositional, objectual relation* between a subject and an item—a method or way of φ-ing, say—that one has in virtue of having an *ability to* φ. On this view, knowing how to φ is grounded in an ability to φ. But importantly, it is not reducible to such ability. Such a view combines anti-intellectualism with a nondispositionalist view of the nature of knowing how.

Alternatively, one might accept intellectualism, thereby holding that one knows how to φ in virtue of having some propositional attitude regarding φ-ing, but reject propositionalism, thereby denying that knowing how to φ is *reducible* to a propositional attitude. For instance, one might hold that knowledge how to φ is a *nonpropositional, objectual relation* between a subject and an item—a method or way of φ-ing, say—that one has in virtue of having a certain *propositional attitude regarding φ-ing*. On this view, knowing how to φ is grounded in a propositional attitude regarding φ-ing. But importantly, it is not reducible to a propositional attitude. Such a view combines intellectualism with a nonpropositionalist view of the nature of knowing how.

These scenarios are possible because of the availability of the following—admittedly heterodox—alternative to propositionalism and dispositionalism:

Objectualism
The relation is a nonpropositional, non-behavioral-dispositional objectual attitude relation (e.g., a *knowledge-of* relation), and the relatum is a nonpropositional item (e.g., a way of φ-ing).[9]

---

8. There are clear precedents for the type of two-debate framework suggested here; see note 11. Both debates about knowing how may be distinguished from debates about skill, expertise, intelligent action, and the semitechnical cognitive scientific notion of "procedural knowledge"—none of which can innocently be assumed to be equivalent with, or bear some other substantive connection to, knowing how. It simply muddies the waters to attempt to collapse these debates (cf. Glick forthcoming). This places a limitation on some otherwise interesting recent discussions of empirical work on expertise and procedural knowledge by Bzdak (2008), Wallis (2008), Adams (2009, §2), Young (2009), and Devitt (forthcoming-a).

9. Later we will refine this thesis and explore its credentials. For now, this statement of the view suffices to get the main idea on the table.

The upshot is that the debate between intellectualists and anti-intellectualists over what is involved in knowing how to φ is to some extent separable from the debate over whether knowing how is reducible to or a "species" of (or "consists" in) knowing that.[10]

One virtue of this way of mapping the philosophical landscape is that it enables the formulation of views that do not make sense within a one-debate framework.[11] This two-debate framework also has the potential to clarify various disagreements about knowing how and, perhaps, create the conceptual space necessary to move the discussion forward. In particular, it makes room for comparatively sophisticated positions that might capture what is all too often felt to be missing in their more orthodox counterparts. For example, no extant theory has seemed capable of respecting all three of the following attractive but prima facie incompatible theses about knowing how:

i. Knowing how is not merely a kind of knowing that.
ii. Knowing how is practical: it bears a substantive connection to action.
iii. Knowing how is a cognitive achievement: its status as a piece of practical *knowledge* is not merely coincidental.

To the extent that *propositionalist* versions of intellectualism take knowing how to be a mere "grasp of true propositions," they have a tendency to do violence to—or render mysterious—(i) and (ii).[12] Yet, insofar as *anti-intellectualist* theses

---

10. One might worry that we are doing an injustice to the fact that the arch-anti-intellectualist Ryle, who in some sense began the discussion, was concerned to undermine the thesis that knowing how is a propositional attitude or relation. However, we should not forget that Ryle's explicit aim was to dispel the "paramechanical hypothesis" of internal mental causes, which he viewed as a product of the "myth" of "hidden" mental "phantasms" that "take place 'in the head'" (see Ryle 1945 and 1949, chs. 1–2), a "doctrine" that is wholly preserved in our (relation-neutral) formulation of intellectualism.

11. Versions of this sort of two-debate framework show up in a variety of metaphysical contexts. For instance, in the philosophy of time, state-of-the-art B-theories of time may accept that tensed propositions/facts are *grounded* in tenseless ones and that time itself is a tenseless, space-like dimension (debate one), though tensed propositions/facts cannot be *reduced* to tenseless ones (debate two). Another familiar example occurs in contemporary philosophy of mind, where one now finds a framework that enables the formulation of "nonreductive physicalism" or a primitive supervenience thesis, according to which the mental is *grounded* in the physical (debate one), though it is not the case that the mental is *reducible* to the physical (debate two). These positions are analogous to nonpropositional intellectualism: knowledge how is *grounded* in propositional attitudes, though it is not the case that knowledge how is *reducible* to a propositional attitude.

12. The quoted expression is Ryle's (1949, 26). Propositionalist intellectualism is treated sympathetically by Stanley and Williamson (2001), Braun (2006, ch. 12), Brogaard (2009, ch. 6), and

narrowly tie knowing how to mere behavioral-dispositional states or powers, they have a tendency to falter on—or render mysterious—(iii).[13] By contrast, as we shall see, the combination of *objectualism* and *intellectualism* provides a natural way of simultaneously accommodating each of (i)–(iii). In our view, this is reason to take the view seriously. (Additional reasons will be advanced later.)

Our aim in this chapter is to further explore this view, which we call *objectualist intellectualism*. One knows how to φ, when one does, in virtue of having certain propositional attitudes regarding φ-ing.[14] But knowledge how to φ is not itself a propositional attitude, nor is it an ability or disposition. Rather, it is a certain kind of objectual attitude. (Likewise, perhaps, for other kinds of knowledge-*wh*—though, for lack of space, here we can do no more than gesture in §4.1 at this extension.)

Later, we suggest reasons for preferring objectualism to both dispositionalism and propositionalism. This discussion should be of interest to intellectualists and anti-intellectualists alike, for as we have illustrated, objectualism is compatible with both intellectualism and anti-intellectualism. However, although objectualism is consistent with anti-intellectualism, we believe that it is best combined with intellectualism. Accordingly, before proceeding to the discussion of objectualism, we first explain one of the main reasons we think that an intellectualist framework is to be preferred.

2. A Structural Flaw in Anti-Intellectualism

Endorsement of anti-intellectualism is sometimes based on a pretheoretical conviction that knowing how to do things just is a matter of having an ability or disposition to do them.[15] This section aims to articulate, in a systematic way, a

---

Stanley (2011, forthcoming-a), among others. Some versions of propositionalism attempt to accommodate (i) and (ii). Nevertheless, in our estimation, these attempted resolutions are neither intuitively compelling nor particularly natural approaches to the problem. See §§3–5.

13. Anti-intellectualism is treated sympathetically by Ryle (1945, 1949), Brandom (1994, 23), Hawley (2003), Noë (2005), Setiya (2009), Wiggins (2009), Devitt (forthcoming a, ch. 14), and Hornsby (1980, ch. 3), among others. Anti-intellectualists often explicitly acknowledge (iii) (see, e.g., Setiya 2009, 405). But behavioral-dispositional states or powers alone are not in our view able to provide a satisfactory treatment. See §2 for critical discussion.

14. Objectualist intellectualism thus fits nicely with the plausible thought that many objectual attitudes bear a tight relation—tighter than supervenience—to propositional attitudes, even though they are not reducible to propositional attitudes. Cf. Crane (2001, 113–114), Szabó (2003), Forbes (2006, ch. 4), Montague (2007), and Bengson, Grube, and Korman (2011, §2.1).

15. Such conviction is sometimes motivated by perceived defects in the intellectualist position, which we aspire to avoid (see §§3–5; cf. BMW 2009 and the state of play essay in this book).

series of worries about this type of view. The intention is to make clear why we find anti-intellectualist approaches unconvincing *in outline*, not simply in detail. This discussion will, at the same time, indicate why we find intellectualism so attractive.

We will approach anti-intellectualism by examining necessary conditions, and then sufficient conditions, for knowledge how in terms of abilities or dispositions. Consider, first, the claim that knowing how to φ requires an ability or disposition to φ. No doubt some abilities are necessary for knowing how (e.g., the ability to think, breathe, or apply concepts). What is distinctive of anti-intellectualism is its commitment to the thesis that knowing how requires the *corresponding* ability or disposition.[16] Focusing on ability, the claim is that:

[AI$_N$] Having the ability to φ, or having had the ability to φ at some time in the past,[17] is necessary for knowing how to φ.

This claim might seem difficult to deny. Yet it appears that some people, such as coaches and instructors, know how to do what they are not able, and have never been able, to do themselves. Consider, for example:[18]

But it is also sometimes asserted without any argument whatsoever. Strangely, it is often simply assumed that knowing how is an ability, or vice versa—or that 'knows how to' is obviously ambiguous and that one of its standard meanings is equivalent to a meaning of 'is able to' (Hintikka 1975, 11; Carr 1981a, 54). For example, Hetherington (2006, 74) asserts without argument that when "you have an ability—in that sense, you know how." Not only is such an assumption dialectically problematic but also it is open to the counterexamples in this section. (The point is significant for Hetherington's discussion in particular because, among other things, it reveals a loophole in his modified regress argument against intellectualism (cf. Williams 2008, §3): because knowing how cannot innocently be assumed to be an ability, the intellectualist may say that when one applies or otherwise exercises one's propositional attitudes, one is *able*—but need not thereby *know how*—to do so, thus avoiding regress. See the state of play essay in this book for related discussion.) At any rate, we have argued elsewhere (BM 2007, §2) that 'knows how to' is not ambiguous in the manner suggested, though our discussion here does not depend on that argument.

16. Among other things, this means that Noë's (2005, 285–286) modified regress argument, which aims to show that some abilities are necessary for knowing that (namely, the ability to apply concepts to objects) on pain of regress, does not motivate anti-intellectualism about knowing how.

17. We include this clause even though we regard past ability as a red herring. Consider an adult human Alpha and his Davidsonesque swampman counterpart Omega, who comes into being at a given time *t*. Presumably, if Alpha knows how to swim at *t*, then so does Omega. But Omega lacks causal-historical connections to abilities Alpha possessed prior to *t* (since Omega, ex hypothesi, has no past at all!). This example highlights why we would not want to account for knowing how in historical terms.

18. An example of this sort is suggested by Stanley and Williamson (2001, 416), who in turn credit Jeff King. We articulate the particular version in the text in Bengson, Moffett, and

168   PHILOSOPHICAL CONSIDERATIONS

Ski Instructor. Pat has been a ski instructor for twenty years, teaching people how to do complex ski stunts. He is in high demand as an instructor, since he is considered to be the best at what he does. Although an accomplished skier, he has never been able to do the stunts himself. Nonetheless, over the years he has taught many people how to do them well. In fact, a number of his students have won medals in international competitions and competed in the Olympic games.

Pat knows how to do the stunts.[19] But he is not able, and has never been able, to do them.

It might be suggested in response that Pat does not know how *to* do the stunts; rather, he simply knows how *one* does the stunts.[20] No doubt this distinction between knowledge how *one* φ-s and knowledge how *to* φ—the *one-to distinction*—is important. However, this distinction does not support [AI_N], for these two kinds of knowledge-how often come apart in a way that is insensitive to the absence or presence of the corresponding ability. This can be seen by reflecting on pairs of cases with the following structure:

Wright [BMW] (2009, §2), which reports the results of a study in which the vast majority of ordinary English speakers judged that the subject in the example both knows how and is unable. See also the examples given by, e.g., Ware (1973, §3), Craig (1990, 158), and Snowdon (2003, §3). We believe that there is an important difference between this type of case and cases involving subjects who are merely unable to act *right now* or *for a spell* (see BM 2007, n. 5); such subjects may simply suffer from an interference in what Honoré (1964, 463; cf. Maier 2010, §1) dubs 'particular' ability (cf. finks, masks, etc.).

19. Suppose a novice ski jumper were to enter the ski lodge and say, "My goal is to learn how to do ski stunts. Who here knows how to do them?" An employee may then reply, while pointing to Pat, "He does." Notice also that it would be more than a little odd for Pat (or the employee) to tell students that Pat does not know how to do the stunts, but he will teach them how to do the stunts anyway.

20. Or that he merely knows how the stunts *are done*, *what it takes* to do the stunts, and so forth. Cf. Noë (2005, 284 n. 4) and Hetherington (2006, 71 n. 2 and §11). Such a distinction is marked by, e.g., Hornsby (1980, 84) and emphasized in §1 of BMW (2009).

Incidentally, it should be plain that Pat does not merely know how the stunts are taught, or how to teach the stunts. Clearly, there is more going on here than that, as evidenced by the considerations in note 19 and the text that follows. Furthermore, as discussed in §3, Pat is in a state that is potentially action-guiding: it could guide someone in the intentional execution of the stunts, even if it does not actually do so for Pat. An adequate treatment must explain this fact about the state that Pat enjoys (vis-à-vis, e.g., the state that Albert, introduced later, has). A natural explanation is that Pat (but not, e.g., Albert) knows how to do the stunts, and knowledge how to do the stunts is potentially action-guiding in this sense. This explanation would be unavailable if we were to adopt the anti-intellectualist position under discussion.

Case A	Case B
A knows how one φ-s.	B knows how one φ-s.
A is not able to φ.	B is not able to φ.
A knows how to φ.	B does not know how to φ.

To illustrate, contrast Pat with Albert, an unathletic (nonskiing) scientist who studies the mechanics of skiing, including but not limited to the mechanics of complicated ski stunts. As a result of his theoretical studies, Albert knows how *one* does the stunts (namely, by contracting such-and-such muscles in such-and-such ways). Suppose that Pat, too, knows the mechanics of the ski stunts he teaches his students (he studies them in his spare time). Then Pat and Albert both know how one does the stunts; neither is able to do the stunts. *But plainly a significant difference remains*: only Pat knows how to do the stunts. Indeed, even though Pat cannot do them, he grasps the stunts in a way that Albert, who only knows the theory, does not.[21] Thus the one-to distinction cannot help anti-intellectualism answer the challenge posed by *Ski Instructor*.[22]

This challenge does not rely on a single, isolated case. There appear to be many further counterexamples to [AI$_N$]. One might know how to run a marathon without being able to (because one has severe asthma). One might know how to dunk a basketball without being able to do so (because one is too short). Or one might know how to sink a very long but perfectly straight putt without being able to do so (because such putts are, in fact, extremely difficult). And so on.

Might all such examples be accommodated by acknowledging the obvious truth that sometimes there are internal or external impediments to action? When those impediments are removed, the thought goes, we see that one who knows how to φ is in fact able to φ.[23] Anti-intellectualists attracted to this response may

---

21. Perhaps made possible by Pat's skiing experience, this not-purely-theoretical grasp is arguably part of what *enables* Pat to teach the stunts to Olympic-caliber students. For this and other reasons, although one might attempt to evade the point in the text by denying that such grasp is properly described in the terminology of 'knowing how to act' it should be clear that the difference between Pat and Albert is not merely terminological but theoretically (e.g., explanatorily) important (cf. note 20). One of the goals of a theory of practical knowledge should be to explicate the nature of this difference. This is our project in §§3–5.

22. In conversation, native German speakers have reported that the one-to distinction goes unmarked in German. They inform us that although they themselves see the difference between Pat and the scientist, all that can be said is that both Pat and the scientist have *wissen wie* and neither has *können*. This illustrates one of the difficulties of drawing substantive philosophical conclusions from cross-linguistic data (cf. Craig 1990, 151–152; Rumfitt 2003; and Stanley 2011).

23. Cf. Noë's (2005, §2) discussion of enabling conditions. Of course, we must beware of trivialities: for example, x knows how to φ only if x is able to φ when conditions are such that x is able

be tempted by Katherine Hawley's (2003) interesting suggestion that, even if the ability to φ is not quite necessary for knowing how to φ, as demonstrated by *Ski Instructor* and various other examples, counterfactual success at φ-ing under normal (ordinary, etc.) conditions is. Call this the *counterfactual success thesis*:

> **Counterfactual Success Thesis**
> x knows how to φ only if: if x tried to φ under normal conditions, x would succeed at φ-ing.[24]

Anti-intellectualists could then hold that [AI_N] is to be understood as equivalent to the counterfactual success thesis.[25]

However, it is not clear that the counterfactual success thesis handles the problem. There need not be anything abnormal (extraordinary, etc.) about the conditions in which ski instructor Pat finds himself, yet he does not successfully do the stunts when he tries. Of course, one might remove the 'under normal conditions' clause in order to arrive at an ordinary counterfactual, whose truth is to be assessed by considering whether x succeeds in φ-ing when she tries to φ in "nearby" or "similar" worlds. While this revision might accommodate Pat, the following case indicates that the basic problem remains:

> *Pi*. Louis, a competent mathematician, knows how to find the nth numeral, for any numeral n, in the decimal expansion of π. He knows the algorithm and knows how to apply it in a given case. However, because of principled computational limitations, Louis (like all ordinary human beings) is unable to find the 10^{46} numeral in the decimal expansion of π.

---

to φ, i.e., when all internal and external impediments to ability are removed. What is needed is a nontrivializing, informative condition that does not simply offer a promissory note that there is some such condition.

24. Hawley (2003, 23) includes the 'under normal conditions' clause (cf. Ryle 1949, 130) partly in order to avoid counterexamples: "The appearance of a counterexample can arise whenever a subject's circumstances are not ordinary circumstances for a given task." However, as we shall see, counterexamples remain. (And they do so even if we weaken the consequent to 'x would *usually succeed* at φ-ing,' as **Williams** (2008, §8 emphasis added) suggests.)

25. The issues are not quite as straightforward as this might suggest, however. There is reason to worry whether this thesis alone would be enough to secure a form of anti-intellectualism, for it leaves the question of *what makes it true* that the counterfactual holds unanswered. If the counterfactual is grounded in propositional attitudes, then the counterfactual success thesis supports intellectualism rather than anti-intellectualism. Consequently, the counterfactual success thesis is consistent with intellectualism and so cannot, by itself, decide the debate. We shall set this issue aside here, though we do think it constitutes a significant challenge to counterfactual versions of anti-intellectualism.

Notice that conditions would have to be extremely *abnormal* for Louis to succeed in finding the 10^{46} numeral in the decimal expansion of π when he tries: he would have to be superhuman, as it were. Presumably, then, we need to consider *very* "distant" or "dissimilar" worlds to locate one in which Louis succeeds in his attempt. In this world, and presumably all others even remotely like it, Louis cannot reasonably hope to succeed in finding the 10^{46} numeral in the decimal expansion of π when he tries. His inability is pervasive. Yet he still knows how to find it. So the counterfactual success thesis—with or without the 'under normal conditions' clause—is false. Call this *the problem of pervasive inability* for the anti-intellectualist thesis that an ability to act is necessary for knowing how to act.

Turn now to the thesis that the ability to act is *sufficient* for knowledge how to act. Since it is implausible that unreliable ability is sufficient for knowing how (as demonstrated by cases of "accidental success"),[26] we focus on a moderately restricted version of the anti-intellectualist sufficient condition for knowing how:

[AI$_s$] Being reliably able to φ is sufficient for knowing how to φ.

Now consider the following example:

Salchow. Irina, who is a novice figure skater, decides to try a complex jump called the salchow. When one performs a salchow, one takes off from the *back inside* edge of one skate and lands on the *back outside* edge of the opposite skate after one or more rotations in the air. Irina, however, is seriously mistaken about how to perform a salchow. She believes incorrectly that the way to perform a salchow is to take off from the *front outside* edge of one skate, jump in the air, spin, and land on the *front inside* edge of the other skate. However, Irina has a severe neurological abnormality that makes her act in ways that differ dramatically from how she actually thinks she is acting. So despite the fact that she is seriously mistaken about how to perform a salchow, whenever she actually attempts to do a salchow (in accordance with her misconceptions), the abnormality causes Irina to unknowingly perform the correct sequence of moves, and so she ends up successfully performing a salchow. Although what she is doing and what she thinks she is doing come apart, she fails to notice the mismatch.

---

26. See, e.g., Ryle (1949, 45–46 and 130), Ware (1973, 161), Carr (1979, 407), Ginet (1975, 6–8), Chomsky (1988, 9ff.), Craig (1990, 159), Hawley (2003, §6), Snowdon (2003, §3), BM (2007, 46), Williams (2008, §2), and BMW (2009, §3).

172   PHILOSOPHICAL CONSIDERATIONS

In this case, it is clear that Irina is reliably able to do a salchow. However, because of her confusions regarding how to execute the move, she cannot be said to know how to do a salchow.

One might propose the following impure (intentional or mentalistic) version of the anti-intellectualist's reliable-ability-is-sufficient thesis in an attempt to circumvent the problem posed by *Salchow*:

[AI$_S$*] Being reliably able to *intentionally* φ is sufficient for knowing how to φ.

This thesis is endorsed even by propositionalist-intellectualists Jason Stanley and Timothy Williamson (2001) and Stanley (2011); the latter explicitly holds that it avoids the challenge posed by *Salchow*.[27]

However, we believe that a restriction to intentional action is no help. This can be seen by considering complex actions constituted by sequences of simpler actions or steps, such that to be reliably able to execute the complex action, one need only be reliably able to execute each of the steps. Let φ be such a complex action. Suppose that φ-ing requires completing four steps, but at the outset, *x* is unaware of this fact: at the outset, *x* is aware only of step one, which *x* is reliably able to intentionally execute. As a matter of fact, after intentionally executing step one, step two will be painfully obvious, and *x* will intentionally do it. In fact, step two is an intentional action that *x* does regularly, and thus *x* possesses a reliable ability to intentionally execute it. And so on for each of the last two steps. So at the outset, *x* is reliably able to intentionally perform each step, and thus reliably able to intentionally φ, though *x* does not at the outset know how to φ—contrary to [AI$_S$*].

This recipe yields concrete examples such as the following:

Kytoon. Chris forms the desire to build a kytoon—a lighter-than-air kite that may, like a balloon, be filled with gas (e.g., hydrogen, hot air, or helium).

---

27. *Salchow* is from BM (2007, 46); it reappears in BMW (2009). Brogaard (chapter 6) suggests that it would be "odd" for a bystander to describe Irina as reliably able to do a salchow even though she does not know how to do one; we provide an explanation of such oddity in BM (2007) and BMW (2009) in terms of a gap between the epistemic grounds for know-how attributions and the metaphysical basis for know-how. Stanley (2011, 218) approves of the example but adds that "Bengson, Moffett, and Wright take Irina to be intentionally performing the Salchow when she performs it." This attribution is mistaken: BMW (2009) do not mention intentional action, and the view of intentional action sketched in BM (2007, §4) as tied to understanding, which Irina lacks, may, perhaps, be taken to imply just the opposite. That said, our argument here does not turn on whether Irina intentionally performs a salchow. The connection between knowing how and reliable ability to intentional action proposed by [AI$_S$*] is critically examined next.

Nonpropositional Intellectualism 173

She has never built a kite before, let alone a kytoon. But she is very good with her hands and thus is confident in her ability to make one. Seeking information about how to build a kytoon, information she currently lacks, Chris goes online and performs a Google search for "building a kytoon." She finds a Web site with instructions. The instructions are long, but she is able to understand and follow each step with a modest amount of effort. Over the course of the next few days, she succeeds in executing the steps. The result of her efforts is her own personal kytoon, which she then proceeds to learn to fly.

At the time of her initial decision to seek further information, Chris does not yet know how to build a kytoon. Indeed, it is easy to imagine her worrying about whether she will locate any usable directions, anxiously hoping that she will. Still, although the information Chris possesses at the time of her initial decision to seek further information is, by itself, inadequate to build a kytoon, there is a clear sense in which her situation is not hopeless. Her current information state, coupled with the information she will encounter once she performs a Google search, will together be sufficient to reliably build a kytoon. Consequently, Chris is, at the time of her decision, reliably able to build a kytoon—which is plainly an intentional action of Chris's. So at the time of her initial decision, Chris is reliably able to intentionally φ (build a kytoon), but at the time of her initial decision, she does not know how to φ (build a kytoon).[28]

Cases like this are not uncommon. But they refute [AI$_S$*], since they show that it is possible to have the reliable ability to intentionally φ without knowing how to φ. This possibility is realized in those cases when one's reliable ability is ignorant, that is, not accompanied by an adequate grasp of the relevant action. Call the problem posed by such cases the *problem of ignorant reliability* for the anti-intellectualist thesis that ability is sufficient for knowing how.

We take the foregoing considerations to identify a serious difficulty for anti-intellectualism. The difficulty is not (or not merely) that (a) anti-intellectualism, by focusing solely on the presence or absence of abilities or dispositions, neglects important nonbehavioral features of—and corresponding

---

28. That Chris requires further information emphasizes the point that Chris does not *at the outset* know how to build a kytoon. Otherwise, subjects would know how to do many things they clearly do not know how to do. For example, my current information state and the mass of information (blueprints, guides, etc.) that I will encounter when I later do extensive research on the Internet are together sufficient to reliably and intentionally build and fly a zeppelin. But sadly, it is not now the case that I know how to build and fly a zeppelin: this is, after all, why I need to do the research. Setiya (2009, 404) offers another type of counterexample to [AI$_S$*], involving defusing a bomb.

similarities and differences between—the practical, epistemic situation of the subjects in the preceding cases. Nor is the difficulty (wholly or merely) that (b) the anti-intellectualist faces the as-yet-unanswered challenge of having to "refine" her view—that is, to clarify or specify the relevant type of ability or disposition to φ—to successfully dispel, or navigate between, the problem of pervasive inability and the problem of ignorant reliability. While these are indeed difficulties facing anti-intellectualism, they do not exhaust the challenge posed by these problems. What the problems of pervasive inability and ignorant reliability seem to show is that (c) there is a *structural flaw* in the anti-intellectualist position. In short, the two problems push anti-intellectualism in opposite directions. The problem of pervasive inability counsels us to weaken the ability condition: we must require *less* than a reliable ability to φ, since a reliable ability to φ is not necessary for knowledge how to φ. But the problem of ignorant reliability counsels us to *strengthen* the ability condition: we must require *more* than a reliable ability to φ, since a reliable ability to φ is not sufficient for knowledge how to φ. In light of this internal conflict, we submit that the prospects of a consistent anti-intellectualist thesis that succeeds in reaching its intended destination are not good.[29]

Yet in our view the mistake is not simply attempting to consistently maintain both the necessity and sufficiency of ability for knowledge how. The mistake goes deeper and can be traced to (d) the misguided project of trying to force knowledge how, which is *cognitive* (recall (iii) from §1), into the mold of a mere power, which is *behavioral-dispositional*. Simply put, anti-intellectualist theories are looking in the wrong place. A subject's knowledge how is not narrowly tied to her abilities or dispositions to behavior (her powers); rather, when one knows how, one has an adequate, though not purely theoretical, grasp of the relevant activity—as illustrated by *Ski Instructor* and *Pi*, in which such grasp (and thus knowledge how) is present, and reinforced by *Salchow* and *Kytoon*, in which such grasp (and thus knowledge how) is absent. Our project in the remainder of this chapter is to explicate the nature of this grasp.

3. *The Practical Character of Knowledge How to* φ

The rejection of anti-intellectualism does not license dismissal of intuitions motivating the anti-intellectualist position. Indeed, our understanding of knowledge how would be severely impoverished were we to fail to acknowledge a crucial

---

29. To the extent that our argument in this section identifies a structural flaw in a style of theory, it does not commit a "counterexample fallacy" (this label is due to Bonevac, Dever, and Sosa forthcoming).

insight behind anti-intellectualism, namely, that knowledge how bears a substantive metaphysical connection to action.[30] Getting this connection right is one of the most significant challenges facing any theorist concerned with the nature of mind and its relation to action.

One hypothesis is that knowledge how to φ is (predicative 'is', here and later) a state such that if one is in (has) that state, then one successfully φ-s. That is:

> [I] Knowledge how to φ is a state σ such that: if x is in σ, then x φ-s.

But merely knowing how to act in a certain way need not entail that one does in fact act in that way, so the hypothesized connection is far too strong. We might weaken the connection as follows:

> [II] Knowledge how to φ is a state σ such that: if x is in σ, then x is able or disposed to φ.

However, this is equivalent to [AI$_N$], which as we have already seen is also too strong: recalling *Ski Instructor*, knowing how to act in a certain way need not entail that one is able or disposed to act in that way. A still weaker connection is the counterfactual success thesis, which is equivalent to:

> [III] Knowledge how to φ is a state σ such that: if x is in σ, then (if x were to try to φ under normal conditions, x would φ).

But as we have seen, even this is too strong.

Still, there is something to the idea that knowledge how implies a certain kind of potential or possibility for successful action. Thus, for example, the fact that one knows how to φ does seem to imply that one is in a state such that it is possible for someone in that state to successfully φ. That is:

> [IV] Knowledge how to φ is a state σ such that: if x is in σ, then it is possible for there to be some y such that y is in σ and y φ-s (where y may but need not be identical to x).

---

30. We discuss *epistemological* lessons to be learned from certain anti-intellectualist intuitions in BMW (2009, 397–398): for example, the information that x is able to φ often provides prima facie evidence that x knows how to φ, and vice versa (cf. Craig 1990, 160). The substantive *metaphysical* connection between knowledge how and action discussed in this section might help to explain such epistemological connections.

Although this is indeed a necessary truth, it lacks the substance required to illuminate the relation between knowledge how and action. After all, nearly every state satisfies the indicated condition, including states—such as Irina's state in *Salchow*, the state of having long hair, and so forth—that are accidentally or fortuitously correlated with successful action. What is needed is a more substantive principle that helps to distinguish knowing how from these other states by providing some insight into the nature of its connection to the possibility of success.

An attractive suggestion is that knowledge how is potentially action-guiding in the sense that it is a state that *can guide successful, intentional action*. That is, the individual's exercise of that state could underlie and explain intentional action, even if it does not in fact do so for any given individual on any given occasion. For example, recalling Pat in *Ski Instructor*, if a ski instructor knows how to do ski stunts, then even if he or she cannot do—and thus never does—them, it remains possible that there be someone in the same state who successfully and intentionally does the stunts, and does so on the basis of exercising that very state: in this way, the ski instructor's state (his or her know-how) is such that it *can* guide the intentional execution of the stunts, even if it does not actually do so for him or her. Similarly, recalling Louis in *Pi*, if a competent mathematician knows how to find the 10^{46} numeral in the decimal expansion of π, then he is in a state such that someone—perhaps not himself, given principled computational limitations—in that state could successfully and intentionally find it, and do so on the basis of exercising that very state: in this way, the competent mathematician's state (her know-how) is such that it *can* guide the intentional calculation of the 10^{46} numeral in the decimal expansion of π, even if it does not actually do so for her.

By contrast, a novice skater confused about the way to do a salchow is not in a state such that some individual in that state could successfully and intentionally do a salchow on the basis of exercising that very state: she lacks a state the exercise of which could underlie and explain the successful and intentional execution of a salchow—no state that carries sufficient information, as it were, to guide the successful and intentional execution of a salchow.[31] Similarly, a subject, like Chris, lacking sufficient information about the way to build a kytoon is not in a state

---

31. Might one perform a salchow on the basis of exercising a composite state consisting of an incorrect belief and neurological abnormality? Such an abnormality, being wholly "subpersonal," cannot be exercised by the individual (either intentionally or subintentionally), even when coupled with a belief. Moreover, the incorrect belief does not carry the information required to guide one to the completion of a salchow. Indeed, someone who acted on the basis of exercising that very state—someone whose intentional action was guided by such a belief—would not successfully and intentionally do a salchow, but an entirely different jump (or nothing properly classified as a jump at all, but rather, say, a mere movement). So Irina in *Salchow* is not in a state that satisfies [V] below.

such that some individual in that state could successfully and intentionally build a kytoon on the basis of exercising that very state: such a subject does not then possess any state that could underlie and explain the successful and intentional building of a kytoon—no state that carries sufficient information, as it were, to guide the successful and intentional construction of a kytoon.

In light of this, we propose the following connection between knowledge how and action:

> [V] Knowledge how to φ is a state σ such that: if x is in σ, then it is possible for there to be some individual y such that y's exercise of σ underlies and explains y's successfully and intentionally φ-ing—that is, σ *guides* y in successfully, intentionally φ-ing.[32]

This connection—an *action-guidingness* connection—is extremely plausible. Although it is weaker than the connection proposed by anti-intellectualism, it is substantive for all that.[33] This is significant for three reasons. First, [V] looks to be a perfect candidate for the source—or inspiration—of the classification of knowledge how as *practical*. Second, to the extent that [V] is consistent with intellectualism, as it appears to be (see §5), the implication is that even intellectualism can explain this classification. Third, and perhaps most important, absent a reason to think that [V] is still not yet substantive enough, stronger connections between knowledge how and action must be regarded as superfluous, in which case anti-intellectualist proposals remain unmotivated by reflection on the practical character of knowledge how.

---

32. Four points of clarification. First, y's exercise of σ must be the explainer (not simply an element in, or enabler of, a complete explanation) of y's intentionally and successfully φ-ing. Second, as we understand the notion, for an individual to exercise a state is for the individual to act upon that state—for her to bring it to bear on subsequent action, perhaps intentionally or subintentionally. Third, the relevant worlds may be restricted in various ways, though we will not pursue these restrictions here. Fourth, [V] identifies a property of knowledge how, rather than a set of necessary and sufficient conditions for the presence of knowledge how. The aim is to identify a substantive necessary connection between knowledge how and action; we do not think that an action-based sufficient condition for knowledge how is available (recall §2), for reasons—centering on the type of *conception* required for knowledge how—that will feature in §5.

33. It is weaker in that it does not require a subject who knows how to φ to possess a power to φ; it requires only that there be *some* subject who does. Notice that [V] makes good sense of the plausible idea that knowing how persists beyond internal or external impediments to a subject's action (recall note 23). But it also reveals that this idea does not motivate anti-intellectualism. Rather, we need to recognize that the impediments might run so deep as to force us to look into modal space, to another subject. These points help to explain intuitions that drive anti-intellectualism (e.g., that knowing how cannot be wholly divorced from ability) without thereby capitulating to anti-intellectualism.

It is natural to wonder what accounts for the connection between knowledge how and action expressed by [V]. Here we encounter the following question, which we will refer to as the 'action-guiding question':

What could or must knowledge how be if it is such that if one has it, then one is in a state that can, but may not in fact, guide successful, intentional action?

An adequate theory of knowing how must supply an answer to this question.

We shall approach an answer in two steps. Recall that in §1 we distinguished between two orthodox views of the nature of knowing how: propositionalism and dispositionalism. The arguments advanced in §2 serve as reasons to reject dispositionalism. If one can know how to φ without being able or disposed to φ—as indicated by examples such as *Ski Instructor* and *Pi*—then it would seem to follow that the relevant *knowing* or *knowing-how* relation cannot be a mere behavioral-dispositional relation (e.g., the *being-able-to* relation). This is reason enough to set dispositionalism aside. Within a traditional framework, this would motivate the attempt to seek a propositionalist explanation of [V]. But we have seen that there is another option, namely, objectualism. In the next section, §4, we sketch a few reasons to pursue this alternative. That is step one. In §5, we take step two: we explain how an objectualist view of the nature of knowing how to φ might account for a variety of heretofore unexplained features of knowledge how, including the substantive connection between knowledge how and action expressed by [V].

4. *From Propositionalism to Objectualism*

4.1 The Uniformity of Knowledge-*wh*

It has been suggested that the uniformity of so-called knowledge-*wh* strongly favors propositionalism over rival approaches. Consider the similarities between (1) and the constructions in (2)–(4):

1. *x* knows how to φ.
2. *x* knows where to φ.
3. *x* knows why to φ.
4. *x* knows when to φ.

Does 'knows' pick out the same relation in each of (1)–(4)? The availability of the following coordination constructions suggests so:[34]

---

34. Suggests, but does not entail: while we find the results of such 'coordination tests' plausible in this case, they are not conclusive. To illustrate, take a simple argument for propositionalism,

5. Martin knows how and why to raise money for Obama's campaign.
6. Martin knows where to meet and how to get there.
7. Martin knows when and how to castle (referring to chess).

In each of (1)–(4), *x* in some sense *knows* that which is designated by the complement clause ('how/where/why/when to do it'). In this respect, at least, these various instances of knowledge-*wh* seem to be uniform.

(A more theoretical reason for adopting this uniformity thesis derives from an influential argument form due to Noam Chomsky [1970], which Edwin Williams [1991] dubs "target syntax" and "target semantics" arguments; see also Goldberg [2006, 23ff.]. Generalizing somewhat, this form of argument says that if two surface forms *A* and *B* pattern in similar ways with respect to their syntactic and semantic behavior, then ceteris paribus both are generated from some underlying form *C*. Applied to the present context, 'knowledge how' and the other *wh*-constructions behave similarly with respect to their surface syntactic and semantic behavior (see, e.g., Lahiri 2002); so, ceteris paribus, 'knowledge how' attributions are generated from an underlying form that is identical to the underlying form from which the other *wh*-constructions are generated.)

Stanley (2011, 208) has argued that this uniformity thesis provides the basis for "a powerful argument in favor of the conclusion that our ordinary folk notion of knowing-how is a species of propositional knowledge," as the propositionalist maintains.[35] For (2)–(4) "involve the ascription of propositional

---

namely, that it is possible to conjoin 'knowledge how' and 'knowledge that' constructions (as in Stanley and Williamson's [2001, 430–431] example, 'John knows that bicycle accidents can happen and also how to avoid them in most cases'); so 'how'-complements in the former constructions, like 'that'-complements in the latter constructions, denote propositions, and 'knows' in both constructions denotes a relation between subjects and those propositions. This is too quick. As is well known, 'that'-complements can be conjoined with complements that denote vastly different types of entity, including propositions, properties, and objects (Sag et al. 1985): consider, e.g., 'John knows that bicycle accidents happen and the best strategies for avoiding them'. For relevant discussion, see Roberts (2009, §1.3) and Ginzburg (chapter 9).

35. Cf. Snowdon (2003, 6–8). Stanley (2011, 208) writes: "It is a common assumption . . . that sentences involving constructions like 'know where + infinitive,' 'know when + infinitive,' 'know why + infinitive,' etc. all can be defined in terms of propositional knowledge. But given that ascriptions of knowing-how in English look so similar to such ascriptions, it is hard to see how they could ascribe a different kind of mental state. This provides a powerful argument in favor of the conclusion that our ordinary folk notion of knowing-how is a species of propositional knowledge." And again (221): "Different views of the semantics of embedded questions all agree that the constructions [in (1)–(4)] call for the same analysis. Since [(2)–(4)] uncontroversially involve the ascription of propositional knowledge, these analyses all agree that [(1)] does as well." But as we will see, nonpropositionalists can accept uniformity: a general objectualist approach is available. (Arguably, Ryle [1949, 146] himself was aware of the indicated coordinations and sought to preserve uniformity through a general dispositionalist approach to all knowledge-*wh*.)

knowledge"; consequently, to preserve uniformity, we must conclude that (1) also ascribes "a relation that holds between a person and a proposition" (226).

But we need not accept propositionalism to preserve the uniformity of knowledge-*wh*. Specifically, an objectualist can easily accommodate the observation that 'knows' picks out the same relation in each of (1)–(4): in all of these cases, one stands in a *knowing* relation to the *nonpropositional* item denoted by the complement clause, for example, a way (1), a location (2), a reason (3), or a time (4).[36] Hence an objectualist may offer the following "paraphrases":

1*. *x* knows the way (in which) to φ.
2*. *x* knows the location (at which) to φ.
3*. *x* knows the reason (for which) to φ.
4*. *x* knows the time (at which) to φ.

There is nothing particularly spooky about such objectual knowledge. Just as one can genuinely know a proof (e.g., Gödel's incompleteness theorem), a route (e.g., the way to the train station), or a person (e.g., one's partner), one can also know a method or way of acting, a place or location, a reason, or a time—and, we might say, know it *as such*.[37] Later, we consider how we should understand the relevant type of objectual knowledge, theoretically speaking. (Spoiler: it is not *mere* objectual knowledge or "knowledge-by-acquaintance." Rather, it is a kind of *understanding*.) For now, it suffices to observe that an objectualist approach defuses this "powerful argument" for propositionalism.

4.2 What Is the Intuitive Meaning of '*x* knows how to φ'?

Propositionalism asserts that knowing how to φ is a relation to a proposition, for example, the proposition that some way *w* is a way of φ-ing.[38] This view appears to

---

36. 'Where to φ' seems to, in some way, be about places, that is, the place to φ. 'Why to φ' seems to, in some way, be about reasons, that is, the reason to φ. 'When to φ' seems to, in some way, be about times, that is, the time to φ. And 'how to φ' seems to, in some way, be about the way or method in which to φ.

37. Forbes (2000) offers a detailed treatment of the as-such modifier, which we will simply use as an (often implicit) placeholder until our own, alternative conceptions-based approach in §5. At any rate, familiar linguistic machinery may be employed to distinguish between various readings of these sentences and to model the appropriate granularity.

38. There are a variety of ways to implement propositionalism. For example, the propositionalist can but need not quantify over propositions. Brogaard (2009, §3) and Kallestrup (2009, n. 2) offer reasons for propositionalists to prefer such quantification (cf. Schaffer 2009b, §1.3).

get knowledge how attributions wrong, descriptively speaking. Consider, for instance, Stanley's (2011, 209–210) claim that "it is fairly uncontroversial, and indeed intuitively obvious, that" the sentence

8. John knows how to find coffee in New York.

"has a reading synonymous" with the sentence

9. For some way w, John knows that he can find coffee in New York in way w.

We find it neither "uncontroversial" nor "intuitively obvious" that (8) and (9) have a reading on which they are *synonymous* or even rough paraphrases of one another. Nor do many prominent linguists (see, e.g., Ginzburg and Sag 2000 and Roberts 2009).[39] In any event, surely it is not the pretheoretical thing to say. If anything, the pretheoretical stance is that they are *not* synonymous.[40]

Compare:

10. John knows the way to find coffee in New York.

To the extent that we can provide a pretheoretical paraphrase of (8), presumably it is (10) or something thereabouts rather than (9).[41] It is not unnatural to speak of a subject who knows how to φ as knowing the way to φ and to speak of a subject who does not know how to φ as not knowing the way to φ. Interestingly, this is what is predicted by the objectualist view that knowledge how to φ is an objectual

---

39. Stanley and Williamson (2001, 440 emphasis added) are simply wrong when they claim that their treatment—exemplified by (9)—of the syntax and semantics of attributions of knowledge how "is *the* account entailed by current theories about the syntax and semantics of the relevant constructions." There are many different theories consistent with many different accounts. See, e.g., Ginzburg (chapter 9) and Michaelis (chapter 11).

40. Just consider the relative popularity of anti-intellectualism and the observation (i) from §1: intuitively, knowing how is *not* a kind of knowing that. We are not alone in this assessment; for example, Soteriou (2008, 480) writes in a similar vein, "Many, I think, share the intuition that there is something unsatisfactory in assimilating know how to straightforward propositional knowledge." At any rate, in our view, claims of synonymy are not to be taken lightly. Semantics is a delicate enterprise, and we theorists must be careful not to abuse or be overhasty with ordinary language or get carried away with currently fashionable linguistic theories.

41. Cf. Ware (1973, 157): "I would suggest that 'knowing how' means something very like 'knowing the way.' Knowing how I do it and knowing how to do it is the same as knowing the way I do it and knowing the way to do it." In (10) and certain statements that follow, we have spoken of 'the way,' though it may be more accurate to speak of 'a way.'

attitude that relates a subject (e.g., John) and a way of φ-ing (e.g., the way to find coffee in New York): in knowing how to φ, x knows the way to φ.[42]

In support of this suggestion, notice that objectualism also tracks the way we are inclined to speak about the cases discussed in §2:

11. Pat knows the correct way of doing the stunts (hence he can teach them).
12. Louis knows the way to find the numeral (since he knows the algorithm).
13. Irina does not know the way to do a salchow (because she is too confused).
14. Chris does not at the time of her decision to seek further information about kytoon-building know the way to build a kytoon (since she lacks sufficient information).

This may be taken as evidence in favor of an objectualist approach: for x to know how to φ is, roughly, for x to stand in a *knowing* relation to *a way of φ-ing*.

4.3 The Relation and the Relatum

An objectualist approach might be further motivated by reflecting on various features of what is known when one knows how to φ, namely, *how to* φ. Interestingly, this entity—how to φ—seems to behave more like a nonpropositional item than a proposition. For example, if it were a proposition, then presumably it could be said to be true or false—that is, it could be attributed the property of being true or the property of being false. But compare the following:

15. Michael knows that w is a way to swim; so it must be true.
16. ? Michael knows how to swim; so it must be true.[43]
17. ? Michael knows a way to swim; so it must be true.

---

42. One might object that from a linguistic point of view, 'how to find coffee in New York' is in this case an embedded question (a "real interrogative"), not a free relative, and thus it must express a proposition rather than a way of acting (as such). However, it is not clear to what extent the *metaphysical* distinction between propositions and ways of acting currently at issue corresponds to the *linguistic* distinction between embedded questions and free relatives. In work in progress, we develop an account of the syntax and semantics of *wh*-constructions consistent with these sorts of distinctions. See also the syntactic and semantic approaches developed by Ginzburg (chapter 9) and Michaelis (chapter 11).

43. On the proposal endorsed by Schaffer (2007, 2009b), x knows how to φ iff KxpQ, where Q is an indirect question regarding φ-ing and p is the answer to Q. To the extent that a question is the salient entity to which Michael is related when he knows how to swim, and questions cannot be true, this view might predict the oddity of (16). However, such a proposal looks to also predict that the following should be acceptable: ? 'Michael knows how to swim; it is easily answered'. It has been suggested to us that Q is for some reason unavailable to be the referent of 'it'. One might then expect p (an answer to Q) to be available instead, but it is not (recall 16). An appeal to type shifting is no help: ? 'Michael knows how to swim; it is nonempty.'

Other propositional predicates such as 'is possible' and 'is necessary' are similar. This disconfirms the prediction favorable to propositionalism while lending favor to objectualism (a way of acting can be neither true nor false, for example).

One might be tempted to think that, regardless, 'how to φ' in '*x* knows how to φ' must pick out a proposition because the question 'How to φ?' expresses a proposition with interrogative force. There is arguably a precedent (beyond familiar applications of Frege's context principle) for the objectualist's reluctance to bow to such temptation. Consider, for example,

18. Martin sees Lucy run.

This plausibly expresses an objectual relation between a subject (Martin) and a nonpropositional item—viz., an event (Lucy running)—even though the declarative sentence 'Lucy runs' expresses a proposition.[44]

Now turn to the relation that one stands in to what is known when one knows how to φ. This relation seems to behave more like an objectual knowledge relation than a propositional knowledge relation. First, if it were a simple propositional knowledge relation, then presumably it would not be gradable. Thus the following, for example, sounds bad:

19. ? Rebecca knows that swimming is a sport far better than Michael does.

By contrast, the relation picked out by 'knows' in '*x* knows how to φ' is gradable.[45] Thus the following sound just fine:

20. Rebecca knows how to swim far better than Michael does.
21. Rebecca knows how to swim far better than she knows how to dive.

Second, if the relation picked out by 'knows' in '*x* knows how to φ' were a simple propositional knowledge relation, then we should expect it to be

---

44. Cf. Crane (2009).

45. Cf. Ryle (1949, 59), Sgaravatti and Zardini (2008, §6), and Roberts (2009, §1.4). See Stanley (forthcoming-b, 33–34) for an attempt to give a propositionalist treatment of such gradability, but that account does not accommodate the possibility of comparing or grading the knowledge itself, not simply what is known. We often say that one *really* knows how, knows *quite well* how, knows *well enough* how, only *kind* (*sort*) *of* knows how, and so forth. These observations, together with the availability of a salient scale (namely, degree of mastery broadly construed), substantiates the gradability of knowing how.

possible to be as it were bumped up to certainty. Thus the following, for example, sounds fine:

22. Rebecca knows that swimming is a sport—in fact, she's certain of it!

But the relation picked out by 'knows' in 'x knows how to φ' cannot be bumped up to certainty. Thus the following sounds bad:

23. ? Rebecca knows how to swim—in fact, she's certain of it!

Presumably this is because, whereas propositional knowledge (knowing that) bumps up to certainty, knowing how bumps up to *mastery*:

24. Rebecca knows how to swim—in fact, she's mastered it!

Compare the following objectualist paraphrase:

25. Rebecca knows a way to swim—in fact, she's mastered it!

In contrast to propositionalism, then, an objectualist approach fits the data.

A related point concerns the matter of justification.[46] There is something odd about the following exchange:

26. a. Martin knows how to get to the airport.
    b. ? Hmm ... is he really justified in believing that?

Compare the following equally odd exchange:

27. a. Martin knows the way to the airport.
    b. ? Hmm ... is he really justified in believing that?

Here we find that an objectualist paraphrase nicely preserves the oddity of the exchange. A propositionalist paraphrase, by contrast, unacceptably relieves the exchange of its oddity:

28. a. Martin knows that following E-470 is the way to the airport.
    b. Hmm ... is he really justified in believing that?

---

46. Cf. Ryle (1949, 28) and Glick (forthcoming, §4).

5. Objectualist Intellectualism

To this point, we have argued that although knowledge how to φ is not merely a behavioral-dispositional state (§2), it is nevertheless fundamentally practical: knowledge how to φ is a state σ such that if x is in σ, then it is possible for there to be some y such that σ guides y in successfully and intentionally φ-ing (§3). We have also articulated the following objectualist hypothesis: for x to know how to φ is, roughly, for x to stand in a *knowing* relation to *a way of φ-ing* (§4). This section aims to improve on this pretheoretical statement of the objectualist position by articulating an account of the relation, as well as ways of acting, which locates the position in an intellectualist setting.

5.1 Understanding

There is reason to think that the type of knowledge in question involves a bit of sophistication, as it were. A natural starting point is the observation, suggested by the discussion in §§4.2–3, that it is at least as strong as objectual knowledge of—or familiarity or acquaintance with—a way of acting: as in (10)–(14), to know how to φ involves knowing the way to φ. On reflection, it is hard to see how the necessity of such *objectual* knowledge for knowing how has so often been suppressed or overlooked (by intellectualists and anti-intellectualists alike). Perhaps it has been hidden from view by its near-triviality: plainly, one could not know how to φ but fail to know any way of φ-ing.[48]

But objectual knowledge of a way of acting is not alone sufficient for knowing how. As it happens, making swimming motions is a way of escaping avalanches. A competent swimmer from the tropics who has never heard of or encountered snow or avalanches can have objectual knowledge of—be familiar or acquainted with—this particular way of acting (namely, making swimming motions), but if

---

47. The discussion in this section suggests that although objectualism is a metaphysical (not specifically linguistic) thesis, broadly linguistic considerations might be adduced on its behalf. This is important insofar as it is widely thought that linguistic considerations clearly favor propositionalism.

48. We recognize that knowing-x (e.g., knowing a way of acting) may differ from knowledge-*of* (e.g., knowledge *of* a way of acting). For ease of exposition, we use 'knowing a way' and 'knowledge of a way' interchangeably, though it should be kept in mind that, where they diverge, we always have in mind the former.

she has no conception of snow or avalanches, then she cannot know how to escape avalanches. Call this example *Swimmer*.[49]

Examples like *Swimmer* show that one fails to know how to φ if one *lacks* a conception of a way of φ-ing. Another route to a failure of knowledge how to φ is to have an *incorrect* conception of way of φ-ing. Recall Irina in *Salchow*. She is mistaken about the way to do a salchow (she conceives of a certain sequence of movements as constituting a way of doing a salchow when they do not) and hence does not know how to do one.[50] Yet a third route to a failure of knowledge how to φ is to have an *incomplete* conception of a way of φ-ing. Recall Chris in *Kytoon*. She lacks sufficient information about the way to build a kytoon (this is why she performs a Google search) and hence does not know how to build one. Irina's conception is incorrect; Chris's conception is incomplete.

A fourth route to a failure of knowledge how to φ is to harbor *conceptual confusion* that prevents reasonable mastery of the concepts in one's conception of a way of φ-ing. Suppose that Irina corrects her mistaken conception of a way of doing a salchow by memorizing her coach's instructions. So she now believes correctly that to do a salchow, one takes off from the back inside edge of one skate and lands on the back outside edge of the opposite skate after one or more rotations in the air. However, she is—á la Tyler Burge's (1979) arthritis patient—deeply confused about certain concepts, specifically, the concepts *back outside edge* and *back inside edge*. In particular, she takes her back outside edge to be her front inside edge and her back inside edge to be her front outside edge. As a result, Irina fails to grasp—that is, lacks reasonable mastery of the concepts in—her otherwise correct and complete conception of a way to do a salchow (failure that would result in substantive mishaps or errors if she were to try to do a salchow or attempt to teach someone else to do a salchow) and hence does not know how to do one. Call this example *Modified Salchow*.[51]

---

49. This example is inspired by Hawley's (2003) very nice avalanche case, developed in BMW (2009, §3).

50. Markie (2006, 126) also argues that a mistaken conception undermines knowledge how. He offers his example in the context of a discussion of learning and practicing complex intentional actions: "Suppose that, in learning to ride a bike, I start with a mistaken conception of correct bicycling. I think that correct bicycling requires moving as slowly as possible with a good bit of wobbling and weaving. The experience of moving very slowly and wobbly becomes a correct-bicycling experience; that of moving at all quickly or steadily an incorrect-bicycling one. I end up not really knowing how to ride."

51. The point of this example is twofold. First, a correct belief—even a knowledgeable belief, contra Stanley and Williamson (2001)—about the way to φ (or that w is a way to φ) is not sufficient for knowing how to φ. Second, simply having a correct and complete conception of a way to φ is likewise not enough; one must *grasp* that conception (i.e., have reasonable mastery of the concepts in that conception). A related example is given in BM (2007), which discusses

To summarize:

    A1. x does not know how to φ if x lacks a conception of a way of φ-ing.
    A2. x does not know how to φ if x has an incorrect conception of a way of φ-ing.
    A3. x does not know how to φ if x has an incomplete conception of a way of φ-ing.
    A4. x does not know how to φ if x fails to grasp a correct and complete conception of a way of φ-ing (i.e., lacks reasonable mastery of the concepts in such a conception).

Therefore,

    A5. Grasping a correct and complete conception of a way of φ-ing is necessary for knowing how to φ.[52]

Moreover, as we have seen, it is a near-triviality that:

    A6. Objectual knowledge of (familiarity or acquaintance with) a way of φ-ing is necessary for knowing how to φ.

So we have identified two necessary conditions for knowing how to φ. But as indicated by examples such as *Ski Instructor* and *Pi* (to which we return in a moment), these conditions are also jointly sufficient. Thus:

    A7. Having objectual knowledge of a way w of φ-ing while grasping a correct and complete conception of w is necessary and sufficient for knowing how to φ.

We believe that this is the key to understanding knowledge how. As we shall see, it provides the basis for explaining, among other things, why knowledge how to φ (i) is distinct from propositional knowledge, (ii) bears a substantive connection to action, and (iii) is a genuinely cognitive achievement.

    It is worth pausing for a moment to reflect on the complex objectual state or attitude invoked in (A7), namely, an objectual knowledge of a way of acting, together with an objectual grasp of a correct and complete conception of that way. Obviously, this complex objectual attitude is more demanding than mere objectual knowledge of

---

the relevant notion of grasping—that is, reasonable conceptual mastery—and, more generally, the role of concept possession in knowledge how.

52. One might worry that this cannot be right because it overintellectualizes knowing how and delivers the wrong verdict about simple-minded creatures who know how while lacking the requisite conceptions and conceptual sophistication. We respond to both objections in BMW (2009): this condition does not overintellectualize knowing how, and it does not wrongly exclude simple-minded creatures.

(familiarity or acquaintance with) a way of acting by itself, since grasping a correct and complete conception of a way of acting involves conceiving of that way in an appropriate manner—conceiving of it *as such* (with reasonable conceptual mastery). So the type of objectual attitude at issue is quite robust. In fact, it is natural to think of it as a kind of *understanding*, specifically, an *objectual understanding* of a way of acting:[53]

Having an objectual understanding of w (where w is a way of φ-ing) = having objectual knowledge of w while grasping a correct and complete conception of w.[54]

The view of knowing how to φ that emerges from this line of reasoning is a version of intellectualism because an understanding of a way, while not reducible to or a species of propositional attitude, is partially *grounded* in propositional attitudes. This can be seen from examples, such as those described previously, involving absent, incorrect, or incomplete conceptions. The problem in each case ultimately can be traced to a problem in certain of one's propositional attitudes or to the absence thereof. The competent swimmer in *Swimmer* does not have any nontrivial propositional attitudes about avalanches (she has never heard of or encountered them); as a result, she lacks any conception of avalanches (including a conception of a way to escape them) and hence fails to know how. Irina in *Salchow* has mistaken beliefs about the way to do a salchow; as a result, she has an incorrect conception of this way and hence does not know how to do one. Chris in *Kytoon* is unaware of certain key facts about the way to build a kytoon; as a result, she has an incomplete conception of this way and hence does not know how to build one. Irina in *Modified Salchow* is deeply confused about the concepts *back outside edge* and *back inside edge*, which confusion looks to imply the absence of certain key propositional attitudes;[55] as a result of her confusion, she fails to grasp a correct and

---

53. The importance of understanding to knowing how is suggested by Ryle (1949, 41ff.), Dreyfus (1992, 3), Hawley (2003, 28), and Noë (2005, 283). We believe that the considerations in §2 reveal the inadequacy of a behavioral-dispositional or successful-action-based treatment of such understanding. For ease of exposition, we will use 'understanding a way' and 'having an understanding of a way' interchangeably, though it should be kept in mind that, where they diverge, we always have in mind the former.

54. Such understanding is a kind of knowledge, but, as emphasized in the text, it is neither propositional knowledge nor mere objectual knowledge (acquaintance, familiarity) alone: rather, it is *objectual-knowledge-of-a-way-of-φ-ing-as-such-with-reasonable-conceptual-mastery*.

55. Which propositional attitudes? If Bealer's (1998) analysis of conceptual understanding in terms of intuitions is correct, some of the relevant attitudes will be intuitions. If Peacocke's (2008) most recent analysis of conceptual understanding is correct, some of the relevant attitudes will be states of tacit propositional knowledge. And so forth. However, the basic idea expressed in this paragraph is that to fix a subject's propositional attitudes *plus the subject's conceptual situation* is to fix their knowledge how.

complete conception of a way of doing a salchow and hence, as in *Salchow*, does not know how to do one. If these defects were not present, then the subjects would know how to perform their respective actions. Recall Pat in *Ski Instructor*: although he has never been able to do the stunts, he has an impressive understanding of their correct execution; as a result, he grasps an adequate conception of the way to do the stunts and hence knows how to do them. (In fact, it is his understanding of a way to do the stunts that enables him to teach Olympic-caliber students how to do them.) Likewise, although Louis in *Pi* is unable to find the 10^{46} numeral in the decimal expansion of π, he grasps the algorithm; as a result, he has an understanding of the way and hence knows how. And so on: the absence or presence of knowledge how is a matter of the absence or presence of a certain kind of understanding (not ability or disposition to behavior), and this ultimately can be traced to the absence or presence of some defectiveness in one's overall propositional attitudes (plus conceptual understanding).[56]

The result is an intellectualist view according to which knowledge how to φ is an objectual attitude or state grounded in (possibly tacit) propositional attitudes, though it is not itself reducible to or a species of propositional attitude. We call this *objectualist intellectualism*:

Objectualist Intellectualism
To know how to φ is to stand in an objectual *understanding* relation to *a way w of φ-ing*,

where such understanding consists in objectual knowledge of *w* together with an objectual grasp of (having reasonable mastery of the concepts in) a correct and complete conception of *w*.

What remains is to clarify this thesis and articulate its virtues.

5.2 Conceptions and Ways

We begin by unpacking the notion of a *conception*, a type of phenomenon that a number of psychologists and philosophers have independently argued is indis-

---

56. In BM (2007, §4), we suggested that the relevant propositional attitude must be knowledge that *w* is a way to φ. However, this perspective is not obligatory; the present approach introduces additional flexibility. As we observed in §1, what is crucial to intellectualism is that knowledge how to φ be grounded in *some propositional attitude or other* regarding φ-ing (see also BMW 2009, n. 3 and especially the state of play essay in this book). Such flexibility allows our intellectualist position to accommodate the alleged cases of knowing how without knowing that discussed by Cath (chapter 5), though we ourselves are not fully convinced by those cases.

pensable in psychological explanation.[57,58] In general, one's conception of some δ is how one conceives or thinks, or is somehow inclined to think, of δ.[59] Such conceptions have the virtue of being not only theoretically useful but also exceedingly familiar. We have conceptions of ourselves, of our environment, of motion (Newton's conception of motion differed from Aristotle's), of higher education, of the proper scope of government, of truth, and of a way of doing a salchow. These conceptions can be accurate or inaccurate, orthodox or unorthodox, liberal or conservative, ambitious or naïve, widespread or idiosyncratic, and explicit or implicit (nonconscious, nondiscursive). They can evolve and change, influence behavior, and affect our well-being.

While there no doubt are interesting differences between these particular conceptions, we find it plausible that these and other conceptions—that is, conceptions in general—possess the following properties:[60]

Nonfactivity: A conception of δ can be incorrect (mistaken).
Nonexhaustiveness: A conception of δ can be incomplete.

---

57. See, for example, the seminal work in psychology on schemata and scripts by Anderson (1977), Schank and Abelson (1977), and Rumelhart (1980). Conceptions and their kin (e.g., stereotypes, views, perspectives, "frames", and "files") have also been invoked in the philosophies of language, action, mind, and fiction; see, for example, Putnam (1975), Brand (1982, 1984, ch. 8), Bratman (1987), Woodfield (1991, §2), Jackson (1998, 31), Peacocke (1998, 2003, 2008, ch. 4), Gendler (2000), Burge (2003, 383ff.), Wiggins (2001), and Gupta (2006, 76ff.). One need not endorse the details of any of these approaches to appreciate the explanatory significance of conceptions.

58. There is an ambiguity in the term 'conception', as in the term 'belief', that can be brought out by considering the difference between *one's having a conception*, which is a mental state or attitude of an individual, and *the conception that one has*, which is a content that might not be had or possessed by any individual at all. Context should serve to disambiguate.

59. As this suggests, conceptions (the attitudes) are not identical to beliefs—at least not outright beliefs—or collections thereof (though they may supervene on beliefs and their kin). Still, as we will see, conceptions resemble beliefs in several respects.

60. It is worth emphasizing the difference between conceptions (the contents), on one hand, and concepts (the nonmentalistic entities), on the other (cf. Higginbotham 1998). One way to see the difference is by noticing that two individuals can possess the very same *concept* of δ, although they do not have the same *conception* of δ. This is illustrated by the patient and doctor in Burge's (1979) famous arthritis example (with respect to their shared concept *arthritis*, however different their conceptions may be), as well as the neuroanatomist and child we describe later (with respect to their shared concept *ear wiggling*, however different their conceptions may be). Conceptions are also distinct from propositions: while the latter are the semantic values of full indicative sentences and canonically introduced by 'that'-clauses, the former are canonically introduced by 'as'- and 'by'-clauses such as 'by contracting the auricular muscles'. We develop a broadly nonreductive theory of conceptions, and propose a general analysis of understanding in terms of conceptions, in work in progress.

Diversity: There can be many distinct conceptions of δ.
Fine-grainedness: Necessarily equivalent conceptions need not be identical.
Nonarticulatedness: A conception of δ can be wholly or partly demonstrative.
Nonovertness: An individual can have a conception of δ either implicitly or explicitly.
Publicity: x and y (x ≠ y) can share one and the same conception of δ.
Nonexclusivity: x can simultaneously have two or more distinct conceptions of δ.

Nonfactivity is illustrated by Irina's conception in *Salchow*, which is incorrect. Nonexhaustiveness is illustrated by Chris's conception in *Kytoon*, which is incomplete. Diversity can be illustrated by considering a neuroanatomist and a child who have differing conceptions of the same way of wiggling their ears, namely, contracting the auricular muscles: whereas the neuroanatomist's conception of this way is the academic and articulated conception *by contracting the auricular muscles*, the child's conception of this way is the casual and unarticulated conception *by doing this to these parts of my body*. The child's demonstrative conception also illustrates nonarticulatedness and nonovertness.[61] The neuroanatomist's conception also illustrates publicity and nonexclusivity: another neuroanatomist might share the same conception and also possess a second, demonstrative conception akin to the child's. Fine-grainedness might be illustrated by the competent swimmer's conception in *Swimmer*: even if her conception of a way of making swimming motions were necessarily coextensive with a conception of a way of escaping avalanches (it is probably not), these conceptions still would not be one and the same.

Ways of acting—or the subclass of such ways relevant here—are *methods*. We take methods to be constituted by a (possibly ordered, possibly singleton) sequence of action types, the execution of which is an act.[62] Methods or ways of acting exhibit several features corresponding to those possessed by conceptions:

---

61. See BM (2007, §4) for further discussion of ear wiggling and the role of demonstrative concepts in knowledge how.

62. While some ways (e.g., impulsively) may be properties of token events, as Stanley and Williamson (2001, 427) suggest, the subclass of ways relevant here, namely, methods, are *not* properties of token events. Nor are methods sets of instructions or regulative propositions: instructions simply *describe* or *command* ways of acting; regulative propositions *represent* or *state* ways of acting; neither are themselves ways of acting.

Diversity: There can be many distinct ways of φ-ing.
Publicity: x and y ($x \neq y$) can φ in one and the same way.
Nonexclusivity: x can simultaneously perform two or more distinct ways of φ-ing.

However, conceptions and ways of acting do not share all of the same features. By contrast with conceptions, ways of acting have the following properties:

Factivity: A way of φ-ing is in fact a way of φ-ing; that is, w is a way of φ-ing only if it is possible that some individual φ-s in way w.[63]
Exhaustiveness: A way of φ-ing must be complete; that is, w is a way of φ-ing only if by acting in way w, one φ-s.
Coarse-grainedness: Necessarily equivalent ways of φ-ing are identical.

Ways of acting differ from conceptions in at least these three respects.

Correct and complete conceptions of ways of acting are related to ways of acting in several ways (beyond the trivial relation *being a correct and complete conception of*).[64] One important relation can be stated once we have the notion of a *guiding conception*:

[GC] ξ is a guiding conception for an action φ for an individual x if ξ is for x a conception of a way of φ-ing and, in attempting to φ, x tries to at least implicitly make x's behavior conform to ξ.[65]

The relation is this:

[R] A conception ξ of a way w of φ-ing is correct and complete only if it is possible for ξ to be some individual's guiding conception in φ-ing in way w.

As we shall see, conceptions and ways of acting and the relations therein play an important role in objectualist intellectualism's explanation of the simultaneously practical and cognitive character of knowledge how.

---

63. Consider: there is no way to square the circle. Cf. Sgaravatti and Zardini (2008, 233–235).

64. For instance, on certain views of analysis (or elucidation), if ξ is a correct and complete conception of a way w of φ-ing, then ξ is an analysis (or elucidation) of w.

65. See BM (2007, §4). As we observed there, guiding conceptions obey the following *exclusion principle*: For any particular attempt α to φ, and for any candidate conceptions ξ and ξ^* of ways of φ-ing ($\xi \neq \xi^*$), if in the course of α, ξ is x's guiding conception, then ξ^* is not.

5.3 Virtues

Objectualist intellectualism has several theoretical virtues. First, by refusing to identify knowledge how to φ with any kind of ability or disposition (power), it avoids the problems of pervasive inability and ignorant reliability. Second, it explains why the relation picked out by 'knows' in '*x* knows how to φ' is gradable, cannot be bumped up to certainty, and renders justification inapplicable: objectual understanding is gradable, cannot be bumped up to certainty, and renders justification inapplicable. Third, as we have seen, it correctly classifies examples of knowing how (or the absence thereof), for instance, *Ski Instructor*, *Pi*, *Salchow*, *Kytoon*, *Swimmer*, and *Modified Salchow*, among others.[66]

Perhaps the most significant virtue of objectualist intellectualism is its capacity to preserve—and, in fact, explain—the three attractive but prima facie incompatible theses listed in §1. First, if knowing how is a nonpropositional, objectual attitude, knowing how is not merely a kind of knowing that. Second, understanding a way of φ-ing (i.e., having reasonable mastery of the concepts in a correct and complete conception of a way of φ-ing) is plainly a nontrivial cognitive state. So objectualist intellectualism makes it easy to see why knowing how is a cognitive achievement. Third, a correct and complete conception of a way of φ-ing is a state that carries sufficient information, as it were, to guide the successful and intentional completion of φ (even if it does not do so for any given individual on any given occasion). Hence knowledge how bears a substantive connection to action.[67]

We can render this objectualist intellectualist treatment of the practical character of knowing how a bit more precise by walking through the steps leading from the nature of conceptions and ways to action-guidingness (where 'CC($\xi w \varphi$)' stands for 'a conception ξ of a way w of φ-ing is correct and complete'):[68]

---

66. Another virtue is that it promises to answer Schaffer's (2007; 2009b §1.2) convergence argument. If we accept Schaffer's judgments of material inequivalence, we must acknowledge the need for conceptions that discriminate properly. See, in particular, Schaffer's (2009b, 479) discussion of proper discrimination.

67. These points also yield an explanation of the one-to distinction discussed in §2: knowledge how *to* φ, but not knowledge how *one* φ-s (or how φ-ing *is done*, *what it takes* to φ, and so forth), requires an objectual grasp of a conception of a way to φ that could guide the successful and intentional completion of φ. This explanation is a further significant virtue. By way of contrast, Stanley and Williamson's (2001) propositionalism—to cite just one example—appears to be unable to explain the one-to distinction, which it basically collapses.

68. In an interesting discussion of what he labels the "directive" character of knowing how, Kumar (2011, §5) objects that our intellectualist view cannot account for the connection between knowing how and action. But insofar as the objection targets our notion of an ability-based concept, a notion that we invoked to an entirely different end (see BM 2007, §3), the objection misunderstands this aspect of our view. It is the notion of *grasping a correct and complete conception of a*

B1. CC(ξwφ) only if it is possible for ξ to be some individual x's conception of w and, in attempting to φ, x tries to at least implicitly make x's behavior conform to ξ. (From [GC] and [R])

B2. x tries to at least implicitly make x's behavior conform to a conception ξ of a way of φ-ing in attempting to φ only if x exercises ξ in attempting to φ. (Premise)

B3. So CC(ξwφ) only if it is possible for ξ to be some individual x's conception of w and x exercises ξ in attempting to φ. (From B1 and B2)

B4. If CC(ξwφ), then w is a way of φ-ing. (Triviality)

B5. So if CC(ξwφ), then it is possible that some individual φ-s in way w. (From B4 and factivity of ways of acting)

B6. So CC(ξwφ) only if: it is possible that some individual φ-s in way w, and it is possible that some individual exercises ξ in attempting to φ. (From B5 and B3)

B7. If it is possible that some individual φ-s in way w and it is possible that some individual exercises a correct and complete conception of w in attempting to φ, then it is possible that some individual successfully and intentionally φ-s in way w by exercising ξ. (Premise)

B8. So CC(ξwφ) only if it is possible for there to be some individual x such that x successfully and intentionally φ-s in way w by exercising ξ. (From B6 and B7)

B9. If x successfully and intentionally φ-s in way w by exercising ξ, then x's exercise of ξ underlies and explains x's successfully and intentionally φ-ing— that is, ξ guides x in successfully, intentionally φ-ing. (Premise)

B10. So CC(ξwφ) only if it is possible for there to be some individual x such that x's exercise of ξ underlies and explains x's successfully and intentionally φ-ing— that is, ξ guides x in successfully, intentionally φ-ing. (From B8 and B9)

It follows that if knowledge how to φ involves a CC(ξwφ)—a correct and complete conception of a way of acting—then [V] is true. In this way, objectualist intellectualism, which says that knowing how involves an objectual grasp of just such a conception, has the virtue of answering the action-guiding question. Thus it explains the substantive connection between knowledge how and action expressed in [V]: knowledge how to φ is a state σ such that: if x is in σ, then it is possible for there to be some y such that y's exercise of σ underlies and explains y's successfully and intentionally φ-ing—that is, σ guides y in successfully, intentionally φ-ing.

---

way of acting (i.e., understanding a way) that explains the connection expressed in principle [V] (as suggested in BM 2007, 53, and made explicit presently).

Objectualist intellectualism offers a unique perspective on the intersection of mind and action—wherein lies teaching, learning, practicing, and other intentional-cum-epistemic phenomena that evince the simultaneously practical and cognitive character of knowledge how. This perspective enables us to escape a false dichotomy between the identification of knowing how with either propositional attitudes or powers. Knowledge how is the property of neither fools nor automata but the achievement of those who *understand*. Thus we can begin to appreciate the idea that knowledge how to act is a form of *practical knowledge*: a cognitive state, distinct from propositional knowledge, that can guide intentional action.[69]

---

69. Thanks to Rachel Briggs, Yuri Cath, Dave Chalmers, Bruin Christensen, David Enoch, Ephraim Glick, Alex Grzankowski, Josh Knobe, John Maier, Aidan McGlynn, Daniel Nolan, Raul Saucedo, Jonathan Schaffer, Anat Schechtman, Susanna Schellenberg, Levi Spectre, and participants in events at the Van Leer Institute, University of Manitoba, ANU Practical Cognition Group, and Kioloa Metaphysics Workshop.

8

Ideology and the Third Realm (Or, a Short Essay on Knowing How to Philosophize)

Alva Noë[1]

> Es geht nicht darum, Philosophie zu kennen; sondern philosophieren zu können.
> MARTIN HEIDEGGER

> No philosophic argument ends with Q.E.D. However forceful, it never forces. There is no bullying in philosophy, neither with the stick of logic nor with the stick of language.
> FRIEDRICH WAISMANN

1. The Problem of the Third Realm

Frege claimed that statements of number are statements about concepts (1884/1978, 59). The statement "the King's carriage is drawn by four horses," for example, is a statement about the concept "horse that draws the King's carriage." It might look as if we are talking about the King's carriage when we use these words, but we aren't. What we are saying, according to Frege, is that the concept "horse that draws the King's carriage" is true of exactly four things.

This is not the only case Frege brings to our attention where, in a sense, we fail to understand what we are saying. Here is another example: we aren't talking about animals when we say that whales are mammals; our topic, rather, is the relation between the two concepts "whale" and "mammal," namely, that anything that falls under the first also falls under the second (1884/1978, 60).

Let's say Frege is right: appearances notwithstanding, a statement of number is a statement about a concept, or we're talking about concepts, not whales, when

---

[1]. Thanks to Nadja El Kassar for helpful discussion.

we say whales are mammals. The questions I pose are these: What sort of discovery is this? How does Frege know? If he were mistaken, what would he be mistaken about? And what kind of mistake is it that we are guilty of when we naïvely find ourselves believing that we are talking about the King's carriage, or horses, when we say, "The King's carriage is drawn by four horses"? Frege's accomplishment is impressive, especially when placed in coordination with his analysis of existence and quantification. But what is his accomplishment exactly?

A reflection on Frege's practice suggests two interesting and puzzling features of his analysis.

First, the proposal that a statement of number is a statement about a concept does not seem to be the sort of thesis that admits of definitive proof. We don't have any idea what such a proof would look like. Frege can give us reasons for agreeing with him, and he does, but he can't quite compel our assent. There isn't anything like a QED in the offing here. We can speak of getting what he's trying to show; we can speak of getting it right; we can speak of being persuaded. But there are no decision procedures here that would enable us to decide, once and for all, that in fact we're talking about concepts and not whales or numbers.

If this is right—and this is hardly shocking—then *analysis*, in the relevant sense, isn't like chemical analysis. In chemistry, we have microscopes that allow us literally to peer into the internal structure of materials, and we have solvents and other chemicals that allow us to break a compound into its component parts. But in the domain of philosophical analysis that is our concern, there isn't anything that plays the role of solvent or microscope. There are no independent or objective measures in this domain.

Second, for all that there are no rules or decision procedures for evaluating claims about what we really mean when we say that the King's carriage is drawn by four horses, it would be crazy to think that Frege isn't offering us a substantive thesis, a thesis that is either right or wrong. We may not know how to settle the matter once and for all, but we can't doubt that we are in a realm of intersubjectively significant discussion; we encounter here the live possibility of agreement and disagreement. Indeed, Frege offers reasons for his proposal; he makes an argument that goes something like this: If we aren't talking about the concept "horse that draws the King's carriage," then, he asks us, what are we talking about? The King's carriage? But there is only *one* of those. The horses? Are we saying that the horses are four? Is this like saying that they are brown? If it is, then it ought to follow that each of them is four, just as it would follow that each of them is brown. But *that* isn't what we want to say. Is four then supposed to be a property not of the horses individually but of the collective? At best, it is arbitrary to assign the number four to the collective. We might just as well assign the number one because there is one collective, or the number two because there are two pair of horses. No, Frege says, we aren't talking about *things* at all, and we aren't ascribing properties to things. Number words are not adjectives. A statement of number is not about a thing; it is, rather, a statement about a way we have of thinking about a thing, which is to say, it is a statement about a concept.

Are you persuaded? I am. But that is of no matter. What is important is that we appreciate that Frege is trying to persuade us of something. He is offering an analysis of what we mean when we engage in a certain type of thought and talk about number. And either he gets it right, or he doesn't.

If we wish to understand philosophical analysis—this is the topic—then we need to understand the distinctively in-between (neither entirely objective nor merely subjective) character of claims about, for example, what we really mean or what we are really talking about. We need to make sense of the fact that analytical insight into the character of our thought and talk, whether Frege's or Socrates', takes place neither in a realm like chemistry, which is, so to speak, straightforwardly objective, nor in a realm that is merely subjective, where there is no call for reason-giving and argument. Frege's insights into our thought and talk belong in neither of these realms but rather in a *third* realm. To understand philosophical analysis, we need to understand the character of this third realm. This is our challenge.

2. *An Inadequate Experimentalism*

I can imagine that there are philosophers—let's call them experimental philosophers—who think Frege should have taken a vote.[2] Their policy would be to send out a questionnaire with a multiple-choice question along these lines:

The sentence "The King's carriage is drawn by four horses" is a statement about which of the following:

1. the King's carriage
2. the horses
3. the concept "horse that draws the King's carriage"
4. none of the above

Once we recognize the third-realm character of Frege's problems, and ours, the misguidedness of this experimentalist approach becomes immediately apparent. The point is not that Frege or we are entitled to be indifferent to what people say or would say in answer to such a questionnaire. The point is that whatever people

---

2. See Bengson, Moffett, and Wright (2009) for an example of experimentalism in action.

say could be at most the beginning of our conversation, not its end; it would be the opportunity for philosophy, not the determination of the solution of a philosophical problem.

The experimentalist displays a naïveté that amounts to a blindness to philosophy and its challenges. The experimentalist's approach is tantamount to denying the third-realm character of the analysis problem. Such a statistical procedure could be justified, after all, only if we think that there is a straightforward decision procedure for deciding what people think (e.g., taking a head count) or, barring that, if we think that there is no fact of the matter at all about what people really mean and that the best we can do is gather data about what people say they mean.

The experimentalist may be motivated by a desire to repudiate dogmatism. When backed into a corner by hostile Indians, the Lone Ranger is said to have turned to Tonto and exclaimed: "What are we to do?" Tonto's reply: "Who do you mean by 'we,' white man?"[3] And so we can appreciate that there is something potentially misguided about thinking that we can decide, from the armchair, what people really mean. If we are interested in what people really mean, then we'd better interrogate people themselves.

A fair point. But what is needed, then, is an interrogation or, better, a conversation or dialogue. The Lone Ranger joke in a way perpetuates a misunderstanding. After all, the Lone Ranger's answer to Tonto ought to have been clear: "Who do I mean by 'we'? I mean, you, Tonto, and me. We're in this predicament together." Whose laughter matters when you tell a joke? The people to whom you tell the joke. And so in the philosophical case. It is *we* who are puzzled by our use of number words. It seems as if we use number words as adjectives, to ascribe properties to things. But this can't be right. Consider my deck of cards. It is *one* deck. But it is fifty-two cards. And who knows how many atoms. What number attaches to the deck of cards *really*? The problem is our problem. And we aren't interested in data points about what people say. We are interested in the question of what we ourselves mean, in why we say what we say, or in why we feel we can't say anything else. It is our puzzlement, sense of surprise, or revelation that is our subject matter. If you say, "It's one thing, the deck," I'll say, "Yes, but then don't you mean that there is one instance of the concept 'is a deck of cards' here? You don't mean that the deck is one, the way the deck is new, do you?" And so we go on and on until we come to a point where we can stop, we lose patience with each other, or we recognize that there isn't a way to settle the issue between us.

---

3. Daniel Dennett told me this joke in 1995. I have the impression that it is widely circulated.

To deny the third-realm character of our puzzle, as the experimentalist does, is to lapse, however unwillingly, into dogmatism. And it is to miss the point of, and the opportunity for, philosophy.

It is perhaps useful to state clearly that to reject the inadequate experimentalism and to insist on the third-realm character of philosophical problems is neither to set philosophy over against the natural sciences nor to deny that mind and experience can be made the subject of natural scientific investigation. To reject the inadequate experimentalism is not to reject naturalism. It is, however, to acknowledge that the demands of naturalism are not always clear and indeed precisely because the study of nature is not itself neatly segregated from philosophy. Philosophical problems are not the property of philosophy professors. Philosophy arises for natural science; it arises within natural science. To insist on the impossibility of reducing philosophy to natural science is to acknowledge that natural science is also and must remain, at least sometimes, a philosophical practice. Philosophy does not stand opposed to natural science. Philosophy is one of science's moments, or better, natural science is one of philosophy's moments. A naturalized philosophy will not seek to replace philosophical conversation with experiments. It will acknowledge the unbreakable marriage of philosophy and natural science.

3. A Misguided Antipsychologism

Frege's insight into the character of our thought and talk was profound. But it turns out that he himself was no better able than the experimentalist to appreciate the third-realm character of his achievements. Frege fails to offer a satisfying account of the status of his own insight.

Frege is sometimes credited with showing that grammatical form is a poor guide to the underlying logical form of our thoughts (see, for example, Anscombe 1959). The problem with this characterization is that it suggests that Frege's conception of the relation between thought and language is coherent, when in fact it would seem to have been anything but. On the one hand, Frege insists that thought is not in any way essentially tied to language. There could be beings who were able to grasp thoughts directly, without needing to clad them in the sensible garb of language (Frege 1924/1997, 288). On the other hand, Frege insists that we are not such creatures. For human beings, at least, the grasping of thoughts is to tied to linguistic understanding.[4] More importantly, his declarations to the

---

4. "There is no contradiction in supposing there to exist beings that can grasp the same thought as we do without needing to clad it in a form that can be perceived by the senses. But still, for us men there is this necessity."

contrary notwithstanding, Frege conceives of thoughts as quasi-linguistic entities. The thought, after all, is the sense of a sentence (Frege 1919/1984, 61), and to the constituents of the thought, there correspond constituents of the sentence (at least a sentence in the language of pure thought, what Frege called the concept-script). A thought, for Frege, then, is the kind of thing whose essence can be exhibited in a suitably clarified formal symbolism.

Part of what prevents Frege from providing an adequate conception of his own analytical insights is his celebrated and, for all that, misguided antipsychologism. Logic has nothing to do with psychology, argued Frege. The logician isn't interested in how we think but in how we ought to think (1919/1984). Psychology is concerned with ideas, which, for Frege, as for Locke or Hume, are purely interior occurrences, rather like tickles or sensations. On Frege's understanding of what an idea is, I have my ideas, and you have yours, and there is no sense whatsoever to the possibility that we might speak about them, compare them, and share them. Ideas are private (Frege 1919/1984, 67). In contrast with ideas, which arise in my head and yours but can never pass between us, thoughts can be communicated. They may be immaterial, like ideas, but unlike ideas, they can be shared and grasped and communicated. Thoughts are not private. Their immateriality is no obstacle to their mind-independence and their actuality.

A thought, for Frege, is real and self-standing, like a walnut or a pistol. And like walnuts and pistols, thoughts can be *grasped*. But unlike walnuts and pistols, thoughts are *immaterial*; they exist outside space and time in what Frege himself called a third realm. And so we can reasonably ask: How do we grasp thoughts? How do we come into contact with them? Frege's attitude to these questions was ambivalent. On the one hand, he insists that these questions are of no relevance to logic; they are the province of psychology. On the other hand, Frege seems to have appreciated that, at least as he sets up the problems, these are questions that can't be answered. Remember, Frege allows the possibility that there might be creatures capable of a direct apprehension of thoughts without any linguistic or communicative setting. For Frege, thoughts and the place they occupy in our lives are a mystery.[5]

---

[5]. "When a thought is grasped, it at first only brings about changes in the inner world of the one who grasps it; yet it remains untouched in the core of its essence, for the changes it undergoes affect only inessential properties. There is lacking here something we observe everywhere in physical process—reciprocal action. Thoughts are not wholly unactual but their actuality is quite different from the actuality of things. And their action is brought about by a performance of the thinker; without this they would be inactive, at least as far as we can see. And yet the thinker does not create them but must take them as they are. They can be true without being grasped by a thinker; and they are not wholly unactual even then, at least if they *could* be grasped and so brought into action" (Frege 1919/1984, 77).

The irony is this: Frege's strange melding of a radically subjectivist view of psychology with a realist/objectivist view of thoughts makes it entirely obscure how Frege's own insight into the structure of our sayings could even be possible. Frege's ontology renders his own analytic practice incomprehensible. What was Frege's investigation other than an investigation into how we understand our thought and talk (about numbers, concepts, etc.)? By insisting that grasping a thought is coming into contact with something whose fundamental nature is independent of our thinking, talking, and understanding (for these are the province of psychology), Frege does not merely render thoughts occult; he renders the very possibility of comprehending the real, transcendent structure of thoughts an enigma, precisely because their nature is now thought of as transcendent. Philosophical analysis, on this view, *is* like chemistry, but it is a mysterious chemistry that requires of us that we achieve bald insight into the mind-independent reality of substances.

4. *The Structure of Our Practices*

I have been speaking of Frege's insight and now also of Frege's mistake. His mistake prevents him from understanding the nature of his own insight. His mistake consists in a failure to bring the third-realm character of his own investigations into focus.

In an effort to bring light to the issue, let us for a moment consider baseball. Baseball is not merely a system of rules and representations. To learn baseball is not merely to learn rules that define a class of events as baseball events (base hits, runs, foul balls, etc.) and that define others as *non*baseball events (foot faults, touchdowns, for example). To learn the game is to learn, among other things, to *perceive* these events, to notice, for example, a missed scoring opportunity or a nicely turned double play. It is also to learn to take an interest in occurrences such as these. The baseball aficionado *cares* whether the pickoff attempt was botched; he or she is emotionally involved in the course of play. To learn baseball is to learn to be engaged with baseball; it is to enter into what we might call *the baseball world*.

There is more to say about this initiation into the baseball world. A striking feature of life in the baseball world is the importance—indeed, the urgency—attached to talk and thought about baseball, about its play, its history, and also its problems. It belongs to life in the baseball world that we engage in elaborate critical discourse *about* baseball. This critical discourse is about baseball, but it is also, I propose, constitutive *of* baseball. In baseball, we not only hit, field, throw, and run but also dispute calls at the plate, question the rules and take sides on hard cases, and even worry about whether rulebook reforms are necessary to avoid certain situations in the future. A crucial feature of the baseball world—and here it is comparable to the legal world, for example, or the art world—is that the first-order practice contains and requires its own metatheory. Or to put the point a different way, baseball requires and nurtures its own ideology.

Are there really home runs and strikeouts, infield pop-ups and outs at home plate? Do these things exist? Of course they do. That the fly ball cleared the wall in fair territory is an intersubjectively assessable matter of fact. Whether it happened is one thing; whether you or I or anyone else believes it happened is another.[6] To doubt the real, mind-independent existence of home runs would be like doubting the reality of taxes, say, or race.

Of course, there are those who insist on the unreality of race (for example) on the grounds that we lack any social practice-independent account of what race is; for example, we lack a plausible biological theory of race. It would be a mistake, though, to think that this fact—that race is not biological—means that there is no race. After all, there is good evidence to the contrary. Race is a statistically significant factor determining measurable features of the lives of real people (e.g., income, life expectancy). Race is something of which we find ourselves drawn to say both that it exists and that it does not exist. "Race is nothing, a figment!" "Race is a defining feature of our lives in modern society!" To understand race, we need to take the measure of this somewhat paradoxical situation.

I think we would all agree that it would be lunacy to reply to the antirealist about home runs or race by insisting that home runs and race are abstract, Platonic phenomena residing outside space and time. What makes this lunatic is that our best hope of understanding what a home run is would be to think about the place of home runs in actual baseball-playing practice. A home run is not something that exists outside baseball, anymore than a checkmate is something that exists within baseball. To try to understand the existence of home runs as entities that are autonomous of baseball practice would be to pull the rug out from under one's only hope of understanding what a home run is. And something very much like this needs to be said about race. Race can be understood only in the context of a set of historical circumstances and conditions, conditions that include among themselves facts concerning social attitudes about, precisely, race. Race is

---

6. Actually, this is a complicated issue, precisely because of the curious status in baseball of the umpire. An umpire calls plays; intuitively, he can get the calls right or wrong. Certainly, baseball audiences frequently criticize umpires for blown calls. But this misunderstands the role of the umpire. He is not an outsider; in a sense, he is not a judge at all. The umpire is not a person with opinions but is rather a mechanism of baseball play. And as a matter of fact, except in exceptional circumstances, an umpire's actions cannot be overturned. The umpire is a mechanism of baseball play. An umpire's call makes it the case, say, that a player is safe or out; it does not record this fact.

something we make in our social practice. We enact race. We do so in millions of ways (some beautiful and some no doubt very ugly).

I would like to suggest that Frege's attitudes about language and thought are comparable to the admittedly lunatic view about baseball. The corresponding lunacy, however, is much harder to appreciate when we turn to language. We take our own ideologies about language so much for granted that we find it literally ridiculous to try to see things from a different point of view. Our entrenchment in the language world is so profound that we find it difficult to appreciate the practice relativity of our linguistic ontologies. Are there nouns and verbs, sentences and truth values, concepts and concept expressions? This question is like the question about fly balls and double plays. Of course there are! It is, however, to misunderstand these questions completely to suppose that linguistic entities have any reality outside the corresponding social practices. But crucially, this is exactly what Frege does when he supposes that a concept, for example, is an abstract constituent of thoughts. (And this is exactly what linguists do when they suppose that language is fixed in the human genome as an element of our biological endowment.)[7]

The basic point here is that our judgments about concepts and meaning, as about grammaticality and words, are judgments we make *within* the language world, just as reflections on baseball are made within the baseball world. Frege's indifference to this point—and as far as I can tell, the indifference of most practitioners of philosophy of language, as well as of "scientific" linguistics—forces him to conceive of language and thought in ways that divorce it from our lives, from our practices, from our actions.

I am not the first to compare language to games. Nevertheless, there is still a great deal to be learned from the comparison. Here is something else. Notice that a home run isn't merely something it is possible to do in baseball. A home run is a thing of a very definite value. If you are batting, a home run is *very* good. If you are pitching, a home run is *very* bad. To understand what a home run is is to understand, inter alia, that every batter wants to hit one and every pitcher wants to do whatever is possible to avoid giving one up. In general, it isn't pos-

---

7. This is a complicated topic that I can't do justice here. But notice, to the linguist's reply that language is universal, one might reasonably respond, no, it isn't! English and Hausa are about as universal as baseball is. To which the linguist is likely to retort: granted, individual languages are not universal, but Language is. And the evidence for this? At this point, the linguist will point to deep structures and principles that are true of all languages. My response, to be filled out elsewhere: these judgments are made within the language world, just as baseball judgments are made in the baseball world. They have no practice-independent plausibility. One example: linguists help themselves to the idea of a "sentence," an idea that is on a par, ontologically, with that of "home run."

sible to separate moves in games from their value, from their point. Exactly the same thing can and ought to be said about linguistic moves. Speech happens in the setting of our active lives. To make a statement is to achieve something, and very often it is also to achieve something else—you inform someone of something; you frighten, threaten, or amuse another; you close a deal or break off relations or invite some further exchange. To understand language is to understand the ways in which language is deployed in the different settings of our active lives.

To learn a language is not only to learn to use words but also to learn to think about, criticize, and reflect on the use of words. This is a striking feature of all linguistic communities and is clearly in evidence when adults talk to children. We don't merely teach kids how to talk; we teach them the concepts "how you say __" and "what __ means," and we teach them to criticize the use of words with expressions such as "no, not like *that*, like *this*." To learn a language is to learn a theory of language, just as to learn baseball is to learn a theory of baseball. Language, like baseball, comes packaged with ideology. There are no ideologically-neutral linguistic judgments.

5. *A Concept Is Akin to an Ability*[8]

We have noticed that Frege's mystical ontology of thought and language blinded him to the status of his own insights about structure and meaning. It also sometimes led him to astonishing and perverse claims. The idea that sentences stand for the True or the False, the way names stand for their bearers, is one such example (Frege 1891/1984, 15; 1892/1984, 34). A perhaps more egregious example is Frege's insistence that concepts must be sharply delimited, that is, defined for every possible object (Frege 1891/1984, 20).[9] A concept such as "is greater than"—as when we say that 3 is greater than 2—is not well-defined, according to Frege, if it is not determinate whether, say, the moon is greater than Julius Caesar. And likewise, we haven't succeeded in explaining what a given number is—the number 1, say—if we can't explain not only why (for example) 1 is the result of subtracting 2 from 3 but also why 1 is not identical to Julius Caesar.

---

8. This is a quotation from Ludwig Wittgenstein's *The Big Typescript*.

9. "This involves the requirement, as regards concepts, that, for any argument, they shall have a truth-value as their value; that it shall be determinate, for any object, whether it falls under the concept or not. In other words: as regards concepts we have a requirement of sharp delimitation..." (1891/1984, 20). He explains that we must be able to say what the sum of the sun + 1 is, if our concept of addition is to be of any use at all. If we can't answer the question of the sum of the sun and 1, then we can't with any confidence speak of the sum of 10 and 1 either.

What is striking, in this demand of Frege's, is the extent to which Frege has severed the link between concepts and our understanding and practice. It would be crazy to tell a child he'd failed to grasp addition because he could make neither heads nor tails of the addition of Julius Caesar and the moon.[10] This would be like criticizing a child for being unable to score a touchdown in baseball. There's no move here, no space in the practice. Concepts are *not* defined over all possible objects; our use of concepts has a point and occurs in a context (just as with strikes and home runs). To miss this is to think of understanding as a matter of the manipulation of formal symbols. But that's to leave understanding out of the story.

A concept is literally a technique for grasping hold of something in thought (as the etymology of the word reveals; compare also the German *Begriff*). Frege, like Kant before him, took for granted that concepts are predicates of judgment. But this is certainly mistaken if it therefore follows that the only use to which we can put a concept is in the making of a judgment. If I have the concept home run, then I can judge of a fly ball that it is a home run. But my grasp of the concept also enables me to see home runs, to encounter them, and to recognize them when they occur around me. And it is surely to *overintellectualize* one's experience of the ball game to suppose that each case of concept-dependent recognition is an *act of judgment*. Indeed, it is precisely this sort of *intellectualist* error that is one of Frege's lasting legacies.

6. *The Intellectualist Mistake*

Frege's mistake—his inability to bring the third-realm character of philosophical discourse into focus—can be called the intellectualist mistake. It forces Frege to conceive of language and concepts as divorced from practice. The puzzle about the strict delimitation of concepts is a clear example of this.

Frege failed to allow for the possibility of a perceptual, nonjudgmental use of concepts. This is a signal commitment of the intellectualist. It is worth noticing that this same mistake is made by many philosophers we might call anti-intellectualist. For example, some philosophers have insisted that to suppose

---

10. In *Foundations*, Frege (1884/1978) insists it is a scandal that no mathematician can state what the number 1 is. Of course, this is hardly a scandal; inability to say what 1 is does not count (not in Frege's day, not now) as evidence that one is deficient in arithmetical knowledge. It is worth noticing, though, that Frege didn't merely insist on pressing this question; he actually devised new conceptual/mathematical tools for framing an answer. *After* Frege, it becomes possible at least to imagine what an answer to the question "What is the number 1?" might look like, even if Frege's own answer can no longer be taken seriously.

that perception is in whole or in part conceptual runs the risk of overintellectualizing perceptual experience, as if the only role for concepts is in the making of explicit deliberative judgments (e.g., Hurley 2001; Dreyfus 2006). But this is precisely to overintellectualize the intellect itself (exactly as Frege did). The use of concepts, like the use of tools, is a practical achievement. It is nonetheless intellectual for all that. Talking, playing chess—these are spheres of intellectual accomplishment par excellence. This is compatible with the thought that these are also spheres where we can act without self-monitoring or deliberation, where we can be in the flow.

Or consider those who object to the idea that experience can be conceptual on the grounds that we don't have concepts of everything we can see (e.g., Evans 1982). Such a view again sees concepts as like words in a dictionary. Of course we don't have, antecedently, words for everything. But that is not to say that we can't embrace what we see in thought (as McDowell 1994 has argued; see also Noë 2004, ch. 6).

Empiricists (such as John Campbell 2002) hold that we need to be able to see without concepts because seeing provides the basis for acquiring concepts. But to see something is anyway just a way of getting a grip on what is there. It is just a special way of thinking about what is there (as I argue at length in Noë forthcoming). It is a kind of thought.

7. *Practical Knowledge*

Intellectualism, of course, is alive and well. This is one of Frege's legacies. Indeed, it is alive and well in good measure because as a culture we have failed to take up the challenge of making sense of the third realm where philosophy happens. And so we continue to shoehorn our problems into one or the other realm, into the objective or the subjective.

An impressive example of this is a recent article by Stanley and Williamson (2001). They declare that it "is *simply false*... that ascriptions of knowledge-how ascribe abilities" (416, my italics). This is like claiming that it is simply false that we are talking about whales when we say that they are mammals. Simply false? As if there were a straightforward, unproblematic standard to which one can appeal, to which one must accede? But the third-realm character of analysis problems consists precisely in the fact that no such standards can be taken for granted. This is not to say that we cannot advocate on behalf of certain standards. But then we need to press forward and argue. We can't appeal to what is *simply* true or false.

Consider the considerations they offer in defense of their claim. They write: "[A] ski instructor may know how to perform a certain complex stunt, without being able to perform it herself. Similarly, a master pianist who loses both of her arms in a tragic car accident still knows how to play the piano. But she has lost her ability to do so" (416).

Good points. But they are not despositive. They do not round off and close down debate; they merely initiate it. Consider that one might respond: abilities have enabling conditions. The fact that there is no water around makes it the case that I cannot swim, even though the absence of water does not deprive me of my ability to swim. That is, the fact that I can't exercise my ability does not make it the case that I have lost the ability. So there are two different ways one can fail to be able to do something. This is relevant to the case of the pianist. In losing her arms, one might argue, she has not lost the ability to play; she just can't exercise the ability (because relevant enabling conditions are not met; she has no arms).

There are other strategies one might explore in an attempt to resist Stanley and Williamson's assertion. One might, for example, concede that loss of the arms is not like the absence of a piano; to lose one's arms is to lose one's ability (not merely an enabling condition of the exercise of the ability). At the same time, one might insist that thus to lose one's ability is to lose one's know-how as well.[11]

Regardless of whether you find this line of reasoning persuasive, what is clear is that it is pointless to suggest that it is *simply false* to think that ascriptions of know-how ascribe abilities. It is of the nature of the case that it is possible reasonably to explain away anything Stanley and Williamson might say to the contrary. Ditto for the case of the ski instructor. Nothing about the way the case is described entails that the ski instructor knows how to perform the stunt. What she knows is how the stunt is done, but to know how something is done is not (necessarily) to know how to do it.

Like Frege and the experimentalists, Stanley and Williamson seem to think there is a big stick they can use to decide hard cases. And the big stick they have in mind is "recent syntactic theory." So much for the worst for this branch of linguistics.

---

11. Bengson, Moffett, and Wright (2009) demonstrate that a significant sample of people find nothing at all strange in the thought that know-how and corresponding abilities come apart. They suggest this undermines the claims of Noë (2005) to the effect that in normal practice ascriptions of know-how do entail ascriptions of corresponding abilities. Bengson, Moffett, and Wright's treatment of these issues is always careful and certainly fair. But I remain unpersuaded by their discussion. What Bengson, Moffett, and Wright give us are data. What we need is insight. This we achieve not by taking data about what people say at face value, for there is no face value to people's words. Context, rhetorical setting, a sense of what is at stake—these are what shape the words we choose, and these are what shape what we say about our choices and understandings. Bengson, Moffett, and Wright's findings do no more than simply kickstart the conversation that still needs to be had about what we mean when we say that you (for example) retain knowledge how to ϕ even when you lose the ability to ϕ.

Part of what makes the case of Stanley and Williamson particularly interesting is that it is their aim not merely to establish the point that there is no special linkage between practical knowledge and the possession of corresponding abilities. They wish to show that there is no *fundamental* distinction between practical and propositional knowledge. And they're right about this, as our reflection on the baseball case allows us to appreciate. If you know how to play baseball, then you can run, throw, field, and catch, but you also know *that* each side has no more than nine players in the game at once and *that* three strikes make an out. Practical knowledge—knowing how to play baseball—consists in both practical abilities and propositional understanding (a point made by Snowdon 2003).

But Stanley and Williamson are not content to leave matters there. When they claim that there is no "fundamental" distinction between knowledge-how and knowledge-that, they mean to insist that propositional knowledge is more basic or fundamental than practical knowledge. They claim that "knowledge-how is simply a species of knowledge-that." In this, they seek to actually defend a kind of intellectualist thesis.

Now, intellectualism is not a doctrine. It is, at best, an attitude. It is Frege's attitude and can be glossed thus: thought and language are autonomous domains; they are formal and are independent of our practical lives, our biology, and conscious experience; what makes humans special, what differentiates us from other animals, is our ability to speak, to grasp propositions. And so Stanley and Williamson's claim that practical knowledge is everywhere an achievement of propositional knowledge can be thought of as a kind of vindication of intellectualism.

In fact, Stanley and Williamson fail to vindicate intellectualism. For one thing, advertising to the contrary notwithstanding, they actually allow that there is a difference between knowledge-how and knowledge-that; after all, what they (seek to) show is that to know how to do something is to grasp a proposition *in a special way*. Moreover, according to their analysis, the difference between knowing how to do something and merely knowing that something is the case has to do precisely with the irreducibly *practical* character of knowledge-how. They insist that to know how to do something consists in knowledge of a proposition that one has grasped *in an irreducibly practical way*. So at the end of the day, Stanley and Williamson, no less than Ryle, support the conclusion that to know how to do something is not *merely* to know that something is the case. As for the assertion that the difference between practical and propositional knowledge is not a fundamental one, this would seem to be belied by their own proffered analysis.

Stanley and Williamson end up offering a technical proposal. They show that it is possible to represent knowledge-how constructions as knowledge-that constructions while at the same time doing justice to their ineliminably practical character. What they fail to show is that to do so is to achieve any insight into the nature of practical or propositional knowledge.

As an afterthought: I find myself sorely tempted to say that if either of the two—"know how," "know that"—has a claim to being more basic than the other, it is surely "know how." After all, to grasp a proposition is to exercise one's know-how (one's understanding of words or concepts, say). But it would be a mistake to give in to this temptation. Although it is true that grasping a proposition is something I achieve thanks to what I know how to do, it is also the case that some of what I know in virtue of knowing how to grasp a proposition p is that (say) it is not the case that not-p. The intellectual is practical, yes. But the practical is a sphere for display of the intellect.

8. Aesthetic Problems in Philosophy

Disputes about meaning are intersubjectively significant and yet immune to the sorts of "objective" criteria that operate in other areas of our epistemic lives. The criteria are always up for grabs. In this, they are like disputes in aesthetics, as Kant understood this domain of inquiry. Aesthetic judgment, Kant insisted, is a matter of feeling. I can't prove to you that something is aesthetically valuable. We are not in the realm of rule-based application of concepts in judgment. And yet aesthetic response is the sort of thing about which it is always intelligible to argue. In contrast with mere expressions of taste—about flavors of ice cream, for example—judgments of the aesthetic value of the work of art happen in a "space of criticism." It is always reasonable to ask someone *why* they respond as they do to a work of art, and it is never reasonable to refuse to take that sort of request seriously (however difficult or impossible it may be to explain or justify oneself). An aesthetic judgment is a cognitively rich perceptual accomplishment, even if it is never the sort of thing that can be autonomously justified, proved, or demonstrated. Aesthetics, for Kant, marks a third realm between the objective and the subjective, between the domain of the rule-governed and the domain of mere feeling.

In arguing for the third-realm character of philosophical problems, I have been suggesting that we take what Kant says about aesthetics and generalize it to embrace philosophical judgment. I propose that we acknowledge the fundamentally aesthetic character of philosophical problems themselves.[12] Debates about what we mean are not debates how we feel. They are not debates about "intuitions."

---

12. The ideas I express in this paragraph display an enormous debt to Stanley Cavell's essay "Aesthetic Problems in Modern Philosophy" (1969).

But nor are they disputes about the structure of Platonic entities in a third realm. They are not the sort of thing that can be decided by appeal to "recent syntactic theory," survey findings, or reflections on our neurobiology or evolutionary history. The question of what we mean when we say "the king's carriage is drawn by four horses" is an opportunity for a kind of stylistic investigation of our intellectual performance. *Are there concepts? Are there home runs?* These, in turn, are comparable to questions such as *Are there plot twists?* and *Is there epaulement?* The place we look to answer such questions is the work of art or, in the case of philosophy, our intellectual work and practices themselves.

The aim of philosophical argument about statements of number or the nature of practical knowledge is understanding. We don't seek to uncover practice-independent truths such as "*really* practical knowledge is a special way of knowing a proposition" or "*really* a statement of number is a statement about a concept." Our aim, rather, is to get a survey of the whole space of possibilities, of the way the different things that we say, or want to say, or feel we could never say, or deny the intelligibility of saying, hang together. We seek an understanding that consists in finding ourselves, in knowing where we are, and in knowing our way about. This has always been the philosophical project. We see this at work in Frege's investigations, and we see it in the work of Socrates.

PART III
Linguistic Perspectives

9

How to Resolve 'How To'

Jonathan Ginzburg[1]

1. Introduction

How do you say 'hello' in Arabic? asks Adam; 'marḥaba,' responds his friend Bilal. After several visits to his local phonetician and no little practice, Adam masters more or less the pharyngeal sound ḥ and can utter 'marḥaba' on cue. He now *knows that* 'marḥaba' is how one says 'hello' in Arabic, he has *learned* to say 'hello' in Arabic, so he *can* start a conversation in Arabic—he *knows* a little bit of Arabic. One way of framing the debate on intellectualism is to ask whether these changes to Adam's cognitive state are to be described in terms of simply one pathway, *the propositional epistemic pathway* (needed in any case to account for the emergence of his knowledge that 'marḥaba' is how one says 'hello' in Arabic), or whether others should also be posited (which one might postulate to account for his having learned to say 'hello' in Arabic and his ability to start a conversation in Arabic, and we could, of course, consider the pathways responsible for the corresponding acquisition for Bilal's infant daughter).

As Abbott (2006) points out, if the answer one is looking for is to be grounded empirically, then given, for example, the solid evidence for various distinct subsystems of memory (e.g., Baddeley 1997; Fletcher 1994), one has to be quite brave to fight for intellectualism. Even limiting one`s gaze essentially to semantics, as I will here, defending *intellectualism* doesn't seem too easy. In §2, I argue for a certain ontology needed to explain the semantics of the attitude predicates involved in epistemic pathways. In particular, I motivate the need for skills/abilities as a distinctive kind of abstract entity. We will see that although there certainly do seem to be attitude predicates that require exclusively one type of entity as their complements (e.g., 'ask' requires questions and 'believe'

---

[1]. I would like to thank Robin Cooper, Shalom Lappin, and Alex Lascarides for a number of very helpful discussions. I would also like to thank the participants of the 2009 Michigan Fall Symposium in Linguistics and Philosophy, where stimulating discussion occurred in reaction to a reading of Zardini (2009), in particular with Barbara Abbott, Nicholas Asher, Craige Roberts, Rich Thomason, and Elia Zardini.

propositions), there are certainly a variety of predicates that can genuinely combine with more than one (e.g., 'be intriguing' with questions and facts or 'learn' with facts and abilities). I will suggest that 'know' happens to be one of the latter—the evidence being stronger in some languages than others. From a semantic point of view, there is nothing very intriguing about that.

And yet, much of the linguistic evidence against intellectualism comes from 'how to' clauses embedded by 'know,' which are commonly analyzed in a way that diverges significantly from the analysis of other types of embedded interrogatives. One motivation for this divergence is that 'how to' clauses do not exhibit the exhaustiveness assumed to characterize interrogatives in a number of influential analyses. In §§3 and 4, I take up the analysis of interrogative constructions and epistemic pathway complementation, respectively, sketching an approach to questions, based on the approach of Ginzburg (1995a, 1995b; Ginzburg and Sag 2000), which rejects the analysis of questions in terms of exhaustive answerhood conditions. In its stead, this approach offers a view of questions as propositional abstracts and proposes *resolvedness*, an agent-relative generalization of exhaustiveness that has a strongly *teleological* nature, as the key notion needed for the semantics of *resolutive* complements (interrogatives embedded by, e.g., 'know,' 'discover,' 'learn,' and 'forget'). I also sketch a formal analysis of the various types of complements at issue: factive, resolutive, and ability-denoting. Although it would be technically straightforward to develop their analysis as ability-denoting complements, in §5 I argue that 'how to' clauses embedded by resolutive predicates can and should be analyzed just like any other interrogative embedded by resolutives. In other words, they are propositional. Or somewhat more precisely, they denote (indefinite descriptions of) facts that resolve the question denoted by the embedded interrogative. My argument relies on data that demonstrate the compatibility of 'how to' with predicates that are *incompatible* with ability-denoting expressions and on a demonstration that ability attributions in 'how to' are often, though not invariably, defeasible (Bengson and Moffett 2007). The account exploits the teleological nature of resolvedness, combined with the fact that the demonstration of an ability is a potentially resolving answer to a 'how to' question.

2. Basic Ontological Picture

An account of the lexical semantics of the epistemic pathway(s) is faced with the problem that the predicates in question combine with a wide range of complements, both clausal (declarative, interrogative, and infinitival) and nominal. What makes this task even more difficult is that there are good grounds for assuming that each of the clausal types is in at least two ways ambiguous, and ditto for some classes of nominal complements. The methodology I adopt in trying to figure out what entities genuinely function as arguments of a given predicate involves using a number of tests, inspired by Quine and Vendler, relating nominal and clausal complements, particularly substitutivity and existential generalization.

2.1 The Propositional Pathway

I start by considering the pathway that starts with an issue being raised and leads, possibly via communicative interaction, to the emergence of knowledge that resolves that issue. Ginzburg (1995b) argued for a class of predicates that combines in a purely referential way with questions, based on data such as (1):

(1) a. **Substitutivity:**
Jean asked/investigated/was discussing an interesting question.
The question was who left yesterday.
Hence: Jean asked/investigated/was discussing who left yesterday.

b. **Existential Generalization:**
Jean asked/investigated/was discussing who left yesterday.
Hence, there is a question/issue that Jean asked/investigated/was discussing yesterday.
Which question?
The question was who left yesterday.

In contrast to the influential analysis of Karttunen (1977), I argue that none of the typically epistemic predicates such as 'know', 'discover', 'forget', 'learn', and 'teach' predicate directly of questions because even when they actually seem to combine felicitously with question nominals, they fail pure referentiality tests, as exemplified in (2):

(2) a. **Substitutivity:** Jean discovered/revealed an interesting question.
The question was who left yesterday.
It does not follow that: Jean discovered/revealed who left yesterday.

b. **Existential Generalization:**
Jean discovered/knows who left yesterday.
It does not follow that: there is a question/issue that Jean discovered/knows.

A common alternative assumption to Karttunen's conception, adopted inter alia by Hintikka (1976) and Groenendijk and Stokhof (1984), is to assume that when predicates such as 'know', 'forget', and 'learn' combine with interrogatives, they predicate of a proposition. Ginzburg (1995b) argued against this strategy because (1) resolutives fail pure referentiality tests with proposition denoting nominals, as in (3a); (2) there are predicates that pass pure referentiality tests with proposition denoting nominals, dubbed truth falsity (TF) predicates, such as 'believe' and 'deny', and indeed such predicates only combine with nominals of which truth/falsity is predicable (see 3b, c); and (3) TF predicates do *not* combine felicitously with interrogative complements, a pattern that holds with a high degree of cross-linguistic regularity. This apparent universal can be explained straightforwardly if one assumes that *interrogatives do not have a proposition-denoting manifestation*:

(3) a. The Fed's forecast was that gold reserves will be depleted by the year 2000. Brendan discovered/was aware of the Fed's forecast.
It does not follow that: Brendan discovered/was aware that gold reserves will be depleted by the year 2000.

b. Brendan believes/denies the Fed's forecast.
Hence, Brendan believes/denies that gold reserves will be depleted by the year 2000.

c. Jackie believed/doubted Billie's story/the claim/the forecast/Bo's weight/my phone number.

d. Bo believes/doubts/supposes/assumes which pitcher will play tomorrow.

Since there is evidence that resolutives do combine in a purely referential fashion with facts, then adopting the Vendlerian assumption (Vendler 1972; Asher 1993; Peterson 1997) that facts and true propositions are distinct, it is natural to assume that resolutive complements denote facts. Which facts? Facts that resolve the question, in a sense; whose precise sense is the topic of §3.

(4) a. Philippe knows/discovered whether Emanuelle was in town.
Hence, Philippe knows/discovered a fact that indicates/proves whether Emanuelle was in town.

b. Philippe knows/discovered who attended the WTO meeting.
Hence, Philippe knows/discovered a fact, one that resolves the issue of who attended the WTO meeting.

c. Dominique revealed to me when the train is leaving.
Hence, Dominique revealed a fact to me, one that resolves the issue of when the train is leaving.

As I mentioned in the introductory section (§1), there is also evidence that some predicates actually combine with more than one type of entity. Ginzburg and Sag (2000) note the existence of a class of predicates, including 'intrigue', 'mystify', and 'puzzle', that are compatible with both questions and facts. These predicates satisfy pure referentiality arguments with interrogatives, though not with declaratives:

(5) a. The question is who entered the building last night.
    That question intrigues me.
    Hence, it intrigues me who entered the building last night.

   b. The claim is that Jerry entered the building last night.
    That claim intrigues me.
    It does not follow that: it intrigues me that Jerry entered the building last night.

   c. That Jerry entered the building last night intrigues me.
    Hence, there is a fact that intrigues me, namely, the fact that Jerry entered the building last night.

Such data are of some theoretical interest. They argue against strategies such as the intensional/extensional strategy of Groenendijk and Stokhof (1984), in which any predicate that selects for facts (or propositions) and combines with an interrogative complement necessarily coerces it to denote a fact (or proposition). It is also telling against the intellectualist mind-set because it indicates that attitude predicates can be perfectly tolerant of distinctive types of entities.

2.2 The Ability Pathway

There is lexical semantic evidence for a more complex pattern among the resolutive predicates with ability/skill nominals and with infinitivals: 'learn' and 'teach' combine with these in a purely referential way, as in (6) and (7); 'understand' and 'explain' resist such complements; whereas with 'know' and 'forget', the evidence is mixed.

(6) a. Bo taught me to swim.

   b. I learned to ride a bike when I was eight.

   c. I acquired the ability to sing a high C at a relatively late age.

   d. Certain abilities cannot be taught.

(7) a. The Vezo people taught me an unusual skill.
That skill was to swim without moving my legs.
Hence, the Vezo people taught me to swim without moving my legs.

b. I learned that particular skill from an old Mapuche guide.
That skill was to ride a bike without making a sound.
Hence, I learned to ride a bike without making a sound from an old Mapuche guide.

In English, 'know' cannot combine with infinitivals like 'learn' and 'teach' can. There are, nonetheless, various languages where the same lexical item is used to describe 'propositional' knowledge and skills or abilities. These include Hebrew, Greek, and Italian,[2] and (8) illustrates this with data from Hebrew:[3]

(8) a. maya yod'at… šebaxoref… yored šeleg.
Maya knows that-in-winter falls snow.
Maya knows that in winter snow falls.

b. maya yod'at lirkav al ofnayim.
Maya knows to-ride on bike.

c. dina yod'at laruc al regel axat.
Dina knows to-run on foot one.

d. hadar yod'at lesaxek squoš.
Hadar knows to-play squash.

Even in English, 'know' seems to have some skill-oriented arguments. In (9a) 'German' clearly denotes neither a proposition nor a fact. Its content arises via some sort of metonymy, akin to (9c) widely discussed since Pustejovsky (1995): in (9d) 'a novel' gets coerced to denote an event. By the same token, 'German' in (9a) would seem to denote a skill/ability, roughly paraphrasable as in (9b):

(9) a. Max knows German.

b. Max can speak/write/understand (read) German.

c. Max began a novel. ↦ Max began reading/writing a novel.

---

2. I became aware of data such as these—about my natively spoken Hebrew—during the discussion period of Zardini's paper (Zardini 2009) in which similar data are provided concerning the Romance verbs 'savoir'/'saber'/'sapere', citing (Rumfitt 2003).

3. It is, of course, a loaded question whether to gloss these in English as 'know how' or 'can.' I won't make that decision here.

This same coercion would seem to apply in (10):

(10) a. Sabine taught me German. ↦ Sabine taught me to speak/understand (read) German.

b. Max learned German. ↦ Max learned to speak/understand (read) German.

Note now that there are resolutive predicates that seem incompatible with skills: (11a, e) illustrate this for 'explain' in English, whereas (11b) is the corresponding example in Hebrew; (11c) illustrates the incompatibility of an ability infinitive with 'understand', with (11d) the corresponding example in Hebrew. Finally, although (11f) is felicitous, it does not seem to involve the skill-oriented coercion we observed earlier:

(11) a. Dina explained to me to swim.

b. dina hisbira li lisxot.
Dina explained to-me to-swim.

c. I understood to ride a bike when I was eight.

d. # maya mevina lirkav al ofnayim.
Maya understands to-ride on bike.

e. Bo explained German to me.

f. Bo understands German. ↛ Bo can speak German.

A possible, if misguided, reaction to (11) is that 'something syntactic' is responsible for the incompatibility. 'forget', however, illustrates that this cannot be the explanation. 'forget' is perfectly compatible with infinitival clauses. However, the only reading (12a) and the corresponding Hebrew datum (12b) obtain is eventive—Bo or Dina forgot to swim on some particular occasion. Similar comments apply to (12c,d).

(12) a. Bo forgot to swim.

b. dina shaxaxa lisxot.
Dina forgot to-swim

c. Bo forgot to show up.

d. Bo forgot to speak German. ↛ Bo cannot speak German.

In the literature, various types of denotation have been proposed for infinitivals. Given our earlier discussion of 'believe', (13a) needs to be propositional; Ginzburg and Sag (2000), inspired by Portner (1997), posit an abstract entity they dub an *outcome*, which serves as the denotation of imperatives and subjunctives and is discussed briefly in §4, as in (13b, c); the close synonymy of (13d) with (13b, c) suggests infinitivals have uses as outcomes. A characteristic of outcomes is futurate temporality: at the time of ordering in (13b, c, d), no money has been transferred, though the intended time can be specified (e.g., 'now'). It is clear that skill infinitivals like (13e) have a very different temporal profile, which if anything is telic and certainly not futurate. Moreover, as (13f) shows, temporal adverbials can only modify the embedding predicate (i.e., the time of learning), not the time in which the skill occurs—the ability clause has no event time of its own. Indeed, neither 'learn' nor 'teach' is compatible with subjunctive clauses, as in (13g). Since subjunctives are syntactically declarative, which 'learn' and 'teach' subcategorize for, this indicates that the problem is semantic—they are semantically incompatible with outcomes. In light of this, it seems clear that skill infinitivals are not outcomes, nor given the incompatibility of 'learn' with truth/falsity nominals (e.g. 'claim', 'forecast') can they be propositions.[4] One possible conceptualization is sketched in §4.

(13) a. Bo believes Mary to have stolen the money.

   b. Jo: give me the money (now)!

   c. Jo ordered that the money be given to him.

   d. Jo ordered Mary to give him the money.

   e. Bo learned to swim.

   f. Bo learned to swim afterward/immediately

   g. Bo taught Jo/learned that he swim.

3. *Resolving Issues in Interaction*

3.1 From Exhaustive Answerhood Conditions to Propositional Abstracts

Some recent analyses of knowing how (e.g., Roberts 2009; Zardini 2009) assume that resolutive 'how to' clauses are somehow exceptional in not exhibiting the exhaustiveness that many formal semantic treatments (e.g., Karttunen 1977;

---

4. Of course, 'learn the forecast/claim' is syntactically well formed, but the nominal is used as a *concealed question* (= 'what the forecast/claim is').

Groenendijk and Stokhof 1997) assume characterizes interrogative clauses. Accounts such as Karttunen's and Groenendijk and Stokhof's specify questions in terms of exhaustiveness answerhood conditions (EACs).

Ginzburg (1995a) and Ginzburg and Sag (2000) argue against an EAC-based approach to questions. One important component of the argument is the claim that the requisite notion of exhaustiveness—that needed for the semantics of resolutive clauses—is an agent-specific notion and, consequently, cannot serve as the *semantic* underpinning of questions.

This claim originates in Ginzburg (1995a), who made it primarily on the basis of examples with 'where,' 'when,' 'why,' and 'who' interrogatives, exemplified in (14):

(14) a. Bo knows where he is (in Helsinki/near the stadium/opposite Nurmi's statue).

b. Bo knows when the train is leaving (At 2:58, 17.333398 seconds, according to our cesium clock/At 2:58/In about an hour/In a short while).

Asher and Lascarides (1998) make analogous claims with respect to (finite) 'how'-clauses in the course of their detailed and insightful account.[5]

Here I briefly mention one motivating example involving 'who' interrogatives. A scientist and a European Union politician are visiting an institute located in a distant country isolated from current academic activity. Both people are taken to visit a local research institute, where the scientist gives a number of lectures. After the last lecture, each asks (15a). It is clear that neither of them will be satisfied with (15b), to which they would be entitled to react with (15c). What the visitors would really have welcomed would be responses of the type provided in (15e, f), which could then be reported as (15d):

(15) a. Q: Who has been attending these talks?

b. The director: (Provides list of names)

c. I asked the director who had been attending the talks. She didn't really tell me. All she did was recite a list of names, none of which meant much to me.

d. The director was asked who had been attending the talks and she told us.

---

5. Asher and Lascarides do not discuss 'how to' clauses.

e. [Querier is the high ranking EU politician.] The director: A number of linguists and psychologists.

f. [Querier is the researcher in the field covered by the institute.] The director: A number of cognitive phoneticians and Willshaw-net experts.

This seems to be the case even despite the fact that neither response conveys information that enables either one of them to determine the extension of the predicate 'has been attending the talks.' Furthermore, unless the scientist is compiling an inventory or the politician an indictment of the skills existing in far-flung territories but not in his own backyard, it is reasonable to assume that they do not presume that all attendees necessarily conform to the descriptions provided. Moreover, permuting the responses results in inappropriateness: providing a specialized domain description to a politician completely unaware of basic information concerning a whole domain of research is pointless, as is the converse, providing a general response to a scientist aware of the intricacies of that field.

These data point to the fact that the semantically absolute notion of exhaustiveness is not appropriate as the notion underpinning the meaning of resolutive clauses—nonexhaustive answers can be *resolving*, and which answers are resolving can vary across agents even in a single discourse context. Moreover, the putative mention-all/mention-some ambiguity—appealed to by Stanley and Williamson (2001) and Roberts (2009) in their accounts of 'knowing how'—is an artifact of EAC-based theories.

It is important to note, nonetheless, that when regarded purely in terms of query-response coherence all of (15b, e, f) *are* equally felicitous. The factors that discriminate in favor of one over the other depend on the belief/knowledge state and purpose of the querier. Hence it seems that on a *semantic level*, the question expressed by uttering (15a) should characterize all of (15b, e, f), if true, as potentially resolving the question asked. Indeed there are propositions that under no conditions resolve a question, yet are *about* the question, emphasizing that *potential resolvedness* and *aboutness* are distinct. Theories of interrogatives such as Karttunen (1977) and Groenendijk and Stokhof (1984, 1997) do not, in fact, accommodate such propositions as answers.[6]

---

6. The problem with accommodating (16a), for instance, is that the partitions corresponding to a polar question p? has only 2 cells, p and $\neg p$. For a more refined theory of answerhood, see Groenendijk (2006).

(16) a. A: Is it going to rain tomorrow? B: Probably.

b. A: Who is coming to the party? B: Few people you know.

Given all this, Ginzburg (1995a) and Ginzburg and Sag (2000) conclude that the motivation for identifying a question—the semantic object associated with the attitude of wondering and the speech act of asking—with an entity that encodes exhaustive answerhood conditions is flawed. Ginzburg (1995a) and Ginzburg and Sag (2000) propose that questions are entities by means of which the various disparate notions of answerhood should be characterized (and not vice versa). They show in detail how this can be done if questions are taken to be *propositional* abstracts. One of the traditional attractions of identifying questions with abstracts has been that they provide the requisite semantic apparatus for short answer resolution (Who left? Bo; Did Bo leave? Yes etc). However, therein also lies danger because this suggests that, for example, unary wh-questions have the same semantic type as properties, which seems counterintuitive, given data such as (17):

(17) a. Some man is happy. So we know that happiness and manfulness are not incompatible. So we know that the question of who is happy and who is a man are not incompatible.

b. A: What was Bill yesterday? B: Happy. B: The question of who is happy.

Ginzburg and Sag develop their account within the situation theoretic-motivated approach to ontology developed in Seligman and Moss (1997). The structure they axiomatize, *a Situational Universe with Abstract Entities (SU+AE)* involves propositions and other abstract semantic entities (e.g, outcomes, the denotata of imperatives; facts, the denotata of exclamatives) being constructed in terms of 'concrete' entities of the ontology such as situations and situation types. An additional assumption made is that the semantic universe is closed under *simultaneous abstraction*, a semantic operation akin to λ-abstraction with one significant extension: abstraction is over sets of elements, including the empty set. Moreover, abstraction (including over the empty set) is *potent*—the body out of which abstraction occurs is distinct from the abstract. Within such a setting, propositions and situation types are naturally distinguished, and hence propositional abstracts (questions) are not conflated with situation type abstracts (properties) and can be assigned a uniform type. Polar questions are 0-ary abstracts, whereas wh-questions are n-ary abstracts for $n \geq 1$. The fact that questions involve abstraction over *propositions*, which will turn out to be of some importance for 'how to' interrogatives, receives empirical support from evidence concerning the distribution of *in situ* wh-phrases in English. In declarative clause-types that in the absence of a 'wh'-phrase denote propositions, the occurrence of such phrases leads to an ambiguity between two readings: a 'canonical' use that expresses a direct query and a use as a *reprise* query to request clarification of a preceding utterance. In all other clause types, ones that denote outcomes (18d), questions (18e), or facts (18f), the ambiguity does not arise; only a reprise reading is available:[7]

(18) a. The bagels, you gave to WHO? (can be used to make a nonreprise query)

b. You gave the bagels to WHO? (can be used to make a nonreprise query)

c. Who talked to WHO? (can be used to make a nonreprise query)

d. Give WHO the book? (can be used *only* to make a reprise query)

e. Do I like WHO? (can be used *only* to make a reprise query)

f. What a winner WHO is? (can be used *only* to make a reprise query)
(Ginzburg and Sag 2000, 282: example 72)

In subsequent work, the reliance on the situation theoretic notion of abstraction has been eliminated. Ginzburg (2005) shows how to formulate a theory of questions as propositional abstracts in Type Theory with Records (TTR) (Cooper 2005), a model-theoretic descendant of Martin-Löf Type Theory (Ranta 1994), while using the standard TTR notion of abstraction. An alternative modeling of the key entities of the situation theoretic ontology in TTR is provided in §4.

3.2 Resolutive Complements: From Exhaustiveness to Resolvedness

The implication from the data discussed previously (examples (15)) would appear to be the following: the notion of *resolvedness* required for capturing certain basic inferences involving interrogatives embedded by propositional attitude predicates is a relative one: information *resolves* a given question relative to an agent's information state. That is, a given question defines a class of true propositions,

---

[7]. A priori, one might expect (18d), for instance, to have a reading as a direct question paraphrasable as 'whom should I give the book to?' if one could simply abstract over the 'wh'-parameter within an 'open outcome.'

each of which is *potentially* resolving.[8] Whether a given member of this class, p, is actually a resolving answer *in a given context* depends on two additional factors fixed by an information state: the goal or desired outcome *o*, which determines a lower bound for *p*, and the inferential capabilities relative to which *p* has *o* as a consequence:[9]

(19) *p* resolves *q* relative to B's information state *I* iff *p* is a potentially resolving answer to *q*, and relative to B's information state *I p* leads to B's desired outcome *o*.

Under reasonable assumptions discussed in Ginzburg (1995a), it is easy to show that if one fixes the contextual parameters to certain 'default settings,' then *resolvedness* reduces to *exhaustiveness*. In other words, resolvedness is an agent-relativized generalization of exhaustiveness.

Since there are good reasons to assume that interrogatives never denote propositions or facts in contexts outside embedding by resolutives,[10] resolutive embedding needs to arise by coercion. Given an interrogative clause S[+Interrog], the coercion needs to yield (a description for) a fact that in that context resolves the question denoted by S[+Interrog].[11] The coercion process will be well defined if and only if the question is resolved. In other words, it is a presupposition of the coercion that there is a resolving fact for the question. Informally, we can specify this as follows, a formulation I refine in §4:

(20) ⌜Bo V S[+Interrog]⌝ denotes $\exists f\ V'(\text{bo},f,I) \upharpoonright \text{Resolve}(f,q,I)$ for I an information state, q the question S[+Interrog] denotes.

---

8. Ginzburg (1995a) suggests that p potentially resolves q if either p strongly positively resolves q (provides a description of a witness for the instantiation of q) or p negatively resolves q (entails the extension of q is empty).

9. The phrase 'p leads to B's desired outcome' is to be understood in terms familiar from planning theory in AI, see Ginzburg (1995a); Asher and Lascarides (2003).

10. Ginzburg and Sag (2000) offer a number of arguments for this conclusion, including the fact that interrogatives cannot be used equatively with fact-denoting nominals (see (i)), nor can they participate in anaphora with such nominals (see (ii)):

(i) # The fact is who vanquished the anti-Leninist faction.

(ii) A: I'd like to point out a crucial fact to you. B: Go on. A: # Who is waiting for you in my office.

11. I assume that this is an indefinite description, given the existence of many resolving facts and, moreover, the possibility of ascribing such knowledge without oneself knowing a resolving fact.

4. Complementation: Ontology and Context

(20) presupposes that *resolvedness presuppositions* emerge in context. These can be explicated very naturally within a questions under discussion (QUD)-oriented view of context. I turn to a barebones sketch of this and, prior to that, to an ontological setting for the concrete and abstract entities that constitute attitudinal objects (events, propositions, questions, etc.).

4.1 An Ontology for Questions, Propositions, Outcomes, and Skills

As the underlying logical framework, I use Type Theory with Records (TTR) (Cooper 2005, forthcoming). This provides a formalism with which to build a semantic ontology, and to write conversational interaction and grammar rules.

The most fundamental notion of TTR is the typing *judgment* a: *T* classifying an object *a* as being of type *T*. A record is an ordered tuple of the form (21)—each assignment to a field constituting a component of the tuple. Crucially, each successive field can depend on the values of the preceding fields. A record type is simply an ordered tuple of the form (21), where again each successive type can depend on its predecessor types within the record. Record types allow us to place constraints on records: the basic typing mechanism assumed is that a record *r* is of type *RT* if all the typing constraints imposed by RT are satisfied by *r*. This is defined more precisely in (21c):

(21) a. $\begin{bmatrix} l_i = k_i \\ l_{i+1} = k_{i+1} \cdots \\ l_{i+j} = k_{i+j} \end{bmatrix}$ b. $\begin{bmatrix} l_i : T_i \\ l_{i+1} : T_{i+1} \cdots \\ l_{i+j} : T_{i+j} \end{bmatrix}$

c. The record:

$\begin{bmatrix} l_1 = a_1 \\ l_2 = a_2 \\ \cdots \\ l_n = a_n \end{bmatrix}$ is of type: $\begin{bmatrix} l_1 : T_1 \\ l_2 : T_2(l_1) \\ \cdots \\ l_n : T_n(l_1, l_2, \ldots, l_{n-1}) \end{bmatrix}$

iff $a_1 : T_1, a_2 : T_2(a_1), \ldots, a_n : T_n(a_1, a_2, \ldots, a_{n-1})$

Cooper (2005) proposes that situations and events be modeled as records. Situation and event types are then directly accommodated as record types. The type of a situation with a woman riding a bicycle would then be the one in (22a). A record of this type (a *witness* for this type) would be as in (22b), where the required corresponding typing judgments are given in (22c):

(22) a. $\begin{bmatrix} \text{x: IND} \\ \text{c1: woman(x)} \\ \text{y: IND} \\ \text{c2: bicycle(y)} \\ \text{time : TIME} \\ \text{loc: LOC} \\ \text{c3: ride(x,y,time,loc)} \end{bmatrix}$ b. $\begin{bmatrix} \ldots \\ \text{x} = \text{a} \\ \text{c1} = \text{p1} \\ \text{y} = \text{b} \\ \text{c2} = \text{p2} \\ \text{time} = \text{to} \\ \text{loc} = \text{lo} \\ \text{c3} = \text{p3} \\ \ldots \end{bmatrix}$

c. a: IND; p1: woman(a); b: IND; p2: bicycle(b); to: TIME; lo: LOC; p3: ride(a,b,to,lo);

TTR offers a straightforward way for us to model propositions (in either their Russellian or Austinian [Barwise and Etchemendy 1987] variants) and questions using records, record types, and functions. An Austinian proposition—employed here for reasons discussed in Ginzburg (2012)—is a record of the form in (23a). The type of propositions is the record type (23b), and truth can be defined as in (23c):

(23) a. $\begin{bmatrix} \text{sit} = r_0 \\ \text{sit-type} = T_0 \end{bmatrix}$ b. $\begin{bmatrix} \text{sit: Record} \\ \text{sit-type: RecType} \end{bmatrix}$

c. A proposition $\begin{bmatrix} \text{sit} = r_0 \\ \text{sit-type} = T_0 \end{bmatrix}$ is true iff $r_0 : T_0$

A question such as (24a) can be identified as a propositional abstract, which in TTR amounts to being a function from records into propositions (24b). In what follows, I often simplify the notation and use the familiar λ notation to denote abstracts, as in (24c).

(24) a. who ran

b. TTR representation—(r : $\begin{bmatrix} \text{x : Ind} \\ \text{rest : person(x)} \end{bmatrix}$) $\begin{bmatrix} \text{sit} = r_1 \\ \text{sit-type} = \begin{bmatrix} \text{c : run(r.x)} \end{bmatrix} \end{bmatrix}$

That is, a function that maps records r : T_{who} $\begin{bmatrix} \text{x : Ind} \\ \text{rest : person(x)} \end{bmatrix}$ = into propositions of the form $\begin{bmatrix} \text{sit} = r_1 \\ \text{sit-type} = \begin{bmatrix} \text{c : run(r.x)} \end{bmatrix} \end{bmatrix}$

c. $\lambda x.run(x)$

Outcomes are closely related to propositions, with the main difference being temporal—outcomes are intrinsically futurate but with a temporal dimension that is typically unanchored (at speech time), which makes them useful theoretical entities for reasoning about future action. Truth is not applicable to such entities; what is applicable is the notion of being fulfilled. We can explicate this in an Austinian fashion—as records whose fields are a situation and a situation type-abstract, of which a temporal argument has been abstracted away. We define the type Irrealis—temporal abstracts over the class of record types in (25a). An outcome will be a record of the form in (25b), the type Outcome given in (25c). The fulfilledness conditions of an outcome $\begin{bmatrix} \text{sit} = s_0 \\ \text{irr-sit-type} = p_0 \end{bmatrix}$ involve the existence of a situation s_1 which is situated temporally after s_0 such that s_1 witnesses an instantiation of p_0. This is the sense in which outcomes are 'futurate.' A simple illustration is provided in (25c, d):

(25) $\quad$ Irrealis $=_{def}$ $([t : \text{Time}])$ RType

a. $\begin{bmatrix} \text{sit} & = r_0 \\ \text{irr-sit-type} = p_0 \end{bmatrix}$

b. Outcome $=_{def}$ $\begin{bmatrix} \text{sit} & : \text{Record} \\ \text{irr-sit-type} : \text{Irrealis} \end{bmatrix}$

c. Jo wants Bo to swim.

d. Want (j,($\begin{bmatrix} \text{sit} = s_0 \\ \text{irr-sit-type} = ([t : \text{Time}]) \begin{bmatrix} a = \text{Bo} : \text{Ind} \\ \text{effect} : \text{swim}(a,t) \end{bmatrix} \end{bmatrix}$)

We can explicate skills/abilities in TTR in a somewhat analogous fashion, though as we noted previously, in contrast to outcomes and propositions, skills and abilities do not intrinsically involve situational reference. (26a) can be conceived of in terms akin to (26b):

(26) $\quad$ a. Bo learned to swim.

$\qquad$ b. Bo learned (what event/situation he needs to be in) to swim.

This suggests conceptualizing abilities as functions relating situations where a certain effect obtains to their preconditions. (27a) gives one toy example relating to (Bo's) swimming, which I abbreviate as (27b)—it maps situations in which Bo is swimming to situations in which his hands and legs are moving at that time. (27c) offers a minimal characterization of the general type as mapping a situation involving an individual and a time into another situation involving that agent and time:[12, 13]

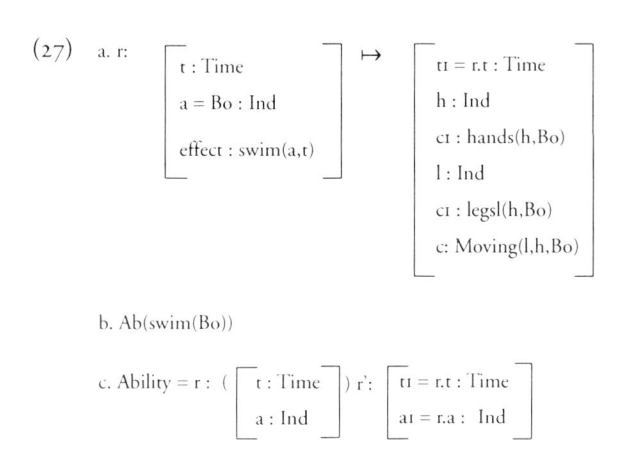

(27) a. r:
$$\begin{bmatrix} t : \text{Time} \\ a = \text{Bo} : \text{Ind} \\ \text{effect} : \text{swim}(a,t) \end{bmatrix} \mapsto \begin{bmatrix} t_1 = r.t : \text{Time} \\ h : \text{Ind} \\ c_1 : \text{hands}(h, \text{Bo}) \\ l : \text{Ind} \\ c_1 : \text{legsl}(h, \text{Bo}) \\ c : \text{Moving}(l, h, \text{Bo}) \end{bmatrix}$$

b. Ab(swim(Bo))

c. Ability = r : ($\begin{bmatrix} t : \text{Time} \\ a : \text{Ind} \end{bmatrix}$) r': $\begin{bmatrix} t_1 = r.t : \text{Time} \\ a_1 = r.a : \text{Ind} \end{bmatrix}$

4.2 Information States in Interaction

As I suggested previously, an analysis of resolutive complements needs to make reference to the cognitive or the *information* states of the participants, given that resolvedness is a notion relativized by the desired outcomes and the inferential abilities of agents. Moreover, we also need a means of explicating how presuppositions concerning the resolvedness of questions enter into context.

---

12. See Cooper's reformalization of Barwise and Perry's notion of constraints (Cooper 2005, 6). (27) employs *manifest fields*—for example, t1 = r.t : Time—to enforce that the time of the effect and its agent can be used in the characterization of the preconditions. See also Fernando (2007) for a detailed treatment of the fine structure of events in a type theoretic framework. The postulated type in (27b) is simplified in a variety of respects.

13. This reverses a common conceptualization of rules in AI as mapping preconditions to effects. And it follows another influential approach in AI—abduction (Hobbs 2004), as pointed out to me by Shalom Lappin. The reason for adopting this tack here is, in part, the fact that linguistically what we are given is the effect (e.g., Bo swimming), whereas the preconditions are implicit. Moreover, in terms of learning, this is not unintuitive: learning can be conceived of as grasping an increasingly refined description of the preconditions for achieving a desired outcome.

The general setting for such a theory needs to be a theory of interaction in which agents interact with each other and, in Hintikka's phrase, with *nature*. I assume here the perspective developed within the KoS framework (Ginzburg 1994; Ginzburg and Cooper 2004; Larsson 2002; Purver 2006; Fernández 2006; Ginzburg and Fernández 2010; Ginzburg 2012), an important characteristic of which is the assumption that a dynamic and partially ordered repository of questions (QUD) is a key component of public context.

The type of such information states is given in (28a). The dialogue game board (DGB), here slightly simplified, represents information that arises from publicized interactions, and for now, we can identify it as the public context. Each DGB is a record of the type given in (28): the *spkr* and *addr* fields allow one to track turn ownership, *Facts* represents conversationally shared assumptions, *Pending* and *Moves* represent, respectively, moves that are in the process of/have been grounded, QUD tracks the questions currently under discussion:

(28) a. TIS = $\begin{bmatrix} \text{dialoguegameboard : DGB} \\ \text{private : Private} \end{bmatrix}$ b. DGB = $\begin{bmatrix} \text{spkr: Ind} \\ \text{addr: Ind} \\ \text{c-utt: addressing(spkr,addr)} \\ \text{Facts: Set(Prop)} \\ \text{Pending: list(Prop)} \\ \text{Moves: list(Prop)} \\ \text{QUD: poset(Question)} \end{bmatrix}$

As for the private part (29), drawing primarily on Larsson (2002): private beliefs is a necessary private counterpart to the public FACTS, whereas AGENDA is a private counterpart to Moves representing those actions the agent desires to perform. GENRE, on the other hand, is a type of information that does not have a public counterpart but plays an important role. It represents the conversational genre characterizing a particular conversation (bakery shopping, courtroom, etc.).

(29) Private =

$\begin{bmatrix} \text{Genre: GenreType} \\ \text{Beliefs: Prop} \\ \text{Agenda: list(Prop)} \end{bmatrix}$

In this setup, the dynamics of resolvedness presuppositions can be explicated roughly as follows: a question q gets introduced into QUD as a consequence of a query or an assertion. q gets downdated from QUD if and when proposition p about q is accepted, insofar as p resolves it sufficiently to fulfill the goal g maximal in the agent's agenda using the assumptions in either Facts or Beliefs. One of the side effects of downdating q is updating FACTS with the corresponding resolvedness presupposition *Resolves(p, q, I$_o$)*, where I_o is the information state at downdate time.

4.3 Factive, Resolutive, and Skill-Oriented Complements

In §2, we saw evidence that attitude predicates have types such as those given in (30), relating an attitudinal type (e.g., a question or proposition), an information state, and an agent (of type Ind). The additional, typically implicit, information state argument assumed here has been motivated in §3 for resolutive complements. Its presence for other attitudes is in light of accounts of the attitudes such as those of Crimmins (1993).

(30) a. Ask : Question, TIS, Ind

b. Believe : Prop, TIS, Ind

c. Explain, Understand : Fact, TIS, Ind

d. Intrigue, Mystify: Fact ∨ Question, TIS, Ind

e. learn : Fact ∨ Ability, TIS, Ind

f. know : Fact ∨ (?) Ability, TIS, Ind

We can characterize three types of predicates: factives, resolutive, and ability oriented. Note that in the current setup a single verb, say, 'learn' or Hebrew 'yodea' or Greek 'ξερω' (both corresponding to 'know') can belong to all three types, **without any assumption of lexical ambiguity.** In (31), I provide lexical types that describe factive verbs, resolutive verbs, and ability-infinitival verbs. In these descriptions, the *spr-dtr* represents the subject argument of the verb, whereas *comp-dtr* its sentential complement.[14] In the case of factives and ability-infinitive predicates, the combinatorial rule is straightforward: predicating that the verb's relation (e.g., 'know') composes with the denotation of the sentential complement and the implicit information state argument.[15] In the case of resolutives

---

14. The types associated with the sentential complements are from Ginzburg and Sag (2000).

15. For simplicity, I have omitted including reference to a factivity presupposition, which would lead to a greater uniformity with the entry for resolutives. Indeed, Ginzburg (1995b) suggested that factives have a presupposition of the form *Prove (f, p, I)*, by analogy with the resolutive case.

complements, as explained previously, a coercion occurs so that for some fact f that resolves the question denoted by the interrogative complement, the verb's relation composes with f and the implicit information state argument.[16]

(31) a. Factive = $\begin{bmatrix} \text{Cat} : \text{V}[+\text{fin}] \\ \text{spr-dtr} = [\text{content} = x : \text{Ind}] : \textit{np} \\ \text{comp-dtr} = [\text{content} = f : \text{Fact}] : \textit{factive-cl} \\ \text{I} : \text{TIS} \\ \text{content} = \text{FactiveRel}(x,f,\text{I}) : \text{Prop} \end{bmatrix}$

b. abilityInfPred = $\begin{bmatrix} \text{Cat} : \text{V}[+\text{fin}] \\ \text{spr-dtr} = [\text{content} = x : \text{Ind}] : \text{np} \\ \text{comp-dtr} = [\text{content} = \text{Ab}(x) : \text{Ability}] : \textit{decl-non-subj-cl} \\ \text{I} : \text{TIS} \\ \text{content} = \text{AbilityRel}(x,\text{Ab}(x),\text{I}) : \text{Prop} \end{bmatrix}$

c. Resolutive = $\begin{bmatrix} \text{Cat} : \text{V}[+\text{fin}] \\ \text{spr-dtr} = [\text{content} = x : \text{Ind}] : \textit{np} \\ \text{comp-dtr} = [\text{content} = q : \text{Question}] : \textit{int-cl} \\ \text{I} : \text{TIS} \\ f : \text{Fact} \\ c0 : \text{In}(\text{I.FACTS},f) \\ c1 : \text{Resolve}(f,q,\text{I}) \\ \text{content} = \text{ResolutiveRel}(x,f,\text{I}) : \text{Prop} \end{bmatrix}$

5. Resolving How to Clauses

The technical apparatus set up in the previous section provides us with the resources to analyze 'how to' clauses, in the life they lead as complements of resolutive predicates, in one of two ways: as canonical (resolutive) *wh*-interrogative complements or as ability-denoting complements. The question is: which is the desirable analysis? I believe the data clearly point to the former as the right answer. However, in contrast to a number of previous works that have assumed a similar strategy (e.g., Stanley and Williamson 2001; Roberts 2009), when I say that 'how

---

16. Although I have offered various empirical motivations for the proposition/fact distinction, it is of little import to the main issues of this chapter. (31a) presupposes a clausal type that is fact denoting. For the fact skeptics, merely assume that facts are true propositions.

to' complements are canonical (resolutive) wh-interrogative complements, I mean just that: I will not exploit distinctive apparatus from that employed to analyze other resolutive clauses.[17] As I emphasized earlier, whether information resolves a question can only be evaluated relative to a desired outcome and background knowledge; we saw in §3 how possession of what is for certain purposes resolving knowledge (that) can fail to provide a resolution of issues like 'who attended the lecture' in the absence of certain background knowledge. The agent-relative, teleological notion of resolvedness enables us to defuse similar recalcitrant cases concerning 'how to.'

For current purposes, I do not need to make strong assumptions about the grammar of 'how' clauses. For simplicity, I assume a Montogovian approach to adverbials (for a recent exposition see Carpenter 1997) in which 'how' introduces a functor 'By' (Goldman 1970; Asher and Lascarides 1998),[18] which relates two properties of an agent a, who may be implicit in the sentence out of which 'how' is extracted, as in (32d), with the first argument the *means* argument being abstracted away:

(32) a. How $\varphi(a)$

b. $\lambda m By(m(a), \varphi'(a))$

c. How did Bo win the race? $\mapsto \lambda m By(m(b), won(b,r))$
By running fast $\mapsto By(fast(run(b)), won(b,r))$

d. How was Bo persuaded to lie? $\mapsto \lambda m By(m(arb), persuade(arb, b, lie(b)))$
By subjecting Mary Smith to torture. $\mapsto By(torture(arb,m), persuade(arb,b,lie(b)))$

---

17. Although I have argued that from a semantic point of view, the intellectualist project is empirically unsustainable, Stanley and Williamson's goal of deriving the semantics of resolutive 'how to' clauses from the semantics for resolutive wh-clauses in general is laudable. However, to achieve this aim, using Karttunen's approach (or by the same token Groenendijk and Stokhof's), they do seem to require to appeal to the additional device of 'practical mode of presentation'— or lose the ability to account for knowledge of practical biking. Beyond this, a misconception that characterizes their project is the assumption of (semantic) parallelism between knowledge that and knowledge wh: as I showed in §4, one can offer an account that differentiates between (declarative) factive clauses and (interrogative) resolutive clauses—for example, only the former manifest resolvedness presuppositions that make explicit reference to an issue—without assuming any lexical ambiguity of 'know.' Roberts' (2009) account appeals to a special interpretation of infinitival questions, an appeal that raises interesting empirical issues discussed soon.

18. I depart here notationally from Asher and Lascarides (1998), who call what I call 'By' 'Can.'

This means, given our earlier discussion of resolutive complements, that the content of a resolutive 'how' clause will be as in (33b):

(33) a. Bilal knows how $\varphi(a)$

b. $\exists f\,\mathrm{know}(\mathrm{B}, \mathrm{f}, \mathrm{I})$, where Resolves$(f, \lambda m \mathrm{By}(m(a),\varphi(a)),I)$

I assume, adapting Asher and Lascarides (1998) slightly, that the relation 'By' satisfies (34). This will be of crucial importance in accounting for—or defusing—the 'ability implication' characteristic of 'how to' clauses.

(34) By$(m(a),\varphi(a)) \vDash$ If m(a) and Intend$(a, \varphi(a))$, then normally $\varphi(a)$ happens.

Note that an entirely analogous approach applies to other adjunct wh-clauses, for instance, 'why,' where 'why' introduces a *Cause* relation, of which the *causer* argument gets abstracted away:

(35) a. Why φ

b. $\lambda r \mathrm{Cause}(r, \varphi')$

c. Why did Bo win the race? $\mapsto \lambda r \mathrm{Cause}(r, won(b, r))$
Because Mary helped him $\mapsto$ Cause(help(m,b),won(b,r))

This approach extends directly to 'how to' or 'why to' clauses—the controller of the agent argument of the interrogative clause being the subject of an embedding predicate if there is one. Just as with finite how clauses, here we can assume that knowing how to V involves knowledge of a fact that resolves the issue how to V:

(36) a. How to V

b. $\lambda m \mathrm{By}(m(a), \mathrm{V}'(a))$

c. Why to V

d. $\lambda r \mathrm{Cause}(r, \mathrm{V}'(a))$

e. Anand knows how to V $\mapsto \exists f\,\mathrm{know}(\mathrm{A}, \mathrm{f}, \mathrm{I})$, where Resolves$(f, \lambda m \mathrm{By}(m(A), V'(A)), I)$

f. Anand knows how to please Joanna $\mapsto \exists f\,\mathrm{know}(\mathrm{A}, \mathrm{f}, \mathrm{I})$, where Resolves$(f, \lambda m \mathrm{By}(m(A), please(A,j)), I)$

Let me now offer empirical justification for this nonexceptionalist approach to 'how to' clauses. For a start, like other interrogatives, 'how to' clauses can appear equatively in denotations as questions, not as facts or skills, and are selectable by all question and resolutive predicates:[19]

(37) a. The question Bo faces is how to ride that bike.

b. The issue that intrigues Bo is how to ride a bike with no pedals.

c. # The fact Bo is aware of is how to ride a bike with no pedals.

d. # The skill Bo possesses is how to ride a bike with no pedals.

e. Bo asked/wondered/investigated/discovered/revealed/understands how to ride that bike.

As expected from this semantics, the resolution of a 'how to' question is often described in propositional terms in conversation. Let me exemplify this with some evidence from the British National Corpus (BNC).[20] In (38), the interlocutors are discussing a test B is about to take at school, and A offers a succinct summary of what it amounts to *know how to cross the road*. Of course, the fact that the knowledge is easy to characterize does not mean its application in practice, with the desired outcome of not getting run over, is easy.

(38) A: I mean you know how to cross the road now, don't ya? Look one way and that

Consider another example from the BNC. It emerges that Anon3 does not know how to get to a particular shop: she is provided with several items of information that apparently resolve the issue: *(starting at Dawson) take the 106 bus to Clapton, cross the street, take an S2 bus (until) the market, and then walk through*. This knowledge is efficacious in resolving the issue of how to get to the shop, but only relative to Anon3's detailed local knowledge, her knowledge of how to use buses and cross roads and the like, and with the aim of getting there by using public transport:

(39) Grace: You don't know where to, you don't know how to get there? Anon3: No. Grace: I (will) tell you. Well if she lives down Dawson, all she has to do is get a one O six to Clapton, right? Anon 3: Yeah. Grace: And just cross

---

19. The idea that 'how to' clauses are ambiguous between a canonical resolutive and an ability-denoting denotation has been floated around repeatedly. For arguments against such an ambiguity, see Bengson and Moffett (2007).

20. These data were found using Matt Purver's search engine SCoRE (Purver 2001).

over, you know. Anon3: And, what, get a number eight bus? Grace: You get S two. Anon 3: S two? Grace: Yeah. (pause) Anon3: And it takes you all the way there? Grace: It takes you straight there. It takes you outside the market and then you walk through.

We now need to tackle the elephant in the room for any nonexceptionalist approach: how do we explicate the existence of the 'ability implication' in resolutive 'how to' clauses? Prototypically, if Bo knows how to ride a bike, then Bo *can* ride a bike (e.g., Ryle 1949; Lewis 1990). A first point to note is that this implication is by no means restricted to 'how to' clauses but applies to a variety of other types of *wh*-phrases, as exemplified in (40).

(40)   a. Bo knows when to press the eject button.

       b. Jo knows where to ride her bike.

       c. Mo knows why to leave work early.

This means that whatever we do, we cannot employ a strategy that involves supplying an *ad hoc* treatment of 'know how to' (for a recent example, see Williams 2007) but need a far more general strategy. One enticing strategy would be to extend the notion of question beyond *propositional* abstracts to include also abstracts over other entities. The most obvious such strategy, given our earlier discussion, would be to assume that wh-infinitivals are abstracts over abilities, as exemplified in (41):[d]

(41)   a. 'how to ride that bike' $\mapsto \lambda m \mathrm{Ab}(By(m(a), ride(a, b)))$

       b. 'why to ride that bike' $\mapsto \lambda c Ab(Cause(c, ride(a, b))$

       c. 'where to ride that bike' $\mapsto \lambda l Ab(Loc(l, ride(a, b)))$

An answer to this type of question would be a(n instantiated) ability. Consequently, 'know wh to' would involve knowledge of an ability, not propositional knowledge, capturing the ability implication directly. Nonetheless, even assuming that technical problems can be overcome,[21] such an approach faces significant empirical challenges. It predicts that predicates incompatible

---

21. In the approach of Ginzburg and Sag (2000), this would entail reformulating a number of the fundamental constraints governing the construction of question meanings so that their input is not solely propositional, the latter assumption having clear empirical justification, e.g., (18).

with abilities should be incompatible with wh-infinitivals, a prediction that is entirely *incorrect*:[22]

(42) a. Bo understands how to ride a bike.

b. Mo explained to me how to construct the platinum airplane.

c. Bo forgot when to press the ejector button.

Moreover, in languages like Hebrew, Greek, and Romance (Rumfitt 2003; Abbott 2006), where simple epistemic ability statements are possible, one typically avoids using 'how to' clauses for similar purposes, as exemplified here for Hebrew. This follows if (43b) has a canonical interrogative denotation from which ability is implied somehow but is surprising if it directly denotes an ability.

(43) a. ani yodea lisxot/lirkav al ofnayim.
    I know to-swim/to-ride on bike

b. ani yodea eyx lisxot/lirkav al ofnayim.
    I know how to-swim/to-ride on bike

Given these intrinsic problems for a reasonably general approach to building in the ability implication to wh-infinitivals, and a fortiori the additional problems more ad hoc approaches face, it is worth checking carefully the extent to which we really want to *grammatically build in* the ability implication. Bengson and Moffett (2007) argue that the ability implication occurs with what they term ability-based concepts (e.g., addition and certain simple logical reasoning), for instance, that:

---

22. Similar considerations apply to the proposal of Roberts (2009), who, building on earlier work of Dowty and Jacobson (1991) on wh-infinitivals, proposes that wh-infinitivals denote abstracts over outcomes (in her terminology *goals*). This makes resolutive complements denote specifications of attaining the goal denoted by the infinitival. Such a proposal faces similar technical issues—allowing for abstraction over outcomes against which there is independent evidence. Given our earlier discussion about the difference between abilities and outcomes, it is questionable whether abstracting over outcomes gives wh-infinitivals the temporal profile needed to characterize abilities, which do not seem to be futurate. Beyond this, there is also the expectation that predicates like 'demand' and 'insist' that combine with subjunctive and infinitival outcomes should combine with wh-infinitivals, were the latter to have outcome-denoting denotations. This expectation is not met:

(i) Bo demanded/insisted to leave immediately.

(i) Bo demanded/insisted that he leave immediately.

(ii) # Bo demanded/insisted when to leave.

(44) If Millie knows how to add small natural numbers, then she can add small natural numbers.

On the minimal semantics of 'by' provided before, if the means clause is fulfilled straightforwardly, the ability follows. It therefore seems feasible to accommodate cases like (44).

Consider pure task predicates—the source of most of the data driving the propositional/ability dichotomy. The first thing to note is that the ability implication does not arise for various resolutive predicates:

(45) a. Jo understands how to ride a bike, though she hasn't ever dared get on one and for all we know would fall off as soon as mounting it.
b. Millie has very patiently explained to me how to play that violin, but I still can't do much with it.

In general, for pure task predicates, the ability implication would appear to exhibit the characteristics of a conversational implicature, namely, cancelability and calculability. Cancelability has been widely discussed in the literature since initially argued for by Ginet (1975)—see Bengson and Moffett (2007) for extensive exemplification, though there is much controversy over judgments. It is worth considering a number of additional examples that bring out how purpose dependent the judgments are, in line with my claim that what is at issue are judgments about the resolvedness of an issue. Consider first a case where I enter a shop and point to a fancy large frame bike that has all sorts of gizmos. I get talking to a petite mechanic there who is, say, 1.55 meters tall and so cannot actually ride the bike. Nonetheless, in such circumstances, the dialogue in (46) seems to be perfectly acceptable, presumably because the desired outcome is that I be able to ride the bike:

(46) Me: Do you know how to ride that bike? Mechanic: Yeah, the only thing you need to know is that the gears and the brakes are merged and that it's got optional electronic gear changing.

Similarly, take Paula, who says (47a). This would seem to justify (47b) but not (47c). Here the desired outcome is theory, not practice—at least in the short term.

(47) a. I've discovered that by running five-minute miles throughout and drinking lots and not starting too fast, I would run a 2:10 marathon.

b. I've figured out how to run a 2:10 marathon.

c. I can run a 2:10 marathon.

Finally, consider me walking in a military command-and-control center where a switch located on a wall in such a way as to be inaccessible is the means for launching a rocket. I can say (48a), which licenses (48b) and—for those who cannot see the placing of the switch but only for them—suggests (48c). That's all assuming discussion is at a theoretical level. Someone can, of course, dispute my assertion of (48b) in this context by uttering (48d) if launching the rocket becomes a practical issue:

(48)   a. I know that by hitting that switch over there I will get that rocket to launch.

        b. I know how to get that rocket to launch.

        c. I can get that rocket to launch.

        d. In theory. Not if you can't figure out how to scramble up that wall and hit the switch.

(47) and (48) illustrate the calculability of the ability implication; it arises also from propositional epistemic reports, whose content approximates the content we postulate for 'how to' clauses. If one indicates a causal chain leading from A to B and A is a feasible state to be in, then there is a clear implicature that B can also be attained.

A crucial issue I have not as yet addressed is this: if resolutive 'how to' clauses are fact denoting, why is it that frequently, particularly when the embedded predicate is task oriented, it is knowledge of the ability that seems to be at issue? On the one hand, in such cases the crucial propositional knowledge is, typically, of little import and difficult to verbalize. Consider the issue of *how to ride a bike* from a child's perspective. This issue is actually a highly complex one, which requires the resolution of a host of subquestions. (49) is an instructional session where the instructor, Dina, sets out the issues to Maya as she sees them and offers her answers:

(49)   Dina: what you need to know is this. Where to put your bum (*Here*), where to put your hands (*Here, on the handlebars*), what to do once you're sitting on the bike (*start waddling, after you've got a bit of momentum, lift your legs and start pedaling*), how to stop (*pedal backwards and then lean the bike to one side*), where to look (*stare right ahead*).

Note that we could report the exchange using (50a). So at least relative to one information state, information resolving the issue has been provided. We could also describe Maya using (50b) and (50c). And relative to Maya's information state, partially resolving information has been provided:

(50) a. Dina explained to Maya how to ride her bike.

b. Maya has a good understanding of how to ride the bike.

c. Maya knows to some extent how to ride her bike: she knows where to put her hands, how to get started,...

And yet an explanation like *after you've got a bit of momentum, lift your legs and start pedaling* is intrinsically vague, so attaining the ability—the desired outcome in such a case—in this way is difficult.[23]

On the other hand, note that for task predicates the demonstration of ability *is* actually an (ostensive) answer to the corresponding 'how to' question, by direct analogy with answers such as (51a, b):

(51) a. A: Who broke the vase? B: [points to C, who is standing nearby]

b. A: Where do I go now? B: [points to a street down which A should ride her bike]

c. A: Can you tell me how to hold the bow? B: Look! [grasps the violin bow appropriately]

d. A: How do you crack open that nut? B: [takes a walnut from a bag and cracks it open with a nutcracker]

Hence, for many practical purposes, providing the answer in this way—or possessing the potential to do so—is the best means to resolve the question.

6. Conclusions

The main conclusions can be summarized briefly:

- Intellectualism is incompatible with the facts about complementation in a variety of languages.
- One of the main empirical bases for anti-intellectualism—the alleged existence of ability-denoting 'how to' clauses—does not survive close scrutiny.

---

23. And probably even if the explanation could be made precise and the teaching involved beeps at the precise moment, that is unlikely to eliminate this problem because attaining abilities typically involves practice.

In this chapter, I have:

1. demonstrated the need to have *abilities* in the ontology of abstract entities that serve as arguments of attitude predicates.
2. exemplified the existence of epistemically oriented attitude predicates that select for both facts and abilities.
3. sketched an ontology formalized in Type Theory with Records for events, propositions, questions, outcomes, and abilities.
4. indicated how a single verb can select for factive, resolutive, and ability-denoting infinitives without assuming lexical ambiguity.
5. shown how a semantic account of resolutive complementation—interrogatives embedded by predicates such as 'know', 'learn', and 'understand'—extends to 'how to' clauses without introducing any additional mechanisms.

10

Knowing How and Knowing Answers

David Braun

I KNOW HOW to drive my car. I also know many propositions about how to drive my car: I know, for instance, that I can start my car by turning its key in its ignition and that I can steer my car right by turning its steering wheel clockwise. My propositional knowledge obviously plays an important role in my knowledge of how to drive my car. Could my knowing how to drive my car simply consist in my knowing propositions?

Propositionalism (as I shall use the term) is roughly the view that knowing how to *G* (for any *G*) reduces to propositional knowledge.[1] I present and motivate a particular version of propositionalism in this paper, thereby following previous advocates, such as Carl Ginet (1975) and Jason Stanley and Timothy Williamson (2001).[2] I then describe how our intuitions about knows-how-to ascriptions vary from context to context. I use this discussion to reply to several objections to my version of propositionalism.

1. Propositionalism

It is easy to motivate propositionalism by examples. Imagine that Jones has arrived at the Holiday Inn in downtown Buffalo and that Smith, a Buffalo resident, phones him to arrange a meeting.

1. SMITH: "I'm trying to think of a place where we can meet. Do you know how to get to the Anchor Bar from your hotel?"

---

1. Noë (2005), Bengson and Moffett (2007), and Fantl (2008) use 'intellectualism' for what I call 'propositionalism'. This use of 'intellectualism' fits well with Ryle's (1949) use of the phrase 'intellectualist legend', but I believe that 'intellectualism' should be reserved for a broader set of views that include propositionalism. Compare Bengson and Moffett (chapter 7, §1) and the state of play essay at the outset of this volume.

2. Snowdon (2003) seems attracted to propositionalism, though he does not explicitly advocate it. Brown (1970) holds that knows-how-to attributions are multiply ambiguous; he (seemingly) thinks that propositional knowledge is sufficient for at least some of these disambiguations to be true.

JONES: "Yes, I do. I turn left when I exit from the front door of my hotel, then right on North Street, then left on Main Street."

SMITH: "Good, you do know how to get there. I'll meet you there."

Suppose that Jones knows that he can get to the Anchor Bar by turning left when he exits the front door of his hotel, and so on.[3] Then (it seems) he is correct when he claims to know how to get to the Anchor Bar, and Smith is reasonable when he concludes that Jones knows how to get to the Anchor Bar. So Jones's knowing that proposition seems sufficient for his knowing how to get to the Anchor Bar from his hotel.

Other examples suggest that propositional knowledge is necessary for knowing how to G. Suppose that Robinson is staying at the same hotel as Jones but is unaware of the Anchor Bar's existence and has no beliefs regarding it or its location. Therefore, he has no propositional knowledge regarding its location. So he does not know how to get to the Anchor Bar from his hotel.[4] Suppose McDonald believes that R is a route to get to the Anchor Bar from his hotel, but he believes this only because he is a victim of a posthypnotic suggestion; he has no good reason to think that there is such a thing as the Anchor Bar or that R is a route to get there. Then he does not know that the Anchor Bar exists or that R is a route to get there. So he does not know how to get there (though he does have a *belief* about how to get there). Suppose that (on a whim) he asks the concierge at his hotel about the Anchor Bar, and the concierge confirms his beliefs about its existence and how to get there. He now has justification sufficient to know the propositions that he believes, and he now also knows how to get to the Anchor Bar.

Reflection on other sorts of knowledge supports propositionalism. A theory of knowing how to G should, it seems, parallel theories of knowing where to G, knowing when to G, knowing what to G, and knowing who to G. But the latter sorts of knowledge all seem to reduce to propositional knowledge.[5] If Jones knows the propositions that he asserts in the (a) examples below, then the (b) ascriptions seem to be true.

---

3. Jones has, in fact, given a correct description of a direct route from the Downtown Buffalo Holiday Inn to the Anchor Bar. The Anchor Bar is famous for being the location where Buffalo chicken wings were invented (in 1964). However, it is controversial among Buffalonians whether the Anchor Bar still makes the best chicken wings in Buffalo.

4. This example and the next resemble examples from Snowdon (2003).

5. Brown (1970), Ginet (1975), Feldman (2003), Stanley and Williamson (2001), and Snowdon (2003) note the parallels. Stanley and Williamson use them to argue for propositionalism.

2. a. JONES: "I can get good chicken wings at the Anchor Bar."
   b. Jones knows where to get good chicken wings.
3. a. JONES: "I should go to the Anchor Bar on Tuesday night."
   b. Jones knows when to go to the Anchor Bar.
4. a. JONES: "I should eat chicken wings at the Anchor Bar."
   b. Jones knows what to eat at the Anchor Bar.
5. a. JONES: "I can ask Smith for directions to the Anchor Bar."
   b. Jones knows who to ask for directions to the Anchor Bar.

Moreover, if Robinson has never heard of chicken wings, then he knows no propositions about them and so does not know where to get good chicken wings. If he has never heard of the Anchor Bar, then he does not know when to go there or what to eat there or who to ask for directions to there. Similarly, McDonald may have beliefs about these matters, but if he has insufficient justification, then he does not know where to get good chicken wings, when to go to the Anchor Bar, what to eat at the Anchor Bar, or who to ask for directions to it.

Therefore, we have good reason to think that knowing how to *G* reduces to propositional knowledge. But what sorts of propositions must one know in order to know how to get to the Anchor Bar from Jones's hotel?

2. *The Answer Theory*

We can get some help by turning to a seemingly related topic, namely, knowledge of questions, or *interrogative knowledge*, as I shall call it. Consider the following dialogue.

6. a. SMITH: "Who went with Chang to the Anchor Bar on Tuesday?"
   b. JONES: "Able and Baker, and no one else, went with Chang to the Anchor Bar on Tuesday."
   c. Jones knows who went with Chang to the Anchor Bar on Tuesday.

The proposition that Jones asserts is an answer to the question that Smith asks. If Jones knows that proposition, then (6c) is true. This suggests that knowing a proposition that answers the question of who went with Chang to the Anchor Bar on Tuesday is sufficient for knowing who went with Chang to the Anchor Bar on Tuesday. Moreover, if Jones does not know a proposition that answers the question that Smith poses, then (plausibly) he does not know who went with Chang to the Anchor Bar on Tuesday. Parallel remarks go for the questions, propositions, and interrogative knowledge ascriptions expressed by the sentences in (7)–(10). In each, the sentence in (b) expresses a proposition that answers the question expressed by (a), and if Jones knows the (b) proposition, then (c) is true.

7. a. SMITH: "What did Chang eat at the Anchor Bar on Tuesday?"
   b. JONES: "Chang ate chicken wings at the Anchor Bar on Tuesday."
   c. Jones know what Chang ate at the Anchor Bar on Tuesday.
8. a. SMITH: "Where did Chang go on Tuesday?"
   b. JONES: "Chang went to the Anchor Bar on Tuesday."
   c. Jones knows where Chang went on Tuesday.
9. a. SMITH: "When did Chang go to the Anchor Bar?"
   b. JONES: "Chang went to the Anchor Bar on Tuesday."
   c. Jones knows when Chang went to the Anchor Bar.
10. a. SMITH: "How did Chang get to the Anchor Bar on Tuesday?"
    b. JONES: "Chang got to the Anchor Bar on Tuesday by driving."
    c. Jones knows how Chang got to the Anchor Bar on Tuesday.

Furthermore, it seems that there are many answers to each of the (a) questions. For instance, one answer to the question asked by Smith in (9a) is 'Chang went to the Anchor Bar at 6:00 P.M. on May 28, 2009.' If Jones knows the proposition that this expresses, then (9c) is true. These observations make the analysis of interrogative knowledge in (11) plausible.[6]

11. The Knowing-an-Answer Theory of Interrogative Knowledge
    For all X, and all questions Q, necessarily, X knows Q iff X knows a proposition that answers Q.

Let us now return to our previous examples to find a more informative description of the sorts of propositions that are necessary and sufficient for knowing how to get to the Anchor Bar from Jones's hotel.

Jones knows a proposition about how to get to the Anchor Bar from his hotel (namely, the proposition that he can get to the Anchor Bar by exiting his hotel and turning left, and so on), and his knowing this proposition is sufficient for his knowing how to get to the Anchor Bar. Moreover, the proposition that Jones knows seems (roughly speaking) to be an *answer* to the *question* of how to get to the Anchor Bar from his hotel. There may be propositions that are *about* how to get to the Anchor Bar that are not *answers* to the question of how to get there: one example may be the proposition that there is some way to get to the Anchor Bar

---

6. Schaffer (2007) has criticized a theory of interrogative knowledge similar to this. I believe that his arguments are flawed, for reasons I cannot take space to discuss here.

from Jones's hotel. If there are such propositions, then knowing them is not sufficient for knowing how to get to the Anchor Bar. There are many other propositions that specify routes from the hotel to the Anchor Bar, and all (or many) of these answer the question of how to get to the Anchor Bar, and if Jones knows any of these alternative propositions, then he knows how to get to the Anchor Bar from his hotel. There may be yet other propositions concerning manners of getting to the Anchor Bar that do not concern routes for getting there and yet count as answers to the question of how to get there, and knowing these is also sufficient for knowing how to get there. For instance, Jones may know how to get to the Anchor Bar because he knows that he can get there by hailing a taxi. All of this suggests that knowing *an* answer to the question is sufficient for knowing how to get there.

Robinson and McDonald do not know any answers to the question of how to get to the Anchor Bar. They also fail to know how to get there from their hotel. So we can reasonably conclude that knowing an answer to the question is also necessary for knowing how to get there.

Generalizing on these thoughts, we arrive at a more informative analysis of knowing how to G.[7]

12. The Knowing-an-Answer Theory of Knowing How to G
    For all X and all G, necessarily, X knows how to G iff X knows a proposition that answers the question of how to G.

At this point, we can reasonably extend the knowing-an-answer theory to knowing when, where, what, and who to G.

13. The Knowing-an-Answer Theory of Knowing When/Where/What/Who to G
    For all X and all G, necessarily, X knows when/where/what/who to G iff X knows a proposition that is an answer to the question of when/where/what/who to G.

In fact, we can subsume both (12) and (13) under the knowing-an-answer theory of interrogative knowledge in (11). Therefore, knowing how to G is a type of inter-

---

7. For many purposes, we can take the variable 'G' to range over properties. But strictly speaking, it ranges over *structured semantic contents*, for I use 'G' to quantify into embedded interrogative phrases that refer to questions (⌜how to G⌝), and questions are more fine-grained than properties. Suppose, for instance, that the property of being a tiger is identical with the property of being an animal with DNA T. Nevertheless, the question of how to catch a tiger by the toe is distinct from the question of how to catch an animal with DNA T by the toe, for an agent could wonder how to catch a tiger by the toe without wondering how to catch an animal with DNA T by the toe. Therefore, 'G' ranges over structured contents appropriate for the contents of verb phrases. These contents, however, determine properties.

rogative knowledge, and propositional knowledge is necessary and sufficient for all such interrogative knowledge. Let us call the version of propositionalism expressed by (12) *the answer theory*, for short.

If I could, I would at this point discuss the nature of the question of how to G and how it differs from questions expressed by unembedded tensed interrogative sentences with explicit subjects (such as 'How can Jones get to the Anchor Bar?'). I would also consider whether there is such a thing as *the* question of how to G and whether phrases of the form ⌜how to G⌝ and ⌜the question of how to G⌝ are ambiguous. But space does not permit this, so I shall move on to other matters.[8]

3. Answers

The answer theory relies on the notion of a propositional answer to a question. Philosophers who accept the answer theory may disagree over which propositions answer which questions. They may also disagree on these matters with theorists who reject the answer theory. To illustrate, let us consider an unembedded tensed interrogative sentence with an explicit subject, such as (14), and some candidate answers to it, such as the sentences in (15).

14. How can Jones get to the Anchor Bar from his hotel?
15. a. Jones can get to the Anchor Bar from his hotel by exiting his hotel and walking a quarter mile north on Delaware Avenue, a half mile east on North Street, and a quarter mile north on Main Street.
    b. Jones can get to the Anchor Bar from his hotel by walking north on Delaware, east on North, and north on Main.
    c. Jones can get to the Anchor Bar from his hotel by asking his concierge how to get there and following her directions.
    d. Jones can get to the Anchor Bar from his hotel by walking there.
    e. Jones can get to the Anchor Bar from his hotel by leaving his hotel.

I suspect that most philosophers would concede that the proposition expressed by (15a) answers the question expressed by (14). But some would deny that (15e) answers (14), whereas I would say that it does.

---

8. Stanley and Williamson (2001) hold that phrases of the form ⌜how to VP⌝ are ambiguous, because they contain occurrences of the pronominal expression 'PRO' and because their infinitival verb phrases are ambiguous. I am agnostic about whether 'PRO' exists and introduces ambiguity. I seriously doubt that infinitival verb phrases are ambiguous in the way that Stanley and Williamson claim. (See Haegeman (1991) and Radford (2004) for mainline theories of 'PRO', and Culicover and Jackendoff (2006) for criticisms.)

Now suppose that the answer theory is true. Then if (15e) answers the question of how to get to the Anchor Bar, and Jones knows the proposition expressed by (15e), then the answer theory entails that (16) is true.

16. Jones knows how to get to the Anchor Bar from his hotel.

Some philosophers who accept the answer theory would find this consequence acceptable (I do), while others would not. Thus disputes over whether a given proposition answers a given question can introduce controversies even among those who accept the answer theory. We should keep this in mind when considering objections to the answer theory, for objections to the theory typically make assumptions about which propositions answer which questions, and these assumptions may be incorrect or debatable.

4. *Contextual Variation in Judgments*

There is another complication that we should keep in mind when evaluating the answer theory and objections to it: our judgments about whether a given agent knows how to *G* vary from context to context. Consider again the sentences in (15) and the ascription of interrogative knowledge in (17).

17. Jones knows how he can get to the Anchor Bar from his hotel.

Notice that (17) is *not* an ascription of knowledge-how-*to*. Suppose that Jones knows the proposition expressed by (15c) but does not know any more detailed proposition about how he can get to the Anchor Bar. Speakers' intuitions about whether (17) is true in such circumstances vary from context to context. In some contexts, typical speakers take (17) to be true if Jones knows the proposition expressed by (15c). But in other contexts, those same speakers think that (17) is true only if Jones knows a proposition that gives more detailed directions, such as proposition (15b).

This is much the same phenomenon that many have noted with 'knows who' ascriptions, such as 'Jones knows who Mark Twain is'. Some speakers in some contexts think that this ascription is true if Jones knows that Twain is an author, whereas in other contexts, those same speakers may take that ascription to be true only if Jones knows that Twain wrote *Huckleberry Finn* (Boër and Lycan 1986). Similar points hold for 'knows how to' ascriptions like those described in the answer theory. In some contexts, typical speakers take (16) to be true if Jones knows the proposition expressed by (15c). But in other contexts, typical speakers take (16) to be true only if Jones knows the proposition expressed by (15b).

There are two views one can take of these contextual variations in intuition. *Contextualism* says that these knowledge ascriptions really do vary in truth value from context to context, because they semantically express different propositions in different contexts. A given ascription varies in its semantic content from context to context because of differences in the interests of the speakers in those contexts. For instance, 'Jones knows who Twain is' semantically expresses different propositions in different contexts. In some contexts, it is true as long as Jones knows that Twain is an author; in others, it is true only if he knows that Twain wrote *Huckleberry Finn*. This variation occurs because (roughly) speakers in different contexts are interested in different sorts of answers to the question of who Twain is. The context sensitivity of 'John knows who Twain is' can be traced to the context sensitivity of 'who Twain is' and ultimately traced to 'who'.[9]

Similarly for ascriptions (16) and (17), on contextualist theories: they express different propositions in different contexts and so can vary in truth value from context to context.[10] The differences in proposition expressed occur because, roughly, the speakers in some contexts are interested in certain sorts of answers to the question of how to get to the Anchor Bar, whereas the speakers in other contexts are interested in other sorts of answers. Presumably the context sensitivity of (16) and (17) can be traced to the context sensitivity of 'how Jones can get to the Anchor Bar' and 'how to get to the Anchor Bar,' and ultimately can be traced to the context-sensitivity of 'how'.

On the alternative view that I prefer, *invariantism*, the sorts of answers that speakers are interested in change from context to context, but this variation does *not* result in changes in the semantic contents of ascriptions from context to context. Therefore, the preceding ascriptions do not change in truth value from context to context. Jones knows who Twain is as along as he knows an answer to the question of who Twain is; what counts as an answer to the question does not vary from context to context. However, in many contexts, the speakers are primarily interested in whether Jones knows certain particular answers to that question. If Jones does not know those answers, then the speakers of those contexts will not judge that Jones knows who Twain is and will not mislead others in the context by saying that Jones knows who Twain is. Similarly, for (16) and (17): these do not vary in content and truth value from context to context. But speakers' interests in particular answers to the relevant questions do vary.

---

9. There is another type of view, which I call *ternarism* (Braun 2006), on which 'Jones knows who Twain is' varies in semantic content from context to context, but 'who Twain is' is *not* context sensitive. I count such views as contextualist here.

10. The alleged context sensitivity of (16) is supposed to hold over and above any of the alleged ambiguities that I mentioned in note 8.

Speakers who are interested in whether Jones knows certain answers to the question of how to get to the Anchor Bar tend not to (misleadingly) ascribe knowledge of how to get there to him if he does not know those answers. But the content and truth value of (16) do not vary from context to context. (See Braun 2006 for more on invariantism.)

Though I prefer the invariantist version of the answer theory, I will try to remain neutral here about the conflict between it and the contextualist version. In much of what follows, it will be simpler to speak as if invariantism is true. I will mention the contextualist version when it makes a difference.

Invariantists and contextualists agree that our intuitions about the truth of a single 'knows how to' ascription can vary from context to context. In my opinion, some who reject propositionalism and the answer theory fail to take this variability into account. It is easy to create contexts in which speakers tend to judge that X knows how to G only if X knows the sorts of propositions about G that (typically) are known only by those who are able to G. In such contexts, it is easy to judge that being able to G is necessary for knowing how to G. Judgments of this sort may seem to conflict with the answer theory. More about this later.

If contextualism is correct, then the sentence I used to formulate the answer theory in (12) is also context sensitive and so expresses different propositions in different contexts. That is obviously undesirable. To correct this problem, we can introduce some new terminology that allows us to reformulate the answer theory without using the allegedly context-sensitive phrase ⌜how to G.⌝ Consider all of the interrogative entities to which ⌜how to G⌝ refers with respect to some context, under some assignment. Call all such entities 'timeless manner questions'.[11] Now reformulate the answer theory as in (18).

18. The Knowing-an-Answer Theory of Knowing How to G, Reformulated
    For all X and all timeless manner questions Q, necessarily, X knows Q iff X knows a proposition that answers Q.

Both contextualist and invariantist theorists can accept this formulation.

---

11. I use the term 'timeless manner question' because the infinitival phrase ⌜how to G⌝ is tenseless and (I assume) the questionlike entities that it denotes lack temporal features possessed by the questions that tensed embedded interrogative sentences denote. In Braun (2006), I argue that contextualists should also hold that 'answer' is context-sensitive, but I ignore that here.

5. Objections to the Answer Theory and Some Replies

I shall now defend the answer theory from several objections, some of which were originally aimed at Stanley and Williamson's (2001) theory. I reformulate them as objections to the answer theory.

5.1 Objection 1: Propositional Knowledge Is Not Necessary

The answer theory entails that knowing a propositional answer to the question of how to G is necessary for knowing how to G. Here are three examples meant to show this is not so. Andrew is a skilled pianist. He knows how to play the piano. But if you were to ask him 'How do you play the piano?', he would not be able to answer. So Andrew does not know a proposition that answers the question of how to play the piano. Suzie is a young girl who can ski, and so she knows how to ski, but she does not know a proposition that answers the question of how to ski (Feldman 2003). Clyde can accurately judge the sex of young chicks, so he knows how to sex chicks. But he cannot say how he does so, and therefore he does not know an answer to the question of how to sex chicks (Schiffer 2002).

In reply, I say (as have others) that the objection overlooks various relevant propositions that the agents know (Ginet 1975; Stanley and Williamson 2001; Snowdon 2003). As Stanley and Williamson point out in similar examples, when Suzie skis, she can know the proposition that she grasps by thinking 'I am skiing by doing *this*' (as she mentally demonstrates the way in which she skis). Going beyond Stanley and Williamson now, if Suzie remembers previous times that she skied, she can think 'I skied like *that* back then'. So she later knows an answer to the question of how to ski. Andrew knows analogous propositions about how he plays the piano, propositions that he would express by using demonstratives, and similarly for Clyde as he sexes chicks ('*This* is how I sex chicks') or as he remembers sexing chicks. So they do know propositions that answer the relevant questions.

This reply is enough to disarm the preceding objection to the answer theory. But I think that it would be misleading to stop there, for Andrew, Clyde, and Suzie know other propositions that they can assert without using demonstratives, and their knowledge of those propositions is also sufficient for them to know how to play piano, ski, and sex chicks. For instance, Clyde knows that he can sex chicks by looking under their tails and looking for features similar to those of male chicks. Suzie knows that she skis by standing up on her skis, holding her poles in her hands, bending her knees, and moving down a slope covered with snow. Andrew knows that he can play the piano by sitting in front of a piano keyboard, pressing the keys hard if he wants a loud sound, pressing the keys softly if he wants a soft sound, pressing on the right-hand pedal if he wants to sustain a sound after he lifts his finger from a key, and so on. These propositions are answers to the questions of how to sex chicks, how to ski, and how to play piano. Their knowing these propositions is sufficient for them to know how to do these things. They can express these propositions without using demonstratives.

The objection plays on the contextual variability in our judgments of knowing-how-to. Insofar as the critic's objection is initially plausible, it is because the critic (implicitly) creates a context in which we become interested in whether Andrew, Clyde, and Suzie know very detailed answers to the relevant questions, namely, answers knowledge of which is sufficient to enable one to play piano, ski, and sex chicks. These are answers that they can express only by using demonstratives. But in other contexts, speakers might be interested in whether Andrew, Clyde, and Suzie know less detailed answers. Imagine, for instance, that Paul has seen a picture of a piano but is otherwise quite ignorant of them and how they work. Suppose he asks Andrew how to play a piano. If Andrew answers that one can play a piano by pressing on its black and white keys, then Paul would be justified in saying that Andrew knows how to play a piano, even if Paul does not know whether Andrew has limbs that allow him to play piano or whether Andrew has demonstrative knowledge of piano playing of the sort I described. Detailed knowledge of the sort that Andrew would express by using demonstratives is not necessary for knowing how to play a piano. Parallel points hold for knowing how to ski and knowing how to sex chicks. Many people who are unable to ski, play a piano, and sex chicks know (relatively undetailed) answers to the questions of how to ski, play a piano, and sex chicks, and therefore also know how to ski, play a piano, and sex chicks.

I spoke as an invariantist in the previous paragraph. A contextualist should hold that there is no context in which (19) is true and (20) is false.

19. Suzie knows how to ski
20. Suzie knows an answer to the question of how to ski.

In some contexts, Suzie's knowledge of rather undetailed propositions concerning skiing is sufficient for both sentences to be true. In nearly all contexts, Suzie's demonstrative knowledge is sufficient to make both true. There are unusual contexts in which (20) is false, despite Suzie's demonstrative knowledge; in some of these unusual contexts, (20) is true only if Suzie knows a highly detailed proposition about skiing that she can express in *non*-demonstrative terms (in the way that good coaches can). But in such contexts (19) is also false, even though Suzie is able to ski. In these unusual contexts, the sentence 'Suzie is able to ski, but she doesn't know how to ski' is true. (Note that it is possible for a thing to be able to

G without knowing how to *G*: my car is able to burn gasoline, but it does not know how to do so.) Speakers have the intuition that (19) is true and (20) is false only when there is a shift in contexts between their two judgments.

5.2 Objection 2: Knowing Answers While Lacking Abilities

I have considered an objection that claims that propositional knowledge is not necessary for knowing how to *G*. The next two objections claim (at least in effect) that propositional knowledge is not sufficient.

John Koethe's (2002) objection to Stanley and Williamson's theory uses a distinction between *basic* and *nonbasic* actions. A nonbasic action is an action that one performs *by* performing another action. Opening a safe *by* turning its knob is a relatively clear example. A basic action is one that is not nonbasic: it is an act that one performs, not by performing another act, but *directly*. For me, moving my hand is a type of basic action. (See Goldman 1970 for more on basic actions.) Koethe suggests that if *G*-ing is a basic action, then being able to *G* is necessary for knowing how to *G*. Furthermore, Koethe says that ear wiggling is a basic action, and so he claims that anyone who is unable to wiggle his ears does not know how to wiggle his ears.[12]

Thus far, we do not have an objection to the answer theory. But we can use Koethe's claims about ear wiggling, and one of his examples, to formulate an objection, as follows. Suppose that John has seen Tom wiggle his ears, and suppose that John knows that *that* way of ear wiggling (pointing at Tom) is a way for him (John) to wiggle his ears. If John knows this latter proposition, then he knows an answer to the question of how to wiggle his ears. So if the answer theory is correct, then John knows how to wiggle his ears. But John is unable to wiggle his ears, and anyone who is unable to wiggle his ears does not know how to wiggle his ears. Therefore, the objection concludes, the answer theory is incorrect.

The objection relies on the general principle that anyone who is unable to wiggle his ears does not know how to wiggle his ears. This is incorrect. Wally was a virtuoso ear wiggler until recently, when he suffered an injury to his scalp muscles that deprived him of his ability to wiggle his ears. He knows how to wiggle his ears but is unable to do so. (See Ginet 1975 and Stanley and Williamson 2001 for similar examples.) In view of this, I will consider a slightly reformulated objection that replaces the previous general principle with the singular claim that if John is unable to wiggle his ears, then he does not know how to wiggle his ears.

---

12. The claim that ear wiggling is a basic type of action is dubious. The same type of action may be basic for one person and nonbasic for another (Goldman 1970). But this claim will play no substantive role in the following objection to the answer theory.

This singular claim has some initial plausibility, even apart from the general principle.

In reply to this last objection, an answer theorist should *either* say that John *does* know how to wiggle his ears (even though he is unable to do so) *or* he should say that John does not know an answer to the question of how to wiggle his ears. I favor the first reply. But which reply an answer theorist prefers should depend on her view of answers and perhaps on whether she takes 'knows how to' ascriptions to be context sensitive.

John is unable to wiggle his ears and knows little about ear wiggling, yet we can think of contexts in which it would be natural to say that he does know how to wiggle his ears. Imagine that John is taking lessons from Ken on ear wiggling.

21. KEN: "If you want to wiggle your ears, it helps to be able to pick out examples of how you should do it. Which of these videos shows how you should wiggle yours ears?" [Ken shows John several doctored videos in which someone moves his ears in physiologically impossible ways and an undoctored video of Tom wiggling his ears by contracting his scalp muscles in the usual way.]
JOHN: "*That* is the way I should wiggle my ears" [demonstrating the video of Tom].
KEN: "Good, you know how to wiggle your ears."

In this context, Ken's attribution seems correct, simply because John knows the proposition that *that* is a way that John should wiggle his ears (demonstrating the way that Tom wiggles his ears). We can imagine other contexts in which it would be natural to say 'John knows how to wiggle his ears' if John merely knows that he should wiggle his ears without touching them or that he should wiggle his ears by moving them back and forth (rather than by flapping their tips up and down).[13] But it has to be admitted that there are also conversational contexts in which a typical speaker would judge that 'John knows how to wiggle his ears' is true only if John is currently able to wiggle his ears or was at one time able to wiggle his ears.

On the invariantist theory that I prefer, the proposition that John knows (namely, that Tom's way of ear wiggling is a way he should do it) is an answer to the question of how to wiggle John's ears. In some contexts, we are interested in whether John knows this answer (or answers like it), whereas in other contexts we

---

13. In the previous dialogue, Ken and John focus on how John *should* wiggle his ears. We can imagine another conversation in which Ken shows the same sequence of videos and asks John to pick out the way in which he *can* wiggle his ears.

are uninterested in whether he knows this answer (or answers like it). Our willingness to say and judge that John knows how to wiggle his ears changes as our interests change, but 'John knows how to wiggle his ears' semantically expresses a true proposition in all of these contexts. Therefore, in reply to the last objection to Koethe, I say that John does know how to wiggle his ears, because he knows an answer to the question of how to wiggle his ears. But Koethe has created a context in which we are uninterested in the answer that John happens to know.

A contextualist answer theorist should say that 'John knows how to wiggle his ears' is true in a context like the one I created by telling the video story but false in a context like the one that Koethe created by telling his (minimal) story. My story created a context in which one needs to know very little about ear wiggling to know an answer to the question denoted by 'how to wiggle John's ear' in that context; Koethe's story creates a (more standard) context in which one needs to know a rather substantive proposition to know an answer to the question denoted by 'how to wiggle John's ears' in that context (these are propositions that people who can, or could, wiggle their ears might express with demonstratives). But the contextualist answer theorist should say that there is no context in which 'John knows an answer to the question of how to wiggle his ears' is true and yet 'John knows how to wiggle his ears' is false. If speakers judge that the first sentence is true and the second false, they are shifting contexts, perhaps in subtle ways.

5.3 Objection 3: Knowing Answers While Being Confused

John Bengson and Marc Moffett (2007) criticize Stanley and Williamson's (2001) theory of knowing-how by arguing (roughly) that knowing an answer to the question of how to G is not always sufficient for knowing how to G. If successful, their argument would also show that the answer theory is incorrect.

Irina's ice-skating coach has told her that one way in which she can do a salchow is to take off from the back inside edge of her skate, jump in the air, spin, and land on the back outside edge of her skate. What the coach says is true, and Irina is justified in believing it. Therefore, Irina knows this proposition. Moreover, this proposition is an answer to the question of how to do a salchow. Therefore, if the answer theory is true, then Irina knows how to do a salchow. However, Irina is confused. She thinks that her skate's front outside edge is its back inside edge, and that her skate's front inside edge is its back outside edge.[14] As a result, she

---

14. This should be understood *de re*: her skate's front outside edge is such that she believes that *it* is her skate's back inside edge, and her skate's front inside edge is such that she believes that *it* is her skate's back outside edge

makes mistakes when she judges whether other skaters are doing salchows, and she gives bad advice to other skaters about, for instance, which way to lean on their skates when they try to do salchows. As Bengson and Moffett say in a parenthetical remark, "in applying her knowledge—e.g., in teaching someone else how to do a salchow—Irina would consistently make substantive errors, errors which would render an attribution of know-how unacceptable." Therefore, Bengson and Moffett claim, Irina does not know how to do a salchow. So the answer theory is untrue.[15]

In reply, I say that Irina does know how to do a salchow. But intuitions about whether she knows how to do a salchow vary from context to context, depending on the interests of the speakers in those contexts. Bengson and Moffett have created a context in which we are interested in whether she knows certain propositions concerning how to do a salchow, and Irina is ignorant of these particular propositions. This may lead some readers to think incorrectly that she does not know how to do a salchow. I shall explain.

Irina knows that to do a salchow, she needs to take off from the back inside edge of her skate. But she does not know that B is the back inside edge of her left skate (where B is, in fact, that back inside edge). In some contexts, we might be particularly interested in whether she knows this proposition, for instance, if we are interested in whether Irina will give useful advice to skilled skaters who wish to do a salchow. Bengson and Moffett emphasize (in their parenthetical remark) that because of Irina's confusion, she is likely to give bad advice to other skaters. The context that Bengson and Moffett create for their readers is one in which her previous ignorance is likely to lead us to judge that she does not know how to do a salchow. But in other contexts, we would be willing to say that she does know how to do a salchow, despite this ignorance, because of her knowledge of other propositions concerning salchows. One such context is the following.

22. ALEX: "I just read a book in which someone did a salchow, but the book did not say much about how to do them. How do you do a salchow?"
    BEN: "You do a somersault on ice."

---

15. Bengson and Moffett also add the following detail to their story, which is inessential to the preceding argument against the answer theory. Irina has a neurological deficit. Whenever she tries to take off from her front outer edge, she in fact takes off from her back inside edge, and whenever she tries to land on her front inside edge, she lands on her back outside edge. So whenever she attempts to do a salchow in the way that she (falsely) believes it should be done, she ends up doing a genuine salchow.

CAL: "No, you do a cartwheel on ice."
DAVID: "No, you ski backward down an ice-covered slope."
IRINA: "No, a salchow is an ice-skating trick. To do it you jump and spin in mid-air in a certain way."
EVE: "Alex, I've watched many winter Olympics on TV. Don't pay attention to Ben, Cal, and David: they don't know how to do a salchow. But Irina does."

Despite her confusion about inside edges, Irina clearly does know that one can do a salchow by jumping and spinning in mid-air in a certain way while skating. (She also knows that she can do a salchow in this way.) In this context, her knowledge of this proposition seems sufficient for her to know how to do a salchow.

Given this contextual variation in our intuitions, what should we say about whether Irina knows how to do a salchow? On the invariantist theory I prefer, we should say that she does know how to do a salchow. In some contexts, the speakers are interested in whether she knows relatively undetailed answers to the question of how to do a salchow. In those contexts, the speakers are inclined to say (and think) that she knows how to do a salchow. Their judgments in these contexts are correct. In contexts in which the speakers are primarily interested in whether she knows more detailed answers, all of which partly concern the inside edges of skates, the speakers might be inclined to say that she does not. But these latter ascriptions are mistaken, even though they may correctly convey the true information that (a) she does not know the detailed propositions concerning skate edges in which the speakers and hearers of the context are interested and (b) she may give bad advice to novice skaters.

On a contextualist version of the answer theory, the sentence 'Irina knows how to do a salchow' genuinely varies in content and truth value from context to context. In one of the contexts that Bengson and Moffett create, the ascription is false. In the context that I set up in my preceding example, it is true. The only worry that Bengson and Moffett raise for the contextualist version of the answer theory is that their argument may lead us first to judge that 'Irina knows an answer to the question of how to do a salchow' is true and then to judge that 'Irina knows how to do a salchow' is false. On the contextualist version of the answer theory, there is no context in which these sentences differ in truth value. In reply to this problem, the contextualist should maintain that Bengson and Moffett subtly shift contexts in the middle of their argument. In the context created by the beginning and middle of their argument, 'Irina knows an answer to the question of how to do a salchow' is true, and so is the sentence 'Irina knows how to do a salchow', though this sentence is not uttered in this context. But Bengson and Moffett change the context when they make their parenthetical remark about her giving bad advice to other skaters. In this context, both sentences are false. But in no context is 'Irina knows an answer to the question of how to do a salchow' true and 'Irina knows how to do a salchow' false.

11

Knowledge Ascription by Grammatical Construction

Laura A. Michaelis

1. Introduction[1]

While little consensus has emerged from the debate about the nature of know-how, the parties do appear to agree about two things: first, folk conceptions of knowledge matter, and second, linguistic analysis is a good way to get at those conceptions. Particular attention has been paid to the syntactic behavior of verbs of knowledge ascription. The rationale is presumably that a verb's grammatical frame (i.e., its complement structure) reveals its conceptual structure—in particular, the repertoire of semantic roles that it evokes—and therefore a theory that captures the syntactic behavior of knowledge-ascription verbs will also explain what kind of relationship verbs of knowledge ascription express. Thus, for example, Stanley (2011) rejects the Rylean view of know-how in part because it must treat as accidental the fact that both procedural knowledge and propositional knowledge are expressed by clausal complements consisting of a question word followed by an infinitive, as in (1) versus (2), respectively:

1. She knows how to go.
2. She knows where to go.

The evidence suggests, however, that grammatical constructions do not provide a transparent window into the meanings of verbs like *know*, because constructions can, and frequently do, alter the combinatoric potential of verbs with which they combine. As a straightforward illustration of this point, consider the activity verb *sweep*. It denotes a relation between a person and a surface in (3), but in (4) it denotes a relation between a person and a substance:

---

[1]. The author gratefully acknowledges help and advice received from Marc Moffett, Knud Lambrecht, Josef Ruppenhofer, and Adele Goldberg.

3. She swept the floor.
4. She swept the dirt into a dustpan.

The semantic difference between (3) and (4) is attributable to syntactic context: in (3), *sweep* occurs in a simple transitive construction; in (4), it occurs in a construction that expresses causation of motion. How do these observations apply to verbs of knowledge ascription? Taking the verb *learn* as illustrative of the class, I submit that one cannot reasonably infer from the usage in (5), in which *learn* clearly denotes a relation between a person and a proposition, that it denotes this same relation in either (6) or (7):

5. I learned that wider tires have better traction.
6. I learned to change a tire.
7. I learned how to change a tire.

Instead, as I will argue, (6) expresses a relation between a person and a procedure and (7) a relation between a person and a method of performing a procedure. In short, the argument is that a verb assigns different roles according to its syntactic context. Does this then mean that the syntactic behaviors of verbs cannot or should not inform our models of knowing how? To the contrary, I will argue: the observed syntactic variability suggests a compromise between the Rylean and intellectualist views: knowledge-ascription verbs assign complements denoting propositions, as per the intellectualist view, whereas infinitival constructions assign complements denoting actions, as per the Rylean view. The analysis that I will offer is based on construction grammar. According to construction grammar, rules of syntactic combination (like that which describes the noun phrase) are directly associated with interpretive and use conditions, in the form of semantic and pragmatic features that attach to the mother or daughter nodes in these descriptions (Goldberg 1995; Kay 2002; Kay and Fillmore 1999; Michaelis 2004; Sag 2010). This amounts to the claim that syntactic rules mean things. Meaning is generally viewed as the exclusive purview of words, and in the prevailing view of meaning composition, syntactic rules do no more than determine what symbol sequences function as units for syntactic purposes. So while syntactic rules assemble words and their dependent elements into phrases, and the phrases denote complex concepts like predicates and propositions, the rules cannot add conceptual content to that contributed by the words, nor can they alter the combinatoric properties of the words. On this view, which Jackendoff (1997, 48) describes as the "doctrine of syntactically transparent composition," "all elements of content in the meaning of a sentence are found in the lexical conceptual structures...of the lexical items composing the sentence." A major problem with this view is that, as first observed by Goldberg (1995), syntactic context can, in fact, alter the combinatoric potential of words, as shown by the following attested examples:

8. Down at the harbor there is a teal-green clubhouse for socializing and parties. Beside it **sparkles** the community pool. (*Vanity Fair* 8/2001)
9. When a visitor passes through the village, young lamas stop picking up trash to mug for the camera. A gruff 'police monk' **barks** them back to work. (*Newsweek* 10/13/1997)

The verbs shown in boldface in (8) and (9), *sparkle* and *bark*, do not usually appear in these particular sentence patterns. By the same token, the sentence patterns exemplified in (8) and (9) usually contain verbs other than these. The pattern exemplified in (8), in which an intransitive verb precedes its subject and follows a location expression, favors verbs of location like *sit* and *lie*. The pattern exemplified in (9), in which a transitive verb is followed by both a direct object and a location expression, favors causative verbs that denote a change of location, such as *move* or *push*. The verb *sparkle* is not a verb of location, nor does *bark* express causation of motion. Counter to the predictions of the syntactically transparent composition, however, such verb-construction conflicts yield not gibberish but new verb meanings: the reader of (8) is inclined to interpret sparkling as the *manner* of location, and the reader of (9) is likely to interpret barking as the (metaphorical) *means* by which motion is effected.

How are the verb-meaning shifts illustrated in (8) and (9) effected? Using basic tools of construction-based syntactic analysis, Goldberg (1995) provided a simple and conceptually satisfying answer: verb-construction conflict resolution. Her explanation starts with the foundational premise of construction grammar—that grammatical patterns like the ones exemplified in (8) and (9) have meanings, as indicated by the following analyses:

10. Locative inversion construction
    Form: a locative expression (A) preceding a verb whose subject (B) follows the verb.
    Meaning: the location denoted by A has (or comes to have) entity B, in it.
11. Caused motion construction
    Form: a verb with a subject (A), object (B), and directional expression (C).
    Meaning: the entity denoted by A causes the entity denoted by B to go to C.

Given these construction meanings, we can view the novel verb meanings in (8) and (9) as predictable by-products of verb-construction combination, or more specifically of verb-construction conflict resolution—an inferential process in which a verb comes to denote the kind of event or state that the construction denotes (Michaelis 2004). In this process, the set of semantic roles associated with the verb is augmented up to that licensed by the construction, as when the verb *sparkle* acquires a location role. Since we need the locative-inversion and caused-motion constructions anyway, we do not need additional constructions to describe the special meanings in (8) and (9), nor do we need to create new verb definitions to describe those meanings. To reconcile the semantic contribution of verb and construction in such instances, the interpreter must relate the verb meaning to the construction meaning via what Goldberg (1995) calls an integration relation. Integration relations include *manner*, *means*, and *precondition*. The manner and means relations are illustrated by (8) and (9), respectively, and the precondition relation is illustrated later.

The construction-based model of argument structure resolves certain otherwise paradoxical properties of verbs. For example, while it seems a priori impossible for the verb *bark* to be transitive and intransitive at the same time, this apparent paradox disappears when we acknowledge the caused-motion construction as the source of the direct object in (9). Crucially for our purposes, the construction-based model of argument structure also suggests an intuitive way to resolve the conflict between the Rylean and intellectualist positions: verbs of knowledge ascription do indeed, as claimed by the intellectualists, take propositions as their second arguments, but whether that proposition actually surfaces as a complement depends on the construction with which the verb combines. When, for example, knowledge-ascription verbs take bare infinitival complements, as in English *I learned to drive* or French *Je sais conduire*, they express a relation between a person and a procedure, as per the Rylean view, rather than a relation between a person and a proposition, as per the intellectualist view. More generally, the appropriate semantic analysis of a verb of knowledge ascription varies according to the complementation pattern in which the verb is encountered. As shown in (5) through (7), there are three major complementation patterns for verbs of knowledge ascription; those examples are repeated here as (12) through (14):

12. **Clausal complement**: I learned that wider tires have better traction.
13. **Infinitival complement**: I learned to change a tire.
14. **WH-complement**: I learned how to change a tire.

In all but (12), we will assume that the verb's proposition argument has been suppressed and that the construction has supplied a distinct second argument. In the case of the infinitival-complement construction exemplified in (13), this second argument is a procedure. In the case of the WH-complement construction exemplified in (14), this second argument is a 'means' variable in an open proposition (i.e., "One changes a tire in x manner"). The remainder of this chapter is devoted to these two English constructions and the manner in which they interact with verbs of knowledge ascription. Section 2 provides an analysis of two major infinitival-complement constructions, object control and subject control. Section 3 provides an analysis of the WH complement construction. Section 4 contains concluding remarks and a brief consideration of the functional contrast between the two apparently synonymous infinitive constructions exemplified in (13) and (14).

2. *Infinitival Complements*

In arguing against the Rylean view of knowing how, Stanley (2011, 232) points out that it entails a counterintuitive ambiguity for verbs of knowledge ascription. He states:

> The Rylean must argue that the English verb "know," and the French word "savoir," as well as their cognates in many other languages, are ambiguous between the propositional knowledge verb, and a verb attributing a distinct cognitive state, which is an attitude towards an action-type.

But in fact on a constructionist approach, *savoir* means the same thing in (15) and (16):

15. Je sais qu'il a raison.
    'I know that he is right.'
16. Je sais nager.
    'I know how to swim.'

Only the construction-integration relations are different in the two cases. Let us concur with Stanley that knowing is a relationship between a person and a proposition. This does not mean, however, that the construction in which a verb of knowledge ascription appears denotes that relationship. As we saw in §1, constructions can alter the relations that verbs express. The examples discussed in that section were of intransitive verbs (*sparkle* and *bark*) to which additional arguments had been added. A more complex case of argument augmentation, and one closer to the case of *learn*, *know*, and other knowledge-ascription verbs, is that in which an already transitive verb takes a direct-object argument distinct from the one it intrinsically assigns. The verbs *win* and *drink* are here used to illustrate this case. Intuitively speaking, the verb *win* expresses a relationship between a contestant and a prize, and *drink* a relationship between a person and a liquid, but these are not the relationships denoted by the constructions in (17) and (18), respectively:

17. He won me a stuffed animal.
18. He drank himself into a stupor.

Sentence (17) illustrates the ditransitive (or 'double object') construction, whose (active voice) form is a verb followed by two noun phrases (in [17], *me* and *a stuffed animal*, respectively) and whose direct object (i.e., *me*) denotes the recipient of a transferred item. Example (18) illustrates the resultative construction, whose form is a verb followed by a noun phrase and directional expression (in [18], *himself* and *into a stupor*, respectively), and whose direct object (i.e, *himself*) denotes something or someone who has undergone a change of state. In each of these two examples, there is a mismatch between the semantic roles that the verb calls for and those that the construction supplies: while winning requires only two participants (the victor and the prize), transfer requires three, and while drinking requires a direct object denoting a liquid, in (18) it gets a direct object denoting a human. Assuming the set of verb-construction integration relations described by Goldberg (1995), we can say that in (17) winning is understood to be a *precondition* for transfer and in (18) drinking is understood to be the *means* by which one moves (metaphorically) from sobriety to stupefaction. Notice in particular that the integration of the verb *drink* and the caused-motion construction in (18) requires the removal of the verb's ordinary second argument (the potable substance) and the replacement of that argument with one licensed by the construction: the affected-party argument. We understand that the *drink*'s potable-substance argument is present conceptually (since one cannot drink without a liquid), but (18) denotes something that someone did to himself rather than to a beverage. In fact, the suppression of participant roles, and the consequent existential interpretation of those roles, is common in English and other languages (Fillmore 1986). For example, the verb *drink* allows null expression of the potable-substance argument in a variety of frames:

19. She drank from a mug.
20. He drinks.

Significantly, argument omission is also licensed by verbs of knowledge like *teach*:

21. She teaches first graders.

While the speaker of (21) does not specify the content that the teacher causes her students to know, the relevant content is presumably inferable from context. Were the content argument to be present, it could be expressed by a noun phrase, as in (22):

22. She teaches first graders reading skills.

Like (18), (22) is an instance of the ditransitive construction. This construction expresses an act of transfer in which the direct object denotes a recipient and the second object (e.g., *reading skills* in [22]) expresses the theme, or item transferred. (Most ditransitive verbs, including *teach*, are compatible with an alternate pattern in which the recipient is expressed by a preposition phrase, such as *She gave a book to me*.) While causing someone to know something is not literally an act of transfer, the fact that *teach* behaves syntactically as a transfer verb indicates that teaching can be construed according to the metaphorical mapping *causation is transfer*, also found in expressions like *She gave me a headache* and *The judge handed him a victory* (Lakoff 1993). Thus, the pattern of argument omission seen in (21) is the same as that in sentences like (23) and (24), in which the theme argument is likewise missing and recoverable from context:

23. She e-mailed me [the news].
24. Give me [that book].

Alternatively, the missing complement of (21) might be reconstructed as a finite clause introduced by the complementizer *that*, as in (25):

25. She teaches first graders that specific letter sequences correspond to words of English.

Whether the content argument of *teach* is expressed by a noun phrase or a clause, it is subject to null expression, in which case it is reconstructed from context. The same analysis of *teach* holds when it is found in the pattern in (26):

26. She teaches first graders to read.

In (26), *teach* takes a subject (*she*) denoting an agent, a direct object (*first graders*) denoting an experience, and an infinitival complement (*to read*) denoting an act. Following terminological tradition, we will refer to this construction as the object control construction. The object control construction is the transitive analogue of the infinitival complement pattern exemplified in (13). Other examples of the object control construction are given in (27) and (28):

27. She convinced me to stay.
28. She forced me to agree.

Now, according to the intellectualist model, the meaning of (26) is captured by the paraphrase in (29):

29. She teaches first graders that there is some x such that x is a way to read.

This analysis is implausible on its face. Instead, I would submit, the meaning of (26) is captured by the paraphrase in (30):

30. She teaches first graders propositional content that is a precondition to the act of reading.

According to the proposed analysis, (26) is an instance of argument augmentation by construction, as in (17) and (18). The added argument is the 'act' argument denoted by the infinitival verb. The construction that contributes this argument is object control. In the object control construction, the verb's direct object is interpreted as both the party affected by the act of teaching, forcing, persuading, and so on and the (potential) doer of the procedure denoted by the infinitival complement. When *teach* combines with the object control construction, two of the arguments of the verb undergo what Goldberg (1995, ch. 2) refers to as *fusion*: they are identified with compatible arguments of the construction. The teacher argument of *teach* is fused with the agent (subject) argument of the object control construction, and the student argument of *teach* is fused with the experiencer (object) argument of the object control construction. Where is the content argument of *teach* in (26)? It is missing: the content argument has not fused with an argument of the object control construction. In other words, the combination of the verb *teach* with the object control construction requires that the content argument be unexpressed: (31) and (32), for example, are ungrammatical:

31. *She teaches first graders reading skills to read.
32. *She teaches first graders that specific letter sequences correspond to words of English to read.

I submit that the ungrammaticality of (31) and (32) has the same source as that in (33):

33. *He drank liquor himself into a stupor.

Sentence (33) is a defective instance of the resultative construction, a well-formed instance of which is shown in (18). Sentence (33) fails because verb-construction integration requires that the *verb's* second argument (*liquor*) be replaced by the *construction's* second argument (*himself*). The second argument assigned by the resultative construction is an entity that undergoes a change of state; it is referred to as a theme argument. The label *theme argument* is used in frame-based semantics to denote a participant role that moves or is moved, either metaphorically, as in (18), where the state of stupefaction is construed as a location, or literally, as in (4), repeated here as (34):

34. She swept the dirt into a dustpan.

When a verb that selects for a specific type of direct object, like *drink* (a liquid) or *sweep* (a surface), appears without that direct object in the resultative construction, the direct object in question is one that is omissible, as shown in (35) and (36):

35. The horses drank (water) thirstily.
36. She swept (the floor) thoroughly.

Crucially, however, while omission of the verb's theme argument is optional in (35) and (36), it is obligatory in the context of the resultative construction, as shown by (33). The same observations can be made, mutatis mutandis, about the ill-formed examples in (31) and (32): verb-construction integration requires that the content argument, which is otherwise subject to omission, be replaced by the infinitival 'procedure' argument of the object control construction. A general susceptibility to null expression is a necessary but not sufficient condition upon an argument's removal during verb-construction integration. As it happens, *teach* allows either the propositional-content argument, the 'student' argument, or both to be unexpressed. The first pattern is exemplified by (21), repeated here as (37). The second and third patterns are exemplified by (38) and (39), respectively:

37. She teaches first graders.
38. She teaches reading skills.
39. She teaches.

But sentence (40), in which the 'student' argument has been removed in the course of verb-construction integration, is ungrammatical:

40. *She teaches reading skills to read.

Sentence (40) is ungrammatical because the object control construction requires an experiencer argument as its second argument, and the 'student' argument of *teach* is the only one of the two nonsubject arguments with the requisite properties of animacy and volition.

Thus far, we have discussed the combination of a transitive verb of knowledge ascription, *teach*, with a construction, the object control construction, that licenses an infinitival complement denoting a procedure. Similar observations apply to the combination of an intransitive verb of knowledge ascription with an infinitival complement. In contrast to French, German, and other languages, where a stative verb of knowing can be combined with an infinitival complement denoting a procedure (as in the French *savoir* example [16]), the only intransitive verb of knowledge ascription that enters into this pattern in English is the change-of-state verb, *learn*, which I will regard as meaning 'come to know some propositional content.' Thus, while (41) means something like 'I came to know something that enables me to make coffee,' (42) does not mean 'I know something that enables me to make coffee'; rather, it means 'I know that I should make coffee under certain circumstances':

41. I learned to make coffee.
42. I know to make coffee.

While this divergence between *know* and *learn* is mysterious, the generally idiosyncratic behavior of verbs leads us to expect such cross-linguistic differences in verb complementation patterns, and the observations made here about the English verb *learn* can easily be applied to French *savoir* or German *wissen*. What is crucial for our purposes is that the grammatical pattern in (41) appears both grammatically and semantically analogous to that in (43):

43. I tried to make coffee.

The grammatical pattern exemplified in both (41) and (43) is referred to in the linguistic literature as subject control. Like object control, the subject control construction requires a single argument, the subject argument, to play a distinct semantic role for each of two verbs, the main verb and its infinitival complement. These roles are the experiencer of the intentional state denoted by the finite verb (*learn* or *try*) and the agent of the procedure denoted by the infinitival verb (*to make coffee*). While in the object control construction this 'double duty' argument is the direct object of the main verb, in the subject control pattern it is the subject of the matrix verb. Like object control, subject control can replace the second argument of a verb with which it combines. In the case of (41), for example, the second argument, the propositional-content argument, is replaced by the infinitival 'procedure' argument of the construction. As in the case of *teach*, we find independent attestation of this argument-omission affordance for *learn*, in examples like (44) and (45):

44. I love to learn [things].
45. Will they ever learn [that crime doesn't pay]?

Thus, as in the case of *teach*, the version of *learn* that combines with the subject control construction is the intransitive one, in which the "content" argument is not overtly expressed but is present at the conceptual level. As in the case of *teach*, the verb-construction integration relation attested in such combinations is the precondition relation: learning some set of propositions (the content) is a precondition for doing things like making coffee.

The addition of an infinitival or clausal complement to the argument array of a mental-state predicator (verbal or adjectival) is a general phenomenon, attested for predicators other than those expressing knowledge states, as in (46) through (48):

46. "I am **slack jawed** to read that members claim to have not understood that the techniques on which they were briefed were to actually be employed...," Mr. Goss wrote in the *Wall Street Journal*. (*New York Times* 5/14/1909)
47. Griffin appears **happy** that he could be heading to Los Angeles.
48. Fergie was **smart** to dye her hair dark before getting married to Josh Duhamel.

Both being slack-jawed and being happy are single-argument property predications. The clausal second argument with which these adjectives are paired in (46) and (47) is licensed by a construction rather than by the particular adjective. The construction exemplified in (46) is that which pairs a mental-state predicator with an infinitival clause denoting an activity that induces this mental state; it is also exemplified by (49):

49. I am embarrassed/shocked/surprised to read this news.

In (46), the state of being slack-jawed (a facial posture) is used to represent the mental state of being shocked, according to the metonymic convention by which the symptom of an emotional state stands for that state. The integration relation illustrated in (46), as in (49), is the manner relation: the facial posture accompanies the state of being surprised. The construction exemplified in (47), described by Moffett (2005), denotes a relation between a thinker or speaker and propositional content believed or stated; the latter is expressed by a finite clause.

Verbs and adjectives that select for this argument array on the basis of their intrinsic semantics are *aware*, *believe*, and *know*. The adjective *happy* differs from the foregoing predicators in that it does not intrinsically select for a propositional argument: being happy is not necessarily the result of knowing some proposition. It is only by virtue of combining with the *that*-clause complementation pattern, as in (47), that *happy* obtains a propositional argument. The integration relation exemplified in (47) is again manner: the emotional state of happiness accompanies the intentional state of knowing (in this case, that one is heading for Los Angeles). The construction exemplified in (48), described by Oshima (2009) as the adj+*to*-inf construction, pairs an adjective that describes a mental or behavioral propensity of an individual (e.g., *intelligence, boldness, bravery, stupidity*) with an infinitival complement denoting an action ascribable to that propensity. In line with the present approach, Oshima describes this construction as follows:

> The traditional argument/adjunct distinction tends to be obscured in 'non-canonical' constructions like the adj-to-inf-cxn. The to-infinitive is an indispensable constituent in the construction, and can be regarded as a complement in that respect; on the other hand, it may be considered an adjunct for the reason that the main predicate (adjective) does not inherently select for it. (2009, 367)

In construction grammar terms, the infinitival complement is licensed by the adj-*to*-inf construction rather than by the adjective itself. In other words, adjectives like *smart, stupid*, and *wise* are not intrinsically relational adjectives; in this respect, they differ from intentional-state adjectives like *eager, prepared*, and *determined*: felicitous use of sentences like *Fred is eager/prepared/determined* requires mutual knowledge of the act that Fred intends to perform, while no such requirement obtains for sentences like *Fred is bold/smart/brave*. Thus, adjectives like *smart* and *stupid* receive an infinitival complement only through the mechanism of word-construction integration. What is the integration relation exemplified by predications like (48)? As in the case of verbs of knowledge ascription, it is the precondition relation: having the relevant propensity is a necessary condition on performing the action, and so one can infer the propensity from the performance of the action. The latter statement captures Oshima's observation that predications licensed by the adj-*to*-inf construction are implicit epistemic conditionals; for example, as he observes (370), the sentence *John was wise to leave early* can be paraphrased as "John must have been being wise, {because/considering that} he left early."

The foregoing observations show that syntactic context, or more specifically constructional context, may alter the array of semantic arguments that a verb or adjective selects. This means that the syntactic context may only indirectly reflect the semantic-role-licensing properties of the predicator. Acknowledging this enables us to strike a compromise between the Rylean and intellectualist views: verbs like *learn* and *teach* do indeed take propositions as their second arguments, but that propositional argument is replaced by one denoting a procedure in the infinitival constructions that have convinced proponents of the Rylean view that verbs of knowledge ascription describe a relationship between a person and a procedure. Instead, as in the intellectualist view, verbs of knowledge ascription denote a relationship between a person and propositional content. Such verbs are compatible with the object control and subject control constructions insofar as propositional knowledge is understood as a prerequisite for performance of the procedure. We here adopt the Rylean rather than intellectualist view of infinitival complements: such complements denote procedures rather than propositions. The present account is thus Rylean with regard to constructional argument licensing and intellectualist with regard to verbal argument licensing. At least in the case of verb phrases like French *savoir nager* and English *learn to swim*, the distinction between 'knowing how' and 'knowing that' comes down to a distinction between verb meaning and construction meaning.

3. WH-Complements

A WH-clause consists of a predication in which a clause-initial question word (*who, what, where, how*, etc.) serves the function of an argument (e.g., agent or patient) or adjunct (e.g., means, manner, purpose). A WH-clause becomes a WH-complement (also known as an *indirect question*) when it serves as the argument of a verb, such as a speech-act verb or verb of knowledge ascription. Sentence (50) is an example of the latter type of embedding context; I will argue that its meaning is captured by (51):

50. John knows how to make good coffee.
51. There is x means by which one makes good coffee, and John knows the value of x.

Similarly, I propose that (52) means something like (53):

52. John wonders how to make good coffee.
53. There is x means by which one makes good coffee, and John wants to learn the value of x.

In other words, WH-complements of verbs of knowledge ascription are just like WH-clauses in general: first, they presuppose an open proposition (i.e., one containing an unbound variable in place of an argument or adjunct), and second, the embedding construction expresses what the speaker's stance[2] toward that variable is: the speaker may have knowledge of its identity, as in (50); express lack of knowledge of its identity, as in (52); or provide its identity, as in (54):[3]

54. What I lost was my wallet.
 a. Presupposed: I lost x
 b. Asserted: x = my wallet

This analysis, while propositional, is distinct from the intellectualist one in that we view the propositional content conveyed by the WH-complement of a knowledge-ascription verb as presupposed rather than asserted. What is asserted is the speaker's stance toward the value of the variable. The assertion of speaker stance is what makes an utterance containing such a clause informative. In other words, a WH-clause alone conveys nothing more than an open proposition (as, for example, *what I lost* in (54) conveys 'I lost x'); it takes an embedding context to make such a clause into an assertion. Such embedding contexts need not be complementation contexts; they may instead be conversational or speech-act contexts. According to Lambrecht and Michaelis (1998), main-clause questions like (55) assert a speaker stance toward the variable, captured by (56):

55. What did you lose?
56. With regard to your having lost x, I am inquiring about the value of x.

---

2. By *speaker stance* here, I mean either the stance of the person denoted by the subject of a verb of cognition or speaking, as in (50) and (52), or the stance of the person uttering the sentence, as in (54) and (55).

3. The analysis given here of (54) is potentially controversial, since (54) is generally taken to exemplify a free relative-clause (i.e., *the thing that I lost*) rather than an indirect question. While the formal similarity between the two constructions creates ambiguities, as in (a), which has both a free-relative and an indirect-question paraphrase, as indicated in (b) and (c), respectively, certain syntactic tests distinguish the two patterns.

(a) I asked what she asked.
(b) I asked the question that she had asked. (free relative)
(c) I inquired about what she had asked. (indirect question)

One such test is described by Zwicky and Sadock (1975): insertion of the modifier *the hell*, as in (d), allows for only the indirect-question interpretation:

(d) I asked what the hell she asked.

While such facts suggest that free relative clauses and WH-clauses are indeed distinct constructions, I maintain that the former can revealingly be treated as denoting an open proposition in equative predications like (54).

In exploiting properties shared by WH-complements across a variety of syntactic contexts, the present account resembles that of Stanley and Williamson (2001) and Stanley (2011), who take the formal similarity of know-how ascriptions to ascriptions of knowing-why, knowing-where, and so forth as evidence that

> knowing how to F is in a family of mental states that include knowing where to F, knowing why to F, knowing when to F, etc., states that involve the normal knowing relation, together with an embedded question. (Stanley 2011, 226: 24)

The current account, however, provides a semanticopragmatic representation of WH-complements that makes sense regardless of the embedding verb; it is unclear whether the same could be said of the intellectualist account. Stanley (2011, 209) asserts, for example, that (57) has the paraphrase given in (58):

57. John knows how to find coffee in New York City.
58. For some way w, John knows that he can find coffee in New York City in way w.

This seems reasonable, and yet the proposed paraphrase relation appears to be restricted to sentences containing factive verbs like *know*. It does not appear to hold, for example, when we replace the verb *know* with the verb *ask*: (60) is not a valid paraphrase of (59):

59. John asked how to find coffee in New York City.
60. For some way w, John asked whether w was a way to find coffee in New York City.

When John asks how to find coffee in New York City, he is not inquiring about the efficacy of a coffee-locating method that he already has in mind (say, using an iPhone application). Instead, he is seeking to discover a method. Because the paraphrase in (60) contains a wide-scope existential quantifier over methods, it does not capture what is going on in a context of inquiry, where the person making the inquiry does not yet know of a particular method but takes for granted that there is one. If, however, we translate the WH-complement *how to find coffee in New York City* as a proposition containing an unbound 'means' variable (i.e., "one finds coffee in x way in New York City") and analyze the matrix verb *ask* as an indicator of the speaker's stance toward that variable, it is easy to describe the meaning of (59): it asserts that John inquired about the value of a 'means' variable, just as (50) asserts that John knows the value of a 'means' variable. In other words, the current account may come closer to the compositional ideal than the intellectualist one in that it gives the same analysis of WH-clauses regardless of embedding context. In the present analysis, the true second argument of the verb *know* in (50), the verb *wonder* in (52), or the verb *ask* in (59) is not an open proposition but the variable contained within that open proposition.

Is an unbound variable the kind of thing that can be an argument? A recent study by Birner, Kaplan, and Ward (2007) suggests that the answer is yes. This study examines the family of argument-structure constructions consisting of *that*-clefts (e.g., *That's John who wrote the book*), equative clauses containing the epistemic verb *would* and a demonstrative subject (e.g., *That would be John*), and simple equatives with demonstrative subjects (e.g., *That's John*). The latter two constructions, they argue, should not be analyzed as truncated clefts (*pace* Hedberg 2000). That is, they reject the view that (61) is an elliptical version of (62):

61. That's John.
62. That's John who's knocking on the door.

Instead, they argue, all three constructions inherit formal, semantic, and information-structure properties from an argument-focus construction used for equative assertions. This construction contains a copular verb and a demonstrative subject, and it presupposes an open proposition whose variable is referred to by the demonstrative subject. The focal expression following the verb *be* provides the value of this variable, as in other argument-focus predications (e.g., *I saw John*). Thus, for example, in (61), the demonstrative subject refers to the variable in a presupposed open proposition, 'x is at the door.'

But if the variable is the true second argument of a verb that takes a WH-complement, where is the propositional content of the WH-complement in our representation? It is in the presupposition, as indicated by the existential clauses in the paraphrases of (50) and (52). For example, (51), the paraphrase provided for (50), *John knows how to make good coffee*, contains the existential clause 'there is x means by which one makes good coffee.' Patterns of ellipsis in WH-complements support the view that the open proposition is presupposed rather than asserted: in a pattern called *sluicing* by Ross (1969), only the question word is present; the predication in which the question word plays an argument role is deleted on the supposition that it is recoverable:

63. Sue can make good coffee but I don't know how....
64. I left my keys somewhere, but I don't know where....

The fact that the open proposition is omissible under conditions of contextual recoverability follows from its status as a topic, that is, the entity or proposition about which the speaker is providing new information (Lambrecht 1994, ch. 4; Lambrecht and Michaelis 1998). Topical arguments are predictable arguments; speakers omit them because hearers can reconstruct them from context. In the case of knowledge-ascription predications like (57), *John knows how to find coffee in New York City*, the topical proposition is the open proposition 'One finds coffee in New York City using x method.' The topic status of the open proposition is further substantiated by synonymy relations like that in (65) and (66):

65. I know how to make good coffee.
66. I know the way to make good coffee.[4]

In (66), a noun phrase is used in place of a WH-complement. It is significant that this noun phrase contains the definite article, which elsewhere evokes an existence presupposition: both (65) and (66) take for granted that there is some way to make good coffee. Thus, while Stanley (2011, 210) is correct in asserting that, for example, the sentence *John knows how to find coffee in New York City* (sentence [57]) "is naturally read as expressing the proposition 'For some way w, John knows that he can find coffee in New York City in way w,'" his analysis fails to distinguish between asserted and presupposed parts of that proposition. This sentence does not assert that John knows that there are ways to find coffee in New York City. Instead, it presupposes that there are ways to find coffee in New York City. It asserts that John knows one or more of those ways, namely, one or more values of the 'means' variable.

4. Conclusion

Neither the intellectualist nor the Rylean model provides an adequate semantic analysis of the two major complementation patterns attested for verbs of knowledge ascription, namely, the infinitival and WH-complement patterns.

---

4. The complementation pattern exemplified by (66) may be unique to English. For example, French native speakers find its direct translation ungrammatical:

(e) *Je sais la manière de faire du bon café.

Such cross-linguistic differences in verb complementation patterns are not unexpected, even in closely related languages. For example, while the complementation pattern exemplified in (64) is also found in French, as in (b), it is ungrammatical in German (c), which requires a finite clause instead, as in (d):

(f) Il ne sait pas comment répondre. ("He doesn't know how to respond.")
(g) *Er weiss nicht, wie zu antworten.
(h) Er weiss nicht, wie er antworten soll. (lit. "He doesn't know how one should respond.")

The intellectualist model perhaps comes closer, in that it correctly assesses such verbs as expressing a relationship between a person and a proposition. The problem with the intellectualist model, as I see it, is that neither the infinitival-complement construction nor the WH-complement construction actually denotes this relationship. I have argued that the infinitival-complement pattern denotes a relation between a person and a procedure, where propositional knowledge represents a precondition for performing the procedure, and that the WH-complement pattern denotes a relation between a person and a 'means' variable in a presupposed open proposition—namely, the ability to identify that variable. We use the former pattern to attribute an ability to someone and the latter to attribute a skill. The moral of this story is that the grammar of knowledge attribution is not monolithic but is instead a constellation of constructions, each with its own array of semantic roles and use conditions.

But why should the grammar of English (or any other language) offer speakers two different ways of saying essentially the same thing? Put differently, what pragmatic considerations induce a speaker to use the infinitival-complement construction rather than the WH-complement construction when formulating a knowledge-ascription predication? We can gain some insight into this question by contrasting reports of mundane abilities, like those in (67) and (68), with reports of refined abilities, like those in (69) and (70):

67. Sue learned to swim.
68. Sue learned how to swim.
69. Sue learned to change lanes quickly.
70. She learned how to change lanes quickly.

While (67), (68), and (70) all assert that Sue attained knowledge required to perform a procedure, (69) seems instead to assert that Sue attained knowledge of when to use an already mastered ability. In this respect, (69) appears similar to (71):

71. Sue knows to swim.

If (71) means anything, it means 'She knows that one ought to swim (under some conditions).' By the same token, (69) means something like 'She learned that one ought to change lanes under some conditions.' The deontic reading of (71) makes some sense in that, as observed in connection with example (42), the English verb *know* otherwise lacks the infinitival-complement pattern. However, the English verb *learn* is clearly compatible with the infinitival-complement pattern. What then accounts for the deontic flavor of (69)? Comparison with French gives some clue. Native speakers report the pattern of grammaticality in (72) and (73):

72. Elle sait (??comment) nager.
    lit. "She knows (??how) to swim."
73. Elle sait *(comment) changer de voie rapidement.
    lit. "She knows *(how) to change lanes rapidly."

As (72) shows, while the bare-infinitive form is preferable to the WH-infinitive form for *nager* ('swim'), the reverse pattern holds for the more complex verb phrase *changer de voie rapidement*, as shown in (73). If, as suggested earlier, the infinitival complement denotes an ability and the WH-complement a skill, this pattern makes sense: an ability is an unrefined (or mundane) skill, and the opposition seen in (69) and (70) and in (72) and (73) may be a case of linguistic iconicity (Haiman 1980, 1983). According to Haiman's quantity principle, linguistic complexity reflects conceptual complexity, and it therefore stands to reason that the less elaborate complementation pattern (the bare infinitive) should denote a mundane skill (i.e., an ability), while the more elaborate one (the WH-complement) should denote a refined one.

PART IV

Implications and Applications

12

Knowing How and Epistemic Injustice

Katherine Hawley

1. Introduction

In her *Epistemic Injustice* (2007), Miranda Fricker argues that people can be distinctively wronged in their capacity as knowers. Perhaps the most obvious type of epistemic injustice occurs when people are unfairly prevented from obtaining knowledge because of their lack of access to education, resources, or social networks. But Fricker brings other types of epistemic injustice to our attention, focusing especially on "testimonial injustice, in which someone is wronged in their capacity as giver of knowledge" (Fricker 2007, 7).

In central cases of testimonial injustice, a speaker's assertions are given unduly low weight because of a listener's prejudices about a social group to which the speaker belongs. If I don't take what you say seriously because you're a woman or because you're Jewish, then I perpetrate a testimonial injustice. People can, of course, suffer in practical terms when they are not properly listened to—for example, they may receive lower quality health care, fail to advance their careers, or be wrongly sentenced to jail. But Fricker argues that, in addition to practical harms, people sometimes suffer distinctively epistemic harms from testimonial injustice because they are wronged as knowers.

What sort of harms are epistemic harms? One aspect of being a knower is being a giver of knowledge: "The capacity to give knowledge to others is one side of that many-sided capacity so significant in human beings: namely the capacity for reason" (Fricker 2007, 44). So wronging someone as a giver of knowledge—by perpetrating testimonial injustice—amounts to wronging that person as a knower, as a reasoner, and thus as a human being.

Fricker does not explicitly discuss knowledge how in the course of her rich and interesting book. This is unsurprising for two reasons. First, knowledge how is rarely the center of epistemological attention outside the context of debate about its relationship with propositional knowledge. Second, Fricker's discussion is framed in relation to the mainstream literature on testimony, which is itself focused on the verbal transmission of articulated propositional knowledge; some of the prima facie differences between knowledge how and (other) propositional knowledge turn on the distinctive ways in which practical knowledge is taught, learned, and transmitted.

Nevertheless, given the significance of Fricker's ideas, and given that knowledge how is surely some form of knowledge, it is worth exploring the ways in which ideas about epistemic injustice may apply to knowledge how. This project is potentially illuminating on several fronts. First, the ways in which Fricker's ideas can or cannot encompass knowledge how may tell us something about their scope or limitations. Second, this gives us an opportunity to investigate aspects of knowledge how without focusing on its relationship with propositional knowledge. Third, if Fricker is right that there are practical, political, and ethical consequences of epistemic injustice, then this in itself gives us good reason to explore whether such injustice can arise in the context of practical knowledge.

2. *Inquirers and Apprentices*

Why is testifying, or the capacity to give knowledge to others, so central to knowing? In addressing this question, Fricker draws extensively on Edward Craig's (1990) 'genealogical' approach to epistemology; both Fricker and Craig are concerned with the practical role played in our lives by the concept of knowledge, and Craig in particular is concerned about how that concept might have arisen in response to our basic epistemic needs in the 'state of nature.'

What might those basic epistemic needs be? Bernard Williams accuses epistemologists of paying undue attention to

> what might be called the *examiner* situation: the situation in which I know that p is true, this other man has asserted that p is true, and I ask the question whether this other man really knows it, or merely believes it. I am represented as checking on someone else's credentials for something about which I know already. That of course encourages the idea that knowledge is belief plus reasons and so forth. But this is far from our standard situation with regard to knowledge; our standard situation with regard to knowledge (in relation to other persons) is rather that of trying to find somebody who knows what we don't know; that is, to find somebody who is a source of reliable information about something. (1970, 146)

Our standard situation is that of the inquirer rather than that of the examiner: I am interested in whether S knows whether p, because I myself would like to know whether p, either for practical purposes or for its own sake. Building on this, Craig argues that our concept of knowledge serves primarily 'to flag approved sources of information' (1990, 11). For Craig, the notion of the inquirer and the related notion of the informant, who can help the inquirer, are key to understanding our concept of knowledge.

Admittedly, there are other reasons for seeking out people who know. Sometimes we seek knowers not because we ourselves want information, but because we seek someone who can teach others. Sometimes we seek knowers because we want them to act as examiners, to evaluate whether others know. And sometimes we seek knowers because of the prestige they may possess, regardless of whether the knowers will in fact provide information to anyone. Nevertheless, the perspective of the inquirer is central to this approach to epistemology.

Following his discussion of the inquirer, who seeks propositional knowledge, Craig develops a parallel notion of the "apprentice, who wants either (i) someone to tell him how to do A, or (ii) someone to show him how to do A. What we want, as apprentices, is to be able to do A ourselves" (Craig 1990, 156). Apprentices seek to acquire knowledge how (or perhaps ability—Craig does not dwell on the difference), either for its practical value or for its own sake.

Admittedly, there are other reasons for seeking out those who know how. Sometimes we seek knowers-how not because we ourselves want to know how, but because we seek someone who can teach others. Sometimes we seek knowers-how because we want them to act as examiners, to evaluate whether others know how. And sometimes we seek knowers-how for their prestige, regardless of whether they will in fact teach anything to anyone else. Nevertheless, the perspective of the apprentice seems central.

Is the apprentice's situation genuinely similar to that of the inquirer? Typically, someone who knows whether p is well-placed to tell an inquirer whether p, even if she is unwilling to do so. But one might think that someone who knows how to X is often poorly placed to tell an apprentice how to A, even if she is willing to try; knowledge how is often thought of as tacit or inarticulable knowledge. Acknowledging this point, Craig suggests that attributions of knowledge how have 'informational' and/or 'capacity' aspects—someone who knows how to A will typically either be able to tell the apprentice how to A, or else be able to do A, and thus transmit know-how by demonstration. Hence the two clauses in Craig's account of the apprentice (quoted earlier).

Craig is surely right that we would hesitate to attribute knowledge how to someone who could neither say what to do nor perform, unless her inability to perform was due merely to physical deterioration. But as he notes (158), witnessing a successful performance will not always enable an apprentice to emulate the expert, and so those who know how are not always able to teach. Yet the same goes for knowledge more generally: even willing, sincere experts are not always capable teachers. In real situations, the inquirer may not know what questions to ask—there are the unknown unknowns—and the expert may not know where best to start. Sometimes the expert may be unable to articulate her knowledge in ways that enable her to transmit it to novices, even if she can articulate it to other experts. (Goldman [2001] explores issues in this area.) There are no clean distinctions to be made around here—what knowledge can be transmitted, and how, depends not just on the form of what is known but on the background knowledge, skills, physical agility, learning (or teaching) style, and vocabulary of both teacher and learner.

In these respects, the situation of the apprentice is relevantly like that of the inquirer. Similarly, both may have difficulties with uncooperative knowers. Any knower might refuse to cooperate with an inquirer or apprentice, either by withholding information or by refusing to demonstrate. Indeed, a malicious knower can actively do damage by lying or by intentionally performing badly. Finding a knower is no guarantee that you will get what you want as inquirer or apprentice. But what other choice is there?

If I want to know whether p, or how to A, someone who knows whether p (how to A) may refuse to tell (or show) me, or else deliberately mislead me—I have no guarantees. But someone who *doesn't* know whether p (how to A) is very unlikely to give me what I want. There is some debate about whether it is possible to gain testimonial knowledge that p from a speaker who says that p, but does not know that p (e.g., Lackey 1999). However, the purported cases of this kind involve speakers who have good evidence that p, yet do not believe that p, yet despite this testify that p. Even if such speakers can provide testimonial knowledge to listeners, this situation is hardly the norm.

So although finding a knower is no guarantee of success as an inquirer or apprentice, it is still overwhelmingly the best strategy where information or skills are not otherwise readily available. The only preferable alternative is to seek a cooperative knower, but this is to narrow the search within the field of knowers, not to abandon the search for a knower altogether. The existence of uncooperative knowers does not diminish the importance of the inquirer's and the apprentice's situations to thinking about knowledge.

Fricker's discussion of testimonial injustice draws significantly on the inquirer's perspective; the close parallels between the inquirer and the apprentice suggest that her discussion might quite easily be extended to encompass knowing how. The inquirer seeks to acquire knowledge from others and may treat them unjustly by unfairly failing to recognize reliable informants; the apprentice seeks to acquire knowledge how from others and may treat them unjustly by unfairly failing to recognize reliable showers or tellers. Yet there are a couple of reasons to hesitate here. First, the kind of interaction involved in the transmission of knowledge how is not always distinctively epistemic—I return to this point toward the end of the chapter. Second, Craig overlooks a further perspective on knowing how, one that may be just as central as that of the apprentice: this is the client's perspective.

3. Clients

I have followed Craig in exploring similarities between the inquirer and the apprentice. There is, however, a further kind of motive for seeking someone who knows how, a motive that may be very central to our thinking about knowledge how. When I seek a plumber, hairdresser, or architect, usually this is because I need the drains fixed, my hair cut, or a building designed. I need have no interest in learning how to do these things myself, nor in finding someone who can either teach or assess others. Perhaps I know how to do such things already but am too busy or too lazy to get them done myself (and I can't reach to cut my own hair). I call this 'the client's situation,' in contrast with the inquirer's and the apprentice's situations.

Craig builds his epistemology through consideration of the inquirer; he extends this to encompass knowing how through consideration of the apprentice (1990, §17), but he overlooks the client. Does this oversight matter? Can consideration of the client's situation tell us anything about knowledge how? You might think not, especially if you think, like Stanley and Williamson (2001), that there can be knowledge how without the corresponding ability, or if you think that ability does not suffice for knowledge how. The client primarily seeks performance, and the bigger the gap between ability to perform and knowledge how, the less central is the client's perspective to our understanding of knowledge how.

Let us suppose that knowing how is not necessary for ability to perform. Why then would the client search for a knower-how rather than settling for a competent performer? This challenge applies distinctively to the client's perspective and not to those of the inquirer or the apprentice. After all, we can explain why the inquirer seeks an informant who knows, not just someone who has a true belief, given that the inquirer seeks knowledge not just true belief and that testimonial knowledge presupposes a knowing testifier. Similarly, perhaps we can explain why the apprentice seeks someone who knows how, rather than someone who merely has ability, if the apprentice seeks to obtain knowledge how not just ability (though see Hawley [2010] for discussion of the limits on strictly testimonial knowledge how).

The client is not an apprentice: she primarily seeks performance, not knowledge. Why then should she make the detour via knowledge? First, the client seeks someone who can control her ability, exercising it at will, repeatedly, and in line with the client's wishes, so far as that is possible. Even if knowing how is not necessary for bare ability or occasional success, it may well be necessary for this kind of intentional, responsive, controlled ability. Second, it may be that knowledge how is easier to detect than is bare ability. Craig makes a similar point in arguing that the inquirer, who seeks information as to whether p, must rely on detecting some property of informants that correlates well with the property of having a true belief as to whether p, because detecting such a property is easier than directly detecting a true belief (1990, 18–19). I return later to issues about how we recognize knowledge, ability, or true belief in others.

So the client may have good reason to seek a knower-how, even if knowing how is not necessary for bare ability. What if knowing how is not sufficient for ability? I have already discussed uncooperative experts who refuse to perform; here the concern is experts who cannot perform. Someone who knows how to fix drains may be unable to do so even if she is willing—perhaps she has lost her plumber's license, her equipment, or her eyesight.

But even if knowledge how is not sufficient for ability, there remains a link between the client's situation and knowledge how—even if some knowers cannot perform, this is no reason to prefer nonknowers. Rather, it is a reason to focus one's search for a knower to those knowers who are able (and willing) to perform, just as the existence of insincere or silent knowers is a reason for the apprentice or the inquirer to narrow the search for a knower to those knowers who are sincere and willing informants, not a reason to look for someone who lacks knowledge.

In this section so far, I have made an initial case for the importance of considering the client's perspective on knowledge how alongside that of the apprentice, which is the perspective more closely analogous to the perspective of the inquirer. We may seek knowers-how for the same reasons we seek knowers more generally—we may want to increase our own knowledge, to arrange for others to acquire knowledge or have their knowledge assessed, or we may simply value knowledge in others for its own sake. But in addition, as clients we often seek knowers-how for their ability to perform; I have argued that even if there are gaps between ability to perform and knowledge how, consideration of the client's situation may provide insight into knowledge how, alongside consideration of the apprentice's situation.

Once we have recognized the client alongside the apprentice, it is natural to return to our starting point and ask whether there is an analogous perspective on knowledge *whether*, one that should be recognized alongside the inquirer's perspective. Knowledge whether is often a central part of knowledge how: the bomb disposal expert knows how to defuse the bomb partly in virtue of knowing whether to cut the red wire first, whereas knowing how to fit in at a formal dinner involves knowing whether to start eating as soon as your food is served. So the client who needs a bomb defuser or an inconspicuous guest needs someone with appropriate knowledge-whether, regardless of whether the client already knows how to defuse bombs, how to fit in at dinner, whether to cut the red wire first, or whether to start eating immediately. Similarly, we may seek someone who knows *where* to buy cheap but reliable cars or someone who knows *when* to invest in the stock market not because we want to acquire this knowledge ourselves (perhaps we already have the knowledge but are short of time), but because we seek an agent who will buy a car or shares on our behalf. Again, this perspective is akin to that of the client rather than that of the inquirer or apprentice.

The distinction between client and inquirer/apprentice is reflected in a phenomenon discussed by John Hawthorne (2000) and taken up by Jason Stanley (2011). There are plenty of situations in which we attribute knowledge whether/where/who/and so on to someone else, but the pragmatics are such that we focus merely on whether the person has a true belief, rather than demanding full-blown knowledge. If I'm interested in whether John knows where to find decent coffee, this may be because I want him to fetch some for me; in such a situation, it's enough that John has a true belief about where to find decent coffee (and that he is willing to help). Stanley writes that "the pragmatics of situations in which we ascribe knowledge-wh often places the focus on true belief, rather than justification." In my terms, at least some such situations are ones in which we adopt the client's perspective rather than that of the inquirer.

Of course, Craig does not claim that the inquirer's situation provides the only possible perspective on knowledge whether, nor does he claim exclusivity for the apprentice's perspective on knowledge how. And the somewhat elusive quasi-empirical status of his genealogy makes it hard to see whether these ideas about clients conflict with Craig's views or merely suggest possible extensions of them.

My ultimate goal is not to pass judgment on the genealogical account, but rather to explore ideas about epistemic injustice and knowledge how against that genealogical backdrop, as Fricker does for articulated propositional knowledge; the following points are relevant to that goal. First, the client's perspective on knowledge how seems at least as significant as the apprentice's perspective. Second, there is a clientlike perspective on knowledge whether (and on knowledge when, knowledge where, knowledge who, etc.). It is not clear how central or significant this is or whether this always arises from a situation in which the client seeks someone who knows how (partly in virtue of knowing whether, etc.). But it is clear that there is a distinction between perspectives on others' knowledge available only to those who lack that knowledge themselves, such as inquirers and apprentices, and perspectives available to those who already possess that knowledge, such as clients (and examiners). As we will now see, this distinction makes a difference to the ways in which we can identify knowers, and this difference can result in different varieties of epistemic injustice.

4. Who Knows?

One central motive for seeking a knower is the desire to acquire knowledge for oneself. The inquirer and the apprentice begin from a state of ignorance and seek informants (or demonstrators) who can provide them with knowledge. As Craig and Williams emphasize, when an inquirer seeks someone who knows whether p, the inquirer does not know whether p and does not know what constitutes a true belief as to whether p. This presents a challenge—how can the inquirer identify someone who has a true belief as to whether p, when the inquirer does not already know the truth of the matter?

This question underpins the distinction between the inquirer's situation and that of the examiner, and it is crucial to Craig's genealogy of our concept of knowledge. The inquirer cannot directly check whether the informant has a true belief as to whether p. The inquirer can, however, check whether the informant is well placed to find out about facts such as whether p, whether the informant has plenty of evidence to hand, whether the informant has a good track record in matters like this, and so on. "We need some detectable property—which means detectable to persons to whom it is not yet detectable whether p—which correlates well with being right about p; a property, in other words, such that if the informant possesses it he is (at least) very likely to have a true belief on that matter" (Craig 1990, 19).

What about knowledge how? As the inquirer stands to knowledge more generally, the apprentice stands to knowledge how. The inquirer wants to acquire knowledge and so seeks someone who has the relevant knowledge; the apprentice wants to acquire knowledge how and so seeks someone who has the relevant knowledge how. The know-how informant may resort to demonstration and nonverbal communication to get her knowledge across, but so, too, informants more generally may need to provide exemplars or draw diagrams in transmit their knowledge.

The inquirer cannot directly check whether the informant has a true belief as to whether p; if she could, she would no longer need to rely on the informant's testimony. The apprentice, however, may be better placed to check whether the supposed expert really knows how to A, for it is often possible to detect whether someone else knows how to A even if you yourself do not know how to A.

I do not know how to drive; nevertheless, I know full well that my mother knows how to drive because she picks me up at the train station every time I visit. A skeptic could challenge my claim to knowledge about my mother—perhaps

I'm being driven by a mule cleverly disguised as my mother; perhaps the car is radio controlled, and my mother merely pretends to drive. But setting these scenarios aside, it seems I know as well as I know most things that my mother knows how to drive. Yet I don't know how to drive.

Or so it seems; perhaps I know that my mother is *able* to drive because I have often seen her do so, but since ability can fall short of knowledge how, I do not thereby know that my mother knows how to drive. This objection is misguided, even if ability can indeed fall short of knowledge how. If I can't tell from seeing my mother drive that she knows how to drive, that is presumably because I need to make further investigations into the source of her ability, the degree to which she can control her ability and adapt to changing circumstances, or (following Craig) her capacity to either show or tell others how to drive. None of this further investigation would require me to learn how to drive myself.

So we can in some cases directly check whether a purported expert knows how to A even though we do not know how to A ourselves. It is true that there are plenty of cases in which someone who does not know how to A also cannot recognize competent performance of A. I do not know how to play the gamelan, and moreover, I cannot even recognize competent gamelan playing. So if I seek an expert gamelan player, I must rely on indirect means such as recommendation and reputation. Yet presumably there are gamelan connoisseurs who can recognize competent performance but do not themselves know how to play the gamelan.

Are there skills for which it is impossible to recognize successful performance without oneself being a successful performer? This looks like an empirical question, one that is complicated by the fact that many sophisticated skills, like gamelan playing, can be acquired at various degrees of excellence. Perhaps there are skills that a complete novice cannot recognize, but where highly skilled practitioners can be recognized by those at less elevated levels of training.

The possession of knowledge how may often be evident even to those who lack it, such as apprentices (who inevitably lack the relevant knowledge how) and some clients. This is worth remarking for at least three reasons. First, as I discuss later, the relative accessibility of some knowledge how has consequences for the ways in which we can think about epistemic injustice in this area. Second, this accessibility contrasts with a common way of thinking about knowledge how. Those who take knowledge how to be distinctive often dwell on its inarticulability, on the difficulty of acquiring and transmitting knowledge how, and on the importance for both teacher and learner of practice and demonstration. (Notice how this line of thought focuses primarily on the apprentice rather than the client.) But as we have seen, knowledge how can be relatively easy to spot, if not always easy to transmit. Third, although I have developed this idea of accessibility by focusing on knowledge how, it also arises in connection with more obviously propositional knowledge, which raises new questions about the inquirer's situation, as I shall now explain.

I see that you brought a coffee to the meeting—now I know that you know *where* to get coffee around here (setting aside weird possibilities), yet I still lack that knowledge myself. I see you arrive on the train from London. Now I know that you know *whether* the train leaves from London Kings Cross or London Euston (setting aside weird possibilities), and I know that you know *which* station the train leaves from; I myself still don't know whether it's Kings Cross or Euston and don't know which station it is.

We can often work out that others have knowledge by inferring from the evidence of their successful action, even when we ourselves lack that knowledge and don't gain it via this process. I argued this in some detail for the case of knowledge how, but the same seems to be true for knowledge-where, knowledge-whether, and so on. We cannot directly attribute knowledge-that to others when we lack it ourselves: "she knows that p, but I don't" has the flavor of 'p, but I don't believe that p.' But the same does not apply to knowledge-wh.

How does this point fit with the Craig-Williams point that the inquirer typically cannot directly detect true belief and Craig's argument that our concept of knowledge has therefore developed to include what Fricker (2007, 114) calls 'indicator properties,' detectable properties of potential informants that correlate well with having a relevant true belief? Craig and Fricker focus on what we might call 'upstream indicators' of true belief, such as being in the right place to see what was going on or, more generally, having a reliable method for acquiring beliefs in that sort of area. Fricker goes on to discuss how, for better or for worse, social status may come to act as a defeasible 'marker' of such indicator properties—we think people from one group are likely to have true beliefs about that sort of thing, and people from another group are not.

My prior discussion placed more emphasis on 'downstream indicators' of true belief; these are typified by successful action of the sort that may best be explained by true belief (or, if we follow Williamson (2000), by knowledge). Your successfully fetching the coffee is good evidence that you have a true belief about where to find coffee near here; your successfully catching the right train is good evidence that you have true beliefs about where and when to catch the train. Such downstream indicators are very often available for knowledge how but are not limited to that realm, as these examples show.

As Craig very nicely shows, the upstream indicators we might rely on to satisfy our basic epistemic needs are just those properties that various epistemologists have drawn on in their attempts to give necessary and sufficient criteria for knowledge—knowledge as true belief acquired via a reliable method, for example.

But downstream indicators are more naturally thought of as consequences of knowledge, not constituents of it: you successfully catch the train *because* you know when it leaves, which is why I can infer to your knowledge as the best explanation of your success. Your knowledge when the train leaves is in no part constituted by your successfully catching the train (although success semantics might complicate this claim; Whyte [1990]).

There is an asymmetry in the relationship between our concept of knowledge and upstream indicators, on the one hand, and the relationship between that concept and downstream indicators on the other. Yet both upstream and downstream indicators seem to play a crucial role in helping us meet our basic epistemic need to identify an informant, as well as helping us meet our nonepistemic needs as clients. The challenge for Craig, then, is to explain the asymmetry: if downstream indicators are just as useful as upstream ones, why haven't they been incorporated into our concept of knowledge? I do not pursue this challenge further in this chapter.

5. *Knowledge How and Epistemic Injustice*

Recall that Fricker (2007) argues that people can suffer distinctively epistemic harms when they are wronged in their capacity as knowers. She focuses in particular on "testimonial injustice, in which someone is wronged in their capacity as giver of knowledge" (7). (She also discusses hermeneutical injustice, which occurs when people are unfairly prevented from accessing the conceptual resources required to make sense of their experiences in society.) Fricker often works within the Williams-Craig approach to epistemology, asking how and why we might have developed our epistemic concepts and what purposes they might serve; in this chapter, I, too, have adopted this approach. Our shared framework indicates a number of ways in which ideas about epistemic injustice—and testimonial injustice in particular—might apply to knowledge how. In the remainder of this chapter, I draw on my earlier discussions to begin this task; much of what I say is inconclusive, but I hope at least to outline the issues for further investigation.

5.1 Underestimating Knowledge How

Testimonial injustice can take a number of forms, but Fricker usefully distinguishes prejudice about ignorance from prejudice about deceit. I can fail to take you at your word because I think you may not know the truth or because I think you may be lying; different ethnic groups, for example, may be prejudicially characterized as ignorant (stupid), as deceitful (cunning), or perhaps via a confusion of the two. It is clear that unfairly underestimating someone's knowledge can constitute a distinctively epistemic injustice, since it involves wronging someone as a knower. This point transfers smoothly to knowledge how—if I unfairly think that you lack knowledge how, then this is a distinctively epistemic injustice, one that wrongs you as a knower.

I argued earlier that we often rely on 'downstream' indicators of knowledge how, that these are often accessible even when we lack knowledge how ourselves, and that these two points apply also to knowledge-whether, knowledge-when, and the like. Understanding this provides fresh insight into the various ways in which epistemic injustice may occur as a result of unfair underestimation of others' knowledge. (I return to the issue of deceit later.)

Fricker raises a number of legitimate concerns about the ways in which we unfairly rely on social status as a marker of knowledge in others (and underestimate others' knowledge when they lack this status)—in my terms, such markers are typically upstream (though attributes such as speaking confidently may be downstream). We might hope that our judgments about downstream markers—successful knowledge-guided action—would be held to more objective standards and be less prone to prejudice and injustice. Surely, if someone gets to display her knowledge in action, it will be harder to ignore her epistemic achievement?

It is, of course, an empirical question how good we are at judging the extent of other people's knowledge how and the extent to which prejudice or implicit bias can affect these judgments. But as philosophers, we can begin to explore the ways in which these judgments and prejudices might arise and interact. For example, it may well be that successful action is sometimes less susceptible to objective measure than we might hope. As Goldin and Rouse (2000) show, when certain American orchestras introduced anonymous auditions—candidates could be heard but not seen—the proportion of women admitted rose significantly, compared with orchestras that continued to audition without screens. It seems that assessors' gender prejudices were affecting their judgments of the musicians' success in performance. (Data on characteristics other than gender were not available for study.)

Another possibility is that prejudice can affect the degree to which successful performance is attributed to underlying skill and knowledge, as opposed to luck or perhaps 'instinct.' In studies involving simulated job applications, Biernat and Kobrynowicz (1997) found that women as compared with men, and black people as compared with white, 'must work harder to prove that their performance is ability-based.' Here, *ability* and *knowledge how* are interchangeable, and both stand in contrast with lucky or accidental success. But philosophers' recent work on the ability–know-how distinction and on the notion of epistemic value could help us think more carefully about this. Fricker is concerned about specifically epistemic injustice because of the significance she attaches to knowledge and knowing; this ties up with the idea that the value of knowledge can outstrip its practical value. Against this backdrop, we may ask how and whether acting out of knowledge how is more valuable than succeeding via luck, ability, or instinct.

I have briefly discussed two examples of epistemic injustice—underrating the performance of female musicians and failing to attribute black and/or female success to underlying knowledge—and both of these focus on knowledge how. However, they illustrate possibilities for epistemic injustice where we use downstream indicators to make judgments about someone's knowledge more generally; knowledge how is often assessed via downstream indicators involving successful action, but as we have seen, other knowledge can also be assessed in this way. For example, in witnessing a colleague's teaching, we may fail to recognize successful classroom interaction or, recognizing this success, we may attribute it to the students' talent rather than the colleague's knowledge when to intervene and when to let discussion run its course.

None of this conflicts with Fricker's claims, but it helps broaden them out. Fricker's work focuses on the opportunities for epistemic (in)justice that arise when we rely on upstream indicators to assess others' knowledge; we should be equally alert to our prejudices when we judge others epistemically by what they can manage to do.

5.2 Underestimating Honesty

Fricker distinguishes prejudice about ignorance from prejudice about deceit. It is clear that unfairly underestimating someone's knowledge involves epistemic injustice, and in the preceding subsection, I explored some ways in which this might arise. But Fricker argues that unfairly treating someone as a liar is also a distinctively epistemic injustice, not just a character slur. This is because being a reliable informant, a giver of knowledge, is inextricably bound up with being a knower, and "since epistemic trustworthiness requires the conjunction of competence and sincerity, a wrongful attack on either component is sufficient for being wronged in that capacity [*qua* giver of knowledge]" (Fricker 2007, 45).

Recall the apprentice and the client, each in search of a knower-how. How might epistemic (in)justice play a role in their searches? The apprentice seeks a teacher, and if she is prejudiced, she may unfairly underestimate how likely someone is to know how to X and/or unfairly underestimate how likely someone is to honestly teach her how to X. (You might think that women are poor drivers and/or that they are devious driving instructors.) The client seeks someone to perform X, and if she is prejudiced, she may unfairly underestimate how likely someone is to know how to X and/or unfairly underestimate how likely someone is to employ that knowledge honestly on the client's behalf. (You might think that Polish builders are incompetent and/or that they cheat.)

As the peculiar notion of the devious driving instructor suggests, this attempt to apply Fricker's competence-sincerity distinction to knowledge how is not entirely successful. First, there is less scope for honesty or dishonesty, sincerity or insincerity, when it comes to knowledge how. Second, possessing knowledge how and being honest typically do not suffice to make someone a good coach or instructor. I next take up these points in turn.

First, honesty. Why, for Fricker, is honesty or sincerity central to being a knower? From the 'genealogical' perspective, the concept of knowledge is understood fundamentally in terms of our need to identify reliable testifiers. Fricker draws on Craig's distinction between sources of information and informants (Craig 1990, §5). When I find out that it is raining from seeing your wet coat, I treat you as a source of information; when I find out that it is raining from accepting your say-so—relying on your accuracy and your sincerity—I treat you as an informant. Unfairly failing to treat others as informants objectifies them, reducing them to mere sources of information at best and undermining their status in the knowledge economy (Fricker 2007, 133). (Moran [2006] puts similar distinctions to somewhat different work.)

Does the apprentice treat the teacher as a source of information or as an informant? I have explored this question in some depth elsewhere (Hawley [2010]) and cannot recapitulate all the details here. But the short answer is that much of the know-how we gain from other people, we gain by treating them as sources of information—sources of information who obligingly make themselves clear to us, to be sure, but sources of information nonetheless.

One aspect of this is that there is less scope for deception in the transmission of knowledge how and correlatively less need for epistemic trust. You may refuse to teach me how to ride a bicycle, but it is difficult for you to mislead me about how to do so; any such deception is likely to be exposed after I have fallen off a few times. I must trust you not to push me under a car while I'm learning, but after a while, I will not need to trust that you have taught me how to ride a bike; it will be obvious that this is what you have done. This flows from the point I made earlier, that we are often in a position to recognize successful performance even before we can achieve this ourselves.

Another aspect of the fact that we typically gain knowledge how from sources of information rather than informants is this: when we learn by emulating an expert, it often doesn't matter whether the expert is intentionally trying to communicate her skill; indeed, it needn't matter whether the expert realizes she has an audience. It may be easier for us to learn if the expert slows down her behavior, but it doesn't matter whether she does this for our benefit or just because she's tired or being extra careful.

I cannot here fully justify my claim that in acquiring knowledge how from other people, we very often treat them as sources of information rather than informants, especially where we are capable of recognizing successful performance ourselves. And the claim is not intended as an exceptionless generalization—sometimes the transmission of knowledge how requires the expert to act as informant, not just source of information. But I hope the claim is plausible or at least interesting enough to justify my exploring its consequences for Fricker's ideas about epistemic injustice.

The apprentice or client may unfairly underestimate someone's knowledge how—this clearly constitutes epistemic injustice. But what about unfair underestimation of someone's honesty in transmitting knowledge how to an apprentice? As discussed, there is often little scope for dishonesty (or honesty) on the part of the teacher—if I ask you to teach me how to ride a bike or drive a car, any attempts to mislead me will soon be evident, since I will be able to tell whether your instructions are helping me succeed. Then in such cases, there is no scope for distinctively epistemic injustice focusing on sincerity. (I do not claim that teaching how never leaves room for dishonesty, only that in many cases there is less scope for dishonesty than in typical cases of teaching that.)

What about the client? The client is interested in finding someone who knows how to X and is willing to exercise that knowledge on the client's behalf. What scope is there for dishonesty in this relationship? Of course, a builder, lawyer, or other expert practitioner may insincerely promise to work for a client and ultimately fail to do so, and there is plenty of scope for financial dishonesty here. In addition, if the client is unable to recognize good work—successful completion of the relevant task—then she must rely on the practitioner's say-so about this (or call in an inspector). But in many cases, a client can recognize good work, regardless of whether she possesses the relevant knowledge how. In such cases, there is no scope for honesty or dishonesty, only good or bad work. Again, in such cases, this limits the scope for distinctively epistemic injustice in the client's relationship with the practitioner.

I do not mean to downplay the role of trust in the relationship between teacher and apprentice or between professional and client. In such situations, we often need to trust one another not to divulge sensitive information, not to cheat financially, not to laugh at our failures, and so on. But unfair mistrust in these respects does not constitute a distinctively epistemic injustice. In addition, there are some situations in which we must take on trust the expert's claim to be providing us with knowledge how or employing knowledge how on our behalf. But this is not an inevitable feature of these relationships, for often a client or apprentice can judge in other ways whether the expert is honestly acting out of knowledge how. Fricker's emphasis on sincerity as central to the transmission of knowledge arises from treating as central the case in which a purported informant says that p and the listener must decide whether to believe that p; many situations in which we rely on the knowledge of others do not fit that pattern.

5.3 Underestimating Effectiveness

Again recall Fricker's requirements of competence and sincerity. The good informant has relevant knowledge and expresses it honestly. As we have seen, there are opportunities for epistemic injustice where we underestimate someone's know-how, and I explored ways in which this might arise. In contrast, I have argued that there is relatively little scope for epistemic injustice focusing on sincerity in cases where we can recognize successful action for ourselves.

But thinking through the needs of the apprentice highlights a third kind of requirement. Not every honest expert is a good teacher. This is especially obvious for know-how experts, but the same is often true for obviously propositional knowledge. On a narrow interpretation of competence, what is required of testifiers is that they know the truth and speak sincerely—that they avoid both ignorance and deception. On a broader interpretation, competence involves both possession of the relevant knowledge and the ability to express and articulate that knowledge in a way that makes it accessible to the relevant audience. Though it's not entirely clear, Fricker's examples and explication of competence suggest the narrower reading. But if we are interested in genuine ability to give knowledge to others and see this as a fundamental part of being a knower, then we should adopt the broader reading—really good testifiers are not just knowledgeable and honest but also talented teachers, writers, or public speakers. In the context of Fricker's book, this raises fascinating but very complex political issues: different social groups may use different styles of communication, allowing for mismatch of style between speakers and listeners from different groups, and different groups may differ in absolute terms in their levels of articulacy, but as a result of earlier injustice, hermeneutical or otherwise.

These thoughts are tailored to evidently propositional knowledge, but what is the role of 'competence' in transmitting or exercising knowledge how? Again, on the narrow reading, this simply amounts to possessing the relevant knowledge how, and so unfair underestimation of this clearly constitutes epistemic injustice. On the broader reading, 'competence' is a question of teaching ability (for the apprentice) or ability to act on knowledge how (for the client). Possessing knowledge how and being able to act on it are closely entwined (even if the relation between them is not identity), so it seems reasonable to count a client's unfair underestimation of someone's ability to act on their knowledge how as constituting epistemic injustice.

Matters are much hazier where an apprentice unfairly underestimates someone's ability to transmit her knowledge how. I may wrong you if I unfairly judge that, though you know how to drive, you are a poor driving instructor, but do I wrong you epistemically? The Craig-Fricker approach suggests that the wrong here is epistemic because part of being a knower is being able to transmit your knowledge. But does the wrong you suffer when I unfairly judge that you are a bad teacher really differ in kind from the wrong you suffer when I unfairly judge that you are a poor cook or are bad at raising your children?

These questions put some pressure on Fricker's notion of testimonial injustice as involving distinctively epistemic harm, which in turn puts pressure on Craig's distinction between informant and mere source of information. There are lots of things we can do with our knowledge, lots of ways in which we can use our knowledge to guide our action—to fetch coffee, catch a train, defuse a bomb, and so on. At a fairly high level of abstraction, testifying is just one more thing we can do with our knowledge—we can use our knowledge to speak truly and induce knowledge in our listeners. But for Fricker, using our knowledge in this way—acting as an informant—is a distinctively epistemic activity, unlike using our knowledge in other ways. This may seem plausible when we focus on the simple case in which the informant knows that p, and says that p—the paradigm case in the literature on testimony—but it is less plausible when we consider cases involving the transmission of complex information, where being a good informant requires much more than simply possessing knowledge and being sincere.

6. Summary

The purpose of this chapter has been to explore how epistemic injustice may arise in the context of knowledge how, though many of the resulting ideas apply to knowledge-wh more generally. I have emphasized the varied purposes for which we seek knowledgeable others, the ways in which we may rely on downstream as well as upstream indicators of knowledge, and the limitations of the 'honesty' requirement in our dealings with one another. Overall, I hope to have illustrated the ways in which taking knowledge how as a case study can help us understand more about knowledge in general, opening up epistemological vistas that are easily neglected when we focus on whether S knows that p.

An ancestor of this chapter was presented at a St Andrews reflectorium; thanks in particular to Yuri Cath and Jonathan Ichikawa for their thought-provoking questions.

13

Knowing What It Is Like

Michael Tye

You and I know the phenomenal or subjective character of the experience of seeing red. What do we know in knowing this? It is tempting to suppose that we know what it is like to see red. After all, the phenomenal or subjective character of the experience of seeing red just is what it is like to see red. So, in knowing one, one knows the other. Unfortunately, this argument is a non sequitur. It assumes that a *wh*-expression may safely be replaced by another coreferring expression within the scope of an intensional verb. And such substitutions are not safe, as the following triples of consistent assertions show:

(1a) Samantha knows the color red.
(1b) Red is what my favorite color is.
(1c) Samantha does not know what my favorite color is.

(2a) Paul knows Ann.
(2b) Ann is who Sebastian loves.
(2c) Paul does not know who Sebastian loves.

The case of Marianna (Nida-Rümelin 1996) makes this point directly for color experience. Marianna is trapped in a black-and-white room and has been there since she was born. One day she is released into another room with a red color patch on the wall. Marianna is not told that the patch is red. Viewing the patch, she has her first experience of red. As she does so, she introspects, and thereby Marianna knows the phenomenal character of the experience of red. But at least if Marianna is in the same boat as Samantha and Paul, it does not follow that she knows what it is like to experience red. How can this be? How can one know the phenomenal character of an experience and not know what it is like to undergo that experience? And what exactly is involved in knowing what it is like? These are the questions with which this essay is concerned.

I

The semantic treatment usually accorded in linguistics to sentences containing embedded questions (that is, embedded clauses that are interrogatives) has it that they are true if and only if the relevant subjects know some proposition that is a legitimate or acceptable answer to the embedded question. Thus,

(3) Rupert knows where the pub is

is counted as true if and only if Rupert knows some proposition that is a legitimate or acceptable answer to the question "Where is the pub?" This proposal is intuitively very plausible, but some philosophers have taken positions directly opposed to it at least in some cases, while others who are sympathetic have supposed that it needs qualification. Consider

(4) Laura knows how to ride a bike.

On the standard semantics, (4) is true if and only if Laura knows some proposition that is a legitimate answer to the question, "How do you ride a bike?" Some philosophers say that this is too intellectualist. Knowing how to do something is simply possessing certain abilities with respect to the thing (Ryle 1945; Noë 2005). It is not a matter of possessing propositional knowledge.

This seems to me implausible. Not only does it fail to come to grips with the linguistic data standardly adduced in defense of the standard semantics for constructions with embedded questions but also it is open to obvious counterexamples. Suppose that Laura recently succumbed to Parkinson's disease. Her uncontrollable twitching now makes it impossible for her to ride a bike without falling off. But she still certainly knows *how* to ride one. After all, if she didn't know how to ride a bike anymore, it wouldn't make any sense for her to think sadly to herself (as well she may), "If only I *could* still ride a bike!" She can't do what she wants to do, what she knows how to do, and so she is sad.

Here is another example. I am not able to read the cooking instructions on the food package. I do not have any reading glasses available, and the print is too small for me to decipher. Still, I certainly know how to read the cooking instructions.

It may seem tempting to suppose that if the present ability is missing, the past possession of the ability is what grounds know-how. Laura *did* have the ability to ride a bike, even though she lacks it now. I *was* able to read the cooking instructions when my eyesight for near things was better. But even this is too strong. Suppose that Laura is an elementary school teacher who has successfully taught generations of schoolchildren how to ride bikes. She has done so not by riding a bike herself, for (let us suppose) she has been confined to a wheelchair from an early age, but by using a variety of teaching aids. For example, she has shown slide shows of children riding bikes, she has used elaborate models, she has brought into class other children who can already ride bikes, and she has explained carefully step-by-step what the various components of bike riding are, using the actions of these children to illustrate her points. Clearly, Laura knows how to ride a bike, even though, given her physical condition, she is unable to ride one.[1]

Some philosophers who accept the propositional line on knowing how claim that the standard semantics needs at least minor qualification (Stanley and Williamson 2001). Here is an example that supposedly brings this out. Jane sees someone riding a bike, and she thinks to herself that *that* is a way to ride a bike. In so thinking, assuming standard viewing circumstances and normal sight, Jane knows that that is a way to ride a bike and thus she knows a proposition that is a legitimate answer to the question "How do you ride a bike?" Still, she may not herself know how to ride a bike.

One way to handle this difficulty is to say that the reason Jane does not know how to ride a bike in the case just broached is that she does not know the relevant action or complex of actions under the right mode of presentation or guise (Stanley and Williamson 2001). What is needed is for Jane to know the action complex under a *practical* mode of presentation.

There is a pressing problem for this view. Just what is a practical mode of presentation? One possibility is that it is a practical concept. But what is that exactly? And what would be an example? I do not know of any satisfying answers to these questions.

Happily, no answers are needed. The supposition that practical modes of presentation are required is mistaken. First, some terminology. In what follows, I shall assume that concepts are mental representations deployed in thought, belief, and knowledge—representations that individuate in a fine-grained way. The concept *the bottle Pablo gave me*, for example, as applied to the last bottle of wine, is a very different concept from the concept *the last bottle of wine*, even if the bottle Pablo gave me is the last bottle of wine. Here the concepts are complex. Atomic concepts with the same referent can differ, too. For example, the concept *Hesperus* is different from the concept *Phosphorus* even though they both refer to the planet Venus.[2]

---

1. That ordinary thought goes against the ability view is brought out convincingly by Bengson, Moffett, and Wright (2009).

2. Some philosophers deny that these concepts really are atomic. For a discussion of this issue, see Sainsbury and Tye (forthcoming).

Consider again Jane. Let us accept that Jane does not lack special practical concepts, whatever these may be. Does Jane really automatically know that that is a way to ride a bike, as she notices someone ride by (where that is indeed a way to ride a bike)? If she does, then she must apply the concept *that* to the *appropriate* action complex. If she doesn't so apply it—if, say, she is actually focusing on the action complex *C* consisting of the biker's breathing methodically and holding his chest out while he is singing and ringing the bell—then if she thinks that *that* is a way to ride a bike, she is wrong. The proposition she entertains is false, and so she does not know it.

Suppose then that she does apply the concept *that* to the right action complex. In these circumstances, surely she does know how to ride a bike. After all, as we have already seen, the ability to ride a bike is not needed to know how to ride a bike. And Jane now has managed to pick out in her thought the appropriate action complex from among the many action complexes the biker is tokening. She sees that that is a way to ride a bike, and in so seeing, she knows that that is a way to ride a bike.

It is worth stressing that, on the propositional view, knowing how to ride a bike does not require a lot of sophistication. Of course, sometimes the relevant person does know a lot. An expert may know, for example, that a way to ride a bike is to grip the handlebars firmly with both hands, balance one's weight evenly, sit on the seat, pedal with both feet, and concentrate not only on the road ahead but also on maintaining one's balance. However, a small child who has just learned how to ride a bike need not know anything remotely that sophisticated. What the small child knows is simply that one rides a bike by doing this, where the concept *this* the child exercises refers to the appropriate action complex she herself is tokening.

In general, what counts as an acceptable answer to an embedded question is context relative. Consider Rupert. Suppose that (3) is true: Rupert knows where the pub is. In knowing this, he knows a proposition that is an acceptable answer to the question "Where is the pub?" But suppose that all Rupert knows is that *here* is where the pub is. Rupert has been blindfolded and taken to the relevant pub. Then what he knows is not an acceptable answer, at least in usual contexts. But we can imagine a context in which it is an acceptable answer. Imagine that Rupert is not blindfolded and that he has been searching for hours for a particular pub. Finally, he sees a side street that seems familiar to him, and convinced that the pub is nearby, he goes into a building with the intention of asking where the pub is. Suddenly, out of the blue, it dawns on him that he is actually inside the relevant pub. "The pub is here!" he announces wearily to a friend. Rupert now knows where the pub is.

Here is another example. Suppose, pointing at the man in front of me, I say to you, "Who is that guy?" You respond by remarking, "That guy is the man in front of you." In responding in this way, you are expressing your knowledge of a proposition that is an answer to the question "Who is that guy?" But this response does not show that you know who that guy is. The proposition you express is not an acceptable answer to the question—unless the context has special features of a sort not yet brought out. Suppose, for example, that you and I are in a hall of distorting mirrors. People typically in this situation do not appear to be located where they are located. At any given time, I can see three different men, all of whom look alike. I know that one of these men is in front of me, one on my left, and one on my right. But I also know that only some of the men are located where they appear to be. I find myself befuddled by the situation, and I wonder whether that guy—the man who *appears* in front of me—is really the man on my left, the man on my right, or the man directly ahead. Knowing that you have managed to grasp how the mirrors shift apparent location, I say to you, "Who's that guy?" You respond by saying, "He's the man standing in front of you." Arguably, hearing your answer, I now know enough to be counted as knowing who that guy is in this special context, even though I may have no idea as to his name, history or character.

We are ready to turn to knowing what it is like.

2

If the standard semantics is correct, knowing what it is like to see red is knowing an acceptable answer to the question "What is it like to see red?" But what is an acceptable answer? Philosophers generally agree that Mary in her black-and-white room does not know what it is like to see red. But of course, Mary does know various facts about the experience of red and its phenomenal character, for she can "triangulate each color experience exactly in a network of resemblances and differences" (Lewis 1990, 502). She knows, for example, that seeing red is like seeing orange but not like seeing green, that seeing red is like seeing purple but not like seeing lime, and so on. So, citing these similarities and differences would not count as providing an *acceptable* answer to the question "What is it like to see red?" What, then, would?

The discussion of the previous section suggests an obvious response: an acceptable answer is that seeing red is (phenomenally) like *this*, where *this* is an experience having the phenomenal character of the experience of red.

It might be objected that one can know what it is like to see a given color at times when one is not experiencing the color either via the use of one's eyes or via a phenomenal memory image. Right now, for example, I know what it is like to experience red, but I am not imaging red, and I am not seeing anything red either.

So it might be held that right now I do not know that seeing red is like *this*, where this is an actual experience of red.

A natural reply is that my knowledge of the relevant demonstrative fact does not require that I now undergo an occurrent, conscious thought deploying the concept *that*. It suffices that I am in a dispositional epistemic state that *can* manifest itself in consciousness in the appropriate demonstrative thought, regardless of whether it actually does so (where the demonstrative concept at play in the thought refers to the phenomenal character of the experience of red). The knowledge state thus is one I can be in, even when I am fast asleep.

There remains a difficulty. The worry is that the conditions on the use of the demonstrative with respect to the phenomenal character of the experience of red have now been so loosened that there is no obvious reason why Mary, in her black-and-white room, should not be truly reported as knowing that seeing red is like this. After all, we may suppose that via a cerebroscope she often views in others the brain state that, according to some physicalists, just is what it is like to experience red. Viewing this brain state, Mary thinks to herself that that is what the experience of red is like. However, she does not know what it is like to experience red.

In my view, the way to meet this difficulty is to distinguish Mary's knowledge in this case from her knowledge when she knows that the experience of red is like this, as she sees a red surface for the first time. This needs a little explanation.

Suppose I see an object from one angle and think of it as *that*. A minute or two later, I see and think of the same object, also thinking of it as *that*. Under what conditions have I used the same concept twice, and under what conditions have I used distinct concepts? Here is one feature that grounds the view that there is but a single demonstrative concept that has been tokened twice: the later use defers to the earlier one, in ways like the following:

- Information from the earlier use is treated as relevant in a certain way. Suppose earlier the subject formed the belief that that is F and is now inclined to believe that that is not F. If she sees that she rationally cannot give in to that inclination without abandoning the earlier belief, then she is treating her that-concepts as the same.
- Information from earlier uses is merged with current information. If she now forms the belief that that is G, she'll be disposed to form the belief that something is F and G.

It is easy to imagine situations having nothing to do with knowing what it is like in which these conditions are not met. A famous example is the case, first introduced by John Perry (1977, 483) and taken up by Gareth Evans (1982, 82), in which a subject, viewing a long ship from one window, forms a belief she is inclined to express by the words "That ship was built in Japan," and seeing the same ship from another window but not realizing it is the same, forms a belief she's inclined to express by the words "That ship was not built in Japan." The beliefs are related as the belief that Hesperus is visible is related to the belief that Phosphorus is not visible. They cannot both be true, but they do not (in her thought) have the form of a contradiction.[3] The subject viewing the ship has distinct concepts of the ship, and that is why the thoughts are not contradictory. The concepts were introduced on different occasions (though close together in time), and the second introduction was independent of the first. This is reflected in the subject's disposition to infer that there are two different ships, for example.

In general, it is plausible to suppose that (atomic) concepts with different origins are distinct concepts, just as it is plausible to suppose that words with different origins are distinct words. Many objects are individuated by their historical origin. Sexual organisms could not have come from gametes other than those from which they actually came. Cladistic classification in biology is historical: a clade is individuated by its historical origin. Concepts are human creations, tools for thought, and as with other tools, they may be used by many and passed from one person to another. Like other artifacts, they have their origins essentially.[4]

Using subscripts to mark the distinct demonstrative concepts, the proposal that the concept *that*$_1$ differs from the concept *that*$_2$ does not demand that the subject a priori associates different properties with the ship on the two occasions. That need not be so. Cases like that of the two tubes (Austin 1990) show that it can be a significant discovery that that is that, even if the subject cannot specify, via a priori means, properties the one referent has that the other lacks.[5]

In the case of Mary, it is evidently a significant discovery for her that *that*, pointing at the brain state indicated by the cerebroscope, is *that*, pointing (mentally) to the phenomenal character of her own experience, as she leaves her room and sees something red. There are two different demonstrative concepts at play in her thought here—concepts, the uses of which are not deferentially connected.

---

3. Thoughts contradict just in case there is a structure of concepts that features unnegated in one and negated in the other.

4. Here I draw on the originalist theory of concepts elaborated in Sainsbury and Tye (forthcoming).

5. Questions can be raised about whether the two tubes example, as presented by Austin, is fully convincing. However, it is not difficult to develop the example further so as to avoid the worries that arise for Austin's presentation. See again Sainsbury and Tye (forthcoming).

In general, there is a perfectly good sense of the term 'discovery' under which someone discovers that *p* just if they come to know that *p* having not previously known that *p*. In that sense, it is a discovery that Hesperus is Phosphorus. The pre-Babylonians may have entertained the thought that Hesperus was Phosphorus, but they did not believe it, or, if they believed it, they did not have sufficient evidence for it to count as knowledge. When it became known that Hesperus is Phosphorus, a new thought came to be knowledge. Let's call this sense of discovery "cognitive discovery."

One might think in a different way of what it is to make a discovery. Suppose we think of the starting point for the acquisition of knowledge as a state of information that excludes no possibilities at all: it's a state that rules out no possible worlds from being actual. When new information is acquired, the set of worlds consistent with our information shrinks. On this picture, a discovery is the addition of a piece of knowledge that shrinks the set of worlds consistent with what we know.

On some views, in the Hesperus-Phosphorus case, there is a discovery in this sense, as well as in the cognitive sense. In the case of Mary, if physicalism is true, her discoveries are not of this sort. However, Mary, after she leaves her room, comes to think new thoughts (thoughts exercising new demonstrative concepts), and thereby she comes to have new true beliefs that are warranted.[6] Thereby she acquires new knowledge. Accordingly, even if physicalism is true and there is nothing new in the world Mary comes to have knowledge about, she makes *cognitive* discoveries.

The upshot is that while Mary, located in her black-and-white room and viewing a cerebroscope trained on the brain of someone experiencing red, does know *an* answer to the question "What is it like to experience red?" this answer would not be counted as acceptable in normal contexts. By the usual standards, the demonstrative concept operative in her knowledge has the wrong origin and thereby is the wrong demonstrative concept.

By contrast, I do know what it is like to experience red, since I know an answer to the prior question that *is* acceptable in normal contexts. What I know is that experiencing red is like *this*, where the demonstrative concept my knowledge draws on originates in an act of attending to the relevant phenomenal character in my own experience. The answer I know here is a *different* answer from the one Mary knows in her room viewing a cerebroscope. It uses a different demonstrative

---

6. Some physicalists hold that Mary acquires new color concepts and/or new general phenomenal concepts for what it is like to see red (green, blue, etc.) when she leaves her room. For detailed criticisms of this way of defending physicalism, see Tye (2009).

concept. So there is no difficulty in holding that my answer is acceptable and Mary's is not.[7]

At the beginning of this chapter, I distinguished between knowing the phenomenal character of the experience of red and knowing what it is like to experience red. The latter knowledge, I have argued, is a certain kind of factual knowledge. The question I want to address in the last section concerns the former knowledge. What is it? Is it factual knowledge? And why exactly does the inference from

I know the phenomenal character of the experience of red

to

I know what it is like to experience red

fail?

3

Let me begin with some general remarks about psychological verbs. In many cases, these verbs are used both with respect to attitudes to objects and with respect to attitudes to propositions or facts. I can fear spiders, like the color purple, and see a cat; equally, I can fear that the plane will crash, like that Cecily is wearing a purple shirt, and see that the cat is shedding hair. Philosophers have often supposed that talk of bearing a psychological attitude to an object is to be understood in terms of bearing such an attitude to a proposition or fact. But it is not in the least obvious that this view is correct. If, for example, I fear that some proposition about an object, x, is true, I need not fear x. Take my dog Quigley. I do not fear Quigley, but I may fear that he has been bitten by a snake, as I see him recoil from a rattlesnake in the grass nearby. And if alternatively I like something x, I need not like that some proposition about x is true. Viewing a swatch of color, I like the shade I am seeing. Even so, in liking the shade, I do not like that the store has no paint left of that shade of color. Nor need there be any other proposition about the shade I like.

---

7. In my (2009), I did not take a definite view on whether Mary is subject to any new demonstrative thoughts when she leaves her black-and-white room. I rejected then (as now) any attempt to appeal to a priori associated properties to pull apart the relevant demonstrative concepts; but I did not offer any positive theory of their nature which would ground the claim that demonstrative concepts with the same referent in the Mary case in the text are different.

In the case of seeing, what might be called the "antireductive view" has significant support. Roderick Chisholm (1957), Fred Dretske (1969), Frank Jackson (1977), and I (1982), among others, have argued that seeing things is not reducible to seeing that things are thus-and-so. To see a thing, it suffices that the thing looks some way to the perceiver; and something can look some way without the perceiver noticing that it is that way and thus without the perceiver seeing that it is that way.

Suppose, for example, a white cube is bathed in red light and that it looks red to Paul, who is viewing it. Paul cannot see that the cube is red, for the cube is white. Perhaps the cube also looks straight ahead when in reality it is off to the right and Paul is seeing it in a mirror placed at a forty-five-degree orientation in front of Paul. Perhaps the cube looks irregular in its shape in virtue of an apparent shape distortion brought about by the mirror. Paul does not see that the cube is off to the right, nor does he see that the object he is viewing has a cubical shape. Still, Paul does see the cube.

The general point here is that one can see an object O without there being any property P, such that one sees that O has P or without there being any property P, such that one sees with respect to O that it has P. This is indicated by the cube example and other such cases of ubiquitous error.

What about the case of knowing? In ordinary English, we talk of knowing things and knowing facts. I know David Chalmers, for example. I know the island of Capri. I know the joy of victory, and I also know the thrill of driving very fast. I know the feeling of anger. I do not know the city of Istanbul, however. Nor do I know the pain of childbirth.

I know *of* the city of Istanbul, and I know *of* the pain of childbirth, for I know truths about these things. I know that Istanbul is located in Turkey. I know that the pain of childbirth is sometimes difficult to bear. I know also that the earth is 93 million miles from the sun, that hydrogen is the first element of the periodic table, and that AIDS is rampant in Africa. Philosophers have typically supposed that knowing things is to be understood in terms of knowing facts—that in the end, all knowing is knowing that. But there have been notable exceptions. Bertrand Russell (1912), for example, comments:

> Knowledge of things, when it is of the kind we call knowledge by *acquaintance*, is essentially simpler than any knowledge of truths and logically independent of knowledge of truths, though it would be rash to assume that human beings ever, in fact, have acquaintance with things without at the same time knowing some truth about them. (46)

Russell is not here claiming that all knowledge of things is separable from knowledge of truths. Obviously, that would be too strong. Clearly, there is a familiar sense of 'know' under which I would not count as knowing David Chalmers if I did not know *any* truths about him. Furthermore, in one sense, I do not know the thrill of driving very fast unless I know with respect to some thrill I have experienced *that* it is the thrill of driving very fast. Russell's thought is that knowing a thing *can* occur without knowing any truth about it simply in virtue of being acquainted with the thing. The corresponding claim about seeing is that one can see a thing without seeing that it is thus and so simply in virtue of its looking some way to one. A stronger but no less plausible thesis is that just as there is a sense of 'see' such that one sees an object if and only if it looks some way to one, so there is a sense of 'know' such that one knows a thing if and only if one is acquainted with that thing.

By acquaintance, Russell himself had in mind acquaintance of the sort that is provided by *direct* awareness and not the sort of acquaintance I have with, say, the city of London. According to Russell, when I see a table, I am directly acquainted with the sense data the table presents and not with the table itself or its facing surface. I know the table indirectly, in Russell's view, *as* the physical object that causes such and such sense-data. I thus know it by description. As Russell puts it:

> All our knowledge of the table is really knowledge of *truths*, and the actual thing which is the table is not, strictly speaking, known to us at all. We know a description and we know that there is just one object to which this description applies, though the object itself is not directly known to us at all. In such a case, we say that our knowledge of the object is knowledge by description. (1912, 47–48)

In Russell's view, we are not only directly acquainted with particulars such as sense data but also directly acquainted with some properties. For example, as I view the table, I am directly aware of a particular shade of color, and in being so aware of it, I know it, according to Russell.

The primary suggestion, then, is that just as one can see an object without seeing that it is any way in particular simply via its looking some way to one, so, according to Russell, one can know an item without knowing any truth about it simply via direct awareness or consciousness of that item. Here, as noted before, one's consciousness of an item, or equivalently one's awareness of it, is taken to be direct if and only if there is no other item such that by being conscious or aware of the latter item one is aware of the former.

Russell assumed that indirect awareness involves inference, and this is why he insisted that things known via such awareness are known by description. But the account of directness just given does not entail that indirect consciousness is inferential. And to the extent that it is not, as (I would say) in the case of the awareness of a material object via awareness of its facing surface, there seems no clear reason to deny that indirect awareness of a thing yields knowledge of it of a sort that can occur without knowledge of truths about that thing.

There is another aspect of Russell's view on acquaintance from which I wish to distance myself. Russell held that "every proposition which we can understand must be composed wholly of constituents with which we are acquainted" (1912, 5). This is sometimes called the principle of acquaintance. On Russell's view, then, Mary, while she is in her black-and-white room, cannot entertain propositions having redness as a constituent. For reasons I have elaborated elsewhere, this seems to me mistaken.

There is much more to be said about the nature of acquaintance and its role in an account of object knowledge. For present purposes, however, it suffices that there is plausibility to the claim that there is a kind of object knowledge that is not a species of factual knowledge. Let me pursue this general point a little further. Suppose that I am conscious of a particular shade of red at a particular moment. Intuitively, at that moment I know the shade just by being conscious of it. I may not know that shade of red a few moments later after I turn away, I may not know any truths about that shade of red, but as I view the shade, know it I do in some ordinary, basic sense of the term 'know'.

Those who oppose the antireductive view of (at least some) object knowledge will insist that in every such case if it is true that I know the thing, I know some truth about it. Such knowledge is really factual knowledge. But what could the fact be in the case that I am conscious of a particular shade of red? That this is what I am seeing (or of which I am conscious), where the demonstrative 'this' refers to the relevant shade? That cannot be right. First, intuitively, it is a precondition of my knowing this perceptual fact that I know the relevant shade. If I didn't know the shade at all, how could I know that this (the given shade) is what I am seeing? My knowing the shade, then, cannot *consist* in my knowing the previous fact. Second, small children are conscious of determinate shades of color, and in being so conscious, they know the shades while they are conscious of them, but they are not capable of higher order consciousness and thus knowledge of such facts as the fact that this is what I am seeing until they are about three to four years of age.

Suppose it is now said that the relevant fact I know in knowing the given shade is simply that this belongs to a surface before me, where this is the shade and I am the relevant perceiver. But again this cannot be right. Maybe I am misperceiving. Maybe the surface I am seeing appears to have the given shade, but in reality it does not; maybe the surface isn't before me but is off to the side, being reflected in a mirror that I have failed to notice; maybe I am hallucinating, and there is no surface before me at all.

What about the fact that this is a shade of red or simply that this is a shade? In the former case, one might easily be conscious of a particular shade of red without realizing that it is a shade of red. Imagine a blind person seeing the shade of red for the first time and not realizing that the relevant shade is a shade of red. In the latter case, surely one can be conscious of a shade of color without having the concept *shade*.

Another possible proposal is that what I know, in knowing the given shade of red, is some fact about the shade to the effect that this is identical with it. But again, what could the fact be? There is no obvious candidate. The fact is that there need be no fact I know in knowing the color. I can know a thing simply by being acquainted with it.[8]

Acquaintance object knowledge, in my view, stands to certain kinds of factual knowledge in something like the relationship that seeing a thing stands to certain kinds of seeing-that. I can see that the gas tank is empty by taking off the cap, directing my flashlight, and peering inside. In this case, I see the gas tank. But I can also see that the gas tank is empty by viewing the pointer on the gauge. Similarly, I can see that the door has been forced by seeing the marks on the door. I do not see the gas tank, nor do I see the forcing of the door. In these cases, my seeing-that is secondary or displaced. I am not aware—I am not conscious of— either the gas tank or the forcing of the door. Nor am I aware of their qualities. I see something else—the gas gauge or the marks on the door—and by seeing this other thing, I see *that* so-and-so is the case. Secondary seeing-that or, more

---

8. Perhaps it will be said that the notion of acquaintance to which I am appealing is insufficiently clear. This charge seems to me unwarranted. It is certainly true that the notion of acquaintance has been understood in different ways, as has the notion of direct acquaintance. On one standard usage, a person *P* is acquainted with an object *O* if and only if *P* has the ability to have *de re* mental states about *O* (Burge 1977; Evans 1982; Pryor 2004). Sometimes it is supposed that this requirement is too demanding and that the ability to have *de dicto* mental states about an object (pretty much) suffices for acquaintance with it (Jeshion 2002). Sometimes it is held that there can be indirect testimonial acquaintance. As I use the term 'acquaintance', the requirement that one has the ability to have *de re* mental states about the relevant object is not demanding enough.

My notion of acquaintance can be illustrated by example. I am acquainted with the color red, the city of Athens, the Apple computer at which I am now typing, the feeling of pain, the urge to gamble a large sum of money, the feeling of jealousy. These are things, all of which I have encountered (or am now encountering) in experience. Where I have not encountered a thing in experience, as is the case with the city of Istanbul and the shape of a chiliagon, I am not acquainted with it in the relevant sense of 'acquaintance'. In such cases, I may have some familiarity with the thing and thereby have knowledge *of* it. But familiarity of this sort essentially involves knowing (or at least believing) truths about the thing, whereas acquaintance with a thing, as I understand it, does not. One can be acquainted with a thing (in my sense, following Russell) without knowing any truths about it.

generally, secondary perceiving-that is a partly experiential state, for it is part and parcel of such a state that something is experienced.

Correspondingly, I know that the tomato is red in part by knowing the tomato by acquaintance. I know that Julius Caesar was a Roman emperor in part by knowing the page in the history book I am reading. In the latter case, my knowledge is secondary: here I know a fact about a thing even though I do not know that thing by acquaintance. Still, such secondary knowledge-that involves knowing *some* thing by acquaintance.

It should now be clear how I distinguish knowing the phenomenal character of the experience of red from knowing what it is like to see red. The former knowledge is object knowledge. It requires personal acquaintance with the given phenomenal character. But it does not require any factual knowledge. The latter knowledge is factual. To know what it is like to experience red, one needs to know that experiencing red is (phenomenally) like this, where the demonstrative concept at play in one's knowledge was introduced into one's mental economy via an act of attending to the relevant phenomenal character in one's own visual experience. By attending to the phenomenal character in this way, one became acquainted with it, and via one's acquaintance, one knows it. So knowing what it is like does involve object knowledge, on my view, or at least requires it. But object knowledge does not suffice for knowing what it is like. The reason, then, that the inference from

I know the phenomenal character of the experience of red

to

I know what it is like to experience red

fails is that the premise demands only nonfactual object knowledge, whereas the conclusion requires factual knowledge.

So that is what knowing what it is like is like.[9] And that is how knowing what it is like differs from knowing phenomenal character.

---

9. On my proposal, knowing what it is like is not an ability. Nor is it knowing how. Nonetheless, knowing what it is like is interestingly similar to knowing how in that both are a species of factual knowledge.

14

Linguistic Knowledge

Michael Devitt

1. Introduction

The folk say that a person competent in a language "knows" the language. What then does that knowledge consist in? It is common in both linguistics and philosophy to think that it consists in "knowledge that," *propositional* knowledge about the language. Sometimes this alleged knowledge is the sort expressed by general statements such as syntactic theories (grammars), truth theories, and theories of reference. Sometimes it is the sort expressed by singular statements about particular linguistic facts, statements that express the person's intuitive judgments about the syntactic, truth-conditional, or referential properties of expressions. Let us call all these views "propositional assumptions" about linguistic competence.[1] My negative thesis is that, with one possible exception, all propositional assumptions are false. The possible exception is that competence involves "tacit" singular propositional knowledge, in some interesting sense of that weasel word. My positive thesis is that, as a first approximation, linguistic competence consists in "mere knowledge how."

I have argued for these theses before (1981, 1997, 2006b, forthcoming-b). Drawing on these earlier writings, my aim in this chapter is to give an assessment of the state of play on the nature of linguistic knowledge.

The distinction between knowledge how and knowledge that is, of course, a folk psychological one captured in English using the very imprecise term *know*. My take on it has always been, in the spirit of Gilbert Ryle (1949, 1945), along the following lines (Devitt and Sterelny 1989 and 1999, 174–175; Devitt 2006b, 46–47 and 50). Knowledge that is essentially cognitive and propositional. So if a person knows that R is a rule of arithmetic, she knows a proposition. Knowledge how is in the same family as skills, abilities, and capacities. Sometimes, it is entirely cognitive, for example, knowing how to play chess. Other times, it may be hardly

---

1. I take it as obvious that propositional assumptions are widespread in linguistics and philosophy. I have elsewhere given lots of evidence of this (in linguistics, 2006b, 3–7 and 95–97; in philosophy, 1981, 95–96; 1996, 52–53 and 172–173; 1997, 268–269).

cognitive at all, for example, knowing how to swim or ride a bicycle.[2] Sometimes, knowledge how may involve knowledge that; for example, chess know-how may involve knowing that the rules of chess are such and such. Other times—and this is the important point for us—it is, as the folk would say, "mere know-how" and prima facie does not involve any propositional knowledge at all, for example, knowing how to swim.

Paul Snowdon (2003) and John Bengson, Marc Moffett, and Jennifer Wright (2009) have made me think that this account is probably *too* Rylean. There is evidence that the folk count a person who can give a full description of an activity as knowing how to perform it, even though the person has no ability to perform it. So perhaps *one* kind of knowledge how is knowledge that. But I still want to maintain that another kind is not. There is a common kind of knowledge how that a person can have simply on the basis of having the ability to perform an activity:[3] the knowledge may be *mere* knowledge how. That is the kind that Ryle had in mind. And it is the kind that I have in mind here.

If we must follow the folk in talking of linguistic competence as knowledge—and I think it would be better if we didn't (2006b, 5 n. 5)—my positive thesis is that we should say, as a first approximation, that it is mere knowledge how of the Rylean kind. However, I have always preferred to say that it is simply a skill or ability, not involving propositional attitudes (1981, 92–110; 1996, 22–28 and 52; 1997, 272–275; Devitt and Sterelny 1999, 187–190). Let us call this the skill assumption.

What skill or ability is competence in a language? Accepting, as we should, intentional realism and the view that language expresses thought, I give the following answer:

> The competence is the ability to use a sound of the language to express a thought with the meaning that the sound has in the language in the context of utterance; and the ability (together with some pragmatic abilities) to assign to a sound a thought with the meaning that the sound has in the language in the context of utterance (similarly for inscriptions, etc.). (2006b, 148)

We can move to a more theory-laden view of competence if we adopt the popular, and in my view correct, representational theory of the mind (RTM), according to which any thought involves standing in a certain functional relation to a mental representation. Competence is then "the ability to *translate* back and forth between

---

2. As these examples illustrate, the concern here is with knowing how *to A* where *A* is some activity.

3. Bengson et al. have conducted an experiment that leads them to doubt this (2009, 397). I am not persuaded by the experiment but will not attempt to argue the matter here.

meaningful mental representations and the sounds of the language" (Devitt 2006b, 148). And if we go further to the controversial language-of-thought hypothesis, according to which the mental representation is languagelike, the translation is "between mental *sentences* and the sounds of the language" (Devitt 2006b, 148). Finally, linguistic competence is complex, consisting of syntactic competence and lexical competence. Thus, going along with the language-of-thought hypothesis for a moment, syntactic competence is the ability to translate back and forth between the syntactic structures of the sounds of the language and the structures of mental sentences. And lexical competence is the ability to translate back and forth between the words of the language and mental words.[4]

Why think that that linguistic competence is just a skill or ability? Briefly, because it has all the marks of one: it has limited plasticity; it is extraordinarily fast; the process of exercising it is unavailable to consciousness; once established, it is automatic, with the result that it can be performed while attention is elsewhere (2006b, 209–210); it is very likely acquired by "implicit learning" (2006b, 219). But shouldn't we suppose that in the case of linguistic competence, the skill involves knowledge that? We should not suppose this unless we have some powerful reasons for doing so. Otherwise, the supposition seems gratuitous. Why suppose that simply in virtue of being competent in a language a person must have propositional knowledge about the language? Why suppose that speakers have this sort of Cartesian access to linguistic facts? Why not suppose, rather, the modest view that any knowledge of these facts that a speaker may have comes from ordinary empirical reflection on linguistic phenomena?

These rhetorical questions reflect a commitment to what I have called Pylyshyn's Razor: "*Representations are not to be multiplied beyond necessity*" (2006b, 51).[5] Assuming RTM, any propositional assumption requires speakers to have certain representations, and Pylyshyn's Razor demands that we posit these *only if they do explanatory work*. The rationale for this Occamist principle is not an a priori assumption that the world is mostly simple, representation-free, and so on. The rationale is primarily methodological:

> If we fail to posit representations where there are some, we are likely to come across evidence that there are some: our explanations are likely to be

---

4. *Represent* and its cognates are used here with their standard senses in philosophy. However, these terms seem to be used sometimes with other sense in AI, linguistics, and psychology (Devitt 2006b, 5–7).

5. I named this razor after Pylyshyn because he urges that "one must attribute as much as possible to the *capacity* of the system...to properties of the *functional architecture*...one must find the least powerful functional architecture compatible with the range of variation observed" (1991, 244).

inadequate. In contrast, if we posit representations where there are none, it may be difficult to come across evidence that there are none, because with enough representations almost any behavior can be explained. (2006b, 52)

Propositional assumptions are very immodest. One would expect, therefore, that they would be well supported by arguments. This is not what we find. Arguments for them, and against the skill assumption, are few and far between and, with one exception, remarkably thin, as we shall see (§3). One gets the impression that propositional assumptions are thought to be too obvious to need argument. Thus, Herbert Heidelberger points out that the propositional assumption about truth conditions seems to be regarded as "uncontroversial...harmless...perhaps unworthy of serious discussion" (1980, 402); Gareth Evans says, "perhaps no one will deny it" (1982, 106).

The exception to my complaint of thinness is a provocative paper by Jason Stanley and Timothy Williamson arguing that "knowledge-how is simply a species of knowledge-that" (2001, 411). Ingenious as this paper is, it is deeply misguided, particularly in its methodology. Or so I have recently argued (forthcoming-a). I shall say no more about it here.

The immodesty of propositional assumptions is a powerful argument against them, but there are others. I start with some in §2. In §3, I discuss such arguments as one can find that have been adduced *for* propositional assumptions. All of these arguments are rather "philosophical" in being distant from empirical evidence. I think that we should give more weight to the relevant sciences. So, in §4 and §5, I summarize some empirical considerations, drawn from the psychology of skills and from psycholinguistics, that support the skill assumption and undermine propositional assumptions.

2. *"Philosophical" Arguments against Propositional Assumptions*

2.1

The case against general propositional assumptions starts from the observation that a speaker's knowledge of her language is so unlike uncontroversial cases of propositional knowledge.[6] Stephen Stich (1971, 1978) made the point nicely against the linguistic view that a speaker's competence involves propositional knowledge of the syntactic rules (or principles) described by a grammar: (1) If a

---

6. Dwyer and Pietroski (1996) argue in the opposite direction. They think that we have such good reasons (of the sort criticized here and in Devitt 2006b) for the view that speakers believe linguistic theory that this view should constrain our theory of belief.

person knows that p, we expect him to be aware of p, or at least to be able to become aware of it when given a suitable prompt; and we expect him to understand expressions of p. The ordinary speaker quite clearly lacks this awareness and understanding for most of the grammar. (2) If a person knows that p, his knowledge should join up with other knowledge and beliefs to generate more beliefs. If a speaker has knowledge of the grammar, it is clearly not inferentially integrated in this way. Consider an example. Without tuition, a speaker is unlikely to have the conceptual recourses to understand even the relatively simple claim that 'NP → Det + Adj + N' is a rule of English. If she knows that this is a rule, her knowledge is largely inferentially isolated from her other beliefs.

Stich's argument would work as well against the philosophical view that a speaker's competence involves propositional knowledge of a semantic theory, for example, against the view, apparent in early Davidson (1967, 310), that competence involves knowledge of a truth theory.[7]

Stich's argument is against general propositional assumptions, but it works better than one might expect against the indubitably popular Davidsonian singular assumption that competence is, at least partly, constituted by knowledge of the *theorems* of a truth theory, by knowledge of "T-sentences." The paradigm of a T-sentence,

'Snow is white' is true iff snow is white,

can beguile us into thinking that this knowledge is easier to come by than it is. If knowledge of this T-sentence is to be part of a speaker's competence, we must take the quoted sentence at the beginning to refer to a type of sound (or inscription, etc.). But types of sounds aren't true simpliciter but true relative to a language. So the T-sentence should really be written:

'Snow is white' is true-in-English iff snow is white.

Now one could not know this unless one had a *concept of English*. So it follows from the Davidsonian assumption that every competent English speaker has that concept. But this flies in the face of developmental evidence that the capacity to think about one's language does not normally come until middle childhood, well after linguistic competence.[8]

---

7. In Davidson's later works, with his insistence that knowledge of a theory of meaning only *suffices* for understanding (1973, 313; 1974, 309), the bearing of a truth theory on actual understanding becomes unclear.

8. See particularly Hakes (1980); Ryan and Ledger (1984); Bialystok and Ryan (1985); Bialystok (1986); Schütze (1996).

Furthermore, we are still far from typical T-sentences. The indexical elements drive us to examples like this (Davidson 1973, 322):

'Es regnet' is true-in-German when spoken by *x* at time *t* iff it is raining near *x* at *t*.

And this is still inadequate: in a suitable context, 'Es regnet' could be made true by rain that is very distant from *x*. Furthermore, this sort of T-sentence is too simple to deal with the problems of ambiguity, which are more widespread than might appear; for example, the sound /snow is white/ can be true-in-English in appropriate circumstances if a person named 'Snow' is identical to a person named 'White,' or if a person named 'Snow' is white-skinned.

In sum, it seems almost as unlikely that competent speakers must have knowledge of T-sentences as that they must have knowledge of rules and theories.

Of course, linguists may not say *simply* that speakers have propositional knowledge of the grammar. And philosophers may not say *simply* that speakers have propositional knowledge of a semantic theory or T-sentences. Rather, linguists and philosophers may emphasize that the propositional knowledge in question is not conscious and "explicit" but only "tacit." Such "tacit propositional assumptions" hope to avoid Stich's criticism. But in what sense of *tacit* could they be both true and interesting?

We note first that these assumptions are not true in the ordinary sense of *tacit*. According to that sense, a person's knowledge of a proposition is tacit in that she has not entertained the proposition but would readily accept it if she did. Clearly, the typical speaker does not have this relation to linguistic rules, truth conditions, and the like. First, she lacks many of the concepts necessary even to understand claims about these. Second, even if she had the necessary concepts, the truth of the claims would seem far from obvious to her.

But what if we simply decide to *call* mere knowledge how "tacit propositional knowledge"?[9] Then the assumptions would not be interesting. As Lincoln pointed out in the famous story, you do not make a donkey's tail a leg by calling it a leg.

However, tacit assumptions do become interesting if we take 'tacit propositional knowledge of *p*' to refer to a representation of *p* at a *subpersonal* level, a representation in some "module" of the mind, perhaps a "language faculty," largely inaccessible to the "central processor" in which conscious propositional knowledge

---

9. Thus in an early paper, Fodor counts an organism that knows how to X as tacitly knowing that S if S specifies a sequence of operations that the organism runs through in X-ing (Fodor 1981, 75).

resides.¹⁰ We might say "the module knows that p" and, on the strength of that, "the person *tacitly* knows that p." But it is important to note that this claim is compatible with the view that the knowledge in question is mere knowledge how. So the assumption should be that where knowledge how involves the representation of p in an underlying module, it counts as a case of tacitly knowing that p.¹¹ And the skill assumption should be read as compatible with such tacit propositional assumptions.

So henceforth, we should distinguish not only general from singular propositional assumptions but also explicit from tacit. And if a speaker's knowledge of her language is seen as tacit, in the sense described, whether that knowledge is singular or general, then that does seem to yield an effective response to Stich's criticism.

2.2

Gilbert Harman has proposed a neat argument against singular and general propositional assumptions (1967, 1975). And it has some force even against tacit assumptions. If a speaker's competence in a language consists in having knowledge that of its rules or truth conditions, then, assuming RTM, she must represent those rules or conditions. Those representations must themselves be in a language. What is it to be competent in that more basic language? If we suppose the more basic language is the same as the original language, then we are caught in a vicious circle. If we suppose that it is some other language ("Mentalese" perhaps), then its rules or truth conditions also have to be represented. This requires a still more basic language. And so on. The only way to avoid a vicious circle or an infinite regress is to allow that we can be competent in at least one language directly, without representing its rules or truth conditions. Why not then allow this of the original language, the one spoken?

2.3

I have raised a related objection (1981, 97–100). It was aimed particularly at semantic propositional assumptions but would work as well against syntactic ones. It is not

---

10. Although the representation of a proposition in a module of the mind is clearly of great theoretical interest, it does seem to me both unnecessary and misleading to call this "tacit propositional knowledge." Martin Davies (1987, 1989) works hard to define an interesting technical notion of *tacit knowledge*.

11. This is what Stich (1980) recommends in his peer commentary on Chomsky (1980b), but Chomsky does not accept the recommendation (1980c, 57).

clear it would work against tacit assumptions. Briefly, a person could not have semantic propositional knowledge without having the semantic vocabulary of some language. That vocabulary is an isolable part of a language, just as is the biological or economic vocabulary. A person could be competent in the nonsemantic part of a language without being competent in its semantic part or in the semantic part of any other language. So competence in the nonsemantic part does not consist in semantic propositional knowledge. So competence in the language as a whole does not either.

2.4

The meaning of a word is presumably constituted by relational properties of some sort: "internal" ones involving inferential relations among words or "external" ones involving certain direct causal relations to the world. In light of this, I have argued against a singular propositional assumption in the process of arguing against a priori knowledge (1996, 53; forthcoming-b). Take one of those alleged meaning-constituting relations, for example, the inferential relation between *bachelor* and *unmarried*. Why suppose that, simply in virtue of the fact that a person understands the word that has that relation, reflection must lead her to *believe that* it does? Even if reflection does, why suppose that, simply in virtue of the fact that the relation partly constitutes the meaning of her word, reflection must lead her to *believe that* it does? Most important of all, even if reflection did lead to these beliefs, why suppose that, simply in virtue of her competence, this process of belief formation *justifies* the beliefs, or gives them any special epistemic authority, and thus turns them into *knowledge*? Suppositions of this sort seem to be gratuitous. We need a plausible explanation of these allegedly nonempirical processes of belief formation and justification and some reasons for believing in them. This argument seems to work against tacit as well as explicit assumptions.

These are a powerful set of arguments against explicit propositional assumptions and should raise questions, at least, about tacit ones. We turn now to arguments *for* propositional assumptions.

3. *"Philosophical" Arguments for Propositional Assumptions*

I begin with two influential arguments for a propositional assumption that come from linguistics.

3.1

Noam Chomsky is irritated by questions about the "psychological reality" of linguistic principles and rules posited by a grammar (see 1980a, 189–201). This irritation reflects a very fast argument that might be seen as being for a propositional assumption. Chomsky points out that a grammar is a scientific theory and so should be treated just like any other scientific theory. And a scientific theory should be treated realistically, for the alternative of treating it instrumentally has surely been discredited. We have good, though not, of course, conclusive, evidence for a grammar's truth, and so we have good evidence for the reality it concerns. And that reality is a speaker's knowledge of her language (1986, 3).

The first problem with this argument is its last line. This line expresses the "psychological conception" of a grammar, according to which linguistics is part of psychology. I have argued that this conception is totally mistaken (2003 and 2006b, ch. 2; see also Devitt and Sterelny 1989). Instead, I urge a "linguistic conception," according to which a grammar is about a nonpsychological realm of linguistic expressions, physical entities forming symbolic or representational systems. The grammar is about the external products of a speaker's knowledge of her language (or competence), not about that state of knowledge.[12] If I am right, Chomsky's argument for the propositional assumption is not just fast but dirty.

The second problem with the argument is that, even if the psychological conception were right, the argument would not be sufficient to establish a propositional assumption.[13] To see this, we need a distinction that comes largely from computer science. It is the distinction between rules that govern by being represented and applied and those that govern by being simply embodied without being represented. This is a distinction between two ways in which certain rules might be real in an object, two ways in which the rules might be embodied in it. Neither of these ways should be confused with a situation where an object simply behaves *as if* it is governed by those rules, for that situation is compatible with those rules *not* being embodied in the object at all.

A simple, old-fashioned mechanical calculator provides a nice example of something governed by rules that are embodied without being represented. When the calculator adds, it goes through a mechanical process that is governed by the rules of an algorithm for addition. But the rules are hardwired, not represented in the calculator. In contrast, the operations of a contemporary general-purpose computer are partly governed by rules of a program that are represented in its RAM and applied. Yet those rules can govern the operations of the computer only because there are other rules that are unrepresented but built into

---

12. My view has received a great deal of criticism (some of it very harsh): Antony (2008); Collins (2007a, 2008a, 2008b); Dwyer and Pietroski (1996); Laurence (2003); Longworth (2009); Matthews (2006); Pietroski (2008); Rattan (2006); Rey (2006, 2008); Slezak (2009); Smith (2006). I have recently responded at length: see my (2006c, 2008a, 2008b, 2008c, and 2009).

13. I make much of this distinction (2006b, 45–52).

its hardware that enable the represented rules to govern. And note an important generalization: any rule that governs the behavior of one object by being represented and applied could govern that of another by being embodied without being represented.

If, contrary to what I have claimed, the fast argument were good, it would establish that the rules (principles) described by a grammar were psychologically real: they are present in the minds of competent speakers. But our distinction shows that there are two ways that they might be present: they might be represented, or they might be simply embodied without being represented. For the argument to support a propositional assumption, it would need to show that the rules are not only embodied but also represented. That requires another step.

3.2

The metalinguistic intuitions of ordinary speakers—intuitions about what expressions are grammatical/acceptable, ambiguous, corefer, and the like—serve as evidence for grammars. Why are they evidence? I take the received Chomskian answer to be that they are evidence because, noise aside, they are provided to a speaker by her linguistic competence, an underlying state of knowledge:

> It seems reasonably clear, both in principle and in many specific cases, how unconscious knowledge issues in conscious knowledge...it follows by computations similar to straight deduction. (Chomsky 1986, 270)

I call this the "voice of competence" view (recently, VoC for short).[14] We can see in this story an argument for a general propositional assumption. The core of a good explanation of why the intuitions of speakers of a language are evidence for its grammar is that speakers have tacit propositional knowledge of the rules and principles of the language. And there is no other explanation. If the intuitions are really derived from this knowledge of the grammatical rules, then they must be true and hence good evidence for the nature of those rules. But if they are not so derived, how could they be good evidence? How could they have this evidential status unless they really were the voice of competence?

---

14. The evidence that VoC is the received Chomskian view is overwhelming (2006a, 482–486; 2006b, 95–97), yet some strangely resist the attribution: Collins (2008a, 16–19); Fitzgerald (2010, 144). I have responded: see my (2010b). Stich has suggested an analogue of VoC to explain why the referential intuitions of the folk are good evidence for a theory of reference (1996, 40); Stich does not endorse the suggestion: speakers derive those intuitions from a representation of referential principles. I argue that we should dismiss this analogue, just as we should VoC (2006d, forthcoming-b).

I have rejected VoC and hence this argument (2006a; 2006b, ch. 7). A problem with VoC is that we are a long way from a plausible account of *how* competence could provide these intuitions.[15] But the main objection to VoC is that we have a better explanation of these intuitions: they are empirical central-processor responses to linguistic expressions. This explanation, unlike VoC, is nicely modest in that it makes do with cognitive states and processes that we were already committed to. On this view, competence provides a speaker with ready access to data, not with any intuitive judgments she makes about the data. Her intuitions can be good evidence because she is likely to be reliable about the simple and obvious properties of these expressions.[16]

3.3

Chomsky dismisses the knowledge how view of linguistic competence as "entirely untenable" (1988, 9) and usually writes as if he endorses a general propositional assumption.[17] He offers an argument for his position that, unlike §§ 3.1 and 3.2, does not depend on his view of linguistics.

Chomsky takes the knowledge how view of linguistic competence to be that competence is a "practical ability" to *use* the language in understanding and speech (hence, in effect, siding with Ryle about knowledge how). He objects:

> Two people may share exactly the same knowledge of language but differ markedly in their ability to put this knowledge to use. Ability to use language may improve or decline without any change in knowledge. This ability may also be impaired, selectively or in general, with no loss of knowledge, a fact that would become clear if injury leading to impairment recedes and lost ability is recovered. (1986, 9)

---

15. Carson Schütze ends a critical discussion of the empirical evidence about linguistic intuitions with this observation: "It is hard to dispute the general conclusion that metalinguistic behavior is not a direct reflection of linguistic competence" (1996, 95). In other words, it is hard to dispute that VoC is false.

16. For some criticisms of my view of linguistic intuitions, see Collins (2006, 2007a, 2008a); Culbertson and Gross (2009); Fitzgerald (2010); Miščević (2006); Pietroski (2008); Rattan (2006); Smith (2006); Textor (2009). I have responded: see my (2006c, 2008c, 2010a, 2010b).

17. As I show (2006b, 3–6, 72–81, 96–97). However, I do not attribute the assumption to Chomsky. Rather, I raise the possibility of another interpretation, according to which the principles and rules are *"embodied somehow"* without being represented" (7). Despite this, Barry Smith (2006) and Peter Slezak (2009) accuse me not only of attributing the assumption to Chomsky but also of basing my whole critique of Chomsky on this attribution. See my (2006c) and (2009) for responses.

Let us start with the differences in ability to speak. Chomsky gives two examples of the sort of difference that he has in mind. The first is the difference brought about by "a public speaking course" (Chomsky 1986, 10). But this is beside the point. The knowledge how for public speaking *requires* ordinary linguistic knowledge how but *is different from* that knowledge how, as the folk plainly acknowledge. The fact that a person competent in a language can gain another competence as a result of a public speaking course or, for that matter, an elocution course or a calligraphy course, does nothing to show that *all* of these competences are not mere knowledge hows.

Chomsky's second example is of the difference between "a great poet" and "an utterly pedestrian language user who speaks in clichés" (1988, 10). But, once again, the difference is in another knowledge how—presumably, largely, a difference in thought—and does not show that knowledge of the language is not knowledge how. To suppose that it is knowledge how is not to suppose that there are no other skills that depend on it.

Consider next Chomsky's claim that a person's ability to use a language can be impaired by brain damage, even though her knowledge of the language remains relatively stable. There can be no disagreement about that. But it does not show that the stable knowledge is not knowledge how because the same can be said of clear cases of knowledge how. A person knows how to ride a bicycle but cannot do so because his leg is broken; a person knows how to catch but cannot do so because she has blisters; a person knows how to touch type but cannot do so because he has a migraine. Indeed, it is presumably the case that exercising any knowledge how requires the satisfaction of some internal background conditions.

Chomsky rightly insists that "to know a language...is to be in a certain mental state, which persists as a relatively steady component of transitory mental states" (1980b, 5). But he writes as if taking this knowledge as mere knowledge how must saddle it with a whole lot of irrelevant features of performance (1986, 10) and must make behavior "criterial" for the possession of the knowledge, not merely evidential (1980b, 5). This is not so. A person's knowledge how can be an underlying steady state abstracted from features of performance. It can be, as Chomsky insists our knowledge of language is, "a *cognitive system* of the mind/brain" (1988, 10) and yet still be akin to a skill or ability. Usually, such an ability gives rise to certain behavior that then counts as evidence for the ability. But the ability may not give rise to the behavior. The behavior is not criterial.

That was my response to Chomsky's argument in *Ignorance of Language* (2006b, 92–93), and it still seems right to me. However, more needs to be said. It looks as if the ability to F cannot be simply identified with knowing how to F because, as we have just seen, one can lose the ability, perhaps even permanently lose it, without losing the knowledge how. We should see the knowledge how as the necessary underlying part of the ability, "a relatively steady component" that can survive where more overt components of the full ability are lost; to take an example mentioned by Stanley and Williamson (2001, 416), it is arguable that a master pianist who loses both of her arms in a tragic car accident still knows how to play the piano, even though she is no longer able to play it. As noted, I have preferred to talk of linguistic competence as simply a skill or ability; that's the skill assumption. However, if we must talk of it as knowledge, we should see it as mere knowledge how (of the Rylean kind). In light of the present discussion, that knowledge how should be seen as the necessary underlying part of the full skill or ability.

3.4

Despite the philosophical popularity of the singular propositional assumption about truth conditions, I have been unable to find anything in the literature that could seriously be called an argument for it. Apparently, it is thought to follow in some obvious way from the claim that speakers "know the meaning" of sentences in their language and from the theoretical slogan that "the meaning of a sentence is its truth conditions." Many passages in the literature hint at this.[18] The challenge then is to construct an argument from these hints that does not turn into a travesty. I made an attempt but failed. The argument I constructed seems like a travesty because it involves a naïve view, first, of an ordinary use of the word *meaning*; second, of the theoretical slogan; and third, of the connection between the ordinary use and the slogan (1997, 270–272). I think that the challenge cannot be met.

3.5

Dummett seems to think that the following consideration favors a propositional assumption: "The reason why we are impelled to speak of *knowledge* here is that speech must be a conscious activity, since it is *the* rational activity par excellence" (1981b, 310–311). Dummett sees this as related to the fact that normally a person knows whether he understands an expression (81).

Speech is indeed a conscious activity (setting aside talking in one's sleep), and a person does normally have the knowledge Dummett mentions; but neither of these facts supports a propositional assumption (Devitt 1997, 274): (1) Speech is conscious in that it requires thought. But the required thought need not be about language. And if it is about language, the thought and speech will exemplify not

---

18. For example, Dummett (1975, 105–109; 1976, 68–69; 1978, 153–155); McGinn (1980, 20); Wright (1976, 221).

the ordinary speaker's understanding, but linguistic theorizing. (2) The fact that we normally know whether we understand an expression shows that this is a piece of linguistic theorizing of which we are mostly capable. Similarly, we may mostly know such profundities as that 'Snow is white' is true-in-English iff snow is white. However, there is no necessary connection between such knowledge and our ordinary understanding. It is possible for someone to understand expressions of *L* without having any concept *of L* and hence without the capacity to have any thoughts about his understanding of *L* (see §2.1).

As far as I know, that is the extent of "philosophical" arguments for propositional assumptions (aside from Stanley and Williamson 2001, which we are not discussing). Given Pylyshyn's Razor, these assumptions need a lot of support. Yet the arguments we have considered in this section are strikingly unpersuasive. In §2, we adduced powerful considerations against these assumptions, at least of the explicit sort. I turn now to more empirical considerations, which I think should carry the most weight against the assumptions.

I noted (§1) that there are good reasons for thinking that linguistic competence is the *skill*, roughly, of moving back and forth between thoughts and their linguistic expression. If this is right, we can expect to learn something about it by considering what psychologists have discovered about skills in general. That is the concern of §4, and §5 briefly considers the psycholinguistic evidence. These sections draw heavily on more detailed discussions elsewhere (2006b, 210–222 and 230–241).

4. *The Psychology of Skills*

The folk distinction between knowledge that and knowledge how is commonly thought to be the same as the psychological one between declarative and procedural knowledge. That distinction originated in AI but is widely acknowledged, frequently applied, and very important in psychology. Thus, John Anderson, a leading cognitive psychologist, writes:

> The distinction between *knowing that* and *knowing how* is fundamental to modern cognitive psychology. In the former, what is known is called *declarative knowledge*; in the latter, what is known is called *procedural knowledge*. (1980, 223)

The distinction between declarative and procedural knowledge also plays a major role in cognitive ethology and there, too, is identified with the folk distinction: "Declarative knowledge is 'knowing that' whereas procedural knowledge is 'knowing how,' or knowing what to do, as in a stimulus-response connection"

(Shettleworth 1998, 5; see also McFarland 1991). Psychologists describe the distinction, rather inadequately, along the following lines: where declarative knowledge is explicit, accessible to consciousness, and conceptual, procedural knowledge is implicit, inaccessible to consciousness, and subconceptual. Although declarative knowledge may play a role in learning a skill, there is a consensus that the skill itself is a piece of procedural knowledge.

This psychological distinction is related to two others. First, there is a distinction between explicit (or declarative) and implicit (or procedural) memory. Declarative knowledge involves explicit memory; procedural knowledge involves implicit memory. Explicit memory holds factual knowledge such as that Washington is the capital of America, while implicit memory holds rules that govern processes, "routinized skills, ... priming, and classical and operant conditioning" (Bjorklund, Sneider, and Hernandez Blasi 2003, 1059). Second, there is a distinction between explicit and implicit learning. Explicit learning is a top-down process that starts from declarative knowledge. Consider, for example, learning to change gears in a stick-shift car by starting with instructions like: "First, take your foot off the accelerator, then disengage the clutch." In contrast, implicit learning is a bottom-up process: we observe, practice, and just pick up the skill. A. S. Reber defines *implicit learning* as follows: "the capacity to pick up information about complex stimulus displays largely without awareness of either the process or the products of learning" (2003, 486). There is much evidence that a lot of skill learning is implicit; see, for example, the evidence cited by Sun, Merrill, and Peterson (2001) that "individuals may learn complex skills without first obtaining a large amount of explicit declarative knowledge...and without being able to verbalize the rules they use" (207).

In brief, these related distinctions between two kinds of knowledge, two kinds of memory, and two kinds of learning are well established in empirical science. As one researcher says, the evidence for them "lies in experimental data that elucidate various dissociations and differences in performance under different conditions" (Sun 2003, 698).[19]

Consider now the psychologists' identification of their declarative knowledge with the folk's knowledge that. There is a consensus in psychology that declarative knowledge involves a *conscious representation* of what is known. Thus, psychologists think that a subject has declarative knowledge of the rules for a task only if she consciously represents them. So the person who has declarative

---

19. See Schacter (1999, 394); the many results cited by Sun et al. (2001, 207); Cleeremans (2003, 492); Mulligan (2003, 1115–1117); Reber (2003, 491).

knowledge that R is a rule of arithmetic must represent that fact in her central processor. If RTM is correct, declarative knowledge can indeed be identified with the folk's knowledge that. And this identification is with propositional knowledge *proper*, not merely tacit.

Psychologists also identify their procedural knowledge with the folk's knowledge how. Since it is central to procedural knowledge that it is not declarative, I think that psychologists would have done better to identify it with one common kind of knowledge how, *mere* knowledge how. As we noted (§1), it is that Rylean kind of knowledge how that is thought not to involve knowledge that. Still, we needn't fuss about this: mere knowledge how is still knowledge how.

Linguistic competence is a skill (set of skills). So we can immediately draw some conclusions about it from this psychological literature. Skills are procedural, not declarative knowledge. So linguistic competence is mere knowledge how, not knowledge that. So the literature supports the skill assumption according to which linguistic competence is simply a skill, not involving explicit propositional attitudes. And it counts against all explicit propositional assumptions, whether general ones that take competence to involve knowledge of linguistic theories, or singular ones, linguistic facts. So these empirical considerations confirm the earlier philosophical ones. I think we should conclude that *explicit propositional assumptions have nothing to be said for them*.

But what about tacit propositional assumptions? These take speakers to tacitly know linguistic theories or facts in virtue of representing them at a subpersonal level in a module that is largely inaccessible to the central processor. This tacit propositional knowledge would be a special sort of knowledge how, and so these propositional assumptions are compatible with the skill assumption (§2.1). Since linguistic competence is procedural knowledge, assessing tacit assumptions requires us to look at the nature of that knowledge.

This is where it gets tricky. We have a long way to go in discovering that nature (Schacter 1999, 395; Sun 2003, 698). The psychological literature reveals a range of interesting ideas but no rational basis at this time for a sweeping acceptance or rejection of the ideas of one or another theoretical camp. It would be nice if there was a firm consensus on one thing at least: on whether procedural knowledge consists in represented rules or simply rules that are embodied without being represented (§3.1). If the rules were represented, then that would confirm tacit general propositional assumptions; if not, that would disconfirm those assumptions. But alas, there is no consensus. There is no persuasive evidence that skills *do* involve representations of the governing rules. But neither is there decisive evidence that the skills do *not* involve these representations. Still, I think the evidence strongly favors the view that skills do not. The evidence is to be found in the literature on motor skills,[20] on dynamical systems theories,[21] on the Gibson-inspired ecological theories,[22] on connectionist theories,[23] on instance theories,[24] on the implementation of skills,[25] and in cognitive ethology.[26] The only support for the idea that skills do involve those representations may come from production systems theories that seem committed to representations of rules in procedural knowledge, albeit representations of a different sort from those involved in declarative knowledge.[27] But, I argue, there are reasons for doubting the appropriateness of this apparent commitment (2006b, 215–217). So I think that the psychological literature counts, even if not decisively, against tacit general propositional assumptions.

This point is strengthened by a brief look at the evidence on implicit learning. Language learning seems to be a paradigm of implicit learning: "Natural languages are acquired with substantial contributions from implicit acquisitional mechanisms" (Reber 2003, 486; see also Cleeremans 2003, 492). And the evidence favors the view that what is acquired by implicit learning does not involve anything so cognitive as a representation of rules. Thus, according to Axel Cleeremans, computer models show that "elementary, associative learning processes (as opposed to rule-based learning) are in fact often sufficient to account for the data" of implicit learning (2003, 496); "it is clear that the knowledge acquired in typical implicit learning situations need not be based on the unconscious acquisition of symbolic rules" (497). Stanley, Mathews, Buss, and Kotler-Cope suggest that the knowledge that is exploited in performing a task is a "memory for past sequence of events related to the task" (1989, 571). Mathews and colleagues suggest that it is "memory-based processing, which automatically abstracts patterns of family resemblance through individual experiences with the task" (1989, 1098). Reber notes that the bottom-up systems of implicit learning

---

20. For example, Brown and Rosenbaum (2003); Mon-Williams, Tresilian, and Wann (2003); Wolpert and Ghahramani (2003).

21. For example, Kelso (1995); van Gelder (1999); Garson (2003); Carlson (2003).

22. For example, Fowler and Turvey (1978); Kugler and Turvey (1987); Newell (1996).

23. For example, Rumelhart and McClelland (1986); Masson (1990); Sun, Merrill, and Peterson (2001).

24. For example, Logan (1988).

25. For example, Yamadori, Yoshida, Mori, and Yamashita (1996); Posner, DiGirolamo, and Fernandez-Duque (1997).

26. For example, Shank (2002).

27. For example, Anderson (1983, 1993); Laird, Newell, and Rosenbloom (1987); Singley and Anderson (1989); Anderson and Lebiere (1998); Masson (1990); Lebiere (2003); G. Jones (2003).

"are rather easily simulated by connectionist architectures" (2003, 487). Mathews, Buss, Stanley, and Chinn (1988) assume something like a connectionist model. Reber points out that even a sea slug can exhibit implicit learning in Pavlovian conditioning (2003, 489). These discussions clearly count heavily against the idea that skills are governed by represented rules and hence against even tacit general propositional assumptions.

So much for tacit general assumptions, but what about singular ones? These ascribe to speakers tacit knowledge of syntactic and semantic facts. The bearing of the psychological literature on these singular assumptions is much less clear. Still, guided by Pylyshyn's Razor (§1), I claim (2006b, 221–222) that the literature, including the just mentioned literature on implicit learning, should make us doubt that language use involves representing such linguistic facts; it makes such a view of language use seem too intellectualist. Those doubts are particularly encouraged by the sheer *speed* of language processing. Much of the literature suggests that skills have fairly brute-causal associationist natures.

I shall turn now to psycholinguistic studies of language use. I don't think that these change this picture.

5. Psycholinguistics

In the last section, I noted that it is early days in discovering the nature of procedural knowledge. So it is not surprising to find that it is also early days in the study of language processing. Jerry Fodor once remarked:

> Very little is known about how [a device for sentence comprehension] might operate, though I guess that, if we started now and worked very hard, we might be able to build one in five hundred years or so. (1975, 167)

Despite years of ingenious and productive experimentation, the consensus is that we still know little about language processing.[28]

But what does psycholinguistics *suggest*, at this stage, about propositional assumptions? I argue (2006b, 230–241) that psycholinguistic studies give further support to the view that general propositional knowledge, even tacit knowledge,

---

28. Some other expressions of this consensus: "we know so little about the actual machinery engaged in human sentence parsing" (Berwick and Weinberg 1984, 35); the relation between the grammar and the parser "remains to be discovered" (Pritchett 1988, 539); "we know very little about the computational machinery involved in language processing" (Matthews 1991, 190–191).

of rules or theories has no place in the explanation of linguistic competence.[29] Singular assumptions are much harder to assess. Still, the studies, particularly the prominence of connectionist models, seem to me to favor a fairly brute-causal view of the speedy automatic parts of language processing over the view that this processing operates on representations of syntactic and semantic properties.[30] If so, the studies count against the view that we have tacit singular knowledge of linguistic facts. But it is clearly far too early to be confident about singular assumptions: judgments against them must be tentative.[31]

What about language acquisition? The evidence does indeed suggest that humans are innately constrained to learn only languages that conform to universal grammar.[32] But, I argue (2006b, 244–271), this evidence gives no support to the view that the initial state of competence involves tacit general propositional knowledge of rules or theories. Even less does the evidence give support to the view that the final state does. A person in the initial state is totally ignorant of the rules of universal grammar. A person in the final state can be totally ignorant of the rules of her language.

6. Conclusion

It is common to hold "propositional assumptions" about a competent speaker's knowledge of her language. These assumptions take this knowledge to be either general knowledge of linguistic theories or rules or singular knowledge of linguistic facts. Sometimes this knowledge is thought of as "explicit," sometimes as "tacit." I have argued that explicit propositional assumptions have nothing to be said for them. Philosophical arguments in favor of them are thin and unpersuasive, whereas those against are powerful. The empirical evidence from psychology is decisive against them, given that linguistic competence is a skill and hence "procedural knowledge."

Tacit assumptions are another story. If we take tacit knowledge to be something that a person has in virtue of representations in a subpersonal module of the mind, then tacit propositional assumptions about linguistic competence are

---

29. For example, Vigliocco and Vinson (2003).

30. On language production, see, for example, Dell (1995); Dell, Chang, and Griffin (1999); Levelt, Roelofs, and Meyer (1999); Stemberger (2003). On language comprehension, see, for example, Tanenhaus and Trueswell (1995); McClelland (1999); Cutler (1999); Tanenhaus (2003).

31. For example, Steedman (2003); Gibson (2003); Pickering (2003).

32. However, Evans and Levinson (2009) have recently made me wonder about this.

certainly interesting. However, I have argued that tacit general assumptions get no support from evidence about skills or from psycholinguistic evidence about language use and acquisition. There is no significant evidence for them, and given what else we know, they are implausible.

It is more difficult to assess tacit singular assumptions. Some may be right, but I think that we can predict with some small confidence that they are not, that we will discover that language processing does not operate on metalinguistic properties of the linguistic expressions but is more brute-causal. So we can have some small confidence that the assumption that we have tacit knowledge of linguistic facts is false. In any case, tacit propositional assumptions are compatible with the skill assumption. If we think of linguistic competence as knowledge, we should think of it as mere knowledge how, not involving any explicit propositional knowledge.

15

Inference, Deduction, Logic

Ian Rumfitt

WITH CHARACTERISTIC CHUTZPAH, Gilbert Ryle tried to carry his 'anti-intellectualist' crusade into the province of logic, long taken to be one of the opposition's strongholds (see especially Ryle 1945, 1946/1971, 1950/2009). Throughout that crusade, Ryle rightly stressed the importance of our various cognitive skills—skills that cannot be reduced to, or codified as, knowledge of propositions.[1] A good logician possesses many skills of this kind; indeed, what distinguishes a master of the subject is not so much his knowing many logical theorems—*knowledge that*, in Ryle's terms—as his knowing how to deploy them in solving problems. All the same, while Ryle could have contented himself with developing these points to amplify and support his claims about the importance and irreducibility of *knowing how to*, he went much further and offered an account of the nature of logic and of its applicability. That account seems to me to be wrong in almost every particular, but elements of it continue to exert an influence. In this chapter, I aim to identify its most basic flaws and to sketch a better treatment of the topic with a view to elucidating the way in which *knowing how to* and *knowing that* interact as we exercise our capacity for deductive argument.

1. Ryle's Account of Logic

What is logic? According to Ryle, the subject centrally comprises "formulations of rules of inference or consistency rules" (1946/1971, 236). These "rules of inference, like the rules of grammar, chess, etiquette and military funerals, are performance-rules" (238). That is to say, they regulate a certain sort of performance: "references to them are references to criteria according to which performances are characterised as legitimate or illegitimate, correct or incorrect, suitable or unsuit-

---

I am grateful for comments by Jonathan Barnes, Jason Stanley, and David Wiggins.

1. For a sympathetic elaboration of this aspect of Ryle's thinking, see Wiggins (2009). In his (forthcoming), Wiggins explores the relationship between Ryle's conception of *knowing how to* and Aristotle's conception of the practical in the *Nicomachean Ethics*.

able, etc." (238). Ryle has various terms for the kind of performance the logician's rules serve to regulate, but the most common (unsurprisingly) is *inference*. Furthermore, the relevant species of legitimacy or correctness is validity: "a breach of a rule of logic is a fallacy; an observance of it is a valid inference. To speak of an inference as an observance or as a breach of a rule of logic is only a condensed way of saying that the author of the inference has made his inference in conformity with or in breach of a rule of inference" (238).

Ryle distinguishes between two kinds of performance rule: Procrustean rules and canons. The inference rules of formal logic belong to the first kind, which "can generally be expressed in brief formulae or terse orders" (240). The "canonical rules, on the other hand, commonly resist codification" (240). The "principles of induction" (Ryle does not tell us exactly what he takes these to be) are canonical, but there are also canons that bear on purely a priori disciplines: "the formal logician himself in selecting, ordering and proving his Procrustean rules of inference is guided by... non-Procrustean canons"—specifically, by canons similar to those that lead to fertile axiomatizations of mathematical theories (241). Indeed, other canons will have been applied, not in devising the optimal theoretical presentation of the rules of inference, but in discovering those rules in the first place. Aristotle's achievement in this area was to begin to "crystallize" performance rules that "were already being applied" (243). That achievement took a skill of discernment, one which surely cannot be reduced to knowledge of a proposition, but which Ryle compares with the skills displayed by similar 'codifiers,' such as Clausewitz (243), Izaak Walton, and Mrs. Beeton (1945, 12ff.). The last comparison inspires a characteristic flourish:

> You couldn't define a good chef as one who cites Mrs. Beeton's recipes, for these recipes describe how good chefs cook, and anyhow the excellence of a chef is not in his citing but in his cooking. Similarly skill at arguing is not a readiness to quote Aristotle but the ability to argue validly, and it is just this ability some of the principles applied in which were extracted by Aristotle. Moral imperatives and ought-statements have no place in the lives of saints or complete sinners.... Logical rules... are in the same way helpful only to the half-trained. (1945, 13–14)

This somewhat deflating account of the value of logic enables Ryle to dispose briskly of what he regards as the pseudo-problem of explaining how logic applies to the world:

> Some people have worried themselves by speculating how or why the rules of inference apply to the world; they have tried to imagine what an illogical

world would be like. But the puzzle is an unreal one. We know already what an illogical man is like; he is the sort of man who commits fallacies, fails to detect the fallacies of others, and so on. The reason why we cannot imagine what an illogical world would be like is that a tendency to flout performance-rules can only be attributed to performers. The world neither observes nor flouts the rules of inference any more than it observes or flouts the rules of bridge, prosody or viticulture. The stars in their courses do not commit or avoid fallacies any more than they revoke or follow suit. (1946/1971, 238–239)

People who construe the logicians' rule-formulae as descriptions of the spine and ribs of the world...assume that a logician's rule-formula "says" something informative. The mistake is not peculiar to them. Other people think that such a rule-formula "says" something uninformative. (1946/1971, 243)

On a right view, Ryle proposes, these formulae do not say anything at all. When he endorses a rule of inference such as *modus ponens*, the logician is not asserting anything; he is not committing himself to the truth of the claim that the consequent of a conditional invariably follows from that conditional in tandem with its antecedent. Rather, he is formulating a rule with which an instance of inferring can comply or fail to comply and recommending that our inferences should comply with it. We see here why Ryle's view of logic was grist to his anti-intellectualist mill. If an endorsement of *modus ponens* is not an assertion, then the questions of whether and how one can know the proposition thereby asserted do not arise. So, in this central area of our cognition, we should not be inquiring into the nature of our knowledge of certain propositions. Rather, we should be inquiring into the nature of the rules by conforming to which we can correctly perform certain mental operations.

Ryle's account of logic is elusive. He offers the reader few arguments but a host of comparisons and similes: all the papers I have cited are littered with occurrences of the expressions 'like' and 'in the same way.' As so often with similes in philosophy, it is hard to know in what respects the things compared are supposed to be alike or how far to press the putative resemblances. In what ways are inference rules like the rules that regulate military funerals? Well, perhaps someone who found himself attending many such ceremonies could discern the operative rules for them, rather as Aristotle discerned some of the rules to which our inferences conform. But the differences between the two cases are more striking than the similarities. The rule that soldiers at a British military funeral carry reversed arms is clearly a local convention; there are countries in which it does not apply. But Ryle, I take it, is not claiming that *modus ponens* is likewise local and conventional. Or if he is claiming that, he needs to give us an argument. The claim is not to be swallowed on the strength of an unsupported assertion of a likeness.

All the same, those with an interest in the relationship between *knowing how to* and *knowing that* will wish to attain an understanding of how the different forms of knowledge interact in the case of logical deduction. Ryle mentions Lewis Carroll's famous puzzle in 'What the Tortoise Said to Achilles' (Carroll 1895), which he takes to refute the hypothesis that "knowing how to reason" is "analysable into the knowledge or supposal of some propositions, namely, (1) the [particular] premises, (2) the conclusion, plus (3) some extra propositions about the implication of the conclusion by the premises, etc., etc., *ad infinitum*" (Ryle 1945, 6–7). That negative conclusion is surely right,[2] and it is also plausible that the codification of logical principles—whether as rules or axioms—must come after we have acquired deductive capacities. But to say this is not to say very much. One wants a detailed account of how those principles emerge from, bear on, or otherwise relate to our deductive capacities. Ryle does not venture such an account. My task in this chapter is to outline one.

2. *Inference versus Deduction*

First, though, we need to clear some ground.

As we have seen, Ryle takes the logicians' rules of inference to be performance rules. Having gone so far, it might seem inevitable that the relevant performances should be inferences. But in fact, if the word *inference* is taken in its primary sense, the claim that it is inferences that inference rules regulate is a mistake. The basic problem is that an inference is not a performance: unlike the railway journeys that fascinate Ryle in "'If,' 'so,' and 'because,'" inferences do not take time, nor are

---

2. Ryle did not contemplate the reduction of *knowing how to* to *knowing that* proposed by Jason Stanley and Timothy Williamson, according to which knowing how to Φ is a matter of knowing that *this* is a way of Φ-ing, where *this* is presented under a practical mode of presentation (see Stanley and Williamson 2001). Such a view perhaps affords a reply to Ryle's invocation of Carroll: Ryle's slow-witted pupil knows that the conclusion follows from the premises, but he does not know that *this* (practically presented) way of doing things is a way of deducing the conclusion from the premises. I am skeptical both about Stanley and Williamson's linguistic arguments for their reductive thesis (see Rumfitt 2003) and about whether the notion of a practical mode of presentation can play the role that they need it to play (see again Wiggins 2009 and forthcoming). But disputes about the ultimate analysis of *knowing how to*, and about its relationship to *knowing that*, are largely orthogonal to the questions addressed in this chapter. Stanley and Williamson will grant that central cases of *knowing how to* differ from central cases of *knowing that* in that the former involve practical modes of presentation of ways of doing things. So an adherent of their position can read the present chapter as an attempt to delineate the practical modes of presentation that are involved in making deductions.

they subject to intentional control. Moreover, *pace* Ryle's position in *The Concept of Mind* (see Ryle 1949, 302–303), an inference is not an achievement of, or an arrival at, a result. An achievement must be something that an agent can try to attain, but it makes no sense to say, "Try to infer 'It is either raining or snowing' from 'It is raining.'" Alan White got much nearer the mark when he wrote:

> To infer is neither to journey towards, nor to arrive at or be in a certain position; it is to take up, to accept or to change to a position. Inference is not the passage from *A* to *B*, but the taking of *B* as a result of reflection on *A*. (1971, 291)

At any rate, this captures one focal sense of *infer*, and throughout this chapter, I use the term strictly in this sense.

All the same, there is a species of intellectual activity that the logicians' rules can be thought of as regulating.[3] Sometimes, a thinker engages in the task of tracing out the implications of some premises. Sometimes, indeed, he does this step-by-step, taking special care to move only to conclusions that the premises really imply. Let us call this activity *deduction*. Unlike inferences, deductions do take time, and they are subject to intentional control. They can also be achievements: an examination question might sensibly instruct 'Deduce Gödel's Second Incompleteness Theorem from Löb's Theorem,' and a candidate might sensibly report, 'I tried to do that but failed.' This sort of intellectual activity is rare in everyday life, but it is central to any discipline—such as mathematics, the sciences, and indeed philosophy—where it is important to draw out the implications of hypotheses in a manner that prevents non-implications from creeping in. Insofar as the term *inference rules* suggests that the rules of logic regulate inferences, it is misleading: *deduction rules* would have been better.

On this way of understanding the terms, there are many cases where *B* is inferable, but not deducible, from *A*. Indeed, there are cases where *B* is inferable from *A* (but not conversely) while *A* is deducible from *B* (but not conversely). White again: "We can contrast 'From your silence I infer that you have no objections' with 'From your lack of objections I deduce that you will remain silent'" (1971, 292).[4] This contrast should occasion no surprise. One often infers *B* from *A* because *B* provides the best explanation of *A*. Thus White's inference is a good

---

[3]. NB, though: for reasons that will emerge in §§3–4, I do not think that the logicians' rules are the *only* rules that regulate deduction.

[4]. White holds that ordinary English speakers respect this distinction between *infer* and *deduce*, a claim that seems to me to be far-fetched. I claim only that a good philosophy of logic will mark the difference.

one if his colleagues' silence is best explained by the hypothesis that they have no objections to his proposal. But that hypothesis explains their silence in part because one of its implications, in tandem with background facts about White's colleagues, is that they will remain silent.

Can we say anything positive about the relationship between inference and deduction (in the senses specified)? Many philosophers write as though deduction is a species of inference, but on the present understanding of the terms, that must be wrong. Since *dog* is a species of *mammal*, every dog is a mammal, but not every deduction is an inference. Indeed, given that every deduction is a performance while no inference is, *no* deduction is an inference. More interesting, some deductions do not even issue in an inference. To infer B from A, we said, is to take up, to accept, B as a result of reflecting on A. But in drawing out the implications of A, one may reach B without accepting it—and, a fortiori, without accepting it as a result of reflecting on A. Sometimes a thinker accepts A and deduces B from it. His acceptance of B is then grounded in, or based on, his acceptance of A, and we may describe him as having deductively inferred B from A. But the deduction of B from A may not issue in this inference. If B is absurd, it may instead issue in the thinker's accepting the negation of A on the basis of the negation of B. But equally, it may not issue in any inference at all. The thinker's deducing B from A may make him aware of a relationship between A and B without leading him to accept, or to reject, either A or B.

One point these cases bring out is that deduction can play the role we expect it to play in our intellectual economy only if it is applicable in drawing out the implications of false premises. Ryle, however, entirely overlooks this important point. Possessing a capacity for deduction, he tells us, is "knowing how to move from acknowledging some *facts* to acknowledging others" (1945, 7, emphasis added). Sometimes he goes further and writes as though deduction were always a matter of drawing out the implications of premises that we actually know:

> As a person can have a ticket [for a railway journey from London to Oxford] without actually travelling with it and without ever being in London or getting to Oxford, so a person can have an inference warrant without actually making any inferences and even without ever acquiring the premises from which to make them. (1950/2009, 250)

Ryle does not say what is involved in "acquiring" a premise, but it appears from the context that knowledge of its truth is required. He would, alas, be far from alone in thinking this. For both Mill and Russell, to deduce is to come to know the conclusion's truth on the basis of prior knowledge of the premises. For Frege, a deduction's premises must be, if not known, then at least asserted.

Even those philosophers who recognize that we deduce things from false premises sometimes fail to press the observation as far as it should be pressed. According to Aristotle, whether we are engaged in "demonstration" (i.e., in drawing out the implications of what we know) or in "dialectic" (an enquiry directed towards deciding between two contradictories) "makes no difference to the production of a deduction... for both the demonstrator and the dialectician argue deductively after assuming that something does or does not belong to something"—that is, after assuming that such-and-such is the case (*Prior Analytics* I, 24 a 25–27). That is right, and deduction often assists dialectic by drawing out an absurd or obviously false implication from one of the pair of contradictories between which we are trying to decide, as when the Socrates of the *Theaetetus* draws out absurd implications from the hypothesis that knowledge is perception. But we can also deduce things from premises that we already know to be false, as when an aged dominie teaching for the fortieth year running Euclid's proof that there is no greatest prime number begins: 'Suppose there were a greatest prime number, N.'

A thinker may, indeed, deduce implications from some premises, whatever his epistemic attitude to them. To infer B from A, one must accept both A and B. But one may deduce B from A regardless of whether one knows, believes, wonders about, or disbelieves A. This partly explains why the basic criterion of success in deduction is the preservation of truth from premises to conclusion, rather than the preservation of knowability or assertibility. Consider the argument 'Suppose Mrs. Thatcher was a KGB agent. In that case, she would have taken great care to destroy all the evidence of her treachery. So no one will ever know that she was a Russian agent.'[5] In an appropriate context, that might be a perfectly good deduction, but the conclusion would make no sense if the argument were understood to be elaborating the hypothesis that we know that Mrs. Thatcher was a KGB agent. In making our deduction, we are drawing out the implications of the truth of the initial supposition, not the implications of our knowing it. To be sure, we sometimes come to know a conclusion by deducing it from premises that we already know, and in §5 I try to explain how we can gain knowledge in this way. But that is not what deduction is. Deduction is a matter of tracing out the implications of premises, whether we know those premises or not, and whether they are true or not.[6]

---

5. Frank Jackson and John Skorupski have made cognate points about related conditionals.

6. Some logic textbooks (e.g., Lemmon 1965, 8) draw a distinction between premises and assumptions. Assumptions can be made, or 'introduced,' at any stage in the deduction, whereas the premises are somehow given at the start. But while the distinction may help to clarify the way deductions are used in inferences, it is of no relevance to their soundness or validity. The logical rules are applied in just the same way to draw out implications of premises and assumptions, so we need not dwell on the distinction here.

3. *The Varieties of Deduction and of Implicative Relations*

The implications of premises that deduction draws out are not always logical consequences of those premises. Consider declarer in a game of bridge who reasons in the following way about a line of play, L, that he is contemplating using:

Either East or West has the king of hearts. Suppose that East has it.... Then, on that supposition, L makes contract. Suppose that West has it.... Then, on that supposition, L makes contract. So, either way, L makes contract.

The reader is asked to imagine the gaps filled in with detailed deductions about how L will play—first under the supposition that East has the king of hearts, then under the supposition that West has it. If the deductions that fill those gaps are sound, then the total deduction will also be sound, and it will owe its soundness partly to its having dilemmatic form. In §4, I consider how that formal feature of the total deduction helps to account for its soundness. But the important point for the present is that the deductive capacity being exercised in our argument is specific to bridge. It is the capacity to deduce whether a line of play will make contract under various suppositions about where the unseen cards are. A good bridge player possesses this capacity to a high degree, a poor player to a lesser degree, and a non-player not at all. It is not a purely logical capacity—although, as our case shows, logical capabilities are involved in it.

Pari passu, the relation of implication, instances of which are traced by exercising this deductive capacity, is not the relation of logical consequence. The implicative relation, too, is specific to bridge. A premise—such as that East holds the king of hearts—will stand in this relation to a conclusion—such as that L makes contract—if there is no possibility of East's holding the king while L fails to make contract *given that the rules of bridge are adhered to*. The premise implies the conclusion, one might say, if there is no possibility *within the rules of bridge* that the premise should be true without the conclusion's being true.

In this simple case, we may define the pertinent implicative relation in terms of logical consequence: some premises will imply a conclusion if those premises, together with the laws of bridge, logically entail the conclusion. So it is feasible to employ here what Timothy Smiley has called 'the enthymematic strategy': some premises X will imply a conclusion B when B follows logically from X together with some further 'tacit' or 'suppressed' premises Y (see Smiley 1995). Even in this case, though, postulating unexpressed premises butchers the surface structure of arguments for no good reason, and there will be circumstances where the strategy cannot be applied.[7] Better, then, to think of our intuitive assessments of argumentative soundness as depending on our ability to latch onto the implicative relation that is relevant in the argumentative context. Having done that, we can appraise arguments more or less as they come.

But if we do think about the matter this way, we shall need to say what is characteristic of our deductive capacities and of the implicative relations that we trace out by exercising them.

Reflection on this problem supports the thesis that implicative relations should have the three 'Tarskian' structural features: they should be reflexive, be monotonic, and manifest the form of transitivity that is captured in the Cut Law.[8] That is to say, where R is any implicative relation, where A and B are individual implicative *relata*,[9] and X and Y are sets or pluralities of such *relata*, we have:

Reflexivity: $A\,R\,A$
Montonicity: If $X\,R\,B$ then $X, A\,R\,B$
Cut: If $X\,R\,B$ for all B in Y, and $Y\,R\,A$, then $X\,R\,A$.

Reflexivity may be justified as follows. Deduction is a matter of tracing out what our premises commit us to; in taking A as a premise, we are thereby committed to the truth of A; so where R is any implicative relation—that is, any relation whose *relata* are traceable by exercising a deductive capacity—we must have $A\,R\,A$. As for the Cut Law, the deductive enterprise of successively elaborating, stage by stage, the commitments of our premises presupposes that the commitments of those commitments are themselves commitments. At least, this is so if commitments really are *implications* of the initial premises, as opposed, say, to things that the initial premises make likely. The Cut Law expresses the relevant form of transitivity, given that many premises collectively imply a single conclusion.

On its face, monotonicity is more doubtful, and in freestyle deductive reasoning, there are many apparent breaches of it. Where the contextually

---

7. If a sound deduction from A to B is always to be representable as a logical deduction involving a suppressed premise, then the logic must license the assertion of a complex premise $A \to B$ whenever B is deducible from A. That is to say, the logic must permit the introduction of an operator $\to$ that validates the deduction theorem. But many logics do not permit this. Only in systems that do permit it will the enthymematic strategy be generally applicable.

8. Actually, the three features might better be called 'Hertzian,' for, as Tarski glancingly acknowledged (1930, 62 n. 1), they had been articulated in earlier publications by Paul Hertz. See Hertz (1922, 1923, and especially 1929). For a rather different—but, I think, complementary—philosophical defense of these three features of implicative relations, see Cartwright (1987).

9. Just for the sake of a name, I shall call such implicative *relata* 'statements.' The arguments of this chapter do not depend on any theses about the nature of these *relata*. See, though, note 12.

relevant implicative relation is that implicit in Euclidean geometry, the deduction 'This triangle is right-angled; so the square on the largest side is the sum of the squares on the other two sides' is sound. But the deduction 'This triangle is right-angled; the internal angles of triangles sum to more than two right angles; so the square on the largest side is the sum of the squares on the other two sides' is unsound. In this sort of case, though, introducing the additional premise forces a change in the contextually relevant implicative relation against which the soundness of the deduction is assessed. In a context where it is not assumed that a triangle's internal angles sum to 180°, we cannot apply the Euclidean implicative relation. Rather, we must switch to another implicative relation, one that takes account of further possibilities that are not contemplated in Euclidean geometry. So far from being a counterexample to monotonicity, then, the case illustrates the way in which the operative implicative relation is sensitive to the context of the argument.

There is a further, non-structural property that it is natural to postulate any implicative relation will possess—that of being *truth-preserving*. By this I mean simply that whenever some premises imply a conclusion, and those premises are true, then the conclusion is also true. As with the structural properties, the use we make of deduction presupposes that implicative relations are truth-preserving in this sense. I said earlier that an adequate account of deduction must account for its role in dialectical reasoning. A striking feature of that role is that deducing a conclusion that we know to be untrue from some premises leads us to infer that at least one of those premises is untrue. That inference, though, would be unwarranted if the pertinent implicative relation were not truth-preserving. Accordingly, I shall take it to be a further feature of an implicative relation that it is truth-preserving.

In further glossing the notion of an implicative relation, it is indeed natural to do as I did two paragraphs back and invoke a restricted space of possibilities. A stands to B in our bridge-specific implicative relation if there is no possibility within the rules of bridge that A should be true without B's being true; A stands to B in the first of our geometric implicative relations if there is no Euclidean possibility that A should be true without B's being true; and so forth. Quite generally, to each space of possibilities, S, that includes the actual circumstances—that is, the way things actually are—there corresponds an implicative relation R as follows:

(*I*) Some premises $A_1, \ldots, A_n$ R-relate to a conclusion B if and only if, for any possibility x in S, if $A_1, \ldots, A_n$ are all true at x then B is true at x, too.

It is easy to verify that a relation defined according to (*I*) will be reflexive and monotonic and will obey the Cut Law. Given that the actual circumstances are in S, a relation defined according to (*I*) will also be truth-preserving.

We often have an antecedent apprehension of a space of possibilities, S, that via (I) gives us a grip on the corresponding implicative relation. We may then think of that relation as setting the standard for the exercises of a certain deductive capacity: a deduction in which the capacity is exercised will be unsound if its premises do not imply its conclusion in the relevant sense. But there is also a converse result that shows how things can work the other way around. That is to say, given a relation, R, that is reflexive and monotonic and obeys the Cut Law, there will exist a space of possibilities, preservation of truth at every member of which is equivalent to R-relatedness. Since, as we saw, exercising a deductive capacity *à outrance* will generate a relation that possesses these three structural features, any deductive capacity is thereby associated with its own characteristic space of possibilities. Furthermore, if R is truth-preserving, then the actual circumstances (i.e., the way things actually are) will be a member of this space.

What guarantees this converse connection is a theorem that Dana Scott attributed to Lindenbaum, but which posterity has insisted on calling the Lindenbaum-Scott theorem.[10] In one form, the theorem says that whenever we have a non-trivial relation, R, that meets the three Tarskian structural conditions, some premises will stand in R to a conclusion just in case they stand to that conclusion in every bisective extension of R. Now given such a relation, R, a bisective extension of R is defined by dividing all the statements of the relevant language into two classes, the first of which is closed under R; some premises then stand in that bisective extension to a conclusion if and only if either the conclusion is in the first class or one of the premises is in the second class. We can think of each bisective extension of a relation as describing a possible circumstance as fully as the relevant language permits; a statement will then belong to the first of the two classes defined by the bisection just in case it is true at that possibility. We can also think of the totality of such bisective extensions as corresponding to the totality of possibilities that respect the underlying relation R. On this interpretation, the Lindenbaum-Scott theorem says that some premises stand in R to a conclusion if and only if the conclusion is true at every one of these possibilities at which all the premises are true. So the theorem guarantees the existence of a space of possibilities S for which (I) holds. Given also that R is truth-preserving, it follows that the actual circumstances will belong to this space. For this gloss on the Lindenbaum-Scott theorem to be legitimate, the underlying implicative relation must apply between things that are merely supposed to be true, as well between things that really are true. But I argued earlier that we should allow this, a

---

10. See proposition 1.3 of Scott (1974). For the version of the theorem employed here, see Koslow (1992, 50–51).

decision that our bridge example confirms, for of the two suppositions made in the course of that argument—that East holds the king of hearts and that West holds it—one must be false.

A judgment that certain premises imply a conclusion must be distinguished from the deduction of the conclusion from those premises. And it is the deduction that comes first. By applying one of our deductive capacities, we deduce a conclusion from premises known or assumed and thereby discover that the premises stand to the conclusion in the implicative relation that corresponds to that capacity. Deduction is the basic method of discovering instances of implication.

Scott (1974) writes of deductions issuing in 'conditional assertions,' and some such notion is apposite here. On the strength of a deduction of B from the assumptions $A_1, \ldots, A_n$, we may say: 'Given all of $A_1, \ldots, A_n$, we have B' or 'B, on the assumptions $A_1, \ldots, A_n$.' Some have found the notion of a conditional assertion obscure, but we may understand it by way of a natural generalization of the norms for the speech act of outright assertion. An outright assertion is governed (at least) by the norm of truth: one should not assert B when B is not true. In making an assertion, we present ourselves as conforming to this norm, even if we breach it. A conditional assertion is governed by the corresponding conditional norm: one should not assert B, on the assumptions $A_1, \ldots, A_n$, when all of $A_1, \ldots, A_n$ are true and B is not true. This norm is appropriate for the speech act in which a deduction issues, for the implicative relation that the deduction traces out is assumed to be truth-preserving, so a sound deduction does indeed exclude the case where all the A_i are true and B is not.

Scott took these conditional assertions to be what Gentzen expressed by his sequents or *Sequenzen*. I shall not try to decide how faithfully this reading captures Gentzen's intentions, but let us write 'B, on the assumptions $A_1, \ldots, A_n$' as

$$A_1, \ldots, A_n : B.$$

Pace Scott, though, the colon here is not a sign for a relation. 'East has the king of hearts: L will make contract' means 'L will make contract, on the assumption that East has the king of hearts'; it is a conditional assertion that L will make contract. It does not mean 'The conclusion "L will make contract" is implied by the premise "East has the king of hearts,"' which is an outright, unconditional assertion that the conclusion stands in a certain logical relationship to the premise. All the same, when using the colon, some implicative relation is to be taken as understood—from the conversational context or background—as setting the standard for making the conditional assertion; this relation will meet the conditions specified earlier.

Scott's metalogical reading of the colon permits him to follow Gentzen further and allow more than one formula to appear after the colon, in the 'succedent' of the sequent. Thus for Scott, the general form of a conditional assertion is '$A_1,\ldots, A_n : B_1,\ldots, B_m$.' He understands this to mean: "*whenever* all the statements $[A_1,\ldots, A_n]$ are true under a consistent valuation, *then* at least one [statement in $B_1,\ldots, B_m$] must be true also" (Scott 1974, 417, emphasis in original). Scott's explanation of '$A_1,\ldots, A_n : B_1,\ldots, B_m$' is fine in its own terms. But it endows the *explanandum* with the sense of a metalogical statement, one that says that a certain relation obtains between the set (or plurality) of premises $A_1,\ldots, A_n$, and the set (or plurality) of conclusions $B_1,\ldots, B_m$. And to assign such a sense is to change the subject from deductions. In making a deduction, we do not merely identify a finite set of conclusions, one or more of which must be true if all the premises are true. Rather, we elaborate those premises—the deduction's initial assumptions—by making specific further assertions within their scope. (While some deductions terminate in a disjunctive conclusion, such a piece of reasoning is adequately represented in the form $A_1,\ldots, A_n : B_1 \vee \ldots \vee B_m$.) For this reason, I confine the subsequent analysis to conditional assertions with a single statement as succedent. Although Scott's own proof of the Lindenbaum-Scott theorem was for the multiple-conclusion case, it is straightforwardly adapted to systems that permit only single conclusions (see Koslow 1992). So for present purposes, we lose no formal power, but maintain the connection with our topic of deduction, by restricting ourselves to succedents with only one member.

4. *The Role of Logic*

How does a thinker's specifically *logical* capability relate to these various deductive capacities?

In addressing this question, it helps to begin by comparing the argument given at the start of §3 with the following deduction, which a judge might make in deciding an insurance case:

> Either the deceased committed suicide, or he went skiing alone off-piste. Suppose that he committed suicide.... Then, on that supposition, his cover is void. Suppose on the other hand that he went skiing alone off-piste.... Then, on that supposition, he was reckless and his cover is void. So, either way, his cover is void.

Here the gaps are to be filled with legal deductions—that is, with exercises of a deductive capacity that lawyers possess but non-lawyers lack; the premises of these subsidiary deductions will include the terms of the relevant insurance policy. This second deductive capacity is quite different from that possessed by a good bridge player (although a single person may possess both), but the two capacities share certain features. In particular, we may think of the legal capacity, too, as answering to a topic-specific implicative relation. Jones's having given Smith £10 in return for Smith's undertaking to deliver certain goods by October 1, together with Smith's failure to deliver those goods by that date, may be said to imply Smith's liability to compensate Jones for the losses he incurred because of that failure. As before, this is not logical entailment: it is logically possible for Smith to behave in that way without incurring any liability. Rather, it is a relation whose extent is determined by the laws and the precedents of the pertinent jurisdiction.[11]

Our two arguments share a dilemmatic form and owe their soundness in part to their having that form. But how does a thinker's mastery of dilemmatic argument help him produce sound deductions? The natural—and, I think, correct—answer runs as follows. In each of our cases, the thinker's possession of a certain topic-specific deductive capacity enables him soundly to deduce a conclusion from each of two premises. His mastery of dilemmatic argument then enables him to splice these two deductions together to produce a new sound argument whose premise is the disjunction of the premises of its components. The new composite argument is in each case as topic-specific as its parts: in the one case, it is an argument in bridge; in the other, it is a legal deduction. A thinker's logical competence, one might say, consists in an ability to splice together deductions in various fields to produce new, more complex deductions in those fields. Logical competence, on this view, is a higher order intellectual capacity: its application yields new deductive capacities from old.

A thinker will possess this higher-order capacity if, in producing new deductive capacities from old, he reliably conforms to certain easily statable rules. And if the colon of the sequent is understood as in §3, these rules are well formalized as the rules of a sequent calculus—or, more exactly, as the rules of a sequent calculus with single-member succedents. Thus the rule that is applied in both of our dilemmatic arguments may be schematized as follows:

(1) $$\frac{X, A: C \qquad Y, B: C}{X, Y, A \vee B: C}$$

Here, A, B, and C are arbitrary single formulae, X and Y are arbitrary sets of formulae, and the horizontal line is read as 'so' or 'therefore.' Again, I do not claim

---

11. For more about dilemmatic arguments in the law, see Rumfitt (2010b).

that Gentzen had this interpretation in mind when he showed how to formalize classical and intuitionist logics as sequent calculi (see Gentzen 1935). All the same, a classical logician will accept the classical sequent rules as sound when they are interpreted as general rules for moving from deductions, or conditional assertions, in a given field to other deductions in that field, so long as the implicative relation corresponding to the relevant deductive capacity is held constant throughout the derivation, and so long as it meets our conditions on implicative relations.[12] In particular, nothing in this way of formalizing logic requires that the colon should be taken to signify a notion of specifically logical deduction. On this conception, logical rules are generally applicable rules for forming new deductions from old, not rules that regulate the activity of specifically logical deduction.

This seems to me to be a significant advantage of the account, for it is not obvious in advance of theory what the activity of specifically logical deduction is supposed to be. In particular, it is unclear in advance of theory which implicative relation specifically logical deduction is supposed to be tracing. In the famous passage where he appropriated the word *entails* from the lawyers to signify the relation of broadly logical consequence, G. E. Moore wrote that we shall

> be able to say truly that '*p* entails *q*' when and only when we are able to say truly that '*q* follows from *p*', . . in the sense in which the conclusion of a syllogism in Barbara follows from the two premises, taken as one conjunctive proposition; or in which the proposition 'This is coloured' follows from 'This is red'. (1922, 291)

Despite the gloss, though, it is hard to be sure what relation Moore had in mind. I know of no logical system that validates the deduction 'This is red; so this is coloured,' and the variety of implicative relations that our ordinary term *follows* signifies on different occasions of use means that a precise apprehension of broadly logical consequence cannot be recovered directly from our understanding of that term.

All the same, even in advance of any delineation of specifically logical deduction, our conception of logical rules makes it easy to see why logic is useful. Being able to deduce conclusions from premises is clearly useful, if only because it often shows that one or another of those premises is false. So any thinker will benefit

---

12. A classical logician may, though, worry about how completeness is to be secured, given that we are eschewing many-membered succedents. In Gentzen's sequent calculus, the operational rules yield intuitionist logic when the system is restricted to single-member succedents; he obtains full classical logic by allowing succedents containing more than one statement. However, we can obtain classical logic with single-member succedents if we take the *relata* of implicative relations to comprise rejections of propositions as false, as well as acceptances of them as true; this is the approach that I recommend to a classical logician in Rumfitt (2000).

from mastering generally applicable techniques for extending his deductive capacities. On the recommended conception, mastery of the logical rules provides such techniques. In learning to reason about physics, say, a thinker may start with a rather limited deductive capacity. We may pretend, just for simplicity, that his competence in this area is confined to deductions in the form: 'A resultant force is acting on body *a*; so *a* is accelerating.' But if the thinker can reliably contrapose, then his competence will extend to that wider deductive capacity that takes one from the premise 'Body *a* is not accelerating' to the conclusion 'No resultant force is acting on body *a*.' What is more, mastery of contraposition, and of other logical rules, also expands his deductive capacities in other fields—indeed, in *all* other fields, given that the logical particles such as 'not' and 'all' are ubiquitous. The theorems of logic may convey no substantive information, but mastery of logical rules expands all a thinker's deductive capacities. Techniques are no less valuable for being applicable only indirectly.

Formula (1) is a rule, not a statement, so it cannot be assessed as true or as false. However, its correctness presupposes the truth of a logical law. Rule (1) will be generally applicable in producing correct new deductions from old only if the following law is true:

(2) Whatever implicative relation R may be, if X, A stand in R to C, and Y, B stand in R to C, then X and Y together with any disjunction of A with B also stand in R to C.

Formula (2) expresses the logical law of dilemma, and it illustrates a general thesis: at least in the first instance, logical laws do not characterize some more or less elusive relation of specifically logical consequence. Rather, they are general laws governing *all* implicative relations. What is transcendent about the law of dilemma is not that it specially concerns some favored relation of logical entailment (although, if there is such a relation, the law will apply to it a fortiori). Rather, its transcendence lies in its concerning *any* implicative relation, whether it be implication in bridge, in the law, or in anything else. Of course, we are not entitled to assert a general law such as (2) simply on the strength of a couple of favorable cases; apparent counterexamples need to be considered, too. In recent discussions, cases involving vagueness and quantum mechanical indeterminacy have been pressed against (2). I cannot discuss these challenges here, but I have tried to show elsewhere how the pressure to restrict law of dilemma when reasoning with vague concepts can be resisted.[13]

---

13. See Rumfitt (forthcoming). See also Rumfitt (2010b), which defends the law of dilemma against a rather different challenge, due to Colin Radford (1985).

On the conception of the subject that I am recommending, the basic logical laws will be highly general. Thus, in a sequent calculus in which one and only one formula appears on the right of the colon, the standard rule for introducing the conditional on the left of the colon (i.e., for constructing deductions with a conditional premise) is:

(3) $$\frac{X, B: C \qquad Y: A}{X, Y, A \rightarrow B: C}$$

The correctness of rule (3) presupposes the following law:

(4) Whatever implicative relation R may be, if X together with B stands in R to C, and Y stands in R to A, then X and Y together with any conditional whose antecedent is A and whose consequent is B will stand in R to C.

Now in the special case where X is empty, where Y is a singleton whose only member is A, and where C is identical with B, rule (3) reduces to

(5) $$\frac{B: B \qquad A: A}{A, A \rightarrow B: B}$$

Given that every implicative relation is reflexive, the conditions above the line will be fulfilled no matter which relation sets the standard for the conditional assertions that the colon signifies, so the special case reduces further to:

(6) $$\frac{}{A, A \rightarrow B: B}$$

Rule (6) is *modus ponens*, and it presupposes the truth of the following law:

(7) Whatever implication relation R may be, a statement B stands in R to any pair of statements comprising A, together with the conditional statement whose antecedent is A and whose consequent is B.

Note that (7)—the traditional logical law of detachment—follows from the more general law (4).

Although I have emphasized the variety of implicative relations that our ordinary deductions trace, the last paragraph points the way to a principled identification of a relation of specifically logical consequence.[14] Law (4) tells us that if certain deductions are sound (by the standards laid down by a given implicative relation), then a related deduction will also be sound (when assessed by the same standards). Some deductions will be sound, though, whatever implicative relation provides the standard for assessing soundness; the conclusion of such a deduction may be said to follow logically from its premises. From (6), we have that, whatever implicative relation sets the standard for assessing soundness, a deduction by *modus ponens* is sound. So the present account yields the reassuring conclusion that in an instance of *modus ponens*, the conclusion follows logically from the premises. Gentzen's way of formalizing logic has accustomed people to the idea that logical truths are simply the by-products of logical rules—by-products that arise when all the suppositions on which a conclusion rests have been discharged.[15] Our analysis has taken us further in the same direction. On the conception I am recommending, the classification of deductions as logically valid is itself a by-product of yet more general principles that tell us which deductions stand or fall together when assessed against a given implicative relation. Ascriptions of logical validity are just a limiting case of this wider, relational concern.

5. *Knowledge by Deduction*

Ryle was wrong, I argued earlier, to say that a deduction must start from facts, or known facts. But we sometimes deduce things from premises that we know, and we value our deductive capacities in part because we can gain knowledge by applying them. So we also need to consider the role that deduction plays in expanding our propositional knowledge.

In some cases, a deductive capacity enables a thinker to gain knowledge that he could not otherwise attain. Suppose I am strapped to the chair in my study. From that chair, I cannot see the street below. I do, however, see that it is raining,

---

14. The relation identified here, though, is 'narrow' logical consequence, not the broader notion invoked by Moore. For an elucidation of that broader notion consonant with the present account of the narrow notion, see Rumfitt (2010a).

15. Thus Michael Dummett: "The first to correct this distorted perspective [in which a logic is conceived primarily as a collection of logical truths], and to abandon the analogy between a formalization of logic and an axiomatic theory, was Gentzen...In a sequent calculus or natural deduction formalization of logic, the recognition of statements as logically true does not occupy a central place...The generation of logical truths is thus reduced to its proper, subsidiary, role, as a by-product, not the core, of logic" (1981a, 433–434).

and thus know that it is raining. Moreover, I know, ultimately on inductive grounds, that if it is raining, the street is wet. Accordingly, I reason as follows:

1. It is raining.
2. If it is raining, the street is wet.

So,

3. The street is wet.[16]

In this case, exercising my deductive capacity has brought me knowledge that (in my current position) I could not otherwise have attained. In making the deduction, I come to know that the street is wet. Ex hypothesi, though, I cannot see the street, so I cannot come to know the conclusion simply by exercising my perceptual capacities, which is how I came to know the first premise. Similarly, I cannot come to know the conclusion on general inductive grounds, which is how I came to know the second premise. Even in England, so pessimistic a view of the weather (or of the wastefulness of the water companies) would not yield knowledge. But by exercising my deductive capacity on the knowledge delivered by perception and induction, I can come to know something that I could not know on either of those bases severally.

All the same, cases such as this raise a question. In our example and in others like it, exercising a deductive capacity certainly yields a belief. But under what conditions does belief in a deduction's conclusion qualify as knowledge?

A natural first shot at stating those conditions—a shot, I shall argue, that is rather better than many now suppose—is what we may call the Deduction Principle:

(DP) If a thinker knows some premises, and comes to believe a conclusion by competently deducing it from those premises, while retaining knowledge of the premises throughout the deduction, then he knows the conclusion.[17]

We clearly need a clause requiring that the thinker should continue to know the premises: if his knowledge of the premises were to be destroyed by misleading counterevidence acquired in the course of making the deduction, then we should not count his belief in the conclusion as knowledge. And we have, I think, enough

---

16. We need not worry what the pertinent implicative relation is. If the rule for introducing → on the left is accepted as regulating the deductive employment of the English conditional, then arguments by *modus ponens* will be sound no matter what the contextually relevant implicative relation may be.

17. Compare the formulation of multi-premise closure in Hawthorne (2004, 33).

of a grip on the notion of deductive competence for the Deduction Principle to be more than a tautology. Whatever implicative relation may set the standard for assessing a deduction as sound, some people will be reliable in making deductions only when the premises really stand to the conclusion in that relation, and others will not. This division gives us our grip on the notion of deductive competence. In fact, in discussing the worries about the Deduction Principle that I wish to address, it helps to focus on the special case where the sort of deduction under consideration is specifically logical deduction; any logic teacher certainly knows how to recognize this kind of deductive competence.

Do we need to add any further conditions to the Deduction Principle to ensure that belief in the conclusion qualifies as knowledge? Perhaps so. Some epistemologists will say that the thinker must not only be deductively competent but also know, or believe, that he is if his conclusive belief is to qualify as knowledge. Others—more cautiously—will say that he needs not to believe that he is deductively incompetent. Whether one imposes these requirements depends on one's general epistemological predilections. But two sorts of case have been thought to cast doubt even on the barebones principle that has been stated.

First, there are the so-called 'Dretske cases,' of which the following is the most famous (see Dretske 1970). At the zoo one day, you glance into a pen labeled 'zebras' and see a black-and-white horselike mammal. The animal is, indeed, a zebra, so you know, it seems, that the animal in the pen is a zebra. That premise logically entails that the animal in the pen is not a non-zebra carefully disguised to look like a zebra. So by competently making a logical deduction, you come to believe the conclusion—the true conclusion—that the animal is not a non-zebra carefully disguised to look like a zebra. Some philosophers, however, share Dretske's intuition that you do not *know* that conclusion. To know it, you would need evidence that excluded the possibility of the animal's being a non-zebra disguised as a zebra, but your inexpert glance into the pen fails to provide such evidence.

A second sort of case involves the accumulation of epistemic risks. A version of the Paradox of the Preface provides a simple example. Suppose you have composed a book comprising only true statements. Suppose, too, that you know each statement in the book to be true. Now a plausible necessary condition for knowing a statement to be true is that there should be very little risk, given your evidence, that the statement is false. Ex hypothesi, then, you meet this condition in respect of each individual statement in his book. Now suppose, however, that you apply the rule of 'and'-introduction to all the statements in the book, thereby reaching a conclusion that is a conjunction of all the individual statements in your book. This seems to be a case of coming to believe a conclusion by competently deducing it (logically) from premises that you know, so the Deduction

Principle tells us that your belief in the conjunction will have the status of knowledge. That claim, though, seems to be inconsistent with the postulated necessary condition for knowledge. Even when the risk of each conjunct's being false is low, the risk of the conjunction's being false will be higher, and if the book contains sufficiently many statements, the latter risk can be high enough to disqualify you from knowing the truth of the conjunction, even though the conjunction is true and you believe it.

What lies at the root of this latter objection is a probabilistic conception of epistemic risk. Some philosophers, anxious to ensure that fallible thinkers can acquire knowledge, will wish to say that I can know that it is raining by looking out of the window, even when I am susceptible to occasional hallucinations of rain, so long as the chance of my hallucinating rain is small. Suppose then that I am prone to occasional brainstorms that can do any of three things: they can make me hallucinate rain, they can make me reach inductive conclusions that are not supported by my evidence, and they can make me deduce conclusions from premises that do not (in the contextually relevant sense) imply them. On the present view, my being susceptible in this way need not preclude me from knowing the premises (1) and (2) or from being deductively competent in the specified sense, so long as the brainstorms have little chance of happening. However, certain events can be individually unlikely without its being unlikely that one of them will happen. On this view, then, an additional condition needs to be met before we can infer that my conclusive belief—my belief that the street is wet—is knowledge. It is not enough that each brainstorm is unlikely to have occurred. There must also be a very low chance that at least one of the brainstorms should have occurred.

How should we react to these cases? Well, we could restrict the original Deduction Principle to exclude the apparent counterexamples. (And if the restriction is effected in the manner just suggested, *some* beliefs deduced from known premises will still qualify as knowledge.) On the other hand, we could resist the claim that the cases lately described are counterexamples to the Deduction Principle. They certainly put it under some intuitive pressure, but before accepting them as counterexamples, we should weigh the theoretical costs of restricting the Principle against those of resisting the counterexamples. This in turn suggests that we should consider what the ground of the Deduction Principle might be. Once identified, that ground ought to show what restrictions, if any, the Principle needs.

A first shot at grounding the Deduction Principle might run like this. If a thinker qualifies as deductively competent (in a given argumentative context), then he will be disposed to deduce a conclusion from some premises only when the conclusion really does stand in R to them, where R is the implicative relation that sets the standard for assessing deductions in that context. Now suppose that a deductively competent person knows the premises of an argument and deduces its conclusion from those premises. Because he knows the premises, those premises are true. And because the premises are true, and the conclusion is *R*-related to them, the conclusion is also true. (Since *R* is a implicative relation, it will preserve truth from premises to conclusion.) Ex hypothesi, our thinker is deductively competent, so he will deduce a conclusion from some premises only if they really imply the conclusion (in the contextually relevant sense of *imply*). Accordingly, when a deductively competent thinker deduces a conclusion from premises that he knows, the belief thereby formed will be true, and it will have been produced in a way that reliably yields true beliefs. Suppose finally that we accept a reliabilist conception of knowledge. On that conception, what endows a true belief with the status of knowledge is precisely that it has been produced in a way that reliably yields true beliefs. So assuming a reliabilist conception of knowledge, belief in a conclusion that has been competently deduced from known premises will have the status of knowledge, so that the Deduction Principle is unrestrictedly true.

As we shall see, the proponent of this argument puts his finger on something important when he focuses on the connection between deductive competence and implication. But the argument as it stands is vulnerable to an objection, even if we accept the reliabilism needed at the last step. The objection is that the putative explanation of the truth of the Deduction Principle cannot be right, for if correct, it would prove too much. In the explanation, the only use that is made of the hypothesis that the thinker knows the premises of his deduction is to derive the claim that those premises are true. So the same account would appear to explain the truth of the Pseudo Deduction Principle:

(*PDP*) If a thinker comes to believe a conclusion by competently deducing it from true premises that he believes, then he knows the conclusion.

But the Pseudo Deduction Principle is patently absurd. Coming to believe a conclusion by competently deducing it from some true beliefs reliably—indeed, infallibly—yields a true belief. But it clearly does not constitute a reliable way of producing true beliefs in the sense needed for a belief that is thereby produced to qualify as knowledge. For (*PDP*) does not require that the thinker should know the premises of his deduction.

I think we can find an improved ground for the Deduction Principle that escapes the objection if we reflect on what Mark Sainsbury (1997) called the Reliability Conditional but which most epistemologists now call the Safety Conditional:

(SC) If a thinker knows that *P*, then his belief that *P* could not easily have been wrong.

The modality here relates to the knowing, rather than to what is known. To put the point in terms of possible worlds, if a thinker knows that *P*, there is no nearby world (no world that could easily have been actual) in which he falsely believes that *P*—or, better, in which he falsely believes that *P* on the same basis as he actually believes that *P*. Although Sainsbury himself advances (*SC*) only as a necessary condition for knowledge, those with reliabilist sympathies in epistemology will take it to be sufficient as well: on this view, a true belief that is formed in such a way that it could not easily be wrong will have the status of knowledge.

How does the Safety Conditional bear on knowledge acquired by deduction? To see how it does, let us return to our original deduction and consider how I could have believed falsely that the street is wet on the same basis as my actual belief (which is true). Now the actual basis of that belief is a deduction in which the bases for my premises are spliced together to form a basis for my conclusion. And we know that if true premises imply a conclusion, then that conclusion will be true. So in any nearby world in which my belief that the street was wet has its actual basis but is false, at least one of the following three conditions must be met:

(1) my belief that it is raining has its actual basis but is false,

or

(2) my belief that the street is wet if it is raining has its actual basis but is false,

or

(3) I deduce the conclusion from my premises, but in fact my premises do not imply my conclusion.

Now we are supposing that I know the first premise of my argument. By the Safety Conditional, then, there is no nearby world in which possibility (1) obtains. Similarly, given that I know the second premise, there is no nearby world in which possibility (2) obtains. Finally, it is a mark of deductive competence that when a thinker deduces a conclusion from some premises, it could not easily have been the case that his premises fail to imply his conclusion. So, given that I am deductively competent, and that *all nearby worlds belong to the space of possibilities associated with the relevant implication relation*, there is no nearby world in which possibility (3) obtains either. There will be cases where the italicized condition does not obtain. However, when we are dealing with logical deduction, as in the special case of (*DP*) that we are considering, the condition will obtain: for any way in which things could easily have been is logically possible. But we said that, in any nearby world in which my belief that the street was wet has its actual basis but is false, at least one of our three conditions must be met. And we have just argued that, when the conclusion is competently deduced from known premises, none of these conditions is met in any nearby world. Accordingly, there is no nearby world in which the conclusive belief has its actual basis but is false. So if we accept the converse of (*SC*), that conclusive belief will qualify as knowledge. Thus (*SC*) and its converse together vindicate the Deduction Principle.

This analysis brings out the special role of deduction in a way that explains why this vindication of the Deduction Principle does not extend to vindicate the Pseudo Deduction Principle. The 'method' of forming beliefs that consists in only believing what follows from true beliefs is reliable, indeed infallible, for a false belief cannot follow from true beliefs. But that 'method' does not deserve the title, for applying it presumes some antecedent criterion for judging whether the premises are true. What a deductive capacity provides, then, is not a new method for forming beliefs per se, but rather a means of combining reliable methods of belief formation that one already possesses to yield a new *method* that has a wider range of application than its components. A deductive capacity, one might say, yields a second-order method of belief formation. This method may itself be applied to establish the truth of certain statements—namely, those implied by all premises (or none) under the relevant implicative relation. But that is not the present case, nor the central one. Instead, the value of such capacities lies in their power to splice together reliable methods of belief formation to yield further reliable methods that have a wider range of application than their components. Once this is clear, it will be clear why our ground for the Deduction Principle does not extend to justify the Pseudo Deduction Principle.

What, though, of the apparent counterexamples to the Deduction Principle? Our analysis gives us the resources, I think, to resist both of them. In the Dretske example, there are two cases to consider. Either there is a joker at the zoo who is disposed to disguise non-zebras as zebras—in which case the subject's belief that the animal in the pen is a zebra could easily have been wrong, so that he does not know the deduction's premise; or there is no such joker—in which case the subject's belief that the animal in the pen is not a non-zebra disguised to look like a zebra could not easily have been wrong, so we may allow that he knows the conclusion. Either way, the case poses no threat to the Deduction Principle. Matters are similar with the Paradox of the Preface. At any possible world where the long conjunction is false, at least one conjunct is false. Now if the long conjunction could easily have been false, there is a nearby possible world at which it is false. At that nearby world, though, at least one of the conjuncts will be false, showing that one of the conjuncts could easily have been false. That is to say, if the long conjunction could easily have been false, then the author does not, after all, know every statement in his book. So either he does know every statement in the book, in which case the long conjunction could not easily have been false, so that we may credit him with knowledge of the conjunction, or his book contains a statement that he does not know, in which case the Deduction Principle is inapplicable. Properly analyzed, then, the Paradox of the Preface also provides no counterexample to the Principle.

My endorsement of the Deduction Principle is tentative. Perhaps there are other examples that expose a flaw in the justification advanced for it and show how it needs to be restricted. Further exploration of the issue must be left to the epistemologists, but it is interesting that we have a justification of the Principle that depends only on what I take to be an attractive general theory of deduction and the plausible epistemological thesis (*SC*). Surprisingly many contemporary epistemologists are willing to reject the Principle. Our analysis at least reveals the high cost of doing so.

6. Conclusion

How does the proffered account of deduction bear on Ryle's general picture of the mind?

At the heart of that picture is the attack on 'intellectualism,' the view that what marks out intelligent behavior is its being "piloted by the intellectual grasp of true propositions" (Ryle 1949, 26), and I think our analysis of deduction can contribute to the Rylean enterprise of subverting that picture. One might put the point this way. On an intellectualist view, the paradigm of intelligent behavior is theory construction, the goal of which "is the knowledge of true propositions or facts" (26). As we have seen, deduction plays an important role in theory construction—both in refuting false hypotheses and in further elaborating what we have come to know. However, deduction itself is not piloted by the knowledge of true propositions. A deductive capacity cannot consist in knowledge of true propositions—whether those propositions are logical truths or propositions to the effect that this statement follows from these others—for a thinker could know the propositions while lacking any capacity to make deductions. That is the moral of Lewis Carroll's fable. Rather, a deductive capacity is an intellectual ability, exercises of which can (among other things) extend our knowledge of premises to yield further knowledge of what those premises imply. As we have seen, such an ability can be turned on itself to yield knowledge of logical truths and knowledge of instances of the relevant implicative relation. But that knowledge is a by-product of a deductive capacity: it is not what pilots the capacity. A thinker could have a deductive capacity even if he had never turned it on itself to attain knowledge of truths implied (in the relevant sense) by all premises or none. And he could have such a capacity even if he lacked the notion of consequence or implication. So at the very basis of the intellectualist theory of the mind is a form of intelligent behavior—namely, the deducing of the implications of premises—which the theory cannot accommodate.

Is a deductive capacity a form of Rylean *knowing how to*? The answer seems unclear. In some respects, it resembles Ryle's paradigms of that kind of knowledge: it is an ability that one acquires—indeed, learns—by practice and that one can improve by drill (or so those of us who are called on to teach elementary logic must hope). On the other hand, the very fact that it is possible to state deduction rules puts it at the other end of the spectrum from such uncodifiable instances of Rylean savoir faire as the abilities to prosecute a war, to fish, or even to cook. But if the answer is unclear, so is the significance of the question. It matters greatly to Ryle's anti-intellectualist crusade that some intelligent behavior should not be piloted by *knowledge that*. But so far as I can see, it matters not a jot that all the intelligent behavior that is not so piloted should be a manifestation of the agent's knowing how to do something.

Without compromising his wider philosophical project, then, Ryle could have said what I have said about deduction and logical rules. I can only hope that what I have said is closer to the truth than what he actually wrote.

References

Abbott, B. 2006. Linguistic solutions to philosophical problems. Paper presented at an American Psychological Association Pacific Division symposium on Philosophy and Linguistics. Portland, OR.

Adams, M. 2009. Empirical evidence and the knowledge-that/knowledge-how distinction. *Synthese*, 170: 97–114.

Alter, T. 2001. Know-how, ability, and the ability hypothesis. *Theoria*, 67: 229–239.

Anderson, J. R. 1980. *Cognitive psychology and its implications*. San Francisco: W. H. Freeman.

Anderson, J. R. 1983. *The architecture of cognition*. Cambridge, MA: Harvard University Press.

Anderson, J. R. 1993. *Rules of the mind*. Hillsdale, NJ: Lawrence Erlbaum.

Anderson, J. R., and C. Lebiere. 1998. *The atomic components of thought*. Mahwah, NJ: Lawrence Erlbaum.

Anderson, R. C. 1977. The notion of schemata and the educational enterprise. In R. C. Anderson, R. J. Spiro, and W. E. Montague, eds., *Schooling and the acquisition of knowledge*. Hillsdale, NJ: Erlbaum.

Andreou, C., and M. Thalos. 2007. Sense and sensibility. *American Philosophical Quarterly*, 44: 71–80.

Annas, J. 1995. Virtue as a skill. *International Journal of Philosophical Studies*, 3: 227–243.

Annas, J. 2001. Moral knowledge as practical knowledge. *Social Philosophy and Policy*, 18: 236–256. Also printed in E. F. Paul, F. D. Miller, and J. Paul, eds., *Moral knowledge*. Cambridge: Cambridge University Press.

Annas, J. 2011. *Intelligent virtue*. Oxford: Oxford University Press.

Anscombe, E. 1957. *Intention*. Oxford: Basil Blackwell.

Anscombe, E. 1959. *An introduction to Wittgenstein's Tractatus*. London: Hutchinson.

Antony, L. 2008. Meta-linguistics: Methodology and ontology in Devitt's *Ignorance of language*. *Australasian Journal of Philosophy*, 86: 643–656.

Archer, M. S. 2000. *Being human: The problem of agency*. Cambridge: Cambridge University Press.

Aristotle. 350 B.C.E./1908. *Nicomachean ethics*. W. D. Ross, trans. Oxford: Clarendon.

Aristotle. 350 B.C.E./2000. *Nichomachean ethics*. R. Crisp, trans. Cambridge: Cambridge University Press.

Aristotle. 350 B.C.E. *Metaphysics*.

Aristotle. 350 B.C.E. *Prior analytics*.

Asher, N. 1993. *Reference to abstract objects in discourse: A philosophical semantics for natural language metaphysics*. Dordrecht, Netherlands: Kluwer.

Asher, N., and A. Lascarides. 1998. Questions in dialogue. *Linguistics and Philosophy*, 21: 237–309.

Asher, N., and A. Lascarides. 2003. *Logics of conversation*. Cambridge: Cambridge University Press.

Audi, R. 2001. *The architecture of reason: The structure and substance of rationality*. Oxford: Oxford University Press.

Austin, D. 1990. *What's the meaning of 'this'?* Ithaca, NY: Cornell University Press.

Bach, K. 2005. Questions and answers: Comments on J. Schaffer's "Knowing the answer." Presented at the Bellingham Summer Philosophy Conference.

Baddeley, A. 1997. *Human memory*. Hove: Psychology Press.

Barber, A., ed. 2003. *Epistemology of language*. Oxford: Oxford University Press.

Bargh, J., and T. Chartrand. 1999. The unbearable automaticity of being. *American Psychologist*, 54: 462–479.

Bartsch, K., and J. Wright. 2005. Towards an intuitionist account of moral development. *Behavioral and Brain Sciences*, 28: 546–547.

Barwise, J., and J. Etchemendy. 1987. *The liar*. New York: Oxford University Press.

Battaly, H. 2008. Virtue epistemology. *Philosophy Compass*, 3: 639–663.

Bealer, G. 1993. The incoherence of empiricism. In S. Wagner and R. Warner, eds., *Naturalism: A critical appraisal*, 99–183.

Bealer, G. 1998. A theory of concepts and concept possession, *Philosophical Issues*, 9: 241–301.

Bechtel, W., and A. Abrahamsen. 1991. *Connectionism and the mind*. Oxford: Blackwell.

Beck, C. M. 1968. Knowing that, knowing how to, knowing to, and knowing how. *Philosophy of Education*, 24: 171–178.

Bengson, J. In progress. Practical perception.

Bengson, J., E. Grube, and D. Korman. 2011. A new framework for conceptualism. *Noûs*, 45: 167–189.

Bengson, J., and M. Moffett. 2007. Know-how and concept possession. *Philosophical Studies*, 136: 31–57.

Bengson, J., M. Moffett, and J. Wright. 2009. The folk on knowing how. *Philosophical Studies*, 142: 387–401.

Bennett, J. 1964. *Rationality*. London: Routledge & Kegan Paul.

Bergman, M. 1997. Internalism, externalism and the no-defeater condition. *Synthese*, 110: 399–417.

Berwick, R. C., and A. S. Weinberg. 1984. *The grammatical basis of linguistic performance: Language use and acquisition*. Cambridge, MA: MIT Press.

Besson, C. 2010. Propositions, dispositions and logical knowledge. In A. Longo and M. Bonelli, eds., *Quid est veritas? Philosophia antiqua genevensis: Essays in honour of Jonathan Barnes*. Naples, Italy: Bibliopolis.

Bialystok, E. 1986. Factors in the growth of linguistic awareness. *Child Development*, 57: 498–510.

Bialystok, E., and E. B. Ryan. 1985. A metacognitive framework for the development of first and second language skills. In D. L. Forrest-Pressley, G. E. MacKinnon, and T. G. Waller, eds., *Metacognition, cognition, and human performance*. New York: Academic Press.

Biernat, M., and D. Kobrynowicz. 1997. Gender- and race-based standards of competence: Lower minimum standards but higher ability standards for devalued groups. *Journal of Personality and Social Psychology*, 72: 544–557.

Bigelow, J., and R. Pargetter. 1990. Acquaintance with qualia. *Theoria*, 61: 129–147.

Birner, B., J. Kaplan, and G. Ward. 2007. Functional compositionality and the interaction of discourse constraints. *Language*, 83: 317–343.

Bjorklund, D. F., W. Sneider, and C. Hernandez Blasi. 2003. Memory. In L. Nadel, ed., *Encyclopedia of cognitive science*, vol. 2. London: Nature.

Blackburn, S. 1996. Securing the nots: Moral epistemology for the quasi-realist. In W. Sinnott-Armstrong and M. Timmons, eds., *Moral knowledge?* Oxford: Oxford University Press.

Block, N. 1981. Psychologism and behaviourism. *Philosophical Review*, 90: 5–43.

Bloomfield, P. 2000. Virtue epistemology and the epistemology of virtue. *Philosophy and Phenomenological Research*, 60: 23–43.

Boër, S., and W. Lycan. 1986. *Knowing who*. Cambridge, MA: MIT Press.

Boghossian, P. 1989. The rule-following considerations. *Mind*, 98: 507–549.

Bonevac, D., J. Dever, and D. Sosa. 2006. The conditional fallacy. *Philosophical Review*, 115: 273–316.

Bonevac, D., J. Dever, and D. Sosa. Forthcoming. The counterexample fallacy. *Mind*.

Braddon-Mitchell, D., and F. Jackson. 1996. *The philosophy of mind and cognition*. Oxford: Blackwell.

Brand, M. 1982. Cognition and intention. *Erkenntnis*, 18: 165–187.

Brand, M. 1984. *Intending and acting: Towards a naturalized action theory*. Cambridge, MA: MIT Press.

Brandom, R. 1994. *Making it explicit*. Cambridge, MA: Harvard University Press.

Bratman, M. 1987. *Intentions, plans, and practical reason*. Cambridge, MA: Harvard University Press.

Braun, D. 2006. Now you know who Hong Oak Yun is. *Philosophical Issues*, 16: 24–42.

Braun, D. Forthcoming. Implicating questions. *Mind and Language*.

Brewer, B. 1999. *Perception and reason*. Oxford: Oxford University Press.

Brogaard, B. 2007. Attitude reports: Do you mind the gap? *Philosophy Compass*, 3: 93–118.

Brogaard, B. 2008. Knowledge-*the* and propositional attitude ascriptions. *Grazer Philosophische Studien*, 77: 147–190.

Brogaard, B. 2009. What Mary did yesterday: Reflections on knowledge-*wh*. *Philosophy and Phenomenological Research*, 78: 439–467.

Brooks, R. A. 1991. Intelligence without representation. *Artificial Intelligence*, 47: 139–159.

Brown, D. 1970. Knowing how and knowing that, what. In O. P. Wood and G. Pitcher, eds., *Ryle*. London: Macmillan.

Brown, L. E., and D. A. Rosenbaum. 2003. Motor control: Models. In L. Nadel, ed., *Encyclopedia of cognitive science*, vol. 3. London: Nature.

Burge, T. 1977. Belief de re. *Journal of Philosophy*, 74: 338–362.

Burge, T. 1979. Individualism and the mental. *Midwest Studies in Philosophy*, 4: 73–122.

Burge, T. 2003. Concepts, conceptions, reflective understanding: Reply to Peacocke. In M. Hahn and B. T. Ramberg, eds., *Reflections and replies: Essays on the philosophy of Tyler Burge*. Cambridge, MA: Bradford.

Bzdak, D. 2008. On amnesia and knowing how. *Techné: Research in Philosophy and Technology*, 12.

Campbell, J. 2002. *Reference and consciousness*. Oxford: Oxford University Press.

Carlson, R. A. 2003. Skill learning. In L. Nadel, ed., *Encyclopedia of cognitive science*, vol. 4. London: Nature.

Carman, T. 2008. *Merleau-Ponty*. London: Routledge.

Carnap, R. 1947/1956. *Meaning and necessity: A study in semantics and modal logic*. Chicago: University of Chicago Press.

Carpenter, B. 1997. *Type driven semantics*. Cambridge, MA: Bradford and MIT Press.

Carr, D. 1979. The logic of knowing how and ability. *Mind*, 88: 394–409.

Carr, D. 1981a. Knowledge in practice. *American Philosophical Quarterly*, 18: 53–61.

Carr, D. 1981b. On mastering a skill. *Journal of Philosophy of Education*, 15: 87–96.

Carr, D. 1984. Dance education, skill, and behavioral objectives. *Journal of Aesthetic Education*, 18: 67–76.

Carr, D. 1987. Thought and action in the art of dance. *British Journal of Aesthetics*, 27: 345–357.

Carr, D. 1999. Art, practical knowledge, and aesthetic objectivity. *Ratio*, 12: 240–256.

Carr, D., and J. W. Steutel, eds. 1999. *Virtue ethics and moral education*. London: Routledge.

Carroll, L. 1895. What the Tortoise said to Achilles. *Mind*, 4: 278–280.

Cartwright, R. L. 1987. Implications and entailments. In *Philosophical essays*. Cambridge, MA: MIT Press.

Cath, Y. 2009. The ability hypothesis and the new knowledge-how. *Noûs*, 43: 137–156.

Cavell, S. 1969. Aesthetic problems in modern philosophy. In *Must we mean what we say?* Cambridge: Cambridge University Press.

Chalmers, D. 2004a. The representational character of experience. In B. Leiter, ed., *The future for philosophy*. Oxford: Oxford University Press.

Chalmers, D. 2004b. Phenomenal concepts and the knowledge argument. In P. Ludlow, D. Stoljar, and Y. Nagasawa, eds., *There's something about Mary: Essays on phenomenal consciousness and Frank Jackson's knowledge argument*. Cambridge, MA: MIT Press.

Chalmers, D. 2006. Perception and the fall from Eden. In T. S. Gendler and J. Hawthorne, eds., *Perceptual experience*. Oxford: Clarendon.

Chalmers, D. 2010. The two-dimensional argument against materialism. In *The character of consciousness*. New York: Oxford University Press.*

Chisholm, R. 1957. *Perceiving*. Ithaca, NY: Cornell University Press.

Chisholm, R. 1976. *Person and object*. London: George Allen & Unwin.

Chisholm, R. 1988. Theory and practice: The point of contact. In B. Smith and J. C. Nyíri, eds., *Practical knowledge: Outlines of a theory of traditions and skills*. London: Croom Helm.

Chomsky, N. 1970. Remarks on nominalization. In R. A. Jacobs and P. S. Rosenbaum, eds., *Readings in English transformational grammar*. Waltham, MA: Ginn.

Chomsky, N. 1975. Knowledge of language. In K. Gunderson, ed., *Minnesota studies in the philosophy of science, vol. 7: Language, mind, and knowledge*. Minneapolis: University of Minnesota Press.

Chomsky, N. 1980a. *Rules and representations*. New York: Columbia University Press.

Chomsky, N. 1980b. Rules and representations. *Behavioral and Brain Sciences*, 3: 1–15.

Chomsky, N. 1980c. The new organology. *Behavioral and Brain Sciences*, 3: 42–61.

Chomsky, N. 1986. *Knowledge of language: Its nature, origin, and use*. New York: Praeger.

Chomsky, N. 1988. *Language and problems of knowledge: The Managua lectures*. Cambridge, MA: MIT Press.

Chomsky, N. 1992. Language and interpretation: Philosophical reflections and empirical inquiry. In J. Earman, ed., *Inference, explanation, and other frustrations: Essays in the philosophy of science*. Berkeley: University of California Press.

Churchland, P. 1996. *The engine of reason, the seat of the soul: A philosophical journey into the brain*. Cambridge, MA: MIT Press.

Churchland, P. 2000. Rules, know-how, and the future of moral cognition. In R. Campbell and B. Hunter, eds., *Moral epistemology naturalized, Canadian Journal of Philosophy*, supplementary vol. 26: 291–306.

Clark, A. 1996. Connectionism, moral cognition and collaborative problem solving. In L. May, M. Friedman, and A. Clark, eds., *Minds and morals*. Cambridge, MA: MIT Press.

Clark, A. 2000. Word and action: Reconciling rules and know-how in moral cognition. In R. Campbell and B. Hunter, eds., *Moral epistemology naturalized, Canadian Journal of Philosophy*, supplementary vol. 26: 267–290.

Clark, A., and J. Toribio. 1994. Doing without representing? *Synthese*, 101: 401–431.

Clarke, R. 2010. Skilled activity and the causal theory of action. *Philosophy and Phenomenological Research*, 80: 523–550.

Cleeremans, A. 2003. Implicit learning models. In L. Nadel, ed., *Encyclopedia of cognitive science*, vol. 2. London: Nature.

Cohen, D., and T. Handfield. 2011. Rational capacities, resolve, and weakness of will. *Mind*, 119: 907–932.

Collins, J. 2006. Between a rock and a hard place: A dialogue on the philosophy and methodology of generative linguistics. *Croatian Journal of Philosophy*, 6: 469–503.

Collins, J. 2007a. Review of *Ignorance of language*. *Mind*, 116: 416–423.

Collins, J. 2007b. Syntax—more or less. *Mind*, 116: 805–850.

Collins, J. 2008a. Knowledge of language redux. *Croatian Journal of Philosophy*, 8: 3–43.

Collins, J. 2008b. A note on conventions and unvoiced syntax. *Croatian Journal of Philosophy*, 8: 241–247.

Conee, E. 1994. Phenomenal knowledge. *Australasian Journal of Philosophy*, 72: 136–150.

Cooper, R. 2005. Austinian truth, attitudes and type theory. *Research on Language and Computation*, 3: 333–362.

Cooper, R. Forthcoming. Type theory and semantics in flux. In R. Kempson, N. Asher, and T. Fernando, eds., *Handbook of the philosophy of science, vol. 14: Linguistics*. Amsterdam: Elsevier.

Correia, F. 2005. *Existential dependence and cognate notions*. Munich: Philosophia Verlag.

Craig, E. 1990. *Knowledge and the state of nature: An essay in conceptual synthesis*. Oxford: Clarendon.

Crane, T. 2001. *Elements of mind*. Oxford: Oxford University Press.

Crane, T. 2009. Is perception a propositional attitude? *Philosophical Quarterly*, 59: 452–469.

Crimmins, M. 1993. *Talk about beliefs*. Cambridge, MA: Bradford and MIT Press.

Cross, R. C. 1959. Ethical disagreement. *Philosophy*, 25: 301–315.

Csikszentmihalyi, M. 1991. *Flow: The psychology of optimal experience*. New York: Harper Collins.

Culbertson, J., and S. Gross. 2009. Are linguists better subjects? *British Journal for the Philosophy of Science*, 60: 721–736.

Culicover, P. M., and R. Jackendoff. 2006. Turn over control to the semantics! *Syntax*, 9: 131–152.

Cummins, R. 1986. Inexplicit information. In M. Brand and R. M. Harnish, eds., *The representation of knowledge and belief*. Tucson: University of Arizona Press.

Cummins, R., and M. Roth. 2011. Intellectualism in cognitive science. In A. Bartels, E. M. Jung, and A. Newen, eds., *Knowledge and representation: New developments*. Stanford, CA: CSLI.

Cunliffe, L. 2005. The problematic relationship between knowing how and knowing that in secondary art education. *Oxford Review of Education*, 31: 547–556.

Cutler, A. 1999. Spoken-word recognition. In R. A. Wilson and F. C. Keil, eds., *The MIT encyclopedia of the cognitive sciences*. Cambridge, MA: MIT Press.

Dancy, J. 2004. *Ethics without principles*. Oxford: Oxford University Press.

Davidson, D. 1967. Truth and meaning. *Synthese*, 17: 304–323.

Davidson, D. 1973. Radical interpretation. *Dialectica*, 27: 313–328.

Davidson, D. 1974. Belief and the basis of meaning. *Synthese*, 27: 309–323.
Davies, M. 1987. Tacit knowledge and semantic theory: Can a five per cent difference matter? *Mind*, 96: 441–462.
Davies, M. 1989. Tacit knowledge and subdoxastic states. In A. George, ed., *Reflections on Chomsky*. Oxford: Basil Blackwell.
Dell, G. S. 1995. Speaking and misspeaking. In L. R. Gleitman and M. Liberman, eds., *Language: An invitation to cognitive science*, 2nd ed., vol. 1. Cambridge, MA: MIT Press.
Dell, G. S., F. Chang, and Z. M. Griffin. 1999. Connectionist models of language production: Lexical access and grammatical encoding. *Cognitive Science*, 23: 517–542.
Dennett, D. 1982. Styles of mental representation. *Proceedings of the Aristotelian Society*, 83: 213–226.
Descartes, R. 1637/1984. *Discourse on the method of rightly conducting reason and of seeking truth in the sciences*. In *The philosophical writings of Descartes*, vol. 1. J. Cottingham, R. Stoothoff, and D. Murdoch, trans. Cambridge: Cambridge University Press.
Devitt, M. 1981. *Designation*. New York: Columbia University Press.
Devitt, M. 1984/1997. *Realism and truth*. Princeton, NJ: Princeton University Press.
Devitt, M. 1996. *Coming to our senses: A naturalistic program for semantic localism*. Cambridge: Cambridge University Press.
Devitt, M. 1997. *Realism and truth*, 2nd ed. Princeton, NJ: Princeton University Press.
Devitt, M. 2003. Linguistics is not psychology. In A. Barber, ed., *Epistemology of language*. Oxford: Oxford University Press.
Devitt, M. 2006a. Intuitions in linguistics. *British Journal for the Philosophy of Science*, 57: 481–513.
Devitt, M. 2006b. *Ignorance of language*. Oxford: Oxford University Press.
Devitt, M. 2006c. Defending ignorance of language: Responses to the Dubrovnik papers. *Croatian Journal of Philosophy*, 6: 571–606.
Devitt, M. 2006d. Intuitions. In V. G. Pin, J. I. Galparsoro, and G. Arrizabalaga, eds., *Ontology studies cuadernos de ontologia: Proceedings of VI International Ontology Congress (San Sebastian, 2004)*. San Sebastian, Spain: Universidad del Pais Vasco.
Devitt, M. 2008a. Explanation and reality in linguistics. *Croatian Journal of Philosophy*, 8: 203–231.
Devitt, M. 2008b. A response to Collins' note on conventions and unvoiced syntax. *Croatian Journal of Philosophy*, 8: 249–255.
Devitt, M. 2008c. Methodology in the philosophy of linguistics. *Australasian Journal of Philosophy*, 86: 671–684.
Devitt, M. 2009. Psychological conception, psychological reality: A response to Longworth and Slezak. *Croatian Journal of Philosophy*, 9: 37–46.
Devitt, M. 2010a. What 'intuitions' are linguistic evidence? *Erkenntnis*, 73: 251–264.
Devitt, M. 2010b. Linguistic intuitions revisited. *British Journal for the Philosophy of Science*, 61: 833–865.

Devitt, M. Forthcoming-a. Methodology and the nature of knowing how. *Journal of Philosophy*.
Devitt, M. Forthcoming-b. The role of intuitions. In G. Russell and D. Graff Fara, eds., *A companion to the philosophy of language*. London: Routledge.
Devitt, M., and K. Sterelny. 1989. What's wrong with 'the right view.' In J. E. Tomberlin, ed., *Philosophical perspectives, vol. 3: Philosophy of mind and action theory*. Atascadero, CA: Ridgeview.
Devitt, M., and K. Sterelny. 1999. *Language and reality: An introduction to the philosophy of language*, 2nd ed. Cambridge, MA: MIT Press.
Dewey, J. 1922. *Human nature and conduct: An introduction to social psychology*. New York: H. Holt.
Dowty, D., and P. Jacobson. 1991. Infinitival questions. Unpublished manuscript for a talk delivered in colloquia at the University of California at Santa Cruz and Cornell University.
Drestke, F. 1969. *Seeing and knowing*. Chicago: University of Chicago Press.
Dretske, F. I. 1970. Epistemic operators. *Journal of Philosophy*, 67: 1007–1023.
Dretske, F. 1998. Where is the mind when the body performs? *Stanford Humanities Review*, 6. Available at www.stanford.edu/group/SHR/6-2/html/dretske.html.
Dreyfus, H. 1967. Why computers must have bodies to be intelligent. *Review of Metaphysics*, 21: 13–32.
Dreyfus, H. 1992. *What computers still can't do: A critique of artificial reason*. Cambridge, MA: MIT Press.
Dreyfus, H. 2002. Intelligence without representation-Merleau-Ponty's critique of mental representation: The relevance of phenomenology to scientific explanation. *Phenomenology and the Cognitive Sciences*, 1: 367–383.
Dreyfus, H. L. 2006. Overcoming the myth of the mental. *Topoi*, 25: 43–49.
Dreyfus, H., and S. Dreyfus. 1982. *Mind over machine: The power of human intuition and expertise in the era of the computer*. Glencoe, IL: Free Press.
Dreyfus, H., and S. Dreyfus. 1991. Towards a phenomenology of ethical expertise. *Human Studies*, 14: 229–250.
Ducasse, C. J. 1964. Substants, capacities, and tendencies. *Review of Metaphysics*, 18: 23–37.
Dummett, M. 1975. What is a theory of meaning? In S. Guttenplan, ed., *Mind and language*. Oxford: Clarendon.
Dummett, M. 1976. What is a theory of meaning? (II) In G. Evans and J. McDowell, eds., *Truth and meaning: Essays in semantics*. Oxford: Clarendon.
Dummett, M. 1978. *Truth and other enigmas*. Cambridge, MA: Harvard University Press.
Dummett, M. 1981a. *Frege: Philosophy of language*, 2nd ed. London: Duckworth.
Dummett, M. 1981b. *The interpretation of Frege's philosophy*. Cambridge, MA: Harvard University Press.

Dummett, M. 1982. Realism. *Synthese*, 52: 55–112.
Dummett, M. 1991. *The logical basis of metaphysics*. London: Duckworth.
Dummett, M. 1993. *The seas of language*. Oxford: Clarendon.
Dummett, M. 2006. *Thought and reality*. Oxford: Oxford University Press.
Dwyer, S., and P. Pietroski. 1996. Believing in language. *Philosophy of Science*, 63: 338–373.
Erion, G. J. 2001. The Cartesian test for automatism. *Minds and Machines*, 11: 29–39.
Evans, G. 1982. *The varieties of reference*. J. McDowell, ed. Oxford: Clarendon.
Evans, N., and S. C. Levinson. 2009. The myth of language universals: Language diversity and its importance for cognitive science. *Behavioral and Brain Sciences*, 32: 429–492.
Fantl, J. 2008. Knowing how and knowing that. *Philosophy Compass*, 3: 451–470.
Feldman, R. 2003. *Epistemology*. Upper Saddle River, NJ: Prentice Hall.
Fernández, R. 2006. Non-sentential utterances in dialogue: Classification, resolution and use. Ph.D. Thesis. King's College, London.
Fernando, T. 2007. Observing events and situations in time. *Linguistics and Philosophy*, 30: 527–550.
Fillmore, C. J. 1986. Pragmatically controlled zero anaphora. In V. Nikiforidou, M. Van Clay, M. Niepokuj, and D. Feder, eds., *Proceedings of the twelfth annual meeting of the Berkeley Linguistics Society*. Berkeley, CA: Berkeley Linguistics Society.
Fine, K. 1985. *Reasoning with arbitrary objects*. Oxford: Blackwell.
Fine, K. 1995. Ontological dependence. *Proceedings of the Aristotelian Society*, 95: 269–290.
Fitzgerald, G. 2010. Linguistic intuitions. *British Journal for the Philosophy of Science*, 61: 123–160.
Fletcher, C. 1994. Levels of representation in memory for discourse. In M. A. Gernsbacher, ed., *Handbook of psycholinguistics*. Burlington, MA: Academic Press.
Fodor, J. 1968. The appeal to tacit knowledge in psychological explanation. *Journal of Philosophy*, 65: 627–640.
Fodor, J. 1975. *The language of thought*. New York: Thomas Y. Crowell.
Fodor, J. 1981. *Representations: Philosophical essays on the foundations of cognitive science*. Cambridge, MA: MIT Press.
Forbes, G. 2000. Objectual attitudes. *Linguistics and Philosophy*, 23: 141–183.
Forbes, G. 2006. *Attitude problems: An essay on linguistic intentionality*. Oxford: Oxford University Press.
Fowler, C. A., and M. T. Turvey. 1978. Skill acquisition: An event approach with special reference to searching for the optimum of a function of several variables. In G. E. Stelmach, ed., *Information processing and motor control*. New York: Academic Press.
Frankfurt, H. 1978. The problem of action. *American Philosophical Quarterly*, 15: 157–162.

Frege, G. 1884/1978. *The foundations of arithmetic.* J. L. Austin, trans. Oxford: Blackwell.
Frege, G. 1891/1984. Function and concept. P. Geach, trans. In B. McGuinness, ed., *Frege's collected papers on mathematics, logic and philosophy.* Oxford: Blackwell.
Frege, G. 1892/1984. Sense and meaning. M. Black, trans. In B. McGuinness, ed., *Frege's collected papers on mathematics, logic and philosophy.* Oxford: Blackwell.
Frege, G. 1918/1956. The thought: A logical inquiry. A. M. and M. Quinton, trans. *Mind*, 65: 289–311.
Frege, G. 1919/1984. Thoughts. P. Geech and R. H. Stoothoff, trans. In B. McGuinness, ed., *Frege's collected papers on mathematics, logic and philosophy.* Oxford: Blackwell.
Frege, G. 1924/1997. Sources of knowledge of mathematics and mathematical natural sciences. P. Long and R. White, trans. In M. Beaney, ed., *The Frege reader.* Oxford: Blackwell.
Fricker, M. 2007. *Epistemic injustice.* Oxford: Oxford University Press.
Gallagher, S. 2005. *How the body shapes the mind.* Oxford: Oxford University Press.
Garson, J. 2003. Dynamical systems, philosophical issues about. In L. Nadel, ed., *Encyclopedia of cognitive science*, vol. 1. London: Nature.
Gaut, B. 2009. Creativity and skill. In M. Krausz, D. Dutton, and K. Bardsley, eds., *The idea of creativity.* Leiden: Brill.
Gauthier, D. 1994. Assure and threaten. *Ethics*, 104: 690–721.
Geach, P. 1966. Dr. Kenny on practical inference. *Analysis*, 26: 76–79.
Gellner, E. 1951. Knowing how and validity. *Analysis*, 12: 25–35.
Gendler, T. 2000. The puzzle of imaginative resistance. *Journal of Philosophy*, 97: 55–81.
Gentzen, G. 1935. Untersuchungen über das logische Schliessen. *Mathematische Zeitschrift*, 39: 176–210, 405–431. Translated as 'Investigations into logical deduction,' in M. E. Szabo, ed. and trans., *The collected papers of Gerhard Gentzen.* Amsterdam: North Holland.
Gibbons, J. 2001. Knowledge in action. *Philosophy and Phenomenological Research*, 62: 579–600.
Gibson, E. 2003. Sentence comprehension, linguistic complexity in. In L. Nadel, ed., *Encyclopedia of cognitive science*, vol. 3. London: Nature.
Gibson, J. 1977. The theory of affordances. In R. Shaw and J. Bransford, eds., *Perceiving, acting and knowing.* Hillsdale, NJ: Lawrence Erlbaum.
Ginet, C. 1975. *Knowledge, perception, and memory.* Dordrecht, Netherlands: Reidel.
Ginzburg, J. 1994. An update semantics for dialogue. In H. Bunt, ed., *Proceedings of the 1st international workshop on computational semantics.* ITK, Tilburg University, Tilburg, Netherlands.
Ginzburg, J. 1995a. Resolving questions, part I. *Linguistics and Philosophy*, 18: 459–527.
Ginzburg, J. 1995b. Resolving questions, part II. *Linguistics and Philosophy*, 18: 567–609.
Ginzburg, J. 1996. Interrogatives: Questions, facts, and dialogue. In S. Lappin, ed., *The handbook of contemporary semantic theory.* Oxford: Blackwell.

Ginzburg, J. 2005. Abstraction and ontology: Questions as propositional abstracts in constructive type theory. *Journal of Logic and Computation*, 15: 113–130.

Ginzburg, J. 2012. *The interactive stance: Meaning for conversation*. Oxford: Oxford University Press.

Ginzburg, J., and R. Cooper. 2004. Clarification, ellipsis, and the nature of contextual updates. *Linguistics and Philosophy*, 27: 297–366.

Ginzburg, J., and R. Fernández. 2010. Dialogue. In A. Clark, C. Fox, and S. Lappin, eds., *Handbook of computational linguistics and natural language*. Oxford: Blackwell.

Ginzburg, J., and I. Sag. 2000. *Interrogative investigations: The form, meaning, and use of English interrogatives*. Stanford, CA: CSLI.

Glick, E. Forthcoming. Two methodologies for evaluating intellectualism. *Philosophy and Phenomenological Research*.

Goldberg, A. 1995. *Constructions: A construction grammar approach to argument structure*. Chicago: University of Chicago Press.

Goldberg, A. 2006. *Constructions at work: The nature of generalization in language*. Oxford: Oxford University Press.

Goldin, C., and C. Rouse. 2000. Orchestrating impartiality: The impact of 'blind' auditions on female musicians. *American Economic Review*, 90: 715–741.

Goldman, A. 1970. *A theory of human action*. Englewood Cliffs, NJ: Prentice-Hall.

Goldman, A. 2001. Experts: Which ones should you trust? *Philosophy and Phenomenological Research*, 63: 85–110.

Gould, J. 1955. *The development of Plato's ethics*. Cambridge: Cambridge University Press.

Greco, J. 2009. Knowledge and success from ability. *Philosophical Studies*, 142: 17–26.

Gregory, R. L. 1970. *The intelligent eye*. London: Weidenfeld & Nicolson.

Griffiths, P. J. 2003. Religion. In C. Taliaferro and P. J. Griffiths, eds., *Philosophy of religion: An anthology*. Oxford: Blackwell.

Groenendijk, J. 2006. The logic of interrogation. In M. Aloni, A. Butler, and P. Dekker, eds., *Questions in dynamic semantics: Current research in the semantics/pragmatics interface*. Amsterdam: Elsevier.

Groenendijk, J., and M. Stokhof. 1982. Semantic analysis of *wh*-complements. *Linguistics and Philosophy*, 5: 175–234.

Groenendijk, J., and M. Stokhof. 1984. *Studies on the semantics of questions and the pragmatics of answers*. Ph.D. Thesis, University of Amsterdam.

Groenendijk, J., and M. Stokhof. 1997. Questions. In J. van Benthem and A. ter Meulen, eds., *Handbook of logic and language*. Cambridge, MA: MIT Press.

Grush, R. 1998. Skill and spatial content. *Electronic Journal of Analytic Philosophy*, 6. Available at http://mind.ucsd.edu/misc/ejap/ejap_6_6_Grush.html.

Gupta, A. 2006. *Empiricism and experience*. Oxford: Oxford University Press.

Haegeman, L. 1991. *Introduction to government and binding*. Oxford: Blackwell.

Haiman, J. 1980. The iconicity of grammar: Isomorphism and motivation. *Language*, 56: 515–540.

Haiman, J. 1983. Iconic and economic motivation. *Language*, 59: 781–819.

Hakes, D. T. 1980. *The development of metalinguistic abilities in children*. Berlin: Springer-Verlag.
Hare, R. M. 1972. *Practical inferences*. Berkeley, CA: University of California Press.
Harman, G. 1967. Psychological aspects of the theory of syntax. *Journal of Philosophy*, 64: 75-87.
Harman, G. 1975. Language, thought, and communication. In K. Gunderson, ed., *Minnesota studies in the philosophy of science, vol. 7: Language, mind, and knowledge*. Minneapolis: University of Minnesota Press.
Hartland-Swann, J. 1956. The logical status of 'knowing that.' *Analysis*, 16: 111–115.
Hartland-Swann, J. 1958. *An analysis of knowing*. London: George Allen & Unwin.
Haugeland, J. 1998. *Having thought: Essays in the metaphysics of mind*. Cambridge, MA: Harvard University Press.
Hawley, K. 2003. Success and knowledge how. *American Philosophical Quarterly*, 40: 19–31.
Hawley, K. 2010. Testimony and knowing how. *Studies in the History and Philosophy of Science*, Part A, 41: 397–404.
Hawthorne, J. 2000. Implicit belief and a priori knowledge. *Southern Journal of Philosophy*, 38: 191–210.
Hawthorne, J. 2004. *Knowledge and lotteries*. Oxford: Clarendon.
Hawthorne, J. 2005. The case for closure. In M. Steup and E. Sosa, eds., *Contemporary debates in epistemology*. Hoboken, NJ: Wiley-Blackwell.
Hawthorne, J., and J. Stanley. 2008. Knowledge and action. *Journal of Philosophy*, 105: 571–590.
Hedberg, N. 2000. The referential status of clefts. *Language*, 76: 891–920.
Heidegger, M. 1926/1962. *Being and time*. J. Macquarrie and E. Robinson, trans. New York: Harper and Row.
Heidelberger, H. 1980. Understanding and truth conditions. In P. A. French, T. E. Uehling Jr., and H. K. Wettstein, eds., *Midwest Studies in Philosophy*, 5: 401–410.
Hellie, B. 2007. 'There's something it's like' and the structure of consciousness. *Philosophical Review*, 116: 441–463.
Hertz, P. 1922. Über Axiomensysteme für beliebige Satzsysteme I. *Mathematische Annalen*, 87: 246–269.
Hertz, P. 1923. Über Axiomensysteme für beliebige Satzsysteme II. *Mathematische Annalen*, 89: 76–102.
Hertz, P. 1929. Über Axiomensysteme für beliebige Satzsysteme. *Mathematische Annalen*, 101: 457–514.
Hetherington, S. 2006. How to know (that knowledge-that is knowledge-how). In S. Hetherington, ed., *Epistemology futures*. Oxford: Oxford University Press.
Hetherington, S. 2008. Knowing-that, knowing-how, and knowing philosophically. *Grazer Philosophische Studien*, 77: 307–324.
Hetherington, S. 2009. Ginet on a priori knowledge: Skills and grades. *Veritas*, 54: 32–40.

Hetherington, S. 2011. Knowledge and knowing: Ability and manifestation. In S. Tolksdorf, ed., *Conceptions of knowledge, vol. 1: Knowledge, abilities, and contexts.* Berlin: Walter de Gruyter.

Higginbotham, J. 1996. The semantics of questions. In S. Lappin, ed., *The handbook of contemporary semantic theory.* Oxford: Oxford University Press.

Higginbotham, J. 1998. Conceptual competence. *Philosophical Issues,* 9: 149–162.

Hintikka, J. 1974a. Practical vs. theoretical reason: An ambiguous legacy. In S. Korner, ed., *Practical reason.* New Haven, CT: Yale University Press.

Hintikka, J. 1974b. Plato on knowing how, that, what. In *Knowledge and the known: Historical perspectives in epistemology.* Boston: D. Reidel.

Hintikka, J. 1975. Different constructions in terms of basic epistemological verbs. In *The intentions of intentionality and other new models for modalities.* Boston: D. Reidel.

Hintikka, J. 1976. *The semantics of questions and the questions of semantics.* Amsterdam: North-Holland.

Hintikka, J. 1992. Different constructions in terms of 'knows.' In J. Dancy and E. Sosa, eds., *A companion to epistemology.* Oxford: Blackwell.

Hobbs, J. 2004. Abduction in natural language understanding. In L. Horn and G. Ward, eds., *Handbook of pragmatics.* Oxford: Blackwell.

Holton, R. 1999. Intention and weakness of will. *Journal of Philosophy,* 96: 241–262.

Holton, R. 2004. Rational resolve. *Philosophical Review,* 113: 507–535.

Honoré, A. M. 1964. Can and can't. *Mind,* 73: 463–479.

Horgan, T. 1984. Jackson on physical information and qualia. *Philosophical Quarterly,* 32: 127–136.

Hornsby, J. 1980. *Actions.* London: Routledge & Kegan Paul.

Hornsby, J. 2005. Semantic knowledge and practical knowledge. *Supplement to the Proceedings of the Aristotelian Society,* 79: 107–130.

Hornsby, J. 2008. A disjunctive conception of acting for reasons. In A. Haddock and F. Macpherson, eds. *Disjunctivism: Perception, action, knowledge.* Oxford: Oxford University Press.

Huemer, M. 2005. *Ethical intuitionism.* New York: Palgrave.

Hunter, D. 1998. Understanding and belief. *Philosophy and Phenomenological Research,* 58: 559–580.

Hurley, S. L. 2001. Overintellectualizing the mind. *Philosophy and Phenomenological Research,* 63: 423–431.

Hursthouse, R. 2009. Virtue ethics. *The Stanford Encyclopedia of Philosophy.* E. N. Zalta, ed. Available at http://plato.stanford.edu/archives/spr2009/entries/ethics-virtue.

Husserl, E. 1901/1913/1973. *Logical investigations.* J. N. Findlay, trans. London: Routledge.

Hyman, J. 1999. How knowledge works. *Philosophical Quarterly,* 49: 433–451.

Ivanhoe, P. J. 1993. Zhuangzui on skepticism, skill, and the ineffable *Dao. Journal of the American Academy of Religion,* 78: 639–654.

Jackendoff, R. 1997. *The architecture of the language faculty.* Cambridge, MA: MIT Press.

Jackson, F. 1977. *Perception.* Cambridge: Cambridge University Press.

Jackson, F. 1982. Epiphenomenal qualia. *Philosophical Quarterly,* 32: 127–136.

Jackson, F. 1986. What Mary didn't know. *Journal of Philosophy,* 83: 291–295.

Jackson, F. 1998. *From metaphysics to ethics: A defence of conceptual analysis.* Oxford: Clarendon.

Jeshion, R. 2002. Acquaintenceless *de re* belief. In M. Campbell, J. K. O'Rourke, and D. Shier, eds., *Meaning and truth: Investigations in philosophical semantics.* New York: Seven Bridges.

Jones, G. 2003. Production systems and rule-based inference. In L. Nadel, ed., *Encyclopedia of cognitive science,* vol. 3. London: Nature.

Jones, K. 2003. Emotion, weakness of will, and the normative conception of agency. In A. Hatzimoysis, ed., *Philosophy and the emotions.* Cambridge: Cambridge University Press.

Kalderon, M. E. 2001. Reasoning and representing. *Philosophical Studies,* 105: 129–160.

Kallestrup, J. 2009. Knowledge-wh and the problem of convergent knowledge. *Philosophy and Phenomenological Research,* 78: 468–476.

Kallestrup, J. 2010. Knowing-wh and the problem about knowledge of knowledge. Unpublished manuscript.

Kamp, H. 1981. A theory of truth and semantic representation. In J. A. G. Groenendijk, T. M. V. Janssen, and M. B. J. Stokhof, eds., *Formal methods in the study of language.* Amsterdam: Mathematical Centre Tracts 135.

Karttunen, L. 1977. Syntax and semantics of questions. *Linguistics and Philosophy,* 1: 3–44.

Kasher, A., ed. 1991. *The Chomskyan turn.* Oxford: Basil Blackwell.

Katzoff, C. 1984. Knowing How. *Southern Journal of Philosophy,* 22: 61–69.

Kaufman, S. J., S. B. Kaufman, and J. A. Plucker. Forthcoming. Contemporary theories of intelligence. In D. Reisberg, ed., *The Oxford handbook of cognitive psychology.* Oxford: Oxford University Press.

Kay, P. 2002. English subjectless tag sentences. *Language,* 78: 453–481.

Kay, P., and C. J. Fillmore. 1999. Grammatical constructions and linguistic generalizations: The 'what's X doing Y' construction. *Language,* 75: 1–33.

Kelly, S. D. 2002. Merleau-Ponty on the body: The logic of motor intentional activity. *Ratio,* 15: 376–391.

Kelso, J. A. S. 1995. *Dynamic patterns: The self-organization of brain and behavior.* Cambridge, MA: MIT Press.

Kenny, A. 1966. Practical inference. *Analysis,* 26: 65–75.

Kim, J. 1974. Noncausal connections. *Noûs,* 8: 41–52.

Kim, J. 1994. Explanatory knowledge and metaphysical dependence. *Philosophical Topics,* 4: 51–69.

Koethe, J. 2002. Stanley and Williamson on knowing how. *Journal of Philosophy,* 99: 325–328.

Korsgaard, C. 1999. Self-constitution in the ethics of Plato and Kant. *Journal of Ethics*, 3: 1–29.

Koslow, A. 1992. *A structuralist theory of logic*. Cambridge: Cambridge University Press.

Kripke, S. 1982. *Wittgenstein on rules and private language: An elementary exposition*. Cambridge, MA: Harvard University Press.

Kugler, P. N., and M. T. Turvey. 1987. *Information, natural laws, and the self-assembly of rhythmic movement*. Hillsdale, NJ: Lawrence Erlbaum.

Kumar, V. 2011. In support of anti-intellectualism. *Philosophical Studies*, 152: 135–154.

Kupperman, J. 1970. *Ethical knowledge*. London: Routledge.

Kvanvig, J. 2003. *The value of knowledge and the pursuit of understanding*. Cambridge: Cambridge University Press.

Lackey, J. 1999. Testimonial knowledge and transmission. *Philosophical Quarterly*, 49: 471–490.

Lahiri, U. 2002. *Questions and answers in embedded contexts*. Oxford: Oxford University Press.

Lai, K. 2007. Understanding change: The interdependent self in its environment. *Journal of Chinese Philosophy*, 34: 81–99.

Laird, J. E., A. Newell, and P. S. Rosenbloom. 1987. Soar: An architect for general intelligence. *Artificial Intelligence*, 33: 1–64.

Lakoff, G. 1993. The contemporary theory of metaphor. In A. Ortony, ed., *Metaphor and thought*. Cambridge: Cambridge University Press.

Lambrecht, K. 1994. *Information structure and sentence form*. Cambridge: Cambridge University Press.

Lambrecht, K., and L. A. Michaelis. 1998. Sentence accent in information questions: Default and projection. *Linguistics and Philosophy*, 21: 477–544.

Larsson, S. 2002. *Issue based dialogue management*. Ph.D. thesis, Gothenburg University.

Laurence, S. 2003. Is linguistics a branch of psychology? In A. Barber, ed., *Epistemology of language*. Oxford: Oxford University Press.

Lebiere, C. 2003. ACT. In L. Nadel, ed., *Encyclopedia of cognitive science*, vol. 1. London: Nature.

Leist, A. 2007. Cognition and action. In A. Leist, ed., *Action in context*. Berlin: Walter de Gruyter.

Lekan, T. 2007. Actions, habits, and practices. In A. Leist, ed., *Action in context*. Berlin: Walter de Gruyter.

Lemmon, E. J. 1965. *Beginning logic*. London: Nelson.

Lepock, C. Forthcoming. Unifying the intellectual virtues. *Philosophy and Phenomenological Research*.

Levelt, W. J. M., A. Roelofs, and A. S. Meyer. 1999. A theory of lexical access in speech production. *Behavioral and Brain Sciences*, 22: 1–38.

Lewis, D. 1982. Whether report. In T. Pauli, ed., *Philosophical essays dedicated to Lennart Åqvist on his fiftieth birthday*, 194–206. Uppsala, Sweden: University of Uppsala

Department of Philosophy. Reprinted in *Papers in philosophical logic*. Cambridge: Cambridge University Press.

Lewis, D. 1983. Postscript to 'Mad pain and Martian pain.' In *Philosophical papers*, vol. 1. Oxford: Oxford University Press.

Lewis, D. 1988. What experience teaches. *Proceedings of the Russellian Society*, 13: 29–57.

Lewis, D. 1990. What experience teaches. In W. G. Lycan, ed., *Mind and cognition*. Oxford: Blackwell.

Lewis, D. 1996. Elusive knowledge. *Australasian Journal of Philosophy*, 74: 549–567.

Lihoreau, F. 2008. Knowledge-how and ability. *Grazer Philosophische Studien*, 77: 263–305.

Loar, B. 1990. Phenomenal states. *Philosophical Perspectives*, 4: 81–108.

Locke, J. 1706/1891. *The conduct of the understanding*. New York: John B. Alden.

Logan, G. D. 1988. Toward an instance theory of automatization. *Psychological Review*, 95: 492–527.

Longworth, G. 2008. Linguistic understanding and knowledge. *Noûs*, 42: 50–79.

Longworth, G. 2009. Ignorance of linguistics: A note on Michael Devitt's ignorance of language. *Croatian Journal of Philosophy*, 9: 23–36.

Lormand, E. 2004. The explanatory stopgap. *Philosophical Review*, 113: 303–357.

Loux, M. J. 2003. Realism and anti-Realism: Dummett's challenge. In M. J. Loux and D. W. Zimmerman, eds., *The Oxford handbook of metaphysics*. Oxford: Oxford University Press.

Lycan, W. 1996. *Consciousness and experience*. Cambridge, MA: MIT Press.

MacIntyre, A. 1960. Purpose and intelligent action. *Proceedings of the Aristotelian Society*, 34: 79–96.

MacIntyre, A. 1999. *Dependent rational animals: Why human beings need the virtues*. Peru, IL: Open Court.

Mackie, J. 1974. A reply to Jaako Hintikka. In S. Korner, ed., *Practical reason*. Oxford: Oxford University Press.Maier, J. 2010. Abilities. *The Stanford Encyclopedia of Philosophy*. E. N. Zalta, ed. Available at http://plato.stanford.edu/archives/spr2010/entries/abilities/.

Markie, P. 2006. Epistemically appropriate perceptual belief. *Noûs*, 40: 118–142.

Martin, C. B., and J. Heil. 1998. Rules and powers. *Philosophical Perspectives*, 12: 283–312.

Masson, M. E. J. 1990. Cognitive theories of skill acquisition. *Human Movement Science*, 9: 221–239.

Mathews, R. C., R. R. Buss, W. B. Stanley, F. Blanchard-Fields, J. R. Cho, and B. Druhan. 1989. Role of implicit and explicit processes in learning from examples: A synergistic effect. *Journal of Experimental Psychology: Learning, Memory, and Cognition*, 15: 1083–1100.

Mathews, R. C., R. R. Buss, W. B. Stanley, and R. Chinn. 1988. Analysis of individual learning curves in a concept discovery task: Relations among task performance, verbalizable knowledge, and hypothesis revision strategies. *Quarterly Journal of Experimental Psychology*, 40A: 135–165.

Matthews, R. J. 1991. The psychological reality of grammars. In A. Kasher, ed., *The Chomskyan turn*. Oxford: Basil Blackwell.

Matthews, R. J. 2006. Could competent speakers really be ignorant of their language? *Croatian Journal of Philosophy*, 6: 457–467.

McClelland, J. L. 1999. Cognitive modeling, connectionist. In R. A. Wilson and F. C. Keil, eds., *The MIT encyclopedia of the cognitive sciences*. Cambridge, MA: MIT Press.

McDowell, J. 1982/1998. Criteria, defeasibility, and knowledge. In *Meaning, knowledge, and reality*. Cambridge, MA: Harvard University Press.

McDowell, J. 1994. *Mind and world*. Cambridge, MA: Harvard University Press.

McDowell, J. 1996. Deliberation and moral development in Aristotle's ethics. In S. Engsrom and J. Whiting, eds., *Aristotle, Kant, and the Stoics*. Cambridge: Cambridge University Press.

McDowell, J. 2007. What myth? *Inquiry*, 50: 338–351.

McFarland, D. 1991. Defining motivation and cognition in animals. *International Studies of Philosophy of Science*, 5: 153–170.

McGinn, C. 1980. Truth and use. In M. Platts, ed., *Reference, truth and reality: Essays on the philosophy of language*. London: Routledge & Kegan Paul.

McGlynn, A. 2007. Is knowledge-how Gettier-susceptible? *Boundaries of language*. Available at http://aidanmcglynn.blogspot.com/2007/08/is-knowledge-how-gettier-susceptible.html.

Mellor, D. H. 1993. Nothing like experience. *Proceedings of the Aristotelian Society*, 93: 1–6.

Merleau-Ponty, M. 1945/1962. *Phenomenology of perception*. C. Smith, trans. New York: Routledge and Kegan Paul.

Mesler, D. 2004. *The act of thinking*. Cambridge, MA: MIT Press.

Michaelis, L. A. 2004. Type shifting in construction grammar: An integrated approach to aspectual coercion. *Cognitive Linguistics*, 15: 1–67.

Millikan, R. 2000. *On clear and confused ideas: An essay about substance concepts*. Cambridge: Cambridge University Press.

Miščević, N. 2006. Intuitions: The discrete voice of competence. *Croatian Journal of Philosophy*, 6: 523–548.

Moffett, M. 2003. Knowing facts and believing propositions: A solution to the problem of doxastic shift. *Philosophical Studies*, 115: 81–97.

Moffett, M. 2005. Constructing attitudes. *Protosociology (Compositionality, Concepts and Representations I: New Problems in Cognitive Science)*, 21: 105–128.

Montague, M. 2007. Against propositionalism. *Noûs*, 41: 503–518.

Mon-Williams, M., J. R. Tresilian, and J. P. Wann. 2003. Motor control and learning. In L. Nadel, ed., *Encyclopedia of cognitive science*. London: Nature.

Moore, A. W. 1997. *Points of view*. Oxford: Oxford University Press.

Moore, A. W. 2003. Ineffability and religion. *European Journal of Philosophy*, 11: 161–176.

Moore, G. E. 1922. *Philosophical studies*. London: Routledge and Kegan Paul.

Moran, R. 2005. Getting told and being believed. *Philosopher's Imprint*, 5.5. Available at http://hdl.handle.net/2027/spo.3521354.0005.005

Mulligan, N. W. 2003. Memory: Implicit versus explicit. In L. Nadel, ed., *Encyclopedia of cognitive science*, vol. 2. London: Nature.

Mumford, S. 1998. *Dispositions*. Oxford: Oxford University Press.

Nadel, L., ed. 2003. *Encyclopedia of cognitive science*. London: Nature.

Nagel, T. 1969. The boundaries of inner space. *Journal of Philosophy*, 66: 452–458.

Nemirow, L. 1980. Review of Thomas Nagel's mortal questions. *Philosophical Review*, 89: 473–477.

Nemirow, L. 1990. Physicalism and the cognitive role of acquaintance. In W. Lycan, ed., *Mind and cognition*. Oxford: Blackwell.

Newell, K. M. 1996. Motor skills. In L. R. Squire, ed., *Encyclopedia of learning and memory*. New York: Macmillan Library Reference.

Nida-Rümelin, M. 1996. What Mary couldn't know. In T. Metzinger, ed., *Conscious experience*. Exeter, England: Imprint Academic Press.

Noë, A. 2004. *Action in perception*. Cambridge, MA: MIT Press.

Noë, A. 2005. Against intellectualism. *Analysis*, 65: 278–290.

Noë, A. Forthcoming. *Varieties of presence*. Cambridge, MA: Harvard University Press.

Nowell-Smith, P. H. 1960. Purpose and intelligent action. *Proceedings of the Aristotelian Society*, 34: 97–112.

Nozick, R. 1981. *Philosophical explanations*. Cambridge, MA: Harvard University Press.

O'Regan, K., and A. Noë. 2001. A sensorimotor account of vision and visual consciousness. *Behavioral and Brain Sciences*, 24: 939–1031.

O'Shaughnessy, B. 1980. *The will: A dual aspect theory*. Cambridge: Cambridge University Press.

Oshima, D. 2009. Between being wise and acting wise: A hidden conditional in some constructions with propensity adjectives. *Journal of Linguistics*, 45: 363–393.

Paillard, J. 1960. The patterning of skilled movements. *American Handbook of Physiology*, 3: 1679–1708.

Paillard, J. 1991. Knowing where and knowing how to get there. In J. Paillard, ed., *Brain and space*. Oxford: Oxford University Press.

Parry, R. D. 1980. Ryle's theory of action in *The concept of mind*. *Philosophy and Phenomenological Research*, 40: 379–392.

Paul, S. 2009. Intention, belief, and wishful thinking: Setiya on 'Practical Knowledge.' *Ethics*, 119: 546–557.

Peacocke, C. 1992. *A study of concepts*. Oxford: Oxford University Press.

Peacocke, C. 1998. Implicit conceptions, understanding and rationality. *Philosophical Issues*, 9: 43–88.

Peacocke, C. 2003. Implicit conceptions, understanding, and rationality. In M. Hahn and B. T. Ramberg, eds., *Reflections and replies: Essays on the philosophy of Tyler Burge*. Cambridge, MA: Bradford.

Peacocke, C. 2008. *Truly understood*. Oxford: Oxford University Press.
Perry, J. 1977. Frege on demonstratives. *Philosophical Review*, 86: 474–497.
Peterson, P. 1997. *Fact, proposition, event: Studies in linguistics and philosophy*. Dordrecht, Netherlands: Kluwer.
Pettit, D. 2002. Why knowledge is unnecessary for understanding language. *Mind*, 111: 519–550.
Piaget, J. 1937/1954. *The construction of reality in the child*.
Pickering, M. J. 2003. Parsing. In L. Nadel, ed., *Encyclopedia of cognitive science*, vol. 3. London: Nature.
Pietroski, P. 2008. Think of the children. *Australasian Journal of Philosophy*, 86: 657–669.
Plato. *Gorgias*.
Plato. *Theaetetus*.
Polanyi, M. 1958. *Personal knowledge: Towards a post-critical philosophy*. Chicago: University of Chicago Press.
Polanyi, M. 1967. *The tacit dimension*. New York: Anchor Books.
Pollard, B. 2003. Can virtuous actions be both habitual and rational? *Ethical Theory and Moral Practice*, 6: 411–425.
Pollock, J., and J. Cruz. 1999. *Contemporary theories of knowledge*. Boston: Rowman and Littlefield.
Portner, P. 1997. The semantics of mood, complementation, and conversational force. *Natural Language Semantics*, 5: 167–212.
Posner, M. I., G. J. DiGirolamo, and D. Fernandez-Duque. 1997. Brain mechanisms of cognitive skills. *Consciousness and Cognition*, 6: 267–290.
Poston, T. 2009. Know how to be Gettiered? *Philosophy and Phenomenological Research*, 79: 743–747.
Powers, L. 1978. Knowledge by deduction. *Philosophical Review*, 87: 337–371.
Price, H. H. 1946. *Thinking and representation*. New York: Haskell House.
Pritchett, B. L. 1988. Garden path phenomena and the grammatical basis of language processing. *Language*, 64: 539–576.
Pryor, J. 2004. An epistemic theory of acquaintance. Unpublished manuscript.
Purver, M. 2001. SCoRE: A tool for searching the BNC. Tech. rep. TR-01-07, King's College, London.
Purver, M. 2006. Clarie: Handling clarification requests in a dialogue system. *Research on Language and Computation*, 4: 259–288.
Pust, J. 2000. *Intuitions as evidence*. New York: Garland.
Pustejovsky, J. 1995. *The generative lexicon*. Cambridge, MA: MIT Press.
Putnam, H. 1975. The meaning of 'meaning'. *Minnesota Studies in the Philosophy of Science*, 7: 131–193.
Putnam, H. 1988. *Representation and reality*. Cambridge: Cambridge University Press.
Putnam, H. 1996. Introduction. In A. Pessin and S. Goldberg, eds., *The twin earth chronicles*. Armonk, NY: Sharpe.
Pylyshyn, Z. W. 1991. Rules and representations: Chomsky and representational realism. In A. Kasher, ed., *The Chomskyan turn*. Oxford: Basil Blackwell.

Radford, A. 2004. *Minimalist syntax*. Cambridge: Cambridge University Press.
Radford, C. 1966. Knowledge—by examples. *Analysis*, 27: 1–11.
Radford, C. 1985. The umpire's dilemma. *Analysis*, 45: 109–111.
Railton, P. 2006. Normative guidance. In R. Shafer-Landau, ed., *Oxford Studies in Metaethic*, vol. 1. Oxford: Oxford University Press.
Railton, P. 2009. Practical competence and fluent agency. In D. Sobel and S.Wall, eds., *Practical reason*. Cambridge: Cambridge University Press.
Radford, C. 1985. The umpire's dilemma. *Analysis*, 45: 109–111.
Ramsey, W. 2007. *Representation reconsidered*. Cambridge: Cambridge University Press.
Ranta, A. 1994. *Type theoretical grammar*. Oxford: Oxford University Press.
Raphals, L. 1992. *Knowing words: Wisdom and cunning in the classical traditions of China and Greece*. Ithaca, NY: Cornell University Press.
Rattan, G. 2006. The knowledge in language. *Croatian Journal of Philosophy*, 6: 505–521.
Raymont, P. 1999. The know-how response to Jackson's knowledge argument. *Journal of Philosophical Research*, 24: 113–126.
Reber, A. S. 1989. Implicit learning and tacit knowledge. *Journal of Experimental Psychology: General*, 118: 219–235.
Reber, A. S. 2003. Implicit learning. In L. Nadel, ed., *Encyclopedia of cognitive science*, vol. 2. London: Nature.
Reitveld, E. 2008. Situated normativity: The normative aspect of embodied cognition in unreflective action. *Mind*, 117: 973–1001.
Rey, G. 2006. Conventions, intuitions and linguistic inexistents: A reply to Devitt. *Croatian Journal of Philosophy*, 6: 549–569.
Rey, G. 2008. In defense of Folieism: Replies to critics. *Croatian Journal of Philosophy*, 8: 177–202.
Reynolds, S. 1991. Knowing how to believe with justification. *Philosophical Studies*, 64: 273–292.
Riggs, W. 2002. Beyond truth and falsehood: The *real* value of knowing that p. *Philosophical Studies*, 107: 87–108.
Roberts, C. 2009. 'know-how': A compositional approach. In E. Hinrichs and J. Nerbonne, eds., *Theory and evidence in semantics*. Stanford, CA: CSLI.
Roland, J. 1958. On 'knowing how' and 'knowing that.' *Philosophical Review*, 67: 379–388.
Rosefeldt, T. 2004. Is knowing-how simply a case of knowing-that. *Philosophical Investigations*, 27: 370–379.
Ross, J. R. 1969. Guess who? In R. Binnick, A. Davison, G. Green, and J. Morgan, eds., *Papers from the fifth regional meeting of the Chicago Linguistic Society*. Chicago: Chicago Linguistics Society.
Ruben, D. H. 2003. *Action and its explanation*. Oxford: Oxford University Press.
Rumelhart, D. 1980. Schemata: The building blocks of cognition. In R. J. Spiro, B. C. Bruce, and W. F. Brewer, eds., *Theoretical issues in reading comprehension*. Hillsdale, NJ: Lawrence Erlbaum.

Rumelhart, D. E., and J. L. McClelland. 1986. *Parallel distributed processing: Explorations in the microstructure of cognition, vol. 1: Foundations*. Cambridge, MA: MIT Press.

Rumfitt, I. 2000. 'Yes' and 'no.' *Mind*, 109: 781–823.

Rumfitt, I. 2003. Savoir faire. *Journal of Philosophy*, 100: 158–166.

Rumfitt, I. 2010a. Logical necessity. In R. L. V. Hale and A. Hoffmann, eds., *Modality: Metaphysics, logic, and epistemology*. Oxford: Clarendon.

Rumfitt, I. 2010b. Ricky Ponting and the judges. *Analysis*, 70: 205–210.

Rumfitt, I. Forthcoming. The logic of boundaryless concepts. In A. Miller, ed., *Logic, language, and mathematics: A Festschrift for Crispin Wright*. Oxford: Clarendon.

Russell, B. 1912. *The problems of philosophy*.

Ryan, E. B., and G. W. Ledger. 1984. Learning to attend to sentence structure: Links between metalinguistic development and reading. In J. Downing and R. Valtin, eds., *Language awareness and learning to read*. New York: Springer-Verlag.

Ryan, S. 1996. Wisdom. In Lehrer et al. K. Lehrer, B. Lum, B. A. Slichta, and N. D. Smith, eds., *Knowledge, teaching, and wisdom*. Dordrecht, Netherlands: Kluwer.

Ryan, S. 1999. What is Wisdom? *Philosophical Studies*, 93: 119–139.

Ryle, G. 1929. Review of Martin Heidegger's *Being and Time*. *Mind*, 38: 355–370.

Ryle, G. 1940. Conscience and moral convictions. *Analysis*, 7: 31–39.

Ryle, G. 1945. Knowing how and knowing that. *Proceedings of the Aristotelian Society*, 46: 1–16.

Ryle, G. 1946/1971. Why are the calculuses of logic and arithmetic applicable to reality? *Proceedings of the Aristotelian Society*, 20: 20–28. Reprinted in *Collected papers*, vol. 2. New York: Barnes and Noble.

Ryle, G. 1949. *The concept of mind*. Chicago: Chicago University Press.

Ryle, G. 1950/2009. 'If,' 'so,' and 'because.' In M. Black, ed., *Philosophical analysis: A collection of essays*. Englewood Cliffs, NJ: Prentice Hall. Reprinted in *Collected essays*, vol. 2. London: Routledge.

Sag, I. 2010. English filler-gap constructions. *Language*, 86: 486–545.

Sag, I., G. Gazdar, T. Wasow, and S. Weisler. 1985. Coordination and how to distinguish categories. *Natural Language and Linguistic Theory*, 3: 117–171.

Sainsbury, M., and M. Tye. Forthcoming. *Seven puzzles of thought (and how to solve them): An originalist theory of concepts*. Oxford: Oxford University Press.

Sainsbury, R. M. 1997. Easy possibilities. *Philosophy and Phenomenological Research*, 57: 907–919.

Sayre-McCord, G. 1996. Coherentist epistemology and moral theory. In W. Sinnott-Armstrong and M. Timmons, eds., *Moral knowledge?* Oxford: Oxford University Press.

Schacter, D. L. 1999. Implicit vs. explicit memory. In R. A. Wilson and F. C. Keil, eds., *The MIT encyclopedia of the cognitive sciences*. Cambridge, MA: MIT Press.

Schaffer, J. 2007. Knowing the answer. *Philosophy and Phenomenological Research*, 75: 383–403.

Schaffer, J. 2009a. On what grounds what. In D. Manley, D. Chalmers, and R. Wasserman, eds., *Metametaphysics: New essays on the foundations of ontology*. Oxford: Oxford University Press.

Schaffer, J. 2009b. Knowing the answer redux: Replies to Brogaard and Kallestrup. *Philosophy and Phenomenological Research*, 78: 477–500.

Schank, R. C., and R. P. Abelson. 1977. *Scripts, plans, goals and understanding.* Hillsdale, NJ: Lawrence Erlbaum.

Schellenberg, S. 2007. Action and self-location in perception. *Mind*, 116: 603–632.

Schiffer, S. 2002. Amazing knowledge. *Journal of Philosophy*, 99: 200–202.

Schiffer, S. 2003. Knowledge of meaning. In A. Barber, ed., *Epistemology of language.* Oxford: Oxford University Press.

Schön, D. A. 1983. *The reflective practitioner: How professionals think in action.* New York: Basic Books.

Schütze, C. T. 1996. *The empirical base of linguistics: Grammaticality judgments and linguistic methodology.* Chicago: University of Chicago Press.

Scott, D. S. 1974. Completeness and axiomatizability in many-valued logic. In L. Henkin, et al., eds., *Proceedings of the Tarski Symposium.* Providence, RI: American Mathematical Society.

Searle, J. 1980. Minds, brains, and programs. *Behavioral and Brain Sciences*, 3: 417–457.

Seligman, J., and L. Moss. 1997. Situation theory. In J. van Benthem and A. ter Meulen, eds., *Handbook of logic and linguistics.* Amsterdam: North Holland.

Sellars, W. 1962. Philosophy and the scientific image of man. In R. Colodny, ed., *Frontiers of science and philosophy.* Pittsburgh, PA: University of Pittsburgh Press.

Setiya, K. 2008. Practical knowledge. *Ethics*, 118: 388–409.

Setiya, K. 2009. Practical knowledge revisited. *Ethics*, 120: 128–137.

Sgaravatti, D., and E. Zardini. 2008. Knowing how to establish intellectualism. *Grazer Philosophische Studien*, 77: 217–261.

Shank, N. 2002. *Animals and science: A guide to the debates.* Santa Barbara, CA: ABC-CLIO.

Shettleworth, S. J. 1998. *Cognition, evolution, and behavior.* New York: Oxford University Press.

Siegel, S. 2006. Which properties are represented in experience? In T. S. Gendler and J. Hawthorne, eds., *Perceptual experience.* Oxford: Clarendon.

Singley, M. K., and J. R. Anderson. 1989. *The transfer of cognitive skill.* Cambridge, MA: Harvard University Press.

Slezak, P. 2009. Linguistic explanation and 'Psychological Reality.' *Croatian Journal of Philosophy*, 9: 3–21.

Smart, J. C. 1950. Reason and conduct. *Philosophy*, 25: 209–224.

Smiley, T. J. 1995. A tale of two tortoises. *Mind*, 104: 725–736.

Smith, B. C. 2006. Why we still need knowledge of language. *Croatian Journal of Philosophy*, 6: 431–456.

Smith, M. 2003. Rational capacities, or: How to distinguish recklessness, weakness, and compulsion. In S. Stroud and C. Tappolet, eds., *Weakness of will and practical irrationality.* Oxford: Clarendon.

Snowdon, P. 2003. Knowing how and knowing that: A distinction reconsidered. *Proceedings of the Aristotelian Society*, 104: 1–29.

Soames, S. 2003. *Philosophical analysis in the twentieth century*, vol. 2. Princeton, NJ: Princeton University Press.

Sosa, E. 2003. Beyond internal foundations to external virtues. In L. Bonjour and E. Sosa, *Epistemic justification: Internalism vs. externalism, foundations vs. virtues*. Oxford: Blackwell.

Sosa, E. 2007. *A virtue epistemology: Apt belief and reflective knowledge*. Oxford: Oxford University Press.

Sosa, E. 2009. Knowing full well: The normativity of beliefs as performances. *Philosophical Studies*, 142: 5–15.

Soteriou, M. 2008. The epistemological role of episodic recollection. *Philosophy and Phenomenological Research*, 77: 472–492.

Stalnaker, A. 2010. Virtue as mastery in early Confucianism. *Journal of Religious Ethics*, 38: 404–428.

Stanley, J. 2005. Hornsby on the phenomenology of speech. *Supplement to the Proceedings of the Aristotelian Society*, 79: 131–145.

Stanley, J. 2011. Knowing (how). *Noûs*, 45: 207–238.

Stanley, J. Forthcoming-a. Intellectualism and the language of thought: A reply to Roth and Cummins. In A. Bartels, E. M. Jung, and A. Newen, eds., *Knowledge and representation: New developments*. Stanford, CA: CSLI.

Stanley, J. Forthcoming-b. *Know how*. Oxford: Oxford University Press.

Stanley, J., and T. Williamson. 2001. Knowing how. *Journal of Philosophy*, 98: 411–444.

Stanley, W. B., R. C. Mathews, R. R. Buss, and S. Kotler-Cope. 1989. Insight without awareness: On the interaction of verbalization, instruction and practice in a simulated process control task. *Quarterly Journal of Experimental Psychology*, 41A: 553–577.

Steedman, M. 2003. Language, connectionist and symbolic representations of. In L. Nadel, ed., *Encyclopedia of cognitive science*, vol. 2. London: Nature.

Stemberger, J. P. 2003. Speech error models of language production. In L. Nadel, ed., *Encyclopedia of cognitive science*, vol. 4. London: Nature.

Steward, H. 2009. Sub-intentional actions and the over-mentalization of agency. In C. Sandis, ed., *New essays on the explanation of action*. New York: Palgrave-Macmillan.

Stich, S. P. 1971. What every speaker knows. *Philosophical Review*, 80: 476–496.

Stich, S. P. 1978. Beliefs and subdoxastic states. *Philosophy of Science*, 45: 499–518.

Stich, S. P. 1980. What every speaker cognizes. *Behavioral and Brain Sciences*, 3: 39–40.

Stich, S. P. 1996. *Deconstructing the mind*. New York: Oxford University Press.

Stillings, N., S. Weisler, C. Chase, M. Feinstein, J. Garfield, and E. Rissland. *Cognitive science: An introduction*, 2nd ed., Cambridge, MA: MIT Press.

Stout, R. 2006. *The inner life of a rational agent: In defence of philosophical behaviourism*. Edinburgh, Scotland: Edinburgh University Press.

Stout, R. 2010. What you know when you know an answer to a question. *Noûs*, 44: 392–402.

Sun, R. 2003. Connectionist implementationalism and hybrid systems. In L. Nadel, ed., *Encyclopedia of cognitive science*, vol. 1. London: Nature.

Sun, R., E. Merrill, and T. Peterson. 2001. From implicit skills to explicit knowledge: A bottom-up model of skill learning. *Cognitive Science*, 25: 203–244.

Szabó, Z. G. 2003. Believing in things. *Philosophy and Phenomenological Research*, 66: 584–611.

Tanenhaus, M. K. 2003. Sentence processing. In L. Nadel, ed., *Encyclopedia of cognitive science*, vol. 3. London: Nature.

Tanenhaus, M. K., and J. C. Trueswell. 1995. Sentence comprehension. In J. L. Miller and P. D. Eimas, eds., *Speech, language, and communication*. San Diego, CA: Academic Press.

Tanney, J. 2000. Playing the rule-following game. *Philosophy*, 75: 203–224.

Tanney, J. 2009. Gilbert Ryle. In E. N. Zalta, ed. *The Stanford Encyclopedia of Philosophy*. Available at http://plato.stanford.edu/archives/win2009/entries/ryle/.

Tarski, A. 1930/1983. Fundamentale Begriffe der Methodologie der deduktiven Wissenschaften I. *Monatshefte für Mathematik und Physik*, 37: 361–404. Translated by J. H. Woodger as *Fundamental concepts of the methodology of the deductive sciences*.

Tarski, A. 1983. *Logic, semantics, metamathematics*. J. H. Woodger and J. Corcoran, eds. Indianapolis, IN: Hackett.

Textor, M. 2009. Devitt on the epistemic authority of linguistic intuitions. *Erkenntnis*, 71: 395–405.

Thompson, M. 2008. *Life and action*. Cambridge, MA: Harvard University Press.

Tolhurst, W. 1998. Seemings. *American Philosophical Quarterly*, 35: 293–302.

Toribio, J. 2007. Nonconceptual content. *Philosophy Compass*, 2: 445–460.

Toulmin, S. 1949. A defence of 'synthetic necessary truth.' *Mind*, 58: 164–177.

Tye, M. 1982. A causal analysis of seeing. *Philosophy and Phenomenological Research*, 42: 311–325.

Tye, M. 2000. Knowing what it is like: The ability hypothesis and the knowledge argument. In *Consciousness, color and content*. Cambridge, MA: MIT Press.

Tye, M. 2004. Knowing what it is like: The ability hypothesis and the knowledge argument. In P. Ludlow, M. Nagasawa, and D. Stoljar, eds., *There's something about Mary*. Cambridge, MA: MIT Press.

Tye, M. 2009. *Consciousness revisited: Materialism without phenomenal concepts*. Cambridge, MA: MIT Press.

Unger, P. 1975. *Ignorance: A case for skepticism*. Oxford: Oxford University Press.

van Gelder, T. 1999. Dynamic approaches to cognition. In R. A. Wilson and F. C. Keil, eds., *The MIT encyclopedia of the cognitive sciences*. Cambridge, MA: MIT Press.

van Willegenburg, T. 2004. Understanding value as knowing how to value, and for what reasons. *Journal of Value Inquiry*, 38: 91–104.

Varela, F. 1999. *Ethical know-how: Action, wisdom, and cognition*. Stanford, CA: Stanford University Press.

Varela, F., E. T. Thompson, and E. Rosch. 1991. *The embodied mind: Cognitive science and human experience*. Cambridge, MA: MIT Press.

Velleman, D. 2000. The possibility of practical reason. In *The possibility of practical reason*. Oxford: Oxford University Press.

Vendler, Z. 1967. *Linguistics in philosophy*. Ithaca, NY: Cornell University Press.

Vendler, Z. 1972. *Res cogitans: An essay in rational psychology*. London: Cornell University Press.

Vigliocco, G., and D. P. Vinson. 2003. Speech production. In L. Nadel, ed., *Encyclopedia of cognitive science*, vol. 4. London: Nature.

Wallis, C. 2008. Consciousness, context, and know how. *Synthese*, 160: 123–153.

Ward, et al. Forthcoming.

Ware, R. X. 1973. Our knowledge and our language. *Canadian Journal of Philosophy*, 3: 153–168.

Weatherson, B. 2006. Ryle on knowing how. Available at http://tar.weatherson.org/2006/07/22/ryle-on-knowing-how.

Weatherson, B. 2007. Doing philosophy with words. *Philosophical Studies*, 135: 429–437.

Whitcomb, D. 2011. Wisdom. In S. Bernecker and D. Pritchard. *The Routledge companion to epistemology*. London: Routledge.

White, A. R. 1971. Inference. *Philosophical Quarterly*, 21: 289–302.

White, A. R. 1982. *The nature of knowledge*. Totowa, NJ: Rowman and Littlefield.

Whyte, J. T. 1990. Success semantics. *Analysis*, 50: 149–157.

Wiggins, D. 2001. *Sameness and substance renewed*. Cambridge: Cambridge University Press.

Wiggins, D. 2009. Knowing how to and knowing that. In H. J. Glock and J. Hyman, eds., *Wittgenstein and analytic philosophy: Essays for P. M. S. Hacker*. Oxford: Oxford University Press.

Wiggins, D. Forthcoming. Practical knowledge: Knowing how to and knowing that. *Mind*.

Williams, B. 1970/1973. Deciding to believe. In H. Kiefer and M. Munitz, eds., *Language, belief and metaphysics*. Albany: State University of New York Press. Reprinted in *Problems of the self*. Cambridge: Cambridge University Press.

Williams, E. 1991. Meaning categories of NPs and Ss. *Linguistic Inquiry*, 22: 584–587.

Williams, J. N. 2008. Propositional knowledge and know-how. *Synthese*, 164: 133–155.

Williamson, T. 1999. Review of Moore's *Points of view*. *Philosophical Books*, 40: 43–45.

Williamson, T. 2000. *Knowledge and its limits*. Oxford: Oxford University Press.

Wilson, C. 1926. *Statement and inference*.

Wilson, R. A., and F. C. Keil, eds. 1999. *The MIT encyclopedia of the cognitive sciences*. Cambridge, MA: MIT Press.

Winch, C. 2009. Ryle on knowing how and the possibility of vocational education. *Journal of Applied Philosophy*, 26: 88–101.

Winograd, T. 1975. Frame representations and the procedural-declarative controversy. In D. Bobrow and A. Collins, eds., *Representation and understanding: Studies in cognitive science*. New York: Academic Press.

Wittgenstein, L. 1953/1968. *Philosophical investigations*. G. E. M. Anscombe, trans. Oxford: Basil Blackwell.

Wolpert, D. M., and Z. Ghahramani. 2003. Motor learning models. In L. Nadel, ed., *Encyclopedia of cognitive science*, vol. 3. London: Nature.

Woodfield, A. 1991. Conceptions. *Mind*, 400: 547–572.

Woozley, A. D. 1953. Knowing and not knowing. *Proceedings of the Aristotelian Society*, 53: 151–172.

Wright, C. 1976. Truth conditions and criteria. *Supplement to the Proceedings of the Aristotelian Society*, 50: 217–245.

Wright, C. 1989. Wittgenstein's rule-following considerations and the central project of theoretical linguistics. In A. George, ed., *Reflections on Chomsky*. Oxford: Basil Blackwell.

Yalowitz, S. 2000. A dispositional account of self-knowledge. *Philosophy and Phenomenological Research*, 61: 249–278.

Yamadori, A., T. Yoshida, E. Mori, and H. Yamashita. 1996. Neurological basis of skill learning. *Cognitive Brain Research*, 5: 39–54.

Young, G. 2009. Case study evidence for an irreducible form of knowing how to: An argument against a reductive epistemology. *Philosophia*, 37: 341–360.

Zagzebski, L. T. 1996. *Virtues of the mind. An inquiry into the nature of virtue and the ethical foundations of knowledge*. Cambridge: Cambridge University Press.

Zardini, E. 2009. Knowledge-how, true indexical belief, and action. Unpublished manuscript.

Zwicky, A., and J. Sadock. 1975. Ambiguity tests and how to fail them. In P. Kimball, ed., *Syntax and semantics IV*. New York: Academic Press.

Index

Abbott, B., 215, 239
Abelson, R. P., 190n57
abilities, dispositions or
  ability pathway and attitude
    predicates, 219–22, 243
  ascriptions of, 78, 130–32, 159–60,
    208n11, 219–22, 238–43, 255–57,
    278–79
  competence and, 45–46, 298, 324, 347
  enabling conditions for, 33–34, 38, 41,
    169–70, 208, 254
  experts/expertise and, 69, 101–2,
    104–12, 285, 288, 297
  folk ascriptions of knowledge how
    and, 208n11
  habituation or training and, 14,
    33n42, 69, 74, 101–3, 108, 335
  Intelligence and, 5n4, 15–17, 19, 24,
    28, 30, 31–38, 66
  knowledge of, 49
  knowledge how and, 14–15, 18–19,
    31–44, 70, 72, 80–82, 84, 93, 127–32,
    136–39, 144–50, 155–60, 161–77, 189,
    207–9, 255–57, 285, 287–88, 291,
    294–95, 301–3, 314–15, 359
  knowledge that and, 12n15, 18n25,
    81, 84
  language and, 50–51, 314–16, 325, 329
  modal auxiliaries and, 14
  moral knowledge and, 48
  practicing and, 33–34, 35n43, 40–41,
    74, 291, 328
  primitive knowledge states and,
    150–60
  Ryle on, 14–15, 81–82, 86
  skill and, 5, 8–9, 10n12, 32, 45–46,
    101–2, 105–6, 110, 278, 298, 328
  varieties of, 38, 159–60, 168n18, 278–79
  virtues/virtue ethics and, 45–48
Abrahamsen, A., 52, 137n1
acquaintance, familiarity or, 25, 28, 185,
  188, 312. *See also* objectual knowledge
Adams, M., 52, 164n8
addiction, compulsion or, 49n62
aesthetic problems in philosophy, 210–11
Alter, T., 51
Anderson, J. R., 190n57, 327–28
Andrée, S. A., 35n44
Andreou, C., 47
animals, 52, 81, 150–60
Annas, J., 25n36, 34–35, 46n59, 48, 52,
  101–12
Anscombe, G. E. M., 12n15, 48–49,
  83n6, 96n17, 200
answer theory, 249–60
anti-intellectualism. *See also* Ryle, G.
  deduction and, 336, 358–59
  dispositionalism and, 163–64
  in epistemology, 45–46
  in ethics (and moral theory), 46–48
  as general theory of Intelligence, 3–4,
    14–19, 54–55
  intellectualism versus, 17–19, 54–55,
    136–39, 162–66

anti-intellectualism (*continued*)
  linguistic evidence for/against, 36–37, 92–93, 138, 178–80, 185n47, 216, 219–21, 242–43, 261, 275–79
  in philosophy of action, 48–49
  in philosophy of language, 50–51
  in philosophy of mind and cognitive science, 51–53
  putative counterexamples to, 31–32, 82, 128–32, 136–38, 159–60, 166–74, 207–8, 301–2, 326
  resolutive complementation and, 242–43
Antony, L., 322n12
apprentices, inquirers and, 284–87, 290–92
Aquinas, T., 46
Archer, M. S., 49n62
Aristotle, 3n1, 33, 46, 86, 102, 104, 112
articulation, expressibility or, 31n41, 34, 78, 89, 108–11, 191, 283–86, 298
artificial intelligence, 51
Asher, N., 215n1, 218, 223, 227, 235–36
Audi, R., 47
automaticity, 52–53, 101–2, 316, 330, 332

Bach, K., 139n3
Baddeley, A., 215
Bargh, J., 102n1
Bartsch, K., 47
Barwise, J., 229–31
Battaly, H., 45n57
Bealer, G., 124, 133n19, 188n55
Bechtel, W., 52, 137n1
Beck, C. M., 18n25, 52n67
Bengson, J., 25, 27, 33n42, 35n43, 37n46, 38, 43, 44n56, 51, 52, 119n6, 126n12, 128–30, 131n17, 132, 134nn20–21, 136, 137, 149–50, 161–95, 198n2, 208n11, 216, 239, 244n1, 257–60, 302n1, 315

Bennett, J., 14n20, 35n43, 47, 50, 52
Bergman, M., 123n10
Berwick, R. C., 331n28
Besson, C., 45
Bialystok, E., 318n8
Biernat, M., 294
Birner, B., 276
Bjorklund, D. F., 328
Blackburn, S., 47
Blanchard-Fields, F., 330, 331
Block, N., 51
Bloomfield, P., 45n57
Boër, S., 250
Bonevac, D., 37–38
Braddon-Mitchell, D., 137n1
Brand, M., 190n57
Brandom, R., 18n25, 50, 137n1, 166n13
Bratman, M., 48n61, 190n57
Braun, D., 139n3, 165n12, 244–60, 251, 252
Brewer, B., 41n53
Brogaard, B., 119n6, 126n12, 138, 139, 142, 149, 160, 165n12, 172n27, 180n38
Brooks, R. A., 51
Brown, D., 244n2, 245n5
Brown, L. E., 330n20
Burge, T., 7n8, 186, 190n57, 190n60, 326n8
Buss, R. R., 330, 331
Bzdak, D., 52, 164n8

Campbell, J., 207
Carlson, R. A., 330nn21–22
Carman, T., 40
Carnap, R., 44
Carpenter, B., 235
Carr, D., 25n36, 31–32, 47, 52n67
Carroll, L., 84, 337, 358
Cartwright, R. L., 342n8
Cath, Y., 30n41, 120–24, 113–35, 137n1, 143–46, 150, 156–58, 164, 189n56

Cavell, S., 210n12
Chalmers, D., 153
Chang, F., 332n30
Chartrand, T, 102n1
Chase, C., 52–53
Chisholm, R., 48n61
Chomsky, N., 50–51, 179, 319–26
Churchland, P., 47
Clark, A., 47
Clarke, R., 49n62, 51
Cleeremans, A., 328n19, 330
clients, 284–87, 290–92
closure principle, 140–41, 352n17
cognitive science, 51–53, 279, 306–7, 312
Cohen, D., 49n62
Collins, J., 43, 322n12
competence, 45–46, 298, 324, 347. *See also* ability, disposition or; skill
complements. *See also* knowledge-*wh*; *wh*-clauses
    complement structure and conceptual structure, 261–62
    complementation, 242–43
    infinitival, 42, 264–73, 277–79
    predicates combined with declarative, 216–17
    reactive, resolutive, and skill-oriented, 233–34
    resolutive complements from exhaustiveness to resolvedness, 226–27
    wh-complement, 42, 179, 139n3, 235, 273–77
    wh-complement and infinitival complement, 42, 235n17, 239n22, 264–73, 277–79
    wh-infinitival, 235n17, 238–39, 279
compulsion, addiction or, 49n62
conceptions. *See also* understanding
    Bengson and Moffett on, 25, 177n32, 185–94
    Markie on, 186n50

concepts. *See also* understanding
    ability and, 193n68, 239
    aesthetic judgment and, 210
    Brandom on, 50
    conceptions and, 190n60
    Frege on, 196–98, 202, 204–6
    knowledge how and, 25, 27–28, 31n41, 32, 36, 39, 136, 149–50, 161, 162n3, 167, 186–89, 191n61, 193, 209, 327–28
    nonconceptual, 31n41, 51, 53n68, 328
    originalist theory of, 306n4
    perception and, 29, 206–7
    third realm and, 199–211
    Tye on, 302–3, 305–6
    Wittgenstein on, 205–6
construction grammar, 262–63
Cooper, R., 226, 228, 231n12, 232
Correia, F., 7n6, 162n3
counterfactuals, 38, 170n25
counterfactual success thesis, 170–71, 175
craft, ancient versus modern notion of, 103nn2–4, 125
techne, 3, 103, 111
Craig, E., 24n34, 175n30, 284–96
Crane, T., 166n14
Crimmins, M., 233
Cross, R. C., 47
Csikszentmihalyi, M., 106–8
Culbertson, J., 324n16
Culicover, P. M., 249n8
Cummins, R., 51, 52
Cunliff, L., 52n67
Cutler, A., 332n30

Dancy, J., 47
Davidson, D., 129, 167, 318–19
Davies, M., 320n10

declaratives, 183, 222
  Anderson on, 327–28
  declarative clause-types, 226
  factive clauses versus resolutive clauses, 235n17
  predicates combined with declarative complements, 216–17
deduction, 86
  human capacity for, and theory building, 358–59
  inference versus, 337–40
  knowledge that and, 347–59
  logical rules for, 347–51
  modus ponens and, 84, 336–37, 351
  varieties of, 341–46
Dell, G. S., 332n30
Dennett, D., 8n9, 52, 53n68, 199n3
Descartes, R., 10n13, 27, 316
  dualism of mental and physical, 10n13, 51, 88n9
  Ryle's anti-Cartesianism, 80, 87–89, 96–98
  tests for Intelligence, 27n38
Dever, J., 37–38, 174n29
Devitt, M., 42, 43, 51, 52, 53n68, 164n8, 166n13, 315, 316, 317n6, 322, 326
Dewey, J., 3n1, 35n43, 47
DiGirolamo, G. J., 330n25
dispositionalism, 163–64. *See also* anti-intellectualism
dispositions. *See* abilities, dispositions or
Dowty, D., 239n22
Dretske, F., 34, 141, 309
  Dretske cases, 353, 357
Dreyfus, H., 40, 47, 51, 188, 207
Dreyfus, S., 47, 51
Ducasse, C. J., 18n25
Dummett, M., 50–51, 326–27, 351n15
Dwyer, S., 317n6, 322n12

epistemic injustice
  underestimating effectiveness, 298–99
  underestimating honesty, 295–98
  underestimating knowledge how, 293–95
Erion, G. J., 27n38
Etchemendy, J., 229–31
ethology, 51–53, 327–28
evaluative epithets, 20n28
Evans, N., 332n32
examples
  Achilles and the tortoise, 84, 85, 337, 358
  animals, 150–58
  arthritis, 190n60
  avalanche, 31, 32, 185–86, 188, 191
  baby and binkie, 150–58
  barn, 148–49
  baseball, 202–3
  basketball, 169
  bicycle riding, 88, 136, 178n34, 186n50, 219–21, 237–42, 296–97, 301–3
  black-and-white room, 54, 300, 304–8
  blue swan, 139n4
  bowling a googly, 114
  brain-damaged speaker, 325
  catch a tiger by the toe, 248n7
  chess, 6, 13–14, 27, 63, 64, 66, 67–69, 70, 82, 88, 161, 179, 207, 314–15, 334
  chicken sexing, 253–54
  dancer, 31–32
  defective reasoner, 67, 69
  directions, 148–49, 156, 158–59, 184, 237, 244–52
  door opening, 22–23, 94–95
  Dretske cases, 353, 357
  driving a car, 101–2, 106–7, 111, 244, 290–91, 295–97, 299, 309–10
  ear wiggling, 190n60, 191, 255–57

Index

English-speaker cursing in Italian, 137
enjoyable activities, 107–8
faucet manual, 143–45, 150
flight simulator, 125–30
fuse box location, 72
Gettier cases, 118–22, 124–25, 143–45, 149
great poet, 325
hallucination, 120–32, 134, 144–46, 150, 156–58
Hesperus-Phosphorus, 306, 307
hiker, 31–32
horse-drawn carriage, 196–98
infants, 150–58
knowing what it is like, 302–4
kytoon, 172–74, 193
lucky light bulb, 120–34
marathon runner, 169
master chef, 31–32
miscellaneous instances of practical expertise, 102–4, 125
miscellaneous things we know how to do, 88, 94, 161
Pi, 170, 174, 176, 178, 187, 189, 193
pianist, 101, 111, 131–32, 134, 208, 253–54
pruning trees or roses, 6, 26, 36, 88, 91–94
race, 203
righty, tighty; lefty, loosey, 8, 22–23
salchow, 128–30, 132, 134, 137, 149, 171–72, 174, 193
salchow (modified), 257–60
ship's pilot, 73–77
skiing/ski instructor, 31, 69, 167–69, 176, 178, 193, 253–55
sleeping, 133n19
stars, 20–22
swimming, 167n17, 182–85, 193, 315
teaching, 267–68, 269–70
timid student, 152
two views of one ship, 306
typist, 91–92
whales and mammals, 196–97, 207
zebra, 353
experts/expertise. *See* competence; skill
expressibility, articulation or, 31n41, 34, 78, 89, 108–11, 191, 283–86, 298

familiarity, acquaintance or, 25, 28, 185, 188, 312. *See also* objectual knowledge
Fantl, J., 14n18, 25n35, 82n4, 244n1
Feinstein, M., 52–53
Feldman, R., 245, 253
Fernández, R., 232
Fernandez-Duque, D., 330n25
Fillmore, C. J., 262, 266
Fine, K., 7n6, 43n54, 162n3
Fitzgerald, G., 323n14, 324n16
Fletcher, C., 215
flow, 106–8, 207
Fodor, J., 8n9, 23, 52, 319n9, 331
Forbes, G., 166n14, 180n37
Fowler, C. A., 328, 330n22
Frankfurt, H., 97n19
Frege, G., 10n13, 141, 153–54, 183, 196–98, 202–5
Fricker, M., 283–86, 289, 292–99

Gallagher, S., 52
Gandhi, M. K., 16n23
Garfield, J., 52–53
Garson, J., 330n21
Gaut, B., 52n67
Gauthier, D., 47
Geach, P., 47
Gellner, E., 45
Gendler, T., 190n57
Gentzen, G., 345–48, 351
Gettier cases, 118–22, 124–25, 143–45, 149
Ghahramani, Z., 330n20

Gibbons, J., 25n36, 49n62, 97n18
Gibson, E., 332n31
Gibson, J., 40
Ginet, C., 21–22, 23
Ginzburg, J., 43, 179n34, 181, 182n42, 215–43
Glick, E., 51, 52, 134n21, 164n8, 184n46
Goldberg, A., 179, 262–66, 282
Goldin, C., 294
Goldman, A., 148–49, 255, 286
Gould, J., 47
Greco, J., 45n57
Gregory, R. L., 40
Griffin, Z. M., 332n30
Griffiths, P. J., 52n67
Groenendijk, J., 36n45, 217–24, 235n17
Gross, S., 324n16
Grube, E., 166n14
Grush, R., 52
Gupta, A., 190n57

Haegeman, L., 249n8
Haiman, J., 279
Haiman's quantity principle, 279
Hakes, D. T., 318n8
hallucinations, 120–32, 134, 144–46, 150, 152–58, 164
Handfield, T., 49n62
Hare, R. M., 50
Harman, G., 320
Hartland-Swann, J., 18n25
Haugeland, J., 18n25, 50, 51, 52, 137n1
Hawley, K., 31–32, 38, 45, 166n13, 170, 185–86, 188n53, 191, 283–99, 287, 296
Hawthorne, J., 97n18, 141n6, 289, 352n17
Hedberg, N., 276
Heidegger, M., 3n1, 37–39, 49, 196
Heidelberger, H., 317
Heil, J., 50

Hernandez Blasi, C., 328
Hertz, P., 342n8
Hetherington, S., 18n25, 37n46, 45, 167n15, 168n20
Higginbotham, J., 139, 190n60
Hintikka, J., 47, 139n3
Hobbs, J., 231n13
Holton, R., 49n62
honesty, underestimating, 295–98
Honoré, A. M., 167n18
Hornsby, J., 37n46, 41n53, 49, 51, 74–76, 97n18, 168n20
Huemer, M., 133n19
Hunter, D., 133n19
Hurley, S. L., 207
Hursthouse, R., 46
Husserl, E., 10n13
Hyman, J., 45n57

implicative relations, 341–46
implicit, tacit or
  conceptions, 27, 161, 190–191
  information states (representations), 52–53, 233
  knowledge, 33, 76, 123, 188n55, 285, 314, 319–20, 323, 328–33
  learning, 52n67, 53n68, 316, 328, 330–31
  memory, 328
  premises, 341
  propositional attitudes, 8n9, 188n55, 189
infants, 150–60
inference, 335
  deduction versus, 337–40
  observation as compared with, 30
infinitival. *See also* complements
  Roberts on, 235n17, 239n22
  wh-complement compared to, 42, 264–73, 277–79
  wh-infinitival, 235n17, 238–39, 279

Index

inquirers, apprentices and, 284–87, 290–92
intellectualism. *See also* answer theory; objectualism, objectualist intellectualism; predicate view; propositionalism
  on ability versus skill, 8–9
  after Ryle, 17–30
  anti-intellectualism versus, 18–19, 30, 136–39, 162–66
  in epistemology, 45–46
  in ethics (moral theory), 46–48
  Gettier cases, 118–22, 124–25, 143–45, 149
  knowledge how and knowledge that, 3–6, 71, 79, 81–82, 113–14, 120, 165, 179, 209, 253–55, 317
  linguistic evidence for/against, 36–37, 92–93, 138, 178–80, 185n47, 216, 219–21, 242–43, 261, 275–79
  on occult episodes, 9, 81, 202
  in philosophy of action, 48–49
  in philosophy of education, 52n67,
  in philosophy of language and linguistics, 50–51
  in philosophy of mind, phenomenology, cognitive science, ethology, and psychology, 51–53
  third realm and, 206–7
Intelligence (and Intelligent action), 3–55, 62–70, 81, 85–88, 93–94, 97–98
  ability and, 5n4, 15–17, 19, 24, 28, 30, 31–38, 66
  cognition (cognitive) and, 28, 35–36, 39–40, 48n61
  distinction between non-Intelligent and, 6–9, 17
  in epistemology, 45–46
  -epithets or concepts, 5, 20n28, 62–63, 66, 87, 272
  in ethics (moral theory), 46–48

  intelligence compared to, 5–6, 62, 87
  intentional action and, 21n30, 48–89, 88
  knowledge how and, 5–6, 8, 14, 18–20, 54–55, 66, 87n9, 102, 112, 164n8
  knowledge that and, 8–9n11, 35–36, 65, 97–98, 108–11
  machines and, 6n5, 51, 161
  marks of, 14n20, 81
  in miscellaneous areas, 52n67
  philosophical theory of, 4–17, 44, 51nn65–66
  in philosophy of action, 48–49
  in philosophy of education, 52n67
  in philosophy of language and linguistics, 50–51
  in philosophy of mind, phenomenology, cognitive science, ethology, and psychology, 51–53
  Ryle on, 4–17, 62–70, 81, 83, 85–88, 93, 94nn14–15, 97–98, 358–59
intentional action, 21n30, 25, 48–49, 88, 126–27, 172–73
  complex, 33–36, 40–41, 53n41, 186n50
  guiding, 25, 176–78
  intelligence and, 21n30, 48–49
  sub-intentional action, 23n31, 176n31, 177n32
interrogative knowledge. *See* knowledge-*wh*
interrogatives, 216–19, 222–26, 228–29, 246–49. *See also* complements; knowledge-*wh*
  free relatives and, 182n42
  resolving questions, 216, 218, 224, 226–27, 231–34, 242
  wh-questions, 42–43, 89–93, 139–42, 179n35, 183, 222n4, 225, 235, 261, 273–78, 301–4, 307–8
Ivanhoe, P. J., 52n67

394 Index

Jackendoff, R., 249n8, 262
Jackson, F., 51, 54, 126n13, 137n1, 190n57, 300, 304–8, 309, 340n5
Jacobson, P., 239n22
Jeshion, R., 312n8
Jones, G., 49n62, 330, 330n27
justification, warrant or
  aesthetic judgment and, 210
  competence and, 321
  demonstrative knowledge and, 307
  inference warrant, 339
  knowledge how and, 45, 49, 117–18, 123–25, 130, 145, 147–50, 160, 184, 245–46
  knowledge-*wh* and, 289
  understanding and, 193

Kalderon, M. E., 45, 50
Kallestrup, J., 139n3, 180n38
Kamp, H., 43n54
Kaplan, J., 276
Karttunen, L., 36n45, 217–18, 222–24, 235n17
Kaufman, S. B., 52n67
Kaufman, S. J., 52n67
Kay, P., 262
Kelly, S. D., 40, 51, 52
Kelso, J. A. S., 330n21
Kenny, A., 47
Kim, J., 162n3
King, J., 31, 167–69, 176, 178, 193
knack
  versus knowledge how and skill, 34–36, 38–40, 45–46, 49, 108
knowledge ascription. See also knowledge how; knowledge that; knowledge-*wh*
  by acquaintance, 115n3, 138, 161, 180, 308–13
  doing ascription and, 73

  folk ascriptions of knowledge how and abilities, 208n11
  by grammatical construction, 261–79
  infinitival complement compared to *wh*-complement, 42, 264–73, 277–79
  in intellectualism versus anti-intellectualism, 36–37, 42–43, 136–38
  via syntactic rules, 261–65
  by syntax, 261–65
  by *wh*-complement, 273–77
knowledge how. See also answer theory; anti-intellectualism; dispositionalism; intellectualism; objectualism; predicate view; propositionalism; Ryle, G.
  abilities or dispositions and, 14–15, 18–19, 31–44, 70, 72, 80–82, 84, 93, 127–32, 136–39, 144–50, 155–60, 161–77, 189, 207–9, 255–57, 285, 287–88, 291, 294–95, 301–3, 314–15, 359
  acquaintance or familiarity and, 25, 28, 185, 188
  client's perspective on, 287–90
  cognition (cognitive) and, 161, 165, 174, 193–95, 265, 314–15, 334
  concepts and, 25, 27–28, 31n41, 32, 36, 39, 136, 149–50, 161, 162n3, 167, 186–89, 191n61, 193, 209, 327–28
  contextual variation in judgments, 250–52
  declarative knowledge compared to procedural knowledge, 52–53, 327–31
  Gettier cases, 118–22, 124–25, 143–45, 149
  Intelligence and, 5–6, 8, 14, 18–20, 54–55, 66, 87n9, 102, 112, 164n8
  knowing rules and, 84–89

knowledge that and, 3–6, 11–12,
    34–35, 71, 79, 81–82, 86–96, 110–11,
    113–14, 120, 165, 179, 209, 244–46,
    253–55, 308–13, 317
  primitive knowledge states and, 150–60
  and skill versus knack, 34–36, 38–40,
    45–46, 49, 108
  stereotypical implicature from, to
    having ability, 131n17
  two debates regarding, 162–66
  underestimating, 293–99
  understanding and, 25, 27–28, 32, 36,
    39, 82, 134n20, 136, 149–50, 161,
    185–89, 195, 209–10
knowledge that
  Anderson, J. R., on, 327–28
  black-and-white room example, 54,
    300, 304–8
  declarative knowledge compared to
    procedural knowledge, 52–53, 327–31
  by inference, deduction, and
    logic, 347–59
  Intelligence and, 8–9 n11, 35–36, 65,
    97–98, 108–11
  knowledge how and, 3–6, 11–12,
    34–35, 71, 79, 81–82, 86–96, 110–11,
    113–14, 120, 165, 179, 209, 244–46,
    253–55, 308–13, 317
  linguistic competence and, 50–51,
    314–17, 322, 329
  memory and, 328
  objectual knowledge compared
    to, 308–13
  Wiggins on habituation and, 72–74
knowledge-*wh*, 36–37, 42–43, 178–80,
    235n17, 238–39, 299. *See also*
    knowledge ascription
  answer theory, 246–50, 253–60
  contextual variation in judgments
    and, 250–52
  justification and, 289

objectualist view, 166, 181–82
  predicate view, 139–43
Kobrynowicz, D., 294
Koethe, J., 25n35, 255–57
Korman, D., 166n14
Korsgaard, C., 23n32
Koslow, A., 344n10, 346
Kotler-Cope, S., 330, 331
Kotov, A., 63n5
Kripke, S., 157
Kugler, P. N., 328, 330n22
Kumar, V., 51, 193n68
Kupperman, J., 47
Kvanvig, J., 115n3

Lackey, J., 286
Lahiri, U., 179
Lai, K., 52n67
Laird, J. E., 330n27
Lakoff, G., 267
Lambrecht, K., 261n1, 274, 277
language, 50–51, 139–43, 315–16, 322, 325
Larsson, S., 232
Lascarides, A., 215n1, 223, 227n9, 235–36
Laurence, S., 322n12
learning
  Aristotle on, 33, 104
  articulation and, 109–11
  of clients versus inquirers/
    apprentices, 284–87, 290–92
  complex intentional actions and,
    33–34, 40–41, 186
  Csikszentmihalyi on, 106–8
  Dretske on, 34
  as grasping increasingly refined
    description, 231n13
  implicit, 52n67, 316, 328–31
  practicing and, 33–34, 35n43, 40–41
  of propositions as precondition for
    ability/doing, 33–34, 40–41, 270–71
  Wiggins on, 74–79

Lebiere, C., 330n27
Ledger, G. W., 318n8
Leist, A., 49n62
Lekan, T., 49n62
Lemmon, E. J., 340n6
Lepock, C., 45n57
Levelt, W. J. M., 332n30
Levinson, S. C., 332n32
Lewis, C. I., 38
Lewis, D., 51, 152, 238, 304
Lihoreau, F., 37n46
Lindenbaum-Scott theorem, 344–46
linguistic competence, 50–51, 314–33. *See also* language
Locke, J., 13n17
Logan, G. D., 330n24
logic
    Dummett on, 351n15
    role of, 346–51
    Ryle's account of inference, deduction, and logic, 334–39
Longworth, G., 322n12
Loux, M. J., 50n63
Lycan, W., 139n3

MacIntyre, A., 51, 52, 53n69
Mackie, J., 37, 47
manifest image, 53
Markie, P., 45n57, 186n50
Martin, C. B., 50
Masson, M. E. J., 328, 330n23, 330n27
Mathews, R. C., 330, 331
Matthews, R. J., 322n12
maxims. *See* rules, maxims or
McClelland, J. L., 330n23, 332n30
McDowell, J., 29, 47
McFarland, D., 328
McGinn, C., 326
McGlynn, A., 114n2
Mellor, D. H., 51

memory
    distinct subsystems of, 215
    explicit and implicit, 326–28
    factual knowledge and, 328
    false memory detector, 116–18
Merleau-Ponty, M., 40
Merrill, E., 328, 330n23
Mesler, D., 51n66
methods. *See* rules, maxims or; ways of acting
Meyer, A. S., 332n30
Michaelis, L. A., 42–43, 261n1, 262, 274, 277, 324n16
Millikan, R., 38
Miščević, N., 324n16
modus ponens, 84, 336–37, 351
Moffett, M. A., 25, 27, 33n42, 35n43, 37n46, 38, 43, 44n56, 51, 119n6, 126n12, 128–30, 131n17, 132, 134nn20–21, 136, 137, 149–50, 161–95, 198n2, 208n11, 216, 239, 244n1, 257–60, 271, 302n1, 315
Montague, M., 166n14
Mon-Williams, M., 330n20
Moore, A. W., 50, 52n67
Moore, G. E., 348, 351n14
Moran, R., 296
Mori, E., 330n25
Moss, L., 225
Müller-Lyer figure, 124
Mulligan, N. W., 328n19
Mumford, S., 40n51

Nagel, T., 23n32
Nemirow, L., 51
Newell, K. M., 330n22, 330n27
Nida-Rümelin, M., 300
Noë, A., 4n2, 37n46, 38, 40, 51, 52, 82n3, 167n16, 168n20, 169n23, 188n53, 196–211, 207, 208n11, 244n1, 301
Nowell-Smith, P. H., 14n20, 51
Nozick, R., 141

objectualism, 164
  objectualist intellectualism, 161–62, 166n14, 185–95
objectual knowledge, 115n3, 138, 161, 308–13. *See also* acquaintance, familiarity or
optimal experience, 106–8
O'Regan, K., 40, 52
originalist theory of concepts, 306
O'Shaughnessy, B., 23n31
Oshima, D., 272

Paillard, J., 52
Parry, R. D., 23n31
Paul, K., 49
Peacocke, C., 29, 190n57
perception, observation or, 7n8, 12–13, 29–30, 45n57, 52, 54, 145, 152–55, 202, 206–207, 210, 309–13
Perry, J., 229–31
Peterson, P., 328, 330n23
Peterson, T., 328, 330n23
Pettit, D., 115n3
Piaget, J., 3n1
Pickering, M. J., 332n31
Pietroski, P., 322n12, 324n16
Plato, 3n1, 10n13, 25n36, 103n2, 111
Plucker, J. A., 52n67
Polanyi, M., 52
Pollard, B., 45n57
Pollock, J., 52
Portner, P., 221–22
Posner, M. I., 330n25
Poston, T., 114, 119–20, 125
powers. *See* abilities, dispositions or
Powers, L., 45
predicate view, 139–43
Preface Paradox, 353–54, 357–58
Price, H. H., 3, 25, 28
primitive knowledge states, 150–60
Pritchett, B. L., 331n28

procedural knowledge, 31n41, 52–54, 75–76, 164n8, 261, 327–32
  declarative knowledge compared to, 52–53, 327–31
propositional attitudes. *See also* knowledge that
  exercise of, 21–24
  Intelligence and, 5–55
  in linguistic competence, 314–17, 329
  Ryle on, 7–16
propositional epistemic pathway, 215
propositionalism, 163–64, 178–85, 244–48. *See also* intellectualism; propositional attitudes
propositional knowledge. *See* knowledge that
Pryor, J., 312n8
psycholinguistics, 331–32
Purver, M., 232, 251
Pust, J., 133n19, 220
Pustejovsky, J., 220
Putnam, H., 51, 190n57
Pylyshyn, Z. W., 316n5
Pylyshyn's Razor, 316, 327, 331

questions. *See* interrogatives
Quine, W. V., 217

Radford, A., 249n8
Radford, C., 152, 349n13
Railton, P., 47
Ramsey, C., 52
Ranta, A., 226
Raphals, L., 52n67
Rattan, G., 322n12, 324n16
Raymont, P., 51
Reber, A. S., 328
reciprocal action, 201n5
reflective versus animal knowledge, 150–60

Reitveld, E., 52
reliability, 152–55. *See also* safety
representational theory of mind (RTM), 315–17, 328–29
resolvedness, 215–16, 240–41
Rey, G., 322n12
Reynolds, S., 45n57
Riggs, W., 45
Rissland, E., 52–53
Roberts, C. 43, 178n34, 181, 183n45, 215n1, 222–24, 234–35, 239n22
Roelofs, A., 332n30
Roland, J., 18n25
Rosch, E., 52
Rosefeldt, T., 25n35, 37n46, 82n3
Rosenbaum, D. A., 330n20
Rosenbloom, P. S., 330n27
Rouse, C., 294
Ruben, D. H., 49n62
rules, maxims or, 10n14, 13, 23, 67, 83n5, 328, 334
    deduction and, 338, 347–51, 359
    ethical, 47
    knowing (or grasping), 25n36, 84–89, 108, 328
    methods versus regulative propositions and instructions, 191n62
    performance-rules, 334–38
    in practice, 41
    and practices, 202
    and procedural knowledge, 53n68, 329–31
    regulative propositions, 7–8, 23, 41, 62, 64, 65, 86, 191n62
    representation of versus embodiment of, 322–23, 329–31
    rule-following, 50
    rule-governed, 210, 322–23
    syntactic or grammatical, 228, 233, 262, 317–24, 331–32
Rumelhart, D., 190n57, 328, 330n23

Rumfitt, I., 37n46, 43, 45, 86n8, 92–93, 169n22, 220n2, 239, 337n2, 347n11, 348n12, 349n13, 351n14
Russell, B., 309–12, 339
Ryan, E. B., 318n8
Ryan, S., 47n60
Ryle, G. *See also* anti-intellectualism
    on ability, 14–15, 81–82, 86
    anti-Cartesianism of, 80, 87–89, 96–98
    anti-intellectualism after, 31–44
    The Concept of Mind, 4–19, 26, 37, 40, 47–48, 51, 61, 80–89, 94nn14–15, 96n17, 97–98, 128n15, 161, 165n10, 179n35, 338, 358
    intellectualism after, 17–30
    on Intelligence, 4–17, 62–70, 81, 83, 85–88, 93, 94nn14–15, 97–98, 358–59
    "Knowing How and Knowing That", 4–19, 41n52, 61–70, 72, 80–87, 94n15, 136–37, 161n1, 165n10, 314
    on inference, deduction, and logic, 334–39
    on moral knowledge, 47–48
    on propositional attitudes, 7–16
    on ways of acting, 82
    Wiggins on, 70–79

Sadock, J., 37n46, 274n3
safety, 152–55, 355–58.
    See also reliability
Sag, I., 178n34, 219, 221–23, 225–27, 238n21, 262
Sainsbury, R. M., 302n2, 306nn4–5
Sayre-McCord, G., 47
Schacter, D. L., 328n19, 329
Schaffer, J., 139n3, 162n3

Schank, R. C., 190n57
Schellenberg, S., 52
Schiffer, S., 25n35, 51, 253
Schön, D. A., 52n67
Schütze, C. T., 318n8, 324n15
Scott, D. S., 344–46
Searle, J., 51
Seligman, J., 225
Sellars, W., 53, 61n2
Setiya, K., 49, 83n6, 166n13
Sgaravatti, D., 183n45, 192n63
Shank, N., 330n26
Shettleworth, S. J., 328
Siegel, S., 29
Singley, M. K., 330n27
skill, 164n8
  ability and, 5, 8–9, 10n12, 32, 45–46, 101–2, 105–6, 110, 278, 298, 328
  ancient versus modern notion of, 103, 125
  animal cognition and, 52
  and knowledge how versus knack, 34–36, 38–40, 45–46, 49, 108
  linguistic competence and, 314–17, 329
  linguistic issues and, 233–34, 264–73, 277–79
  psychology of, 327–31
Skorupski, J., 340n5
Slezak, P., 322n12
Smart, J. C., 47
Smiley, T., 341
Smith, B., 322n12, 324nn16–17
Smith, M., 49n62
Sneider, W., 328
Snowdon, P., 5n4, 14n18, 21n29, 31–32, 33n42, 51n65, 59n1, 80n1, 87n9, 159–60, 168n18, 179n35, 209, 244n2, 245nn4–5, 253, 315
Soames, S., 13n16
Socrates, 3, 103n2, 111
Sosa, D., 37

Sosa, E., 45–46, 152, 174n29
Soteriou, M., 45, 181n40
speaker stance, 274
Stalnaker, A., 38, 52n67
Stanley, J., 4n2, 13n16, 21n30, 23, 25, 27, 31, 36, 42, 51, 71, 80n1, 82n3, 89–95, 97, 113–14, 116–17, 118, 119, 121–22, 124–30, 131–32, 133n20, 136, 137, 138–39, 143, 149, 160, 162n3, 163n7, 165, 167n18, 169n22, 172, 179, 181, 183n45, 186n51, 191n62, 193n67, 207–10, 224, 234, 235n17, 244, 245n5, 249n8, 253, 255, 257, 261, 265, 275, 277, 287, 289, 302, 317, 326, 327, 337n2
Stanley, W. B., 330, 331
Steedman, M., 332n31
Stemberger, J. P., 332n30
stereotypical implicature, 131n17
Steutal, J. W., 47
Steward, H., 23n31
Stich, S. P., 320, 323n14
Stillings, N., 52–53
Stoics, 112
Stokhof, M., 36n45, 217–24, 235n17
Stout, R., 51n66
sub-intentional actions, 23n31, 176n31, 177n32
Sun, R., 328, 330n23
supervenience, 14, 32, 162n3, 165n11, 166n14, 190n59
syntax
  context examples, 263–73
  knowledge ascriptions and, 179, 261–65
  of knowledge how ascriptions, 36–37, 89–90, 92–93, 179, 181n39, 262, 275–77
  rules and, 228, 233, 262, 317–24, 331–32
Szabó, Z. G., 166n14

tacit. *See* implicit, tacit or
Tanenhaus, M. K., 332n30
Tanney, J., 50, 53n68
Tarski, A., 342, 344
techne, 3, 103, 111. *See also* craft, ancient versus modern notion of; experts/expertise; skill
Textor, M., 324n16
Thalos, M., 47
third realm
    aesthetic problems in philosophy, 210–11
    baseball example, 202–3
    and practices, 202–5
    experimentalism and, 198–200
    intellectualism and, 206–7
    antipsychologism and, 200–202
    practical knowledge and, 207–10
    problem of, 196–98
Thompson, E. T., 52
Thompson, M., 48n61
token events, 89–98, 191n62
Tolhurst, W., 133n18
Toribio, J., 51
Toulmin, S., 45
Tresilian, J. R., 330n20
Trueswell, J. C., 332n30
truth-functional contexts, 139–43
T-sentences, 318–19
Turvey, M. T., 328, 330n22
Tye, M., 300–313

'under normal conditions' clause, 170
understanding
    Annas on, 25n36, 104–5, 108–10
    Bengson and Moffet on, 25, 27, 134n20, 136, 149, 161, 185–89, 190n60, 193, 195

Descartes on role in action, 27
Heidegger on, 39
knowledge how and, 25, 27–28, 32, 36, 39, 82, 134n20, 136, 149–50, 161, 185–89, 195, 209–10
linguistic, 115n3, 200, 205, 318, 324, 327
Merleau-Ponty on role in action, 39
Noë on, 203–6, 209–10
practical expertise and, 104–5, 108–10
Unger, P., 45

van Gelder, T., 330n21
van Willegenburg, T., 47
Varela, F., 47, 52
Velleman, D., 48n61
Vendler, Z., 7n8, 36n45, 217, 218
Vigliocco, G., 332n29
Vinson, D. P., 332n29
virtue/virtue ethics, 46–48, 103, 112
voice of competence view, 323–24

Waismann, F., 196
Wallis, C., 52, 164n8
Wann, J. P., 330n20
Ward, G., 276
Ware, R., 167n18
ways of acting
    Bengson and Moffett on, 25, 27, 33–34, 43, 182–92
    Braun on, 255–56
    Hornsby on, 88–95
    Michaelis on, 43
    Ryle on, 82
    Snowdon on, 69
    Stanley and Williamson on, 89–90, 97, 337
Weatherson, B., 14n21, 128n15
Weinberg, A. S., 331n28
Weisler, S., 52–53

wh-clauses. *See* complements; infinitival; knowledge-*wh*; interrogatives
Whitcomb, D., 47n60
White, A. R., 76, 78
Whyte, J. T., 293
Wiggins, D., 59, 62n3, 70–79, 96n16
Williams, E., 179
Williams, J. N., 25, 162n5, 166n15, 170n24, 185n26
Williamson, T., 4n2, 21n30, 25, 27, 31, 36, 42, 50, 51, 80n1, 82n3, 89–95, 97, 113–14, 116–17, 118, 119, 121–22, 124–29, 130n16, 131–32, 133n20, 136, 137, 138–39, 143, 149, 151–52, 160, 162n3, 163n7, 165, 167n18, 169n22, 172, 179n34, 181, 186n51, 191n62, 193n67, 207–10, 224, 234, 235n17, 244, 245n5, 249n8, 253, 255, 257, 275, 287, 292, 302, 317, 326, 327, 337n2
Wilson, C., 10n13

Winch, C., 52n67
Winograd, T., 51, 52
wisdom, 5, 47n60, 62, 66, 272
Wittgenstein, L., 205–6
Wolpert, D. M., 330n20
Woodfield, A., 190n57
Woozley, A. D., 152
Wright, C., 326n18
Wright, J., 37n46, 47, 119n6, 129, 134n21, 167n18, 172n27, 208n11, 302n1, 315

Yalowitz, S., 45
Yamadori, A., 330n25
Yamashita, H., 330n25
Yoshida, T., 330n25
Young, G., 52, 164n8

Zagzebski, L. T., 45n57
Zardini, E., 183n45, 192n63
Zwicky, A., 37n46, 274n3

CPSIA information can be obtained at www.ICGtesting.com
Printed in the USA
BVOW02s1730210514

354058BV00001B/1/P